Citizenship Curriculum in Asia and the Pacific

CERC Studies in Comparative Education

22. David L. Grossman, Wing On Lee & Kerry J. Kennedy (eds.) (2008): *Citizenship Curriculum in Asia and the Pacific*. ISBN: 978-962-8093-69-4. 268pp. HK$200/US$32.

21. Vandra Masemann, Mark Bray & Maria Manzon (eds.) (2007): *Common Interests, Uncommon Goals: Histories of the World Council of Comparative Education Societies and its Members*. ISBN: 978-962-8093-10-6. 384pp. HK$250/US$38.

20. Peter D. Hershock, Mark Mason & John N. Hawkins (eds.) (2007): *Changing Education: Leadership, Innovation and Development in a Globalizing Asia Pacific*. ISBN: 978-962-8093-54-0. 348pp. HK$200/US$32.

19. Mark Bray, Bob Adamson & Mark Mason (eds.) (2007): *Comparative Education Research: Approaches and Methods*. ISBN 10: 962-8093-53-3; ISBN 13: 978-962-8093-53-3. 444pp. HK$250/US$38.

18. Aaron Benavot & Cecilia Braslavsky (eds.) (2006): *School Knowledge in Comparative and Historical Perspective: Changing Curricula in Primary and Secondary Education*. ISBN 10: 962-8093-52-5; ISBN 13: 978-962-8093-52-6. 315pp. HK$200/US$32.

17. Ruth Hayhoe (2006): *Portraits of Influential Chinese Educators*. ISBN 10: 962-8093-40-1; ISBN 13: 978-962-8093-40-3. 398pp. HK$250/US$38.

16. Peter Ninnes & Meeri Hellstén (eds.) (2005): *Internationalizing Higher Education: Critical Explorations of Pedagogy and Policy*. ISBN 962-8093-37-1. 231pp. HK$200/US$32.

15. Alan Rogers (2004): *Non-Formal Education: Flexible Schooling or Participatory Education?* ISBN 962-8093-30-4. 316pp. HK$200/US$32.

14. W.O. Lee, David L. Grossman, Kerry J. Kennedy & Gregory P. Fairbrother (eds.) (2004): *Citizenship Education in Asia and the Pacific: Concepts and Issues*. ISBN 962-8093-59-2. 313pp. HK$200/US$32.

13. Mok Ka-Ho (ed.) (2003): *Centralization and Decentralization: Educational Reforms and Changing Governance in Chinese Societies*. ISBN 962-8093-58-4. 230pp. HK$200/US$32.

12. Robert A. LeVine (2003): *Childhood Socialization: Comparative Studies of Parenting, Learning and Educational Change*. ISBN 962-8093-61-4. 299pp. HK$200/US$32.

11. Ruth Hayhoe & Julia Pan (eds.) (2001): *Knowledge Across Cultures: A Contribution to Dialogue Among Civilizations*. ISBN 962-8093-73-8. 391pp. HK$250/US$38.

10. William K. Cummings, Maria Teresa Tatto & John Hawkins (eds.) (2001): *Values Education for Dynamic Societies: Individualism or Collectivism*. ISBN 962-8093-71-1. 312pp. HK$200/US$32.

9. Gu Mingyuan (2001): *Education in China and Abroad: Perspectives from a Lifetime in Comparative Education*. ISBN 962-8093-70-3. 252pp. HK$200/US$32.

8. Thomas Clayton (2000): *Education and the Politics of Language: Hegemony and Pragmatism in Cambodia, 1979-1989*. ISBN 962-8093-83-5. 243pp. HK$200/US$32.

7. Mark Bray & Ramsey Koo (eds.) (2004): *Education and Society in Hong Kong and Macao: Comparative Perspectives on Continuity and Change*. Second edition. ISBN 962-8093-34-7. 323pp. HK$200/US$32.

6. T. Neville Postlethwaite (1999): *International Studies of Educational Achievement: Methodological Issues*. ISBN 962-8093-86-X. 86pp. HK$100/US$20.

5. Harold Noah & Max A. Eckstein (1998): *Doing Comparative Education: Three Decades of Collaboration*. ISBN 962-8093-87-8. 356pp. HK$250/US$38.

4. Zhang Weiyuan (1998): *Young People and Careers: A Comparative Study of Careers Guidance in Hong Kong, Shanghai and Edinburgh*. ISBN 962-8093-89-4. 160pp. HK$180/US$30.

3. Philip G. Altbach (1998): *Comparative Higher Education: Knowledge, the University, and Development*. ISBN 962-8093-88-6. 312pp. HK$180/US$30.

2. Mark Bray & W.O. Lee (eds.) (1997): *Education and Political Transition: Implications of Hong Kong's Change of Sovereignty*. ISBN 962-8093-90-8. 169pp. [Out of print]

1. Mark Bray & W.O. Lee (eds.) (2001): *Education and Political Transition: Themes and Experiences in East Asia*. Second edition. ISBN 962-8093-84-3. 228pp. HK$200/US$32.

Order through bookstores or from:

Comparative Education Research Centre
Faculty of Education, The University of Hong Kong, Pokfulam Road, Hong Kong, China.
Fax: (852) 2517 4737; E-mail: cerc@hkusub.hku.hk; Website: www.hku.hk/cerc

The list prices above are applicable for order from CERC, and include sea mail postage. For air mail postage costs, please contact CERC.

No. 7 in the series and Nos. 13-15 are co-published with Kluwer Academic Publishers. Books from No. 16 onwards are co-published with Springer. Springer publishes hardback versions.

CERC Studies in Comparative Education 22

Citizenship Curriculum in Asia and the Pacific

Edited by

David L. Grossman
Wing On Lee
Kerry J. Kennedy

Springer

Comparative Education Research Centre
The University of Hong Kong

SERIES EDITOR
Mark Mason, *Director, Comparative Education Research Centre*
The University of Hong Kong, China

FOUNDING EDITOR (AND CURRENTLY ASSOCIATE EDITOR)
Mark Bray, *Director, International Institute for Educational Planning (IIEP)*
UNESCO, France

ASSOCIATE EDITOR
Anthony Sweeting, *Comparative Education Research Centre*
The University of Hong Kong, China

INTERNATIONAL EDITORIAL ADVISORY BOARD
Robert Arnove, *Indiana University, USA*
Beatrice Avalos, *Santiago, Chile*
Nina Borevskaya, *Institute of Far Eastern Studies, Moscow, Russia*
Michael Crossley, *University of Bristol, United Kingdom*
Gui Qin, *Capital Normal University, China*
Gita Steiner-Khamsi, *Teachers College, Columbia University, USA*

Comparative Education Research Centre
Faculty of Education, The University of Hong Kong
Pokfulam Road, Hong Kong, China

© Comparative Education Research Centre
First published 2008

ISBN 978 962 8093 69 4

All rights reserved. No part of this publication may be reproduced, stored in a retrieval system or transmitted in any form or by any means, electronic, mechanical, photocopying, recording or otherwise, without the written permission of the publisher.

Contents

List of Tables

List of Figures

List of Abbreviations

AP	Advanced Placement
APEC	Asia Pacific Economic Cooperation
ASEAN	Association of South East Asian Nations
AYP	Adequate Yearly Progress
CER	Commission on Education Reform
CICED	Centre for Indonesian Civic Education
CIDE	Comparative and International Development Education
CIRCLE	Centre for Information & Research on Civic Learning & Engagement
CME	Civics and Moral Education
CMI	Chinese-Medium Instruction
CPC	Communist Party of China
DPP	Democratic Progressive Party
EI	Education Index
EMI	English-Medium Instruction
EPA	Economics and Public Affairs
EU	European Union
GPA	Government and Public Affairs
IEA	International Association for the Evaluation of Educational Achievement
IMF	International Monetary Fund
JAIE	Japan Association for International Education
KLA	Key Learning Area
KMT	Kuomintang (Nationalist Party)
LDP	Liberal Democratic Party
MEXT	Ministry of Education, Culture, Sports, Science and Technology
MOE	Ministry of Education
NAEP	National Assessment of Educational Progress
NAFTA	North Atlantic Free Trade Association
NCSS	National Council for the Social Studies
NEA	National Education Association
NGO	Non-governmental Organization
NICT	National Institute for Compilation and Translation
OECD	Organization for Economic Cooperation and Development
PAP	People's Action Party
PSHE	Personal, Social and Humanities Education
ROC	Republic of China
TIMSS	Third International Mathematics and Science Study
TOC	Target Oriented Curriculum
TTRA	Target and Target Related Assessment
UN	United Nations
UNESCO	United Nations Educational, Scientific and Cultural Organization

| WB | World Bank |
| WTO | World Trade Organization |

Series Editor's Foreword

In governments, ministries and departments of education the world over, citizenship education is increasingly viewed by politicians, policy makers and other stakeholders as a panacea, if not the panacea, for the ills that are perceived to plague contemporary society, its young and their youth culture, and which education is expected to ameliorate. The loss of community associated with the disembedded nature of modern existence and the ensuing alienation and disaffection of many young people; the disenchantment of the world that has followed modernity's undermining of established and traditional sources of meaning; the factors associated with what has been called the 'risk' society of late modernity and the increased vulnerability of young people; the fragility of identity in a world of contested authority and the attraction to young people of other forms of identity constituted in terms of consumer choices, for example, rather than in national and patriotic terms – these are among the chief concerns that have led educational policy makers to citizenship education in their search for solutions. Citizenship education is expected to contribute substantially to the development of young people more at home in their communities, societies and nations, who are more patriotically loyal but who also see themselves as global citizens concerned about and committed to the solution of planetary problems of sustainable existence, intercultural conflict, environmental destruction, disease and poverty. Citizenship education is expected to produce young people with a stronger sense of cultural and national identity, but who are also more culturally sensitive, planetarily committed and globally fluent. It has become, to cite the classic expression, all things to all men.

In this book, David Grossman, Wing On Lee and Kerry Kennedy examine the ways in which these multiple and conflicting demands on citizenship education are translated – or not – into the citizenship curricula of a diverse group of societies in Asia and the Pacific. The book follows their successful volume, *Citizenship Education in Asia and the Pacific: Concepts and Issues*, which was published as Number 14 in this series. Here the editors, who are widely regarded as leaders in the field, have gone beyond broad citizenship education frameworks to examine the realities, tensions and pressures that influence the formation of the citizenship curriculum. They asked their chapter authors from these different societies to consider two fundamental questions in this domain: (1) how is citizenship education featured in the current curriculum reform agenda in terms of both policy contexts and values; and (2) to what extent do the reforms in citizenship education reflect current debates within the society? The editors' comparative analysis of these case studies renders a complex picture of curriculum reform that indicates deep tensions between global and local agendas. On one hand, there is substantial evidence of an increasingly common policy rhetoric in the debates about citizenship education – those planetary commitments and responsibilities, those aspirations to global fluency through 'lifelong learning' for a 'globally competitive' 'knowledge society'. On the other hand, it is evident that this discourse does not necessarily extend to citizenship curriculum, which in most places continues to be constructed according to distinctive social, political and cultural contexts. Whether the focus is on Islamic values in Pakistan, an emerging discourse about Chinese 'democracy', a nostalgic conservatism in Australia, or a continuing nation-building project in Malaysia – the cases show that distinctive social values and ideologies construct national citizenship curricula in Asian contexts even in this increasingly globalized era.

It is a pleasure to see this book in the CERC Studies in Comparative Education Series – not only for the continuity it represents with its earlier companion volume in the series, but also because its editors are old friends of the Comparative Education Research Centre (CERC) at the University of Hong Kong. One of the editors, Wing On Lee, was in fact CERC's founding Director.

CERC has recently been described, by the Co-Editor of the *Comparative Education Review*, David Post, as "one of the world's most important publishers of research in the field of comparative education". This volume, in its application of comparative education's research methods to the intersection of the fields of citizenship education and curriculum, is another reason why.

Mark MASON

Editor
CERC Studies in Comparative Education Series

Director
Comparative Education Research Centre
The University of Hong Kong

Introduction

David L. GROSSMAN

Like the first book in this series, *Citizenship Education in Asia and the Pacific: Concepts and Issues* (Lee, Grossman, Kennedy & Fairbrother, 2004), this book originates from a desire upon the part of the editors to encourage dialogue among scholars in the Asia-Pacific region about the nature of citizenship education. The first book focused on conceptions of citizenship education in the region that took into account local and indigenous contexts, traditions, knowledge and values. Its chapters included analysis and reflection on the conceptual debates in citizenship education along with historical and policy studies, studies of key contemporary issues and comparative studies of citizenship education. In the second book, however, it was decided to put the central focus on curriculum issues related to citizenship education, hence the title, *Citizenship Curriculum in Asia and the Pacific*.

The decision to make curriculum the focus was a measured one, based on the editors' observation of some highly visible and common trends in the region, if not internationally. Much of the Asia-Pacific region has witnessed massive curriculum reform over the past five years. Often fuelled by a neo-liberal reform agenda, the purpose of these reforms has been to align the school curriculum with the assumed needs of the "knowledge economy." Reform objectives have focused on the preparation of future citizens who are creative, innovative problem-solvers capable of contributing to future economic growth. "Lifelong learning" has become a mantra of the reforms and the creation of "learning societies" is seen to be one way to develop human capital that can continually generate new ideas and innovations. Beneath these slogans, these so-called "knowledge societies" seem to demand the development of a critical mass of educated citizens to engage in entrepreneurial and innovative activities directly related to economic growth and development.

These trends in curriculum reform are by no means isolated phenomena. Fiala (2006) argues that a global ideology of education has emerged. In brief, this "ideology" presses education systems to pursue:

1. Full development of the individual
2. Development of the nation and the economy
3. Recognition of the importance of the values of equality, democracy and the broad rights of human beings for education (p.30)

It is now common to find these three trends represented in some form in curriculum policy documents across the Asia-Pacific region, if not globally. However, in constructing a formal curriculum the reality is that it is difficult to balance these three ends, and curriculum debates often reflect the differing priorities put on each one of these. For example, as Fiala (2006) points out, less developed countries have a tendency to put more emphasis on national identity and economic growth. In fact, in many cases the more Utopian goals of full development of individuals, equality, democracy and human rights may in the end have only a loose connection to the formal curriculum.

As this volume will illustrate, these global themes are central to issues surrounding citizenship education debates in the Asia-Pacific region, and gave rise to a number of key questions for us to consider. How has citizenship education fared in the process of the broad curriculum reforms across the region? Where has citizenship education curriculum been located within these new educational contexts? How has citizenship education been modified to meet new ideological purposes? What kinds of citizens are needed for these knowledge societies that are being developed throughout the region?

In this context, we invited prospective authors to submit proposals for chapters that would respond to the following set of questions:

1. How has citizenship education featured in the current curriculum reform agenda in terms of its policy contexts and values?
   1.1   At the level of policy;
   1.2   At the level of syllabus design;
   1.3   At the level of teaching materials and schools and classrooms.
2. To what extent do the reforms to citizenship education reflect the current debates within society?

Upon completion of a draft that addressed these questions in terms of their own societal context, authors were invited to a seminar to share their draft chapters in the interests of serving the agenda for cross-regional dialogue and indeed to enhance their chapters through the cross-fertilisation of ideas.

Before outlining the set of chapters that resulted from this process, I would like to take the opportunity to make some brief comments about the conceptual, geographical and political aspects of this endeavour.

The Curriculum Focus

There is not a lot of agreement about the term curriculum and its usage in the literature. For example, Glatthorn (1999) identifies eight conceptually different types of curriculum: hidden (unintended), excluded (what has been left out intentionally or unintentionally), recommended (advocated by experts), written (as found in official documents), supported (as found in textbooks, software and media), tested (embodied in tests), taught (what teachers actually deliver), and learned (what students learn). As Glatthorn points out, there is a challenge into bringing these wide range versions of what is taught into congruence. In a useful definitional exercise, Kennedy (2005c, p.84) describes four broad dimensions of the curriculum that taken together reflect for him the totality of the curriculum.

1. Curriculum as a prescribed plan for learning;
2. Curriculum as all the learning experiences encountered at school, planned and unplanned;
3. Curriculum as a reflection of the expectations that society has for young people; and
4. Curriculum as a statement of values.

Kennedy's definition assumes that curriculum takes place in a political context and represents a selection from the culture. As individuals and groups in a society will want their say, there will be different and often conflicting interests at work. According to Wood (1998), we argue for competing conceptions of the curriculum on the basis of our view of a just society and a good life, and thus every proposed curriculum formation carries a distinct social outcome, "a notion of what body of knowledge, skills, attitudes, and values students should gain in order to live in a particular social order" (p.177). The crucial question, as Kennedy points out, is who selects the knowledge, skills and attitudes that make up the school curriculum. In this context we should not be surprised if there are vociferous debates over the curriculum.

Ross (2002) reminds us that no curriculum is a neutral document; any statement of what is to be learned is permeated with objectives and intentions that in turn embody values, whether implicit or explicit.

The current curriculum reform movements only reinforce the reality that curriculum is far from a fixed entity. Curriculum policies and frameworks will be altered from time to time as their purposes and emphases evolve through societal and political shifts, and in some cases, regime change. In the cases presented in this book, readers will find rather dramatic evidence of the variability of curriculum and its impact on citizenship education engendered by wide-ranging curriculum reforms in a number of societies. What are the educational goals and/or motivation behind reconstructing the curriculum? Ross (2002) argues that there are three distinct approaches to constructing a given curriculum:

1. Content-driven curriculum, a construction of formally delimited zones of subjects or disciplines (knowledge as a distinct body of data);
2. An objectives-driven curriculum, built around specific needs, for competencies of society, of the economy, or of the individual (knowledge as a commodity); or
3. A process-driven curriculum, principally concerned with or guided by processes of learning (knowledge as how to learn).

As Ross concludes, citizenship education does not fall neatly into any one of these three types, and confusingly, can be described as any one of them. Citizenship education variously can be seen as a body of knowledge, or as useful to the individual and socially desirable, or as nurturing a student's value system. The current motivation in the curriculum reform movements seems to focus on the second of these approaches. However, as

Ross points out, in the current assessment environment, there will always be a tendency to migrate towards a content-driven curriculum for testing purposes.

Faced with the ambiguity of the linkage between citizenship education and the curriculum, the editors of this book purposely did not impose on the authors any definition of curriculum. Rather, we challenged them to explore the tensions between these three dimensions of content, objectives and process in the formation of the citizenship education curriculum. We asked them to explore the ongoing debates about both the form and substance of citizenship education, and to give voice to the various stakeholders.

The Geographical Scope

As the reader can determine from a perusal of the table of contents, the societies covered are drawn from four geographical regions including South Asia (Pakistan), Southeast Asia (Indonesia, Malaysia, Singapore), East Asia (Hong Kong, Taiwan, China, Japan), and three "Pacific Rim" countries (United States, Australia, New Zealand). These 11 "societies" (technically we cannot use the term countries because of the inclusion of Hong Kong and Taiwan) are found in this volume as the result of a long search on the part of the editors for appropriate authors in the region. This search was not always successful, and we failed in efforts to obtain chapters from several places, e.g., Thailand, South Korea and two Pacific Island nations.

To capture this geographically diverse set of societies, we have opted to use the term "Asia and the Pacific" in our title. There is a great deal of terminological confusion over terms such as Asia-Pacific, Pacific Rim, etc., and a great deal of debate over their meaning and usage (see for example, Dirlik, 1998). It is not our purpose here to engage in this debate. To be sure, the studies in this book cover a wide geographic range. Yet, despite the spatial diversity, there are some underlying connections among these places, notably economic. With the exception of Pakistan, these societies are all member "economies" of APEC, but in fact this was not a conscious criterion for the selection of the cases. In reality, our notion of "Asia and the Pacific" is a construction, based largely on our own location in Hong Kong. Like most geographical designations, it is not real, natural or essential. It is socially constructed and can be politically contested. At the same time, it is a highly relevant construction if it is viewed from the perspective of Hong Kong as the geographical centre, notably because it is derived from the agenda of our work and existing networks in our Centre for Citizenship Education (see the Centre website for further information: http://www.ied.edu.hk/cce/).

The Political Scope

Perhaps more significant than the geographical diversity is the range of political systems found in these case studies. In no sense can we characterise all of these societies as "democratic." They range from highly authoritarian states to highly developed democracies, and variations between these two poles. The poles are comparatively easy to identify and label, but states that combine democratic and non-democratic elements, or so-called hybrid regimes, are more difficult to categorise. In the literature they are variously categorised as semi-democracies, illiberal democracies, semi-authoritarian regimes, or authoritarian democracies, but the underlying point is that a considerable number of political regimes are neither purely authoritarian nor purely democratic. Munck and Snyder (2004) suggest a four-point scale along a continuum that includes authoritarianism, semi-authoritarianism, semi-democracy and democracy, built along Dahl's notion of the twin dimensions of participation and contestation. However, they also indicate it is very difficult to define the critical and perhaps multiple thresholds that separate authoritarian from democratic regimes even on these two dimensions. They further argue the need for more nuanced measures that distinguish between authoritarian and democratic participation and contestation. They find that a focus on electoral politics neglects extra-electoral factors. They suggest four extra-electoral dimensions that should be considered in understanding the variety of non-democratic regimes: Who rules (e.g., a party, the military, or a person), how do rulers rule (e.g., networks, ethnic ties, mass-based party), why do rulers rule (e.g., religion, ideology, greed), and how much do rulers rule (e.g., the degree of state control)?

It is certainly beyond the scope of this study to resolve the highly complex and contentious task of labelling political regimes. Authors were asked to take into account the political context of the citizenship education curriculum, and this necessarily involved the use of their own labels. While we leave aside the question of whether predominantly Western liberal and highly legalistic notions of democracy can serve as templates for political regimes worldwide, we must point out that in several of the chapters we are examining citizenship education in the context of non-democratic or at best quasi-democratic regimes. In other words, in this book we allow for the possibility of non-democratic citizenship education as well as its democratic counterpart. This is by no means an endorsement of non-democratic regimes or their practices. In this regard the reader should know that there was considerable discussion of the decision to include the cases of the two most authoritarian regimes on the political continuum, China and Pakistan, in a book devoted to citizenship education curriculum. To the editors the alternative, i.e., to narrow the scope of the book by excluding the most extreme cases while including some societies whose political regimes have different blends and mixes of authoritarian and democratic elements (e.g., Singapore, Malaysia, Hong Kong), seemed untenable. In the end, the interests of casting a wide net of inquiry covering a range of regimes across the authoritarian-democratic spectrum seemed more appropriate, and served the larger agenda of increasing dialogue across traditional boundaries.

Synopses of the Chapters

In the opening chapter Kennedy introduces some underlying issues that provide a broad context for the more specific curriculum discourses found in the succeeding chapters. He provides us with an impressive list of policies and legislation that demonstrate the pervasiveness of the curriculum reform agenda across the Asia-Pacific region. He examines how key elements of both the macro context of the "new" global economy and the micro level of the school curriculum are likely to continue to affect citizenship education. Next he considers competing influences on national citizenship education and whether these, rather than more liberalizing tendencies of economic and curriculum reform, will shape citizenship education in the future. Kennedy worries that if social and political values rather than economic values drive curriculum, pedagogy and assessment for citizenship education in the future, the result will be a citizenry ill-equipped to make judgements about the role of the nation states in complex and uncertain global contexts. Kennedy argues that citizenship education needs to encompass both the nation state and global realities, and must rest on the development of these multiple perspectives. Kennedy concludes that it remains an open question whether nation states are capable of reconstructing citizenship education along these lines.

The next four chapters are case studies from East Asia: Hong Kong, Taiwan, China and Japan. Focusing on *Hong Kong*, in Chapter 2 Lee discusses how the dynamic sociopolitical and economic changes in Hong Kong since 1997 have had impact on citizenship education in schools. In particular, he points to the interplay of globalisation and localisation in citizenship curriculum development. On the one hand, he highlights how a growing concern about national identity in the aftermath of the return to Chinese sovereignty has penetrated curriculum documents and generated several governmental and semi-governmental initiatives. On the other hand, he notes the emphasis that government curriculum reform documents have put on meeting the challenges of globalisation and the development of a knowledge economy through global citizenship education. Lee finds that the tensions between the competitive globalisation and localisation agendas are complicated by the process of Hong Kong's repoliticisation after its return to China. Ultimately how citizenship curriculum will develop in the future in Hong Kong will depend on how these tensions are resolved.

In Chapter 3 Doong shows how the new decentralised school-based curricula system in *Taiwan* has redefined the field of citizenship education at the elementary and junior high school levels, and has dramatically changed the citizenship curriculum's scope and sequence, as well as school and classroom practice. This has generated a number of heated debates, including controversies over citizenship education as a separate versus integrated subject and the emphasis on national versus nativist awareness. The debates clearly demonstrate the political nature of the reforms where the citizenship curriculum has been used as a battlefield by contending political parties. According to Doong, Taiwan's citizenship curriculum has now reached a crossroads in which it is too early to tell whether the new reform policies will survive the challenges.

In Chapter 4 Zhong and Lee report that civic education is still in its infancy in mainland *China*, though voices advocating it are growing. In the context of its existing one-party state, the Chinese leadership acknowledges that there is still a long way to go in building a political democracy (while emphasising that by democracy they mean "socialist democracy with Chinese characteristics"). Still, rapid changes in the social and economic fabric of Chinese society have led to dramatic changes in the government's definition of the essential qualities of citizenship. Zhong and Lee track the changes in emphasis in the citizenship curriculum discourse since the adoption of the "open door" policy in 1978, and discuss the recent development of three themes in citizenship curriculum, namely nationalistic education, democratic education and psychological health education. They note that there has been a remarkable shift in the government's framework for citizenship education that now includes an emphasis on the rule of law and legal education. Although in many ways this shift remains at the level of rhetoric, the authors feel that the widening discourses on civic and moral education in China are at least indicative of a nascent trend towards democratisation, linked to China's rapid modernisation and the development of a market economy.

In Chapter 5 Otsu introduces the historical and educational background of educational reforms in *Japan* and the impact of these reforms on citizenship education. She decries Japanese students' lack of knowledge of the very meaning of citizenship, and the confusing use of different terms for "citizen." She shows how government revisions in the Courses of Study have resulted in the first opportunity for schools to create individual classes through the introduction of a new subject, integrated study. After examining Japan's current curriculum policies in citizenship education, Otsu discusses the controversies over how to foster citizenship education, especially in the new subject of integrated study. Otsu argues that a democratic and peaceful nation in a global era requires an education that is much broader than the curriculum prescribed by the government. She concludes by presenting an alternative approach to citizenship curriculum built around international education themes and objectives.

The next section of the book shifts the focus to South and Southeast Asia: Pakistan, Indonesia, Malaysia and Singapore. In Chapter 6 Ahmad introduces the reader to the factors that underlie Islamic ideology as the raison d'être of *Pakistan* and the central organizing principle of the citizenship curriculum. He argues that the contemporary national policy debate on citizenship education curriculum epitomises the tempestuous character of the nation's policy itself. He examines the existing national curriculum policy of citizenship education and shows how that policy is implemented through the social studies textbooks. Through content analysis Ahmad identifies a set of values that textbooks seek to transmit for creating a Muslim citizen, and concludes with a discussion of the tensions between theology and citizenship education over the definition of a good citizen. He concludes that the Islamic model of citizenship education has neither taken into consideration the needs of a developing society nor presented Islamic civilisation as a progressive alternative. He urges curriculum policy-makers in Pakistan to recognise that citizenship education is not theology.

In Chapter 7 Fearnley-Sander and Yulaelawati explain that after the end of Soeharto's 32-year rule in 1998, the *Indonesian* government launched democratizing policies in electoral politics, governance and education. They examine how the contemporary citizenship curriculum has been designed to accommodate these dramatic political changes, as well as the underlying state philosophy of *Pancasila*. They describe the Indonesian government's introduction of radically democratising policies in the areas of governance and education that stress political decentralisation. In education Indonesia's policies have mandated participative school-based management and a new curriculum framework based on competency attainment for all school subjects, including citizenship. Through textual analysis and interviews with key curriculum policy-makers, the authors then examine the degree of integration between the new citizenship curricula and other reforms of schooling that are consistent with an expanding democratic agenda in Indonesia. They are hopeful that what has been put in place will help restructure civic identity and opportunity in directions supportive of democratisation.

In Chapter 8 Bajunid describes the continuing debates in the political arena over citizenship and nationhood in *Malaysia* since its founding in 1957. He traces the impact of initiatives in the wider society on citizenship education over the last 50 years. Bajunid highlights the continuing challenges of developing citizenship education in Malaysia in order to foster a sense of multi-racial, multi-religious and multi-lingual nationhood in an enlightened citizenry where all peoples are equal before the law. He examines current citizenship education initiatives and their potential to achieve these lofty goals. In response to these challenges Malaysia has adopted a national philosophy based on the principle of "unity in diversity." To foster collective values, education policy has adopted a standardised approach to the process of education with a common curriculum and co-curriculum for all; a common medium of instruction from secondary level onwards; common textbooks and other educational resources; common public examinations; common teacher education; common school rituals and ceremonies; and even common school uniforms. Since the challenges of creating a civil and knowledge society with a participative and enlightened citizenry remain complex and continuing, Bajunid argues that there is no space for complacency or neglect of citizenship education and human rights.

In Chapter 9 Tan and Chew review values teaching in *Singapore* through its rather brief history and highlight the curriculum shifts made to meet changing cultural and political circumstances. The authors argue that in Singapore historically values teaching has been geared solely towards national expediency without reverence for moral understanding and truth. In this regard, values teaching is more appropriately labelled "statecraft." Further, when "statecraft" is substituted for citizenship education the result may be trained but uneducated citizens. In this context the authors analyse the Civics and Moral Education programme currently in use and find it lacking. According to the authors, like previous curricula this programme is just another example of a government policy of training Singaporeans not to be educated citizens, but rather to be people who fit their concept of nationhood narrowly conceived in terms of economic survival and progress.

The final section of case studies deals with what we have called the Pacific Rim countries: the United States, Australia and New Zealand. In Chapter 10 Scott and Cogan first briefly summarise the history of civic education in the *United States*, and the current controversy between liberals and neo-conservatives over what constitutes the most appropriate citizenship curriculum for the 21st century. They see the United States as a much divided nation over such fundamental issues as what it means to be a "citizen" and a "patriot." They argue that tensions in citizenship curriculum policies and practices are mirror images of tensions in the divided society at large, and as such are not easily resolved. Their analysis is illustrated through a discussion of the development of guidelines in the areas of civics and government at the secondary school level. The authors discuss how citizenship education reforms reflect the current initiatives under the *No Child Left Behind* federal legislation that has instituted a high-stakes testing programme across all subjects, including civics. Scott and Cogan then discuss how the ideological debates, emphasis on testing, teacher preparation and traditional constraints in schools inhibit the development of a coherent curriculum framework for civic education. They conclude by offering suggestions for a practical approach to an "advanced" citizenship education framework for the 21st century.

In Chapter 11 Kennedy discusses how the "renaissance" of civic and citizenship education in *Australia* has failed to keep up with changes in the social, political and economic landscape. The consequence, according to Kennedy, is that civic education in the school curriculum reflects a conservative vision of how schools should prepare citizens. In the aftermath of dramatic global events that have had great impact on Australia, Kennedy describes a divergence between the curriculum discourse on civics and the community discourse on civic issues and discusses why it is that Australia's civic education seems incapable of dealing with community concerns and issues. To bridge this gap, the author argues that teachers need a broader conceptualisation of civics and citizenship education. In conclusion he offers a dynamic (as opposed to static) curriculum framework that expands the key domains of civics and citizenship so that education can engage with current issues and priorities and remain relevant for both students and society.

In Chapter 12 Mutch examines the relationship between educational policy and education for citizenship in *New Zealand* through three lenses: the past, the present and the future. Mutch describes how in the 1980s and 1990s, as a result of ideological tensions between the "new right" economically-driven agenda and the country's liberal progressive educational traditions, no real consensus has emerged about how citizenship education should be implemented. As a result citizenship education is not a compulsory curriculum area though it is embedded in several key curriculum areas, such as social studies and health education. The author includes a case study showing how citizenship education in its current form is interpreted by schools and implemented in classrooms. She notes that while currently there is no specific provision for citizenship content, there are indications that discussions about the formal inclusion of citizenship in the curriculum are becoming stronger. The author concludes that the debate over explicit versus embedded citizenship education is still open.

In the concluding and capstone chapter of the book, Lee further builds on themes in citizenship education discourse he introduced in the first book in this series. With input from the preceding chapters, he applies these themes to the domain of curriculum. Using examples from several case studies in this volume, Lee explores what he calls the "tensions and contentions" in the orientation of the curriculum and its responsiveness (or lack thereof) to rapid social change. He describes a number of fault lines that are commonly contested domains, e.g., cultural heritage, civic and moral education, language, religion and ideology. He finds that there are always tensions and contentions when curriculum policy decides what is to be taught and how it is to be taught, and these contentions are even stronger when curriculum policy is linked to citizenship education. Though these cases are drawn from the Asia-Pacific region, they are not unique to the region. In fact, the author argues that while citizenship concepts can be quite different between Asia and the West, the "tensions and contentions" faced in constructing citizenship curriculum in these case studies have significant commonalities. Though situated in very different sociopolitical contexts, each society must deal with ideological and cultural fault lines as well as global and local pressures in the construction of citizenship education.

Lee's analysis offers further evidence that much of the debate about citizenship curriculum in the Asia-Pacific region seems to be increasingly part of or perhaps a variation of the global discourse about citizenship education. Evidence from this volume and elsewhere clearly suggest that national approaches to school curricula are increasingly forged within wider regional, cross-regional and global contexts (see for example, Benavot & Braslavsky, 2006). At the very least we can say that despite the diversity among citizenship curricula in these Asia-Pacific societies, there is strong evidence of an increasingly common policy rhetoric found in the debates over citizenship education. In this context it is the editors' hope that this impressive collection of chapters from a diverse set of societies can inform and enrich understanding of the complex relationship between citizenship education and the curriculum both regionally and globally.

Conceptual Overview

1

Globalised Economies and Liberalised Curriculum: New Challenges for National Citizenship Education

Kerry J. KENNEDY

Introduction

The focus of this book is on citizenship education in the school curriculum of societies in the Asia-Pacific region. As important as this emphasis may be, it is not a common one in the discourses that have attempted to construct and understand the region. During the last decade of the twentieth century, the Asia-Pacific region—or at least parts of it—became a major focus of attention largely because of the spectacular rates of economic growth that were achieved by societies such as Singapore, Hong Kong, Korea and Taiwan. The so-called 'Asian miracle' was brought to an abrupt end in 1997 with the Asian financial crisis. Yet the crisis did not mean the end of economic growth in the region, although it did signal a pause. As will be suggested later, the crisis itself led many societies in the region to focus on micro economic issues, such as education and human capital development, to provide a better foundation for the macro policy settings designed to strengthen their growing market economies. After 1997, change became the dominant *motif* of education policy since traditional, elitist education systems could no longer meet new human capital requirements.

The link between education and the economy is not new (Easton & Klees, 1992) but, in the 1990s, it took on a new form. The 'new' global economy required ideas, innovation, creativity and critical thinking to ensure economic competitiveness (Ritchie, 2003; Romer, 1994). Thus, schools had to become the engine rooms that would produce these outcomes. This objective required large scale change at all levels of education systems, but in particular it required significant curriculum change. These broad changes at both the macro level of the economy and the micro level of the school curriculum are still under way and there is little indication that they will become less important as the new century moves towards the end of its first decade. Such changes will continue to provide the macro and micro contexts in which citizenship education for the future will be constructed.

These changes are generally in the direction of liberalisation—a freer economy at the macro level and a freer curriculum at the micro level to meet new economic priorities.

It might be expected that citizenship education, as a key component of the school curriculum, would be influenced by such changes. Yet citizenship education has traditionally been rooted in the conservative values and priorities of nation states. A key issue for consideration, therefore, is to consider the challenges to national citizenship education presented by the liberalizing discourses of economic and curriculum reform.

The argument in this chapter will be that the macro and micro contexts referred to above create a particular discourse about learning, individuals and the desired outcomes of schooling. A key issue to understand is the nature of this discourse—its theoretical underpinnings and its practical implications since there is little doubt that national citizenship education, as a component of the school curriculum, has the potential to be influenced by it. Given the centrality of this issue, it seems important to have a good understanding of the kind of changes at different levels that have the potential to affect citizenship education.

The purpose of this chapter, therefore, is to explore two related topics that will help provide a foundation for understanding the issues raised above:

- The micro and macro contexts influencing citizenship education in the future will be examined to identify the key elements likely to affect citizenship education in the future; and
- The strength of the liberalizing tendencies of economic and curriculum reform will be assessed by considering other possible influences on national citizenship education in the future.

The following sections in this chapter will examine:

- the discourse related to macro level economic change to highlight its relationship with learning and therefore with schools;
- the way in which this broader macro context has influenced education with a focus on curriculum reform agendas, in a number of countries in the region;
- competing influences on national citizenship education and whether these, rather than the liberalisation that characterises economic and curriculum reform, will continue to shape citizenship education in the future.

New Economic Thinking: The Need for 'Learning How' rather than 'Learning What'

The 1980s saw the emergence of a new theory of economic growth that focused on the internal workings of the economic system rather than on external factors influencing the system. This new emphasis, that came to be called the "new growth theory,"[i] was not so much on "exogenous technological change to explain why income per capita has increased. … (rather) it tries instead to uncover the private and public sector choices that cause the rate of growth of the residual to vary across countries" (Romer, 1994, p.3).

This did not mean that technological change was unimportant as a factor influencing and explaining economic growth. It did mean, however, that the focus of new growth theory was on the mechanisms by which such changes were generated. The ideas that created the new technologies, rather than the technologies themselves, came to be seen as key economic drivers. Without ideas, there is no technology!

The important issue to understand about this new emphasis is that mechanisms for change and, therefore, growth were seen to reside within the economic system. This focus gave education and training a new role in relation to economic growth. Within new growth theory, 'learning' was seen as an important 'externality' influencing not just personal growth and development or even just social growth and development, as in traditional education theories. Rather, learning was seen to be at the heart of economic growth and consequently economic competitiveness. Ritchie (2003) explained it this way:

> …a key driver of innovation and technological progress is the supply of and demand for a large and competent pool of intellectual capital—the knowledge and skills found in the local labor pool. This is not to say that physical capital, investment, and macroeconomic stability are no longer necessary for economic growth. Rather, they are no longer sufficient. Whether they positively impact long-term technological upgrading (as opposed to only aggregate growth) depends largely on the creation of new knowledge and skills in the local economy. (p.3)

Ritchie's reference here to new forms of human capital development based on knowledge creation rather than plant and investment is a reflection of the economic essentials of new growth theory. Patrinos (1994) described this as an "ideas based model" of economic growth:

> Ideas based models [as opposed to capital based models] give emphasis to a factor that opens up new investment opportunities, alternatively known as innovation, invention or technological change … Ideas drive both growth in income and capital accumulation. The discovery of ideas is treated as being endogenous rather than exogenous in the new theories. … ideas are not the same as physical or human capital … they come about as intentional attempts to make discoveries. (p.3)

According to this view, ideas, creativity and innovation are the drivers of economic growth and these require problem solving and critical thinking skills. The result is that new ways of doing things can be developed, new approaches to old problems can be adopted, and entirely new products can be developed to create new markets and demand. These processes and outcomes are seen to be essential for modern economies competing in the global market place where competitive advantage leads to success. As Ritchie (2003) pointed out, it is intellectual capital rather than physical plant that is more likely to give this important advantage, thus, the term "knowledge-based economy", an economy driven by ideas rather than by investment in physical plant and infrastructure alone.

This term is now part of international discourse and its roots lay in new growth theory as outlined above.

Ritchie's (2003) contribution to a better understanding of the relationship between new growth theory and education policy was to mark the Asian financial crisis in late 1997 as a turning point. He has argued that, prior to that date, the governments of Malaysia, Singapore and Thailand, for example, had relied excessively on foreign capital and a low-level skills base for economic growth in an increasingly technologically sophisticated world. There was some commitment to human capital development in education policy prior to 1997 yet "in virtually every country the crisis elevated the issue to prominence as part of a strategic imperative to transition from manufacturing-based economies to 'knowledge-based' economies" (Ritchie, 2003, p.4). Thus after 1997, education and the economy in many Asian countries became inextricably linked—education became part of micro-economic reform designed to support new imperatives in the macro economy. One of the best examples of this agenda for micro-economic reform is the school curriculum and some examples of this will be provided in the next section.

Links between human capital formation and economic growth are not new. It is important to understand, therefore, the difference between this new ideas based version of human capital development that now fuels the development of knowledge-based economies and more traditional approaches. Both economists and educators have recognised at least since the 1960s the importance of human capital to economic development. One economist has put it this way:

> … many economists have pointed out that education and training create assets in the form of knowledge and skills which increase the productive capacity of manpower [*sic*] in just the same way as an investment in new machinery raises the productive capacity of the stock of physical capital. (Woodhall, 1987, p.1)

A good deal of work has been done by economists to show how investment in different kinds of education (primary, secondary, tertiary) has different rates of return (Psacharopoulos, 1993). Thus investment in primary education on the part of governments has very high rates of return both for society and for individuals. Yet investment in university education has lower social rates of return than primary education but higher private rates of return for individuals. This helps to explain why governments are relatively happy to invest in the universalisation of primary education but charge higher fees for university education. As individuals such as doctors, lawyers and engineers benefit considerably from university education, it seems reasonable for governments to assume that university students should make a personal contribution to its costs. This approach to understanding human capital development, and even the methodology used to reach conclusions about the contribution of human capital to economic growth, is not uncontested (Bennell, 1998; McMahon, 1998; Toh & Wong, 1999). Yet there is a common understanding that education influences economic growth indirectly through the creation of skilled labour.

It follows from this traditional approach to human capital development that the actual substance of education, and in particular the substance of the school curriculum, is of little interest to human capital theorists. They are more likely to be interested in the aggregate level of education in a society, the length of schooling undertaken, the physical stock of education facilities or the gender distribution of educational opportunities. All of these are important, but they are static variables that provide no insight into students' educational experiences while they are at different stages of schooling. Hanushek and Luque (2002) attempted to address this problem by using the results of the Third International Mathematics and Science Study (TIMSS) as a quality measure of educational provision. Yet the TIMSS results focus on learning outcomes—they do not tell anything about learning inputs. Traditional approaches to producing human capital have been curriculum neutral. An educated workforce in such a context is one that has benefited more from the amount of time spent in education than exposure to a particular kind of education.

It is at this point that traditional approaches to human capital development differ most markedly from ideas based approaches referred to earlier. These traditional approaches looked to human capital variables that were external to the economic system. Ideas based approaches, on the other hand, "focus … on the acquisition of knowledge that can lead to individuals becoming innovative and creative—knowledge producers rather than knowledge consumers" (Kennedy, 2005a, p.9). Knowledge and learning characterise these new approaches but it is not just any knowledge and it is certainly not traditional academic forms of knowledge.

The knowledge being referred to in new growth theory is scientific knowledge that is publicly available and capable of being applied to the creation of new ideas. Thus science is privileged in an ideas-based or knowledge-based economy because it is seen as the source of innovation. New scientific ideas can be applied in different contexts to enhance productivity and ideas successful in one context can be transferred to others. Productive learning that takes place in one company can quickly be adopted in another. There is no end to these creative processes—they can continue unabated, unlike the kind of static variables associated with traditional approaches to human capital development. What is more, these knowledge-based processes are internal to the economic system. They operate within companies, organisations and governments, thus giving rise to the concept of the 'learning organisation' and, as will be shown later, even to the concept of the 'learning nation'. Learning is at the heart of the ideas based economy.

Learning is not a new concept for school educators, but a focus on learning as distinct from schooling has not always characterised school experiences either within the Asia-Pacific region or beyond it. Yet learning has become part of the discourse of current educational policy and 'lifelong learning' is now almost a mantra emanating from international agencies such as UNESCO and OECD, as well as governments and Ministries of Education. The extent to which this renewed focus on learning, a focus that is primarily economic in nature, is now reflected in regional curriculum reforms efforts will be addressed in the following section.

Curriculum Reform across Asia-Pacific Societies

There is considerable evidence to suggest that the post-1997 period in the Asia-Pacific was characterised by widespread curriculum reform as suggested by Ritchie (2003). Table 1.1 sets out policies and legislation that have signalled curriculum reform in different societies. It is not a comprehensive coverage across the region but it does show the pervasiveness of curriculum reform agendas.

Table 1.1   The Scope of Education Reform in the Asia Pacific Region, 1997-2002

Country	Policy	Year
China	Curriculum Reform of Basic Education	2001
Hong Kong SAR	Learning for life – learning through life	2000
	Learning to learn: The Way Forward in Curriculum Development	2001
Indonesia	Competency Based Curriculum	2002
Japan	The Education Reform Plan for the 21st century	2001
Korea	Adapting Education to the Information Age	1998
Malaysia	Smart School Curriculum	1999
Philippines	Restructured Basic Education Curriculum	2002
Singapore	Thinking Schools, Learning Nation	1997
	Master Plan for IT in Education	1997
Taiwan	Moving Towards A Learning Society	1998
	Action Plan for Educational Reform	1998
Thailand	National Education Act, 1999	1999

There is also ample literature to indicate the extent to which policy-makers have engaged with the reform agenda and how academics have reviewed and evaluated the same agenda (APEC Education Network, 2000; Bagnall, 2000; Byron, 1999; Conference of Asia Pacific Curriculum Policy Makers, 2002; Kennedy, 2005a; Lee, 2001; Pennington, 1999; Peters, 2001). Drawing on the policy initiatives outlined in Table 1.1, curriculum reform across the region seems to be characterised by:

- a discourse of lifelong learning
- more integrated forms of curriculum
- less emphasis on examination and more on assessment for learning
- an emphasis on generic skills
- some focus on vocational education
- some focus on more cooperative forms of learning
- the need for learning to be extended to more students

The reforms in different jurisdictions do not give equal prominence to all of these dimensions. In different ways, however, the need to move away from examination dominated and overly academic curricula towards more flexible approaches to content, assessment and, therefore, to learning seems to be common. A common feature of the societies referred to in Table 1.1 is that they have an Education Index (EI)[ii] above 0.80. Some 73% of societies in the region, as defined by the United Nations Development Program, also have EIs in excess of 0.80 (United Nations Development Programme, 2005). That is, the kind of reform agenda outlined above appears to be one for those countries that already have made sound provision for educational opportunity. Why, then, do countries that already have high levels of educational development seem to embrace the kind of curriculum reform agenda outlined above?

An invariant reason provided by policy-makers in the region is linked to the needs of economic restructuring and in particular the so-called 'knowledge economy'. The rationale for the reforms provided by the Secretary of Education and Manpower in Hong Kong was quite specific in its emphasis:

> … to ensure that Hong Kong will not lose out in a knowledge-based, globalized economy, the Hong Kong Special Administrative Region has made education and skill training the number one priority of our social policy. (Law, 2002)

Such an emphasis had already been made even more explicitly by Singapore's then Prime Minister:

> A nation's wealth in the 21st Century will depend on the capacity of its people to learn. Their imagination, their ability to seek out new technologies and ideas and to apply them in everything they do will be the key source of economic growth. Their collective capacity to learn will determine the well-being of a nation. (Goh, 1997)

The discourse in these two brief quotations is reflected in reform documents across the region. The relationship between this kind of discourse and the basic tenets of ideas based human capital theory as outlined in an earlier section of this chapter is unmistakable. New approaches to learning are seen to be an essential prerequisite if the needs of the new economy are to be met. No matter how well-developed education systems are, if they are characterised by traditional academic curriculum, traditional forms of rote learning, traditional examination based assessment practices, they are not likely to produce citizens who can contribute to a new ideas based economy. This is a fundamental plank in current curriculum reform agendas in those parts of Asia where further development is premised on technology-driven economic development. Education might already seem to be well developed in these countries—but it needs to be better and it needs to be different for the future.

Yet how are the proposed reforms linked to the needs of a technology-driven economy? There may seem to be some dichotomy between the kind of reforms referred to above and the needs of an ideas based economy. Changes such as integrated curriculum, student focused learning and formative assessment can easily be framed within a progressivist educational framework, with its roots deep in the history and philosophy of education rather than the needs of the 21st century. Kennedy (2005a) has argued that the proposed reforms are indeed progressivist, but that they represent not just a single progressivist tradition (e.g., child development) but a blending of the multiple traditions of progressivism as outlined by Kliebard (1986). Table 1.2 shows these different traditions with their competing philosophical underpinnings.

Table 1.2   Kliebard's Classification of Rationales for Progressive Approaches to the School Curriculum

Focus	Exponent	Emphasis
Child Development	William Kilpatrick	The child rather than the subject provides the rationale for the school curriculum. Pedagogies are also child-focused.
Social Efficiency	David Snedden	Preparing workers who can contribute to the efficient and smooth running of society.
Social Reconstruction	Harold Rugg	The preparation of future citizens as agents of social change and social justice.

Source: Based on Brady & Kennedy, 2003, p.82

Kennedy (2005a) has argued that these apparently competing views of progressivism have coalesced to underpin the current curriculum reform agendas in the region. "Social efficiency" clearly drives the need for workers who are creative and innovative yet "developmentalism" can be detected in the student focus of the reforms. The call for critical thinking and problem solving skills has the potential to underpin a broad "social reconstructionism." It is not one of these traditions that dominates the current curriculum agenda in the region—it is an amalgam and pastiche of them all.

This pastiche has been called the "new progressivism" (Kennedy, 2005a). It typifies what might be called a postmodernist approach to curriculum that is more eclectic, less reliant on a single essentialist perspective, more pragmatic, more diverse and capable of meeting the needs of multiple stakeholders. At the same time, such reforms also likely to challenge existing practice and even threaten community values and norms. In this sense the reforms are radical. Yet the dominant human capital perspective underpinning them often makes them seem somewhat conservative to the educational community. What seems to be the case is that the reforms are both radical and conservative at the same time. They represent the often competing and conflicting demands of postmodernist societies. It is against this background that the future role of citizenship education can now be evaluated.

Citizenship Education in an Environment of Reform

The contexts that are bound to influence citizenship education—the macro economy and micro level curriculum reform—have been described in the previous sections. The character and direction of these reforms deserve further consideration. The dominant characteristic of economic reforms has been liberalisation—the economic system is seen to be open to the intervention of new ideas, thus highlighting the important role of individuals and of learning in the economic system. A similar emphasis can be seen in the reform of the school curriculum. Across many societies in the region, curriculum is now designed to be less academic, less examination-oriented, less elitist, more inclusive, more integrated, more learning-oriented, more creative and more critical. Even the regimes of testing in countries like the United States, Australia and New Zealand do not negate the kind of freedom envisaged for the school curriculum designed for knowledge societies.

Yet it is a curriculum that is at odds with traditional conceptions of citizenship education. Contrary to the prediction of globalisation theorists (e.g., Ohmae, 1996) that the nation state would wither away, citizenship education has continued to promote the supremacy of the nation state. It often does so with values and priorities that are in contradiction to a policy environment where liberalisation rather than uniformity has become the driving force. Given that this liberalising agenda is primarily economic in nature and that it is not the only discourse capable of influencing national citizenship education, what are the competing discourses and how might they provide alternative constructions of citizenship education? This question will be addressed in the following section under three broad sub-headings.

Geo-political Realities Have Strengthened the Nation State

If the speed and pace of globalisation in the twentieth century seemed to suggest that nation states would play a diminished role in determining issues related to their development and growth, then catastrophic events of the early 21st century suggested an altogether different scenario. The emergence of a new form of international terrorism in September 2001 and subsequent acts of global terrorism in Bali, London, Spain and Saudi Arabia have led to a strengthening of nation states in their resolve to combat terrorism and protect citizens. New security legislation in places like the United States, Australia and the United Kingdom has restricted individual liberties and rights while giving to the state powers of coercion and detention that are often outside the purview of both legislative and judicial review. Individual nation states have waged wars without the backing of the United Nations and often in violation of international legal agreements. Despite widespread domestic opposition and even opposition from members of the international community, these wars have continued unabated. There is little doubt that at the mid-point of the 21st century's first decade, nation states are as strong as they ever were.

Experience with Supra-national Governance Reinforcing Role of Nation States

The growth of supranational entities characterised the decades following the Second World War. Whether it was the United Nation (UN), the European Union (EU), the

Organization for Economic Cooperation and Development (OECD), Asia Pacific Economic Cooperation (APEC), the North Atlantic Free Trade Association (NAFTA), the Association of South East Asian Nations (ASEAN), the World Bank (WB), the International Monetary Fund (IMF) or the World Trade Organization (WTO), the virtue of working outside the nation state and embracing a more global, or at least supranational, perspective was embraced. Yet none of these bodies has really emerged as more than a collection of nation states rather than global bodies taking a global perspective. The U.S. rebuff to the UN over the war with Iraq demonstrated this, but so, too, did the rejection of the proposed EU Constitution by member states such as France and the Netherlands. At the same time ASEAN's inability to deal with Myanmar and the internal tensions in the WTO between rich and poor nations demonstrated the limits of supranational bodies to take a global perspective. Supranational bodies have not moved towards international governance in the sense that national priorities become submerged into global priorities. The priorities of nation states, not those of the global community, continue to drive supranational bodies.

Liberalisation May Serve to Reinforce Nation Based Values

The protracted debate on "Asian values" in the last decade of the twentieth century (Kennedy, 2005a) demonstrated in part the schizophrenic approach of many Asian leaders who wanted the benefits of economic globalisation, but not the social dislocation that seemed to accompany it in the West. The reassertion of traditional Confucian values that featured so strongly in the debates was an attempt to counter more liberal Western values that were seen inevitably to accompany economic globalisation. Many Asian leaders saw that it was possible to embrace the global economy, but not the values of many Western countries. Thus increasing liberalisation of trade was not seen in any way to be in opposition to the retention of traditional values—indeed, in the minds of many leaders there seemed to be an inverse relationship. The freer and more globalised the trading environment, the more necessary it has been to retain local values.

Nation states in the region may well have given priority to a global economic agenda, yet it is clear from the above that such a priority does not extend to social and political dimensions of life. Nation states may want to produce global workers, but they will be global workers with national values. These workers will in all probability experience a liberalised school curriculum, compared to the kind of curriculum their elder family members experienced, but their citizenship education is not likely to be more liberal. The citizenship education component of the school curriculum is likely to be deeply embedded in the social and political values of the nation state rather than reflected in its economic values. This means there will always be a continuing tension between a liberalised economy, a liberal curriculum and conservative citizenship values. This is likely to be a key issue for educators in this new century and it will manifest itself in a number of different ways. The final section of this chapter will explore the challenges associated with this issue.

Conflicting Visions for Citizenship Education for the Future

There are three broad areas that will challenge citizenship education in the future: content or curriculum, pedagogy and assessment. Each of these areas has a distinctive role highlighted by reform agendas across the region and in different ways the reform trends are often not consistent with the objectives of national citizenship education. The unique challenges of each will be discussed in turn.

The Content of Citizenship Education

During the last three decades of the twentieth century educators often made the case for global education or a globalised civic education to be part of citizenship education or even to replace traditional citizenship education programmes. The views of these educators were often driven by commitments to 'one world' philosophies or simply by the desire to break down the negative effects of nationalism. Increasingly globalised economies would also seem to signal some support for a citizenship education that was more global in nature if citizens were to have the capacities and understandings to interact successfully on the global stage. Yet is this a powerful enough rationale for new forms of citizenship education?

Will education for global citizenship be as elusive in the future as it has been in the past? The answer may seem counterintuitive, yet it can be better appreciated once it is accepted that nation states are concerned with more than their economies, even though this concern might often seem to dominate public discourse. In most societies there is also a concern for stability, social cohesion, shared values and social justice, and these are more likely to drive citizenship education than a state's commitment to free market economics. This is particularly so in the light of increasing geo-political instability. Therefore, local values that have dominated citizenship education in the past are not likely to be easily discarded while even nation states are under threat. If this analysis is correct, it suggests national rather than global citizenship education will dominate the agendas of nation states.

The real challenge for citizenship education in the content domain will be the tension between these local values and increasing global commitments. Future citizens will increasingly find themselves involved globally whether it is for work, leisure, business, politics or humanitarian purposes. They will inevitably be called upon to make judgements about global events. They will need to be able to play a role on the global stage, understand global issues and appreciate the perspectives of others in seeking to solve global problems. The challenge for national citizenship education will be to consider how it can deliver these outcomes in an increasingly globalised environment and amidst global instability and upheavals.

Pedagogy

The thrust of curriculum reforms in relation to pedagogy is towards student-centred teaching and active inquiry-oriented learning and away from transmission modes, rote learning and drill. As shown earlier in the chapter, this kind of pedagogy is associated with the development of creativity, problem solving and critical thinking—the ingredients of the 'new' economy. On the other hand, its links with progressivist pedagogies and constructivist ideas about teaching and learning are also obvious. In the broader framework of this chapter, this kind of pedagogy can be considered a liberal pedagogy that acknowledges the student as a "knowledge maker," the teacher as a facilitator of learning and classrooms as communities of learners.

Can such pedagogy contribute towards citizenship education in the future? This kind of pedagogy would be more than appropriate for a citizenship education that was committed to the development of creative and critical citizens. Yet it is a particular challenge when citizenship education is conceived of as a 'received' body of citizenship knowledge and skills that students must master. When, for example, citizenship education consists of a single national history, understandings about the political system, participation in symbolic ceremonies and even prescribed service activities that demonstrate students' commitment to other members of the community, then there is not much room for an active pedagogy. Students are usually not given much choice about these areas of the curriculum—they are not meant to be knowledge constructors in citizenship education lessons. Thus a liberal pedagogy runs into the problem of conservative content that favours a more restrictive pedagogy.

It is likely that a conservative pedagogy will contribute to the development of a passive and uncritical citizenry rather than an active one. Yet, as this new century has already shown, these new times are ones that demand much more from citizens than uncritical acceptance of government actions and societal values. The challenge for national citizenship education will be to produce citizens who value their nation and embrace its values to the point where they can make judgements about infringements of those values and then take action to defend them. This is too big a task for pedagogy alone and a simple change in pedagogy will not necessarily achieve the desired outcome. Thus the challenge remains of building an active citizenry with a conservative pedagogy based on national values and priorities: It is perhaps the greatest challenge that can be undertaken by citizenship educators in the future.

Assessment

The curriculum reforms envisage assessment that is formative rather than summative, focused on learning rather than selection, and portfolio based rather than examination based. The direction of these reforms is on individual achievement and monitoring the progress of individual students towards learning outcomes. Individual differences in learning are expected and the role of teachers is to monitor these differences and provide the appropriate learning support to help students progress towards the desired outcomes. These principles are based on the assumption that learning is the key to success in the future—for both individuals and societies. It is not enough any longer to rank and select individuals since societies in the future will need all citizens to learn and contribute productively, not just the elite.

This approach to learning highlighting individual student progress is barely a reality in most classrooms across the region since that is still characterised by examination cultures and selection procedures at different stages of schooling. Where these cultures are less obvious, such as in the United States, Australia and New Zealand, there are now testing regimes imposed on schools and classrooms by governments that do not trust classroom assessment processes to deliver the kind of accountability seen to be necessary in today's environment. Citizenship education has not been immune from these testing procedures as evidenced by the civic education component of the National Assessment of Educational Progress in the United States and the Citizenship Assessment Project in Australia. Governments appear to want aggregated data about student learning outcomes and they want it for citizenship outcomes as much as they do for Mathematics or Literacy. This trend is likely to continue in the future as governments increasingly seek confirmation that future citizens are being prepared to support the values of the nation state. Assessment is not only an educational tool but a political one as well.

Rigid assessment regimes usually focus on prespecified outcomes stressing knowledge rather than action. This kind of assessment is unlikely to support the development of individuals who can take their role in civil society as informed citizens capable of understanding complex, multifaceted citizenship issues. Yet in the future, all citizens will need to have knowledge, skills and dispositions that will enable them to engage with civic issues. The kind of assessment associated with the reforms can achieve this objective because it is focused on the individual, but external tests imposed on schools for accountability purposes cannot. Aggregated data might provide indicators of system level learning, but they cannot help individuals to learn. Assessment needs to provide feedback to individuals so that they can improve their learning and, unless it does this, learning becomes defined by test results. Such an approach to assessment cannot contribute to the development of citizens and it cannot help future citizens to be prepared for the challenges that will inevitably confront them.

Conclusion

More liberal economies and more liberal curricula will provide the contexts for citizenship education in the future. The history of the 21st century to date suggests that more will be needed than the traditional approaches to national citizenship education. Issues that will confront governments in the future will require citizens who are not only loyal to the nation state, but who can make judgements about the role of the nation state in complex and uncertain global contexts.

What kind of citizenship education can achieve this objective? This is an issue of choice for nation states since there is nothing inevitable about the form and purposes of citizenship education. In this postmodern world, ways need to be found to integrate national values education with skills and capacities that will assist future citizens to be appropriately loyal to the nation state, but not necessarily blind to its faults. This will require, in Stiglitz's (2002, p.x) words, a capacity "to view problems in a dispassionate way, to put aside ideology and to look at evidence before making a decision about what is the best course of action." This may require too much from politicians for whom ideology rather than objective decision making is the norm. Yet there needs to be a commitment to produce citizens who are loyal and critical, national and global, and culturally sensitive but questioning. They need to have a concern for their own communities but also for the international community. Without such citizens, politics and ideology will continue to dominate both national and global contexts. The current state of citizenship education in this regard can be judged from the following chapters in this book.

To avoid this outcome does not necessarily require an "end to ideology." It does mean, however, that policy-makers and politicians need to be more cognisant of their capacities to construct citizenship education in different ways. In the future, citizenship education needs to support the nation state as well as recognise new global realities that are both economic and political in nature. Whether nation states are capable of reconstructing citizenship education remains an open question. The case studies to be reported in this book will provide part of the answer since they will show how different countries are travelling on this journey. Multiple realities and perspectives existing side by side are the hallmark of national and global living in the 21st century. A key issue for politicians and policy-makers is whether they can construct citizenship education in the same way or whether the traditions of national citizenship education will continue to hold sway in these uncertain and unpredictable times. It is a matter of choice, since policies are human constructs rather than inviolable laws, and it is a matter of choosing a direction, since curriculum reform in general has already charted the course.

Notes

[i] Sometimes called "modern growth theory" as opposed to neoclassical models of economic growth.

[ii] The Education Index is defined by the United Nations Development Programme as "(an) index [that] measures a country's relative achievement in both adult literacy and combined primary, secondary and tertiary gross enrolment. First, an index for adult literacy and one for combined gross enrolment are calculated. Then these two indices are combined to create the education index, with two-thirds weight given to adult literacy and one-third weight to combined gross enrolment." (United Nations Development Programme, 2005)

East Asia

2

The Development of Citizenship Education Curriculum in Hong Kong after 1997: Tensions between National Identity and Global Citizenship

Wing On LEE

Background

The Hong Kong education system has experienced dramatic changes in the periods before and since its return to Chinese sovereignty in 1997. For the former colonial government, 1997 seemed to be a deadline for educational reforms. The colonial government attempted to initiate various changes in the education system, and these changes were both broad in scope and quick in pace. For example, obvious changes were made in the contents and teaching approaches in a number of subjects such as History, Geography, Economics and Public Affairs (EPA), Government and Public Affairs (GPA) and Social Studies in secondary school, and a new subject General Studies was introduced in primary school (Curriculum Development Council, 1997). A new approach to the curriculum, namely Target and Target Related Assessment (TTRA), later renamed Target Oriented Curriculum (TOC), was enforced within a span of 2-3 years after the inception of the idea in 1992. In higher education, a unified three-year university system was forced upon all higher institutions, all aligned to the British university system. A policy to increase university places to 18% of the relevant age was introduced as a means of reducing the emigration flux. Further, a unitary university system was adopted to allow most former polytechnics and colleges to be converted to universities to upgrade the higher education system in Hong Kong (Lee & Bray, 1995).

If 1997 provided a deadline for the colonial government to complete its reforms before departure, it also provided the legitimacy and momentum for the new Hong Kong government to mark off its own reform agenda after the change of sovereignty. Soon after the handover, the new government embarked on a series of reforms in the education system which led to controversies and debates in Hong Kong. The highlights were the enforcement of mother-tongue medium education in 70% of schools in Hong Kong and a curriculum restructuring proposal for secondary schools with a ten-year progression plan. A new civic education syllabus for junior secondary school was issued in 1998 (Curriculum Development Council, 1998a), and national identity was set as one of the five core values in the curriculum reform documents (e.g., Curriculum Development Council, 2001, 2002c). A document on restructuring the education system was published, and one of its aims was to expand the university system by introducing a four-year system, and also a 3-3 system for junior and senior secondary education (vis-à-vis the existing 3-2-2 system, of which the 2-2 represents senior secondary and sixth form education). The government also actively supported privatisation (or marketisation) in the education system by encouraging more schools to join the Direct Subsidy Scheme in the school sector, and requiring universities to raise funds in order to obtain matching government funding in the higher education sector.

The background for these various reform measures in Hong Kong was complicated and multifaceted. It was partly political, triggered by the change of government in 1997. It was also partly economic, resulting from the downturn of the economy that led to the reduction of funding, and the economic restructuring of Hong Kong (that triggered a curriculum review emphasising the development of generic skills, curriculum integration and lifelong learning). Moreover, it was also partly influenced by global trends in educational development, as many features of the reforms in the curriculum and the restructuring of the educational system reflected common reform agendas in other parts of the world (Miralao & Gregorio, 2000).

These complicated reasons were expressed in a nutshell in a reform document published by the Education Commission in 2000, entitled *Learning for Life, Learning through Life*. It says:

> *The world is undergoing unprecedented changes*, and Hong Kong is no exception. We are seeing substantial changes in the *economic structure and the knowledge-based economy* is here to stay. Hong Kong is also facing tremendous challenges posed by a globalized economy. *Politically*, reunification with China and democratisation have changed the ways Hong Kong people think and live. Our social structure is fast evolving, and there is an urgent need to alleviate the disparity of wealth. The society is adapting its culture and mindframe to these changes. The rapid development of information technology has opened up new domains in all aspects of our lives and creating new challenges. (Para. 2.1, p.3, emphasis mine)

> In the tide of changes, everyone has to meet new challenges. Adaptability, creativity and abilities for communication, self-learning and cooperation are now the prerequisites for anyone to succeed, while a person's character, emotional qualities, horizons and learning are important factors in achieving excellence. "Lifelong Learning and All-round Development" is our expectation of everyone in this era. Education is infinitely important for everyone. (Para. 2.2, p.3)

The development of citizenship curriculum in Hong Kong has to be understood within this multifaceted context of change in Hong Kong. Citizenship education has become a contentious topic since the change of sovereignty was confirmed in 1984 by the Joint

Declaration of the British and Chinese governments. Before the handover in 1997, debates and discussions pervaded society over how citizenship education should be develop thereafter. This led to the government's publication of the *Guidelines on Civic Education in School* in 1996 (Curriculum Development Council, 1996), which attempted to set the tone for citizenship education beyond the Handover. Since 1997, the degree of intensity of the debate about citizenship education has lessened, but the change of sociopolitical and economic circumstances has had an impact on the development of citizenship education in schools. On the one hand, curriculum development reform documents invariably justified their reform proposals by citing the need to face the challenges of globalisation, such as the emergence of the knowledge-based economy (Kennedy & Sweeting, 2003). The citizenship curriculum also stressed the need to develop global awareness among students (e.g., Curriculum Development Council, 2003). On the other hand, since the change of sovereignty in 1997 patriotic groups have pushed for the strengthening of national identity education, and the government also tried to show an effort in fostering national identity in Hong Kong. For example, national identity was mentioned as one of the five core values in a curriculum reform document (Curriculum Development Council, 2001). In 2001 the government established a National Education Centre in collaboration with the Federation of Education Workers, a teachers' organisation, in order to promote national identity among students. Against this background, this chapter aims to delineate and analyse the development of a citizenship curriculum in the context of political change in Hong Kong, and how the concern for national identity and globalisation both compete with and are integrated into the citizenship curriculum.

National Identity and China Elements in School Subjects and Curriculum Guides

The promotion of national identity education has become an obvious agenda in curriculum development since 1997. In fact, the government's publication of the *Guidelines on Civic Education in Schools* (Curriculum Development Council, 1996) in the year prior to the change of sovereignty has been regarded as the first governmental civic education document that directly acknowledged the significance of fostering national identity in civic education in Hong Kong. According to Dong (1999), the 1996 *Civic Education Guidelines* are characterised by two outstanding features. First, there is direct address of the significance of political education and nationalistic education. Second, there is direct mention of the implications of "one country, two systems" for civic education, i.e., civic education should enhance students' understanding of Hong Kong's system of government and the principles of a democratic society in order to implement the policy of "one country, two systems."

In 1998 the government issued a Civic Education syllabus for junior secondary schools, facilitating the implementation of civic education as an independent subject. While national identity is studied in the context of Chinese culture in the primary curriculum, it is studied in the context of a nation state in the senior secondary curriculum. Under the topic "Nation State," issues covered are the ethnic groups of China, major Chinese thoughts and beliefs, inventions and their worldwide impact, and knowledge about China, such as its national symbols, important achievements, prominent political figures, socioeconomic conditions, and political system (Curriculum Development Council, 1998a). It is worth noting that the discussion of national identity shifts

Table 2.1   China Elements in Various Subjects in Hong Kong

Social Studies	The Chinese people: My Country and My People (include: geographical background of China, relief, climate, land and climate as resources) Culture and Customs of the Chinese People (origin of the Chinese civilisation, languages and dialects, customs, festivals and different forms of arts)
	My Country and My People Structure of the Central People's government The Economy of the Mainland of China
Economic and Public Affairs	Hong Kong as a part of China; identity as a Chinese Citizen of the HKSAR
	The Relationship Between the CPG of the PRC and the Government of the HKSAR
Government and Public Affairs	Resumption of the Exercise of Sovereignty over Hong Kong by the PRC The PRC and the HKSAR
	The Government and Politics of the PRC
Geography	Population problems in China
Liberal Studies	China Today: The philosophies and principles that underlie the political structure and the modernisation drive of China since 1978 The latest developments in economic restructuring and economic development strategy; the aspirations and reactions of the people; the impact of the latest developments upon the lives of the people The latest developments in political and legal reforms; the aspirations and reactions of the people; the impact of the latest developments upon the lives of the people The issues arising from the population size of China; the way of government to address these issues; the role of education in resolving these issues and in improving people's quality of life The way forward for China in terms of national reunification and ethnic harmony How do the current developments in China affect its participation in the international arena?
Chinese Language	The characteristic of Chinese Language is to preserve Chinese traditions, and to develop students' national identity implicitly. Through the learning of language, students can grasp and appreciate Chinese culture and tradition.
Chinese History	The curriculum of Chinese language and Chinese history are interconnected so as to strengthen students' understanding of Chinese history and culture. At the same time, it is not only acquiring knowledge and increasing ability, but also strengthening their sense of belonging towards one's country and nation. Through the learning of Chinese history, students are able to understand Chinese history, culture and tradition more deeply.

Source: Education and Manpower Bureau, 2004a.

from a cultural approach in the primary curriculum to a political approach in the junior secondary curriculum.

In the same year, the Curriculum Development Institute established a working group, examining China elements in the curriculum. The working group completed a report entitled *China Elements in the School Curriculum: Curriculum Examination Report* (Curriculum Development Council, 1998b). The report pointed out that there were relatively more China elements in humanities subjects compared to the other school subjects. The report recommended that other subjects should work towards increasing China elements in their subject contents. The Curriculum Development Institute conducted a more detailed review of subject contents, and identified the China elements in other subjects, as shown in Table 2.1.

In 1999, the Curriculum Development Council launched a "holistic review on school curriculum" (Education Commission, 2000). It argued for the need to develop generic skills among students through subject integration. The review took two years to complete and the Council published a curriculum reform report in 2001, following the publication of the Education Commission's (2000) education reform proposal *Learning for Life, Learning through Life*. The report, entitled *Learning to Learn: Lifelong Learning and Whole-person Development* (Curriculum Development Council, 2001), attempted to group existing subjects into eight key learning areas (KLAs), namely "Chinese Language Education," "English Language Education," "Mathematics Education," "Personal, Social and Humanities Education", "Science Education," "Technology Education," "Arts Education" and "Physical Education." Of these eight KLAs, Personal, Social and Humanities Education (PSHE) has a more direct link to citizenship education as it develops a framework for studying China and the nation as a part of national identity education. The framework covers three themes, namely "time, continuity and change," "culture and heritage" and "social systems and citizenship." The curriculum closely resembles that of the primary curriculum of General Studies. The junior primary curriculum focuses on Chinese culture, national symbols and some major historical events. The senior primary curriculum studies significant historical figures and events, ideas that have influenced China in different periods of time, and the uniqueness of Chinese culture. PSHE is extended to cover the junior secondary curriculum, covering such topics as world history, other cultures, and their impacts on Hong Kong (Curriculum Development Council, 2002b).

Learning Tasks and Priority Values in the Curriculum

As its title indicates, the *Learning to Learn* document suggests that effective learning is to be achieved by developing students' ability of learning how to learn. The document redefines the scope of learning in schools, and moral and civic education is regarded as a key scope, as expressed in the four key learning tasks proposed in the document:

- Moral and civic education, to help students establish their values and attitudes;
- Reading, to learn broadly with appropriate strategies to learn more effectively;

- Project learning, to develop generic skills, acquire and build knowledge; and
- Information technology, for interactive learning.

The Curriculum Development Council further published a series of curriculum guides in 2002. Five priority values are proposed in the moral and civic education curriculum guide:

- Perseverance
- Respect for others
- Responsibility
- National identity
- Commitment

The Guide stipulates that,

> These priority values and attitudes are proposed with due consideration given to students' personal and social development and to the changes in the local context … and global context, with a view to preparing our students to meet the challenges of the 21st century. The values are interconnected and if fostered, should help students to become informed and responsible citizens committed to the well-being of their fellow humans. (Curriculum Development Council, 2002c, p.2)

It is obvious that national identity is propounded as one of the priority values in the new curriculum. When elaborating on this particular value, the Guide says that,

> The return of Hong Kong to China since 1997 calls for a deeper understanding of the history and culture of our motherland. There is a need to strengthen the sense of national identity among our young people. It is imperative to enhance their interests and concern for the development of today's China through involving [the young people] in different learning experiences and lifewide learning. Instead of imposing national sentiments on them, we must provide more opportunities for young people to develop a sense of belonging to China. (ibid., p.3)

The government has also made efforts to enforce national identity education in a wide spectrum of areas beyond curriculum revisions. Law (2004) comments that the Chinese Hong Kong government has politicised the school curriculum by enhancing the public's understanding of China and Chinese culture and by strengthening its sense of belonging. This is in clear contrast to the earlier colonial policy of depoliticisation, delocalisation and disaffiliation from the Chinese mainland.

Promoting National Identity outside the Formal Curriculum

The government has made strenuous efforts to develop national identity among students in geographic, cultural, language and political terms. Geographically, the government has encouraged students to visit the Chinese mainland through exchange programmes so they would gain a better understanding about the current development of China, and more importantly, to develop a sense of national identity through personal experience. Many of the visits were organised by individual schools as their own initiative, but the government subsidised these activities in one way or another through various grants. In July 2004, the Education and Manpower Bureau (2004b) launched a high profile national education programme as part of the youth leadership award scheme. One hundred and seventy student leaders from local schools enrolled in an 11-day programme, held in Beijing. The programme covered a series of lectures and visits, introducing the participants to China's governmental structure, culture and major achievements. The students visited major historical sites. On another front, the government began to subsidise training programmes for staff and principals, co-organised by local universities and mainland universities, such as East China Normal University, Beijing Normal University and Guangdong College of Education. These co-organised training programmes all included on-site training in Mainland China.

Culturally, as the above documentary analysis has shown, there were deliberate additions of China elements in the post-1997 curricula, many focused on introducing Chinese culture. The *Report on China Elements* (Curriculum Development Council, 1998b) mentioned that China elements have permeated over 100 syllabi of more than 40 school subjects. Moreover, Chinese history and culture are specifically designated as core learning elements in the Personal, Social and Humanities Education (PSHE) KLA. In school, extracurricular activities related to Chinese culture have also been intensified through establishing Chinese orchestras and bands, Chinese dance clubs, and kung fu classes (Law, 2004, p.266).

With respect to language, the government proposed a language policy directive, asking schools to develop biliterate and trilingual abilities for Hong Kong students, with the former referring to Chinese and English, and the latter to Cantonese, Putonghua and English. A "firm guidance" report (showing the government's determination) entitled *Medium of Instruction: Guidance of Secondary Schools* (Education Department, 1997) was issued soon after the handover, and was seriously enforced by the government. Under firm guidance, English-Medium Instruction (EMI) schools were drastically reduced from about 90% to 30%, and only 112 secondary schools out of nearly 450 were allowed to be designated as EMI schools. Conversely, the remaining 70% of schools in Hong Kong were designated Chinese-Medium Instruction (CMI) schools, and the number of CMI schools grew dramatically from 70 to about 300 in Hong Kong (Education and Manpower Bureau, 2004c). However, as Hong Kong schools were not yet ready for the implementation of instruction in the national language, i.e., Putonghua, CMI actually means Cantonese-medium instruction. However, there were obvious efforts to promote Putonghua as the medium of instruction. The number of schools using Putonghua as the medium for Chinese classes grew from 12 in 1998 to 40 plus in 2000, and schools were starting to implement Putonghua-medium instruction school-wide (Law, 2004, p.266).

Politically, soon after the handover, government circulars (e.g., Education and Manpower Bureau, 1998; CM294/2001) were issued to remind schools to raise the national flag on significant occasions, such as on National Day, Handover Day, New Year's Day, the first day of every school year, open day, sports day, speech day, etc. On June 21, 2004, the government required all government schools to fly the national flag on National Day. The government further issued guidelines on using national symbols, such as flag raising rituals for schools, to implement the policy (Education and Manpower Bureau, 2004d). Invariably, curriculum revision across subjects includes the study of "one country, two systems" and China's political system. China is no longer described as another country, but as a nation state with sovereignty over Hong Kong (Law, 2004, p.266). The government established a National Education Centre, the announcement of which was given a high profile. The Centre was put under the auspices of a pro-China education body, the Federation of Education Workers, in October 2004. The Centre offered courses to raise the national awareness of Hong Kong people (National Education Centre, http://www.hknec.org/main.php).

Hongkongers' Ambivalence about National Identity

The above discussion shows that efforts to strengthen national identity education have been pervasive and explicit in Hong Kong since the handover. National identity has become a public concern, although its interpretations vary greatly within the society. Since 1997 a number of polls and surveys have been conducted to tap into and track changes in Hong Kong people's sense of national identity. In another paper (Lee, 2003), I have summarised these various studies, as shown in Table 2.2:

Table 2.2 National Identity of People in Hong Kong

Year/Month	Hongkonger	Chinese	Hongkonger> Chinese	Chinese> Hongkonger
1997/08	60%	38%	---	---
1998/01	50%	50%	---	---
1998/10	---	---	57%	29%
1998/11	33.9%	39.9%	15.8%	10.4%
1999/06	62%	34%	---	---
2000/05	---	---	40%	49%
2000/05	---	---	52.9%	37.7%
2000/06	82.8%	83.3%	---	---
2001/09	---	---	54%	38%
2001/10	60%	19%	---	---
2002/08	25%	21%	---	---
2002/09	50%	40%	---	---
2002/09	51%	48%	---	---

Source: Lee (2003, p.122)

These represent 13 different studies between 1997 and 2002. As the sample size, target respondents and questionnaires varied, the figures are not truly comparable. Still, they provide some information about how people in Hong Kong perceived their national identity at different points in time. In general, if the questionnaires did not force the respondents to choose between Hongkonger and Chinese, they had a tendency to choose both. If they were forced to choose either Hongkonger or Chinese, the proportions fluctuated and no identifiable trend was found. This shows Hong Kong people's sense of national identity continues to be ambivalent. Because of this ambivalence, the government has expended strenuous efforts to promote national identity education. However, the continued fluctuations in people's sense of national identity show that while government efforts to strengthen a sense of national identity may continue, they may not be able to change the way people define themselves.

The above review shows that national identity is a distinctive theme in the development of the citizenship curriculum after the handover of sovereignty to China in 1997. The concern with national identity was not restricted to subjects or areas of study that have a more direct relationship with citizenship, such as General Studies in primary schools, Civic Education in junior schools, and Personal, Social and Humanities Education. It also penetrates all related curriculum guidelines, such as the Education Blueprint for the 21st century *Learning for Life, Learning through Life* (Education Commission, 2000), the curriculum reform document *Learning to Learn* (Curriculum Development Council, 2001), and the curriculum guides for various key learning areas (Curriculum Development Council, 2002a, 2002b, 2002c). Emphases and approaches vary across these curriculum documents. General Studies adopts a cultural approach while Civic Education employs a political approach. PSHE approaches national identity education from a historical and cultural heritage perspective. The *Learning to Learn* document defines national identity as a key learning task, and various curriculum guides issued in 2002 regard national identity as one of five priority values. In addition, there were deliberate efforts made to review the China elements in the Hong Kong curriculum (Curriculum Development Council, 1998a).

Globalisation as a Justification for Curriculum Reform

In addition to national identity, another equally explicit theme in curriculum development in post-1997 Hong Kong is globalisation. As mentioned above, the Education Commission's Education Blueprint for the 21st century *Learning for Life, Learning through Life* attempted to justify its reform initiatives in the globalisation context, arguing the need to reorientate education to face changes brought about by the emergence of the knowledge-based economy and global economy. The document says:

> The world is undergoing fundamental economic, technological, social and cultural changes. The world economy is in the midst of a radical transformation, and the industrial economy is gradually being replaced by the knowledge-based economy. ... Rapid developments in information technology have removed the

boundaries and territorial constraints for trade, finance, transport and communication. As communication links become globalised, competition is also globalised. (Education Commission, 2000, pp.27-28)

The above review shows that the government has made great efforts to include national identity elements in curriculum revisions. However, as compared to national identity, facing up to the challenges of globalisation seems to be a more compelling theme and/or justification for curriculum reform. For example, the Curriculum Development Council's *Learning to Learn* document is prefaced by a strong reference to the need for developing global awareness. In its opening paragraph of the first chapter, the Chairman of the Curriculum Development Council says:

> To cope with the challenges of the 21st Century, education in Hong Kong must keep abreast of the global trends and students have to empower themselves to learn beyond the confines of the classroom. The school curriculum, apart from helping students to acquire the necessary knowledge, should also help the younger generation to develop a global outlook, to learn how to learn and to master lifelong skills that can be used outside schools. (Curriculum Development Council, 2001)

This view is repeated in the summary that precedes the document proper:

> The Curriculum Development Council has conducted a holistic review of the school curriculum during 1999 and 2000 in order to offer a quality school curriculum that helps students meet the challenges of a knowledge-based, interdependent and changing society, as well as globalisation, fast technological development, and a competitive economy (Curriculum Development Council, 2001, p.i).

Curriculum Reform with Global Skills and Values as the Focus

The *Learning to Learn* document suggests that the future focus of learning and teaching in Hong Kong should be placed upon the development of generic skills. Of the various generic skills mentioned in the new curriculum, many can be generally classified as citizenship skills, such as collaborative skills, communication skills, critical thinking skills and problem-solving skills. Although national identity is regarded as an important area to cover, among the values and attitudes advocated to be developed through the new curriculum, as tabled in the document (Appendix II), there are many which in fact are global citizenship values, such as plurality, democracy, freedom and liberty, common will, tolerance, equal opportunities, human rights, responsibility, etc. Of the 80 values tabled in the appendix, only a handful were related to national identity, namely patriotism, culture and civilisation, and heritage and sense of belonging (Curriculum Development Council, 2001, p.II-2).

In the General Studies curriculum in primary school, global awareness is mentioned at least as much as national identity, if not more. The core elements of Strand 6,

"Global Understanding and the Information Era" attempt to bring about awareness of different cultural groups in the world, similarities and differences among cultures (and their causes), attitudes towards cultural differences (e.g., respect), ways of interacting with other cultural groups, the interconnectedness and interdependence of the world, the role of information technology in global communication, and major historical and international events (Curriculum Development Council, 2002b, pp.48-49).

The notion of global citizenship is introduced in the primary General Studies curriculum. The themes are "wonderful world" (Primary 4), "life in the city" (Primary 5) and "global perspectives". Issues discussed under these major themes include the physical environment, technology and culture, and common global issues and concerns (Curriculum Development Council, 2002b, p.58).

General Studies adopts a cultural approach to global citizenship education. The section on global understanding in the General Studies curriculum guide is full of expressions implying cultural perspectives, such as "characteristics of people of different cultures" "cultural differences which affect the lives of different peoples" "the ways we perceive other culture groups" "respecting cultural differences" "ways people interact with other cultural groups" "influences of the physical environment social conditions on cultural developments of the world" and "effects on cultural interaction on cultures and societies" (Curriculum Development Council, 2002b, pp.48-49).

Global citizenship is also taught in the 1998 junior secondary Civic Education syllabus as one of the six themes of the subject, namely family, neighbouring community, regional community, national community, international community, and civic quality and civil society (Curriculum Development Council, 1998a). Related topics are pluralistic world, global citizenship, heritage of human civilisation, significant historical events and global issues (Curriculum Development Council, 1998a). It can be seen that the primary curriculum focuses on an awareness of cultural diversity and the interconnectedness and interdependence of countries, whereas the secondary curriculum begins to introduce the concepts of civil society and globalisation in the context of human civilisation and relationships between the national community and the international community. The political dimension of global citizenship is gradually added to the senior citizenship curriculum.

As mentioned above, Personal, Social and Humanities Education has a more direct link to citizenship education compared to the other KLAs introduced in Hong Kong's curriculum reform. The PSHE curriculum guide suggests a curriculum framework on globalisation, covering such topics as McDonald's and the global village, globalisation and interdependence, cultural exchange and cultural imperialism, poverty, unequal distribution of resources and dependence, war and peace, and international organisations (Curriculum Development Council, 2002b, Appendix 2).

The government introduced a new subject called "Integrated Humanities" in 2003 in senior secondary schools (Curriculum Development Council, 2003). Its curriculum guide states that the subject aims to widen students' perspectives to help students know more and to care about the world, to understand the process of globalisation and to provide multiple perspectives to think about controversial issues. Two topics are particularly relevant to this aim, namely globalisation and the human-environment relationship. The former focuses on the impact of globalisation, in particular discussing whether globalisation will bring forth more conflict or peace. The latter examines problems facing our environment and the economy, values related environmental protection, and possible solutions (Curriculum Development Council, 2003). Both PSHE and Integrated Humanities adopt an issues-based approach, inviting discussion and critique of the impact of globalisation.

Conclusion: Tensions in Citizenship Curriculum— The Paradox of Globalisation and Localisation

The above examination shows the national identity and global citizenship features in the development of citizenship curriculum in post-1997 Hong Kong. However, the two themes emerge in different ways. National identity education emerges in the citizenship curriculum in a very deliberate and contrived way. As a response to the change of sovereignty, the government has tried to demonstrate its efforts in including national identity elements in the curriculum. It published a review of the China elements, and it carefully inserted China elements and national identity into the curriculum framework—in the key learning tasks, in the core values of the curriculum, and also as a distinctive topic to be taught in the curriculum. National identity has been made visible and accompanied with corresponding activities, such as flag raising and visits to China. On the other hand, the globalisation theme is less deliberate and contrived, yet was a more compelling driver of Hong Kong's curriculum development. Major education reform documents, such as *Education Blueprint for the 21st Century* and *Learning to Learn*, are prefaced with references to globalisation as main course and justification for the reform proposals. Commenting upon the development of lifelong learning in post-1997 Hong Kong, Kennedy (2004) comments that the government presents education reform as a "narrative of inevitability" against the background of globalisation as "non-negotiable exogenous economic constraints." If the need to strengthen national identity education was compelled by national and political imperatives, the need to launch education reform was compelled by global pressure.

These two forces, the global and the local (or more correctly, national), comprise a dual causality underlying education reform and curriculum development in post-1997 Hong Kong. National identity and global citizenship appear to be quite equally emphasised in curriculum reform. However, rather than being integrated, the two are presented in the curriculum documents in a rather disjointed and dichotomised manner. The dichotomy is manifested in its separate justifications for the two kinds of citizenship education. Global citizenship is justified in economic terms, and is, according to Kennedy (2004), a matter of non-negotiable inevitability if Hong Kong is to maintain her competitiveness in the global economy. Globalisation powerfully penetrates the new curriculum documents. It sets the scene for the curriculum reform, which places strong emphasis, as mentioned above, on generic skills and global citizenship values, such as plurality, democracy, freedom, liberty and human rights.

On the other hand, national identity education is justified in political terms and presented as obligatory. The power of the political is particularly manifested in the way that national identity has been made explicit in curriculum documents. However, as powerful as the political force might be, national identity education has not enjoyed the same status that globalisation has because globalisation forms the justification of education and curriculum reform, and directly shapes the curriculum documents (in promoting generic skills and the necessary values to be acquired). Globalisation and national identity, although both presented as important themes in the curriculum, actually compete subtly with each other in impacting on the post-1997 curriculum reform. This also reflects the underlying political tensions between the two themes.

The literature on globalisation has identified that localisation develops alongside globalisation. However, localisation is very often developed to counterbalance the impact of globalisation on a locality; thus, the two tend to exist in competition, as a dichotomy and with tensions (Pitchon, 1997; Dale & Robertson, 2004). Educational responses to the tension between globalisation and localisation are multifaceted and complicated. Law (2004, pp.254-255) has identified three types of response to the global-local tensions. The first response refers to the power of the nation state. According to this perspective, citizenship is understood as a basis for community, a source of personal identity and a model of social organisation. The second response refers to the decreased power of the nation state in defining citizenship. According to this perspective, the power of the nation state is transferred downward to non-governmental institutions and upward to transnational agencies (such as the World Trade Organization) or a supranational power (such as the European Union). The third response recognises multiple citizen identities of an individual, such as an individual being a member of the community, the nation, the region, the globe, etc. (for the third response, see also Lee, 2002c).

"Delocalised Nationalisation"

The Hong Kong case shows features of these three responses, but this study adds more complexity to the global-local tensions. On the one hand, the deliberate emphasis on national identity in the citizenship curriculum is a demonstration of Hong Kong's attempt to reinstate the power of the nation state in defining citizenship. On the other hand, the emphasis on globalisation as the background of curriculum reform (which is not confined to citizenship reform) shows a clearer awareness of Hong Kong as an international city with an identity of its own. However, the global-local agenda in the Hong Kong curriculum is much more complicated than the apparently parallel emphasis of the two kinds of forces that shape its curriculum. The emphasis on the power of the nation state in defining citizenship in Hong Kong is certainly a demonstration of the nationalisation of the curriculum, but this does not necessarily mean localisation. The deliberate emphasis on national identity obviously propagates the desirability of a Chinese identity over a Hong Kong identity, as if the government were not content with the situation that Hong Kong citizens identify themselves as Hongkongers rather than Chinese. This explains why surveys conducted in Hong Kong since the handover always asked whether Hong Kong people identify themselves as "Chinese," "Hongkongers," "Chinese Hongkongers" or "Hong Kong Chinese." However, Hong Kong people continue to be ambivalent regarding their national identity as no consistent shifts in self-identification were found in the first five years after the handover (see Table 2.2). Unlike the pre-1997 Hong Kong citizenship curriculum, which was depoliticised and disaffiliated Hong Kong from the Chinese mainland, post-1997 Hong Kong citizenship is politicised and affiliated with the Chinese mainland. This is a reinstatement of the power of the nation state and a demonstration of the nationalisation of the curriculum, but to Hong Kong people this kind of nationalisation is delocalised, or more correctly a kind of "delocalised nationalisation."

"Localised Internationalisation"

While nationalisation may not mean localisation in Hong Kong, globalisation can be seen as quite a "localised" agenda. The education and curriculum reform documents in Hong Kong adopt a social and economic perspective in their justification of the need to change in order to meet globalisation challenges. It is worth reiterating that although national identity is one of the four key elements of education, the major skills to be developed according to the curriculum reform, such as collaborative skills, communication skills, critical thinking skills and problem-solving skills, are more relevant to global citizenship. The curriculum drafters in Hong Kong, in this sense, are quite ready to be integrated with the world, attempting to develop skills in meeting the needs of the global challenges. The identification of global citizenship values, such as plurality, democracy, freedom and liberty, common will, tolerance, equal opportunities, human rights and responsibility, as mentioned above, is another illustration of adopting global values in the curriculum. The integration of these global values and skills into the curriculum is very much a kind of local choice. In this sense, the local response to globalisation can be viewed as a kind of localised globalisation.

This study shows the complicated interplay of globalisation and localisation in its citizenship curriculum development. Not only are there tensions between the two, the process of repoliticisation of Hong Kong since its handover adds complexities to the tensions between the two. That is, in the process of nationalisation and affiliation with the Chinese mainland, the encouragement given these two movements has become so strong that Hong Kong's local identity is being weakened. However, being an international city in its own right, Hong Kong's integration with the global market and adoption of global development trends have been so clear that globalisation has never been doubted as a Hong Kong agenda, and its desire to be part of globalisation is thus very much a local choice.

In summary, this study of the Hong Kong case reveals a complex picture of conflicting forces in citizenship education. While a form of *delocalised nationalisation* underlies government attempts to promote national identity education, in contrast a kind of *localised globalisation* forms the background to the government's curriculum reforms and support for global citizenship education.

3

Taiwan's New Citizenship Curriculum: Changes and Challenges

Shiowlan DOONG

Introduction

Every curriculum has a particular educational function that upholds the values of educational developers and society at large. In the past, due to the military confrontation between the two sides bordering the Taiwan Strait and its concerns over national security, Taiwan developed a very rigid, centralised school curriculum to control educational processes and practices. After the suspension of martial law in 1987 and the subsequent advent of free speech and a free press, increasing public criticism has been made of Taiwan's education for its inflexibility and for failing to cope with the particular needs of Taiwan's rapidly changing society. In response to public expectations and national development needs, the Ministry of Education (MOE) has adopted some measures to deal with problems in different aspects of the educational system. The development of a curriculum for citizenship education, i.e., the nine-year integrated curriculum for social studies, is one of those measures. This new curriculum not only redefines the field of citizenship education at the elementary and junior high school levels, but also changes dramatically what the field used to be in terms of scope and sequence, school and classroom practice, and the like.

This chapter seeks to explore Taiwan's citizenship curriculum development, implementation and major challenges, focusing on the elementary and junior high school levels. The analysis presented in this chapter encompasses five critical aspects. First, the analysis inquires into the contexts and underlying values of citizenship curriculum in Taiwan. Second, the analysis of the development of citizenship curriculum distinguishes between three periods and discusses these in turn. Third, the analysis examines the implementation of the current citizenship curriculum reform. Fourth, it focuses on the controversies and challenges confronting Taiwan's new citizenship curriculum. Finally, suggestions are made regarding what needs to be done in citizenship education in order to help resolve the above issues.

The Cultural and Sociopolitical Contexts

Taiwan's population (22.6 million) is comprised almost entirely of Han Chinese, with the exception of over 450,000 indigenous people (Ministry of Interior, 2004).[i] Historically, Taiwan has been an island of immigrants. Early Han Chinese immigrants were principally from two groups: the Fujianese, from China's southeastern coastal province of Fujian, and the Hakka, mostly from Guangdong Province.[ii] Together, these two groups are referred to as "native Taiwanese." The last group of immigrants came to Taiwan from various parts of China with the Kuomintang (KMT, also known as the Nationalist Party) in 1949. This group is generally referred to as "mainlanders."[iii]

Chinese Culture Heritage

When the early Han Chinese immigrants came to Taiwan, they brought with them Chinese lifestyles and cultural traditions. Chinese culture comprises a variety of philosophical systems such as Confucianism, Taoism, Buddhism and the like. Of these, Confucianism has been the most influential.

Based on Confucianism, traditional moral behaviour was governed by relations and respect. Confucius proposed five moral roles in human relations: the relationships between ruler and ruled, father and son, older brother and younger brother, husband and wife, and friend and friend. Each is set forth as a pair of social statuses with rights and duties that obtain between them. The first in each pair is to be benevolent to the second, and the second is to be loyal to the first. Consequently, a person's value and identity could be secured or identified only in relation to a complex web of social relationships; loyalty, obedience, filial piety, conformity and sincerity are the values emphasised in Chinese society. Thus, it is argued that Confucianism, as well as Chinese society, has a strong tendency toward collectivism (Ip, 1996).

In order to build a harmonious and peaceful society based on moral rules governing human relations, Confucianism also places great emphasis on education. Confucius believed that the purpose of education was to cultivate decency and benevolence in students and that it is of great importance to teach ethical and moral values to the young. Furthermore, it was Confucius' view that all people should have an equal and fair chance to succeed in education. His view later led to the development of an open, meritocratic examination system in the Han Dynasty (206 BC-AD 220). This examination system was the basis of the educational system and served as a means of potential upward mobility that still prevails in Taiwan today. It also impacts heavily on the way the curriculum is implemented in the classroom.

Japanese Colonialism

In 1895 Taiwan was ceded to the Empire of Japan under the Treaty of Shiminoseki after the Sino-Japanese War and became a Japanese colony for 50 years till the end of World War II. The goal of Japanese colonialism in Taiwan was to establish a unified and easily managed industrialised society from which Japan could reap benefits. Therefore the Japanese rulers engaged in remarkable efforts to develop Taiwan's industry, creating the first system of national public schools and enforcing the use of the Japanese language as the sole medium of communication and instruction in Taiwan (Chen, 1968; Kiang, 1992; Smith, 1991; Tsurumi, 1977).

Although Taiwan was oppressed and subject to the rule of force at that time, Japanese colonialism had a critical influence on the development of Taiwan society. First, the rapid expansion of industrialisation improved standards of living across the island, creating an expanding middle-class and bringing about a Taiwanese lifestyle that differed strongly from that of the traditional Chinese lifestyle on the Mainland (Kiang, 1992). Second, before Japanese colonial control, the Fujianese, the Hakka and the Indigenous Taiwanese often could not understand one another's language. The language training imposed by the Japanese on the Taiwanese people, however, produced a common medium of communication among the Taiwanese. Also, the imposition of Japanese history and values taught in local schools served to further distinguish the knowledge the Taiwanese acquired from that of the Chinese. Together, these influences gradually created a new sense of Taiwanese consciousness differing from that of the Mainland Chinese (Kiang, 1992), and this eventually became the origin of the conflicts over national identity found in today's Taiwanese society.

Sociopolitical Transformation

Taiwan was returned to the Republic of China (ROC) under the leadership of the KMT in 1945. Nevertheless, Japanese colonial approaches distanced the Taiwanese locals from their former Mainland counterparts, and the February 28 Incident[iv] escalated the hostility between the locals and the new arrivals from the Mainland.

The KMT government withdrew from continental China to Taiwan in 1949 after being defeated by the Communist regime in the civil war. Under immense and continuous threat from the Communist regime, the KMT government resolved to develop Taiwan into a fortress in the Taiwan Strait and to achieve national development through a series of measures. The KMT transplanted the constitution and state structure of the ROC from Mainland China to Taiwan. The main purpose of this measure was to maintain the fiction that Taiwan was a province of the ROC and the KMT regime was its sole legitimate government (Chen, 1997). In addition, mass media and education were used to (a) eradicate Japanese influence, (b) re-identify with Chinese tradition, (c) inculcate Taiwanese people with the concept of Taiwan as a bastion of anticommunism, (d) instil a nationalist spirit in the people, and (e) reinforce the legitimacy of the KMT regime (Chen, 1997; Xu, 1993). Moreover, martial law was imposed to direct control of Taiwan by the military and to suppress all organisations, groups and activities challenging the leadership of the KMT.

In the 1980s, a political transition began to take place in Taiwan. This transition can be characterised by two related directions: democratisation and Taiwanisation. The development of these two directions is intertwined with the KMT's striving to maintain its leadership of Taiwan and the issue of Taiwan's national identity.

Democratisation. The KMT maintained authoritarian rule by enforcing martial law for four decades. It was not until the mid-1980s that a series of critical events gave rise to the dawn of a political transition. The KMT took a series of democratisation measures to ease the increasing challenges from a grass-roots movement of political opposition. The first political opposition party in Taiwan, the Democratic Progressive Party (DPP), was established in 1986. One year later, martial law was lifted, which led to more liberalisation measures, including the abolition of bans on the mass media, official tolerance for public demonstrations, legalisation of public discussion of Taiwan's independence, and the institutionalisation of multiparty competition in elections. On March 18, 2000, the citizens of Taiwan voted to choose the first president from the DPP, Chen Shuibian, who advocates the independence of Taiwan. The peaceful transfer of power from the KMT to the DPP indicated Taiwan's political transition from an authoritarian dictatorship to a pluralistic representative system. The democratisation also resulted in the loosening of the government's central control and the gradual formation of an autonomous civil society. Different pressure groups have emerged that have played a more active role in the discussions and formulation of public policies, which eventually led to the recent educational reform in Taiwan.

Taiwanisation. After being expelled from the United Nations in 1971, the KMT began to employ a policy of Taiwanisation to promote the idea of Taiwan as homeland of Taiwan's people. Therefore, more native Taiwanese were recruited into the higher echelons of the state structure. Especially the promotion of Lee Tenghui in 1984 to become the first native Taiwanese Vice-President, and later President and leader of the KMT in 1988, were important milestones. After taking up the presidential office, Lee started to redefine the national identity of Taiwanese people, and marginalise the political claims of his KMT predecessors to the leadership of the KMT over the whole of China. It was the first time the KMT recognised the fact of a "divided China." Since then the consciousness of Taiwan as an independent political entity has been stressed and is carried on by President Chen Shuibian. This development also further deepened the conflicts over national identity among the Taiwanese people and influenced the curriculum reform concerning citizenship.

The Development of the Citizenship Curriculum

Citizenship curriculum is political by its nature. The knowledge that becomes embodied in the citizenship curriculum is a significant historical and sociopolitical artefact (Kliebard, 1992). The development of citizenship curriculum in Taiwan also corresponds to Taiwan's sociopolitical transition, for which three main periods can be distinguished: the nationalistic citizenship curriculum (1950s to mid-1980s), the transitional citizenship curriculum (mid-1980 to 1990s), and the integrated citizenship curriculum (2000 to present).

The Nationalistic Citizenship Curriculum

The period of the nationalistic citizenship curriculum in Taiwan was obviously bound by Taiwan's politics and Chinese culture. Because of the strong tendency towards collectivism in Chinese culture heritage and out of concern for national security, during this period Taiwan developed a very rigid, centralised educational curriculum to control educational processes and practice. Taiwan's central government has long played an important and decisive role in education. It has engaged in substantial efforts to shape its contents and methodology via national standards and unified government-published textbooks. The MOE was authorised to set up national curriculum standards to guide most educational activities. All textbooks were published by the National Institute for Compilation and Translation (NICT), a governmental educational institute under the MOE. Besides, due to the desire to eradicate Japanese influence, re-identify with Chinese tradition and the view to "reconstruct the Mainland in the future" held by the late President Chiang Kaishek[v], the citizenship curriculum had a strong China-centred and anticommunist orientation.

In 1953, Chiang Kaishek published *The Supplementary Statements on Education and Recreation for the Principle of Livelihood*, in which he defined and analysed the goals, scope and contents of citizenship education. Taiwan's citizenship curriculum was guided by this document for decades (Huang & Chiu, 1991). Chiang argued that education was responsible for the KMT government's being defeated by the Chinese communists. The failure of education on the Mainland was especially related to the fact that young people lacked national spirit and did not truly understand traditional Chinese moral virtues and the Three Principles of the People (Tsai, 2002), the teaching of Dr Sun Yatsen that became the foundation of the ROC. From this point of view, citizenship curriculum should place emphasis on fostering students' national spirit and moral values, based upon the teaching of Dr Sun Yatsen and Chinese culture heritage. This view of citizenship curriculum, which centred on a nationalistic education, was clearly reflected in an official document of the Ministry of Education (1972):

> In our education, common courses shall be based both on the teaching of Dr. Sun Yatsen and on the Eight Chinese Moral Virtues: loyalty, filial piety, mercifulness, love, faithfulness, righteousness, harmony, and peacefulness. (p.3)

School subjects related to citizenship curriculum included "Life and Ethics" and "Social Studies" in the elementary school, along with "Civics and Morality," "History," and "Geography" at the junior high level. These subjects generally aimed at developing students' (a) understanding of the development of the Chinese nation and the change of its territory, (b) understanding of the importance of Taiwan as a base for recovering Mainland China, (c) appreciation of Chinese superior nationality and national spirit, (d) comprehension of the teachings of Sun Yatsen and Chiang Kaishek and their contribution to the nation, (e) willingness to love and build the local community and the nation, and (f) appreciation of Chinese culture, modern world culture and democracy. The content of each subject is summarised as follows (Ministry of Education, 1975, 1983):

- Life and Ethics: 18 key moral virtues, including filial piety, diligence, cooperation, observance of the law, bravery, patriotism, honesty, frugality, responsibility, sense of shame, perseverance, justice, peace, etc.

- Social Studies: knowledge of history, geography, civics and government, as well as the teachings of Sun Yatsen and Chiang Kaishek
- Civics and Morality: civic knowledge regarding education, society, politics, economics, law, and culture, along with "Code of Daily Life Behaviour" which encompassed moral virtues similar to those of "Life and Ethics" at the elementary level
- History: national (China) history, world history; a very small portion of post-1949 Taiwan history was covered in national history
- Geography: national (China) geography, world geography; a very small portion of Taiwan geography was covered in national geography

In sum, from the 1950s to the mid-1980s, the policy of "Recovery of the Mainland" had a significant impact on the design of citizenship curriculum. Education was to become a "symbolic battlefield" in fighting against Communism (Tsai, 2002). Thus, citizenship curriculum in this period was regarded as a means of building a "mental defence" that protected Taiwan through an invisible fortress of loyalty and an ever-present sentinel of caution in every citizen's mind. It legitimised the ruling authority of the KMT government and built national identity in Taiwan's people by cultivating students' appreciation of Chinese culture heritage and the teachings of Sun Yatsen and Chiang Kaishek. The content of the curriculum was China-centred, ideology-driven and morality-based. The primary intent of the curriculum was to inculcate students with the so-called responsibilities of recovering lost territory and freeing their compatriots in the Motherland and ending their enslavement by the evil communists. As a result, although the development of democratic citizenship was cited in the curriculum standards, the cultivation of loyal citizens who were law-abiding, patriotic and respected the government's authority was indeed the real focus of citizenship curriculum in this period (Doong, 2002). It was nationalistic and by its very nature a case of moral education.

The Transitional Citizenship Curriculum

With the termination of martial law in 1987, the opposition determined to challenge and change the KMT-monopolised education system. From the opposition's perspective, the educational establishment in Taiwan was one of the most conservative institutions utilised by the KMT as a means of brainwashing and political socialisation. Citizenship curriculum was especially criticised for indoctrinating students with the authoritarian nationalist ideology (Wu, 1998). Meanwhile, in 1988, the power of the KMT government was passed to Lee Tenghui. Because of Lee's background and attitude towards national identity,[vi] the government took several major steps to "de-Sinicise" the citizenship curriculum. The revision of citizenship curriculum standards in 1993 (elementary level) and 1994 (junior high level) emphasised nationalistic education and ideological indoctrination much less. Nationalistic terminology, such as "Chinese superior nationality," "national spirit," "anticommunism" and "recovering Mainland China" was downplayed or even excluded from the curriculum. Instead, space was created for local identities, issues and characteristics, which had been suppressed in the past, to be reinstated, such as the history of pre-1949 Taiwan, local ethnic identity and local cultures.

There were changes made in the school subjects related to citizenship curriculum during this period. At the elementary level, "Life and Ethics" was merged with "Health Education" into a new subject titled "Morality and Health." In addition, because of the rise of Taiwanese consciousness, two new subjects were officially incorporated into school citizenship curriculum, "Homeland Studies" for elementary level from third to sixth grades and "Understanding Taiwan" for junior high level in seventh grade. These two subjects were regarded as remedies for students' lack of knowledge of local history, geography, culture and the contemporary development of Taiwan. Also, due to the teaching of "Understanding Taiwan" in seventh grade, "Civics and Morality," "History," and "Geography" were taught only in eighth and ninth grades. The following points summarise the content of the citizenship-related subjects in the transitional period (Ministry of Education, 1993a, 1994):

- Morality and Health: 8 key moral virtues, including filial piety, observance of the law, patriotism, honesty, frugality, humanity, courtesy, and justice
- Social Studies: history, geography and social sciences regarding individual, family, school, local community, Taiwan, China and the world
- Civics and Morality: social sciences, knowledge of anthropology, sociology, psychology, political science, economics, law and culture, along with "Codes of Daily Life Behaviour" which encompassed honesty, patriotism, observance of the law, humanity, filial piety, courtesy, frugality, justice, social morality, responsibility, cooperation, and respect
- Understanding Taiwan: Taiwan's society, geography, and history
- History: national (China) history and world history
- Geography: national (China) geography and world geography

Comparing this list to the citizenship curriculum in the nationalistic period, several observations can be made based upon the content analysis of curriculum documents and textbooks. First, the teachings of Sun Yatsen and Chiang Kaishek were no longer emphasised in the citizenship curriculum, and the amount of overtly ideological content declined notably. The citizenship curriculum in this period was more social science-oriented and organised as a simplified introduction to the social sciences. Second, this was the first time the history of Taiwan was made a subject of study in the citizenship curriculum in Taiwan. Third, Chinese history and geography were still referred to as "national" history and geography in those subjects; however, in the subject "Understanding Taiwan," Taiwan was no longer described as a periphery of the ROC, but as a political entity. Besides, learning about historical Taiwan and the spirit of Taiwan changed from being forbidden to being legally recognised knowledge. Fourth, the concepts of "anticommunism" and "recovering the motherland" were removed from the curriculum; instead, "defending Taiwan with determination" and "courage against external military threat" (referring to Mainland China) became two of the emphases. Fifth, the interdisciplinary curriculum pattern at the junior high level was first shown in the subject "Understanding Taiwan." Finally, moral education remained one of the foci of the curriculum but its weight was reduced.

The Integrated Citizenship Curriculum

Before the new millennium, education in Taiwan was a highly centralised institution. The Constitution of the Republic of China makes it clear that education is of such great importance to the nation that it was placed under the central government and funded by the nation's broad-based tax structure. Beginning from the early 1990s, a wide range of social groups were formed which devoted themselves to making changes in formal education. Among those groups, the Humanistic Education Foundation, the Housewives League, the Academy for Invigorating Teachers, and the April 10 League of Educational Reform Movement are most identifiable. These reformist groups found different interests at different levels and in types of education, but they spoke with one voice in their challenge to the legitimacy of the old-time "monocracy," which had implanted nationalism in all aspects of formal education. Hence, they were earnestly eager to remove the old-fashioned mechanisms and to free Taiwan's education systems completely from the control of centralised administration. They were particularly keen to abolish the joint entrance examinations, deregulate the textbook policy and remove the government's control over school curricula (Liu & Doong, 2002; Yang, Wu, & Shan, 2001).

In 1994, the Seventh National Education Conference pointed out the need for improving the rigid, centralised education system as a response to reform requests. The Premier then established a cabinet-level ad hoc Commission on Educational Reform (CER) to take on the task of identifying practical strategies for restructuring the education system to meet the need of the new century. After two years of study and inquiry, the *Consultants' Concluding Report on Education Reform* (Commission on Educational Reform, 1996) was released. The report highlighted five major reform recommendations: deregulation, engaging students, making education accessible, raising education quality, and promoting a society of lifelong learning. To implement the reform proposals, the *Twelve Education Reform Mandates* were approved to be accomplished within a five-year period (Educational Reform Task Force Committee, 1998). Among the reform programmes and policies, the nine-year integrated curriculum was of most importance in bringing about radical changes in elementary and junior high school education.

Previously the junior high school subjects were taught separately and were not linked with elementary subjects in function. In the new curriculum, the traditional subjects were replaced by seven major learning areas so as to avoid confining students within the boundaries of a subject and overlooking students' ability to integrate what they have already learned. The seven learning areas include "language arts," "health and physical education," "social studies," "arts and humanities," "mathematics, science and technology," and "integrated activities."

This new curriculum attempts to reduce the number of school subjects by integrating subjects of a similar nature. In the citizenship education domain, "Morality and Health," "Civics and Morality," "Geography," "History," and "Understanding Taiwan" at elementary and junior high levels are all integrated as "Social Studies." Moreover, the traditional, centralised curriculum standards were replaced by non-prescriptive *Grade 1-9 Curriculum Guidelines*. The content of the new citizenship curriculum is organised around nine thematic strands to integrate the concepts and generalisations of the history subject and the social science disciplines. The goals and the nine thematic strands of the new curriculum are listed in Table 3.1.

Table 3.1   Goals and Thematic Strands of Taiwan's New Citizenship Curriculum

Category	Content
Goals	To understand the environment, humanity, diversity and issues of local and other communities. To comprehend the interaction of people, society, culture and ecology, and the significance of environment protection and resource exploitation. To enrich the essential knowledge of social sciences. To develop the identity and concern of homeland and nation, and global views. To cultivate democratic literacy, appreciation of the rule of law, and responsible attitudes. To nurture self-understanding and self-realisation, as well as positive, self-confident and open attitudes. To develop abilities of critical thinking, value judgement and problem solving. To strengthen abilities of social participation, decision making and action. To cultivate abilities of expression, communication and cooperation. To develop interest in and abilities of inquiry, and information processing.
Thematic strands	People and time People and space Change and continuity Meaning and values Individuals, groups and interpersonal interactions Power, rule and human rights Production, distribution and consumption Science, technology and society Global connection

There are some other significant characteristics found in the new curriculum guidelines. First, the new curriculum adopted a flexible and integrated approach to meet individual needs, social needs and to cultivate competent citizens with international vision. Critical thinking, problem solving, civic participation and social concern are stressed more than acquiring knowledge of the social sciences. Second, in social studies the new curriculum distinguished between several stages of learning according to the structure of knowledge concerned, and recognised the continuity principles of the psychological development of learning. Third, competence indicators were set for each thematic strand in each learning stage. The expression "competence indicator" was a new phrase proposed in the *Grade*

1-9 Curriculum Guidelines. A competence indicator is operationally synonymous with the learning goal. Rhetorically, competence indicators serve to define a common language among their users, such as textbook editors and reviewers, teachers, students, parents, administrators and test developers. All of the nine thematic strands comprise different numbers of corresponding competence indicators.[vii] Fourth, the new curriculum identifies six major issues teaching is to be infused by, namely gender education, environmental education, information technology education, human rights education, home economics education and career development education. Fifth, moral education, which was an explicit emphasis in the old curriculum, was dramatically reduced in importance in the new curriculum, while social diversity and multicultural issues were highlighted more than ever before. Citizenship curriculum becomes an arena for the consolidation and transmission of democratic ideals and for engendering respect for ethnic differences and cultures. Finally, according to the competence indicators the proportion of time devoted to Taiwan's culture, history and geography is larger than that devoted to China. Nevertheless, the issue of national identity became more implicit and appears only once in the curriculum goals, but never in the competence indicators.

The Implementation of the New Citizenship Curriculum

The new citizenship curriculum began to be implemented simultaneously in Grade 1, Grade 4 and Grade 7 in August 2002. Since then, a series of new steps have been taken in schools, including the introduction of flexible integrated curriculum, the development of school-based curriculum and the decentralisation of textbook control.

Flexible Integrated Curriculum

Ideally, the purposes of the nine-year integrated curriculum are to simplify the learning content, reduce students' heavy learning load, provide students with flexible curricular options, improve students' abilities to integrate knowledge, think critically and solve problems, and foster basic skills and the lifelong learning attitude necessary for modern citizenship (Ministry of Education, 2003a). Therefore, the flexible integrated curriculum captures the fundamental spirit of the new curriculum.

Instead of regulating rigid learning periods for every learning area, every grade and every school, the curriculum guidelines empower the Committee of School Curriculum Development for each school to determine the learning periods to be assigned for each learning area, based on the following rules[viii] (Ministry of Education, 2003a):

- Learning periods of Language Arts account for 20%-30% of the area learning periods, while the learning periods of the following six learning areas account for 10%-15% of the area learning periods respectively: Health and Physical Education, Social Studies, Arts and Humanities, Mathematics, Integrative Activities.

- Schools calculate the total number of learning periods for each learning area for the whole school year or a semester, according to the above proportions. Schools arrange weekly learning periods according to their real situation and the needs of instruction.
- The time for each period should be approximately 40 minutes for elementary schools and 45 minutes for junior high schools. However, schools may adjust the time for each period, the weeks of each semester, and the arrangements of grades and classes according to specific circumstances of curriculum implementation and the needs of students.
- Schools are empowered to organise and conduct activities for alternative learning periods (including activities for the entire school or all the grades).

Additionally, the curriculum guidelines make it very clear that the implementation of each learning area should follow the principles of integration and include the adoption of team teaching. The policy of flexible and integrated curriculum has led to a major change in the practice of citizenship curriculum. That is, teachers are encouraged to teach more than one subject area to meet the goal of curriculum integration. For example, teachers of "Civics and Morality" need to teach "History" and "Geography" simultaneously, and vice versa. This change not only reshapes the teaching profession in citizenship education but also causes some problems, which will be discussed later.

School-Based Curriculum Development

School-based curriculum is one of the intended goals of the new curriculum reform in Taiwan. It is carried out as part of the policy of curriculum decentralisation with the hope of making every school a centre for curriculum innovation and every teacher a curriculum designer. The *Grade 1-9 Curriculum Guidelines* provide a greater degree of autonomy for teachers and schools in designing their own curriculum and teaching activities to meet the diverse needs of pupils, schools and communities. Thus, the new curriculum consists of alternative learning periods, which account for 20% of the total learning periods for the development of school-based curriculum. According to the curriculum guidelines, schools are empowered to organise and conduct activities for alternative learning periods, carry out curriculum or activities designed to correspond to goals and objectives of the school, provide optional courses for learning areas, implement remedial teaching programmes and conduct group counselling or self-learning activities.

Based on the *Guidelines* and for the development of school-based curriculum, each school is required to set up its own Committee of School Curriculum Development, and give teachers and parents enough flexibility to work together to design 20% of the curriculum. The functions of this committee are to (a) complete the school curriculum plan for the coming semester by the beginning of the current semester; (b) determine the learning periods for each learning area for each grade; (c) review textbooks written by the school staff; (d) develop topics and activities for teaching; and (e) be responsible for the curriculum and instruction evaluation (Ministry of Education, 2003a). Members of the Committee of School Curriculum Development include the representatives of school administrators, teachers for each grade and each learning area, and parents. Scholars and professionals may also be invited to join the committee for counselling when necessary.

Furthermore, to encourage development and innovation of school-based curriculum, measures for school-based curriculum evaluation are also proposed by the MOE and local government authorities. The MOE is responsible for setting up Academic Attainment Indicators to evaluate the implementation of curriculum by local government authorities and individual schools. Local government is responsible for visiting schools on a regular basis in order to understand the implementation of curriculum, and to provide solutions for problems occurring in the implementation process. Government funding for school-based curriculum development is provided by both the central government and by local government.

Although Taiwan does not have a strong tradition of teachers' involvement in curriculum decision-making and innovation, these policy decisions taken by governments have indeed generated some encouraging changes, especially in elementary schools. More and more principals support and are involved in school-based curriculum development. Teachers are more aware of their role in professional development, and their sense of curriculum ownership has increased. Parents have also been welcomed to participate in curriculum innovation and practice to a greater degree (Chen & Chung, 2002). Furthermore, to better utilise limited resources, some schools located in the same geographical area have been working co-operatively to modify the school-based curriculum and turn it into a community-based curriculum. The result has been very beneficial to all the school teachers and students who have participated in the innovation of the community-based curriculum (Ministry of Education, 2003b).

Decentralisation of Textbook Control

Completely opening up the junior high textbook market to private publishers has been one of the critical policies of the nine-year integrated curriculum. Before the 1990s, all textbooks for primary and secondary schools were compiled and published by the NICT. Teachers were required to cover the same material in the same time frame with the same textbooks. Under this policy of centralised control, teachers did not have the opportunity to design their own sets of materials to meet the needs of their students, taking into account individual differences.

In 1991, the MOE took the first step towards the eventual lifting of its ban on textbook writing and publishing. Aside from the standardised version published by the NICT, privately published textbooks for arts and craft were first approved and adopted in junior high schools. Later, in 1995, the MOE extended its policy of deregulation to elementary schools by giving them a free hand to select any MOE-approved textbook. In 1999, the MOE took a further step by granting the right to choose textbooks to senior high schools. However, it was not until the implementation of the nine-year integrated curriculum in 2002 that the MOE completely opened up the junior high textbook market to private publishers as well (Ministry of Education, 2002e).

The ultimate goals of the decentralisation of textbook control was to replace the government's domination of curriculum development with a school-based system and to ensure that teachers assumed the central role in curriculum design (Shan, 2000). The shift in the power to write and publish textbooks from the central government to the private sector signifies today's much greater freedom in Taiwan's educational system.

Controversies and Challenges

The introduction of the nine-year integrated curriculum is the biggest curriculum reform in Taiwan's education history. However, there are gaps between goal and practice, ideal and reality. This curriculum reform, implemented in a short period of time, has had to confront severe challenges.

Controversies over Curriculum Guidelines and Patterns

There have been a number of controversies over the new curriculum guidelines in terms of the appropriateness of curriculum integration, the "Americanised" direction of the curriculum, vagueness of the guidelines, decline in teaching time and avoidance of national identity issues.

Appropriateness of curriculum integration. One major criticism is that integrating primary and junior high school curricula is inappropriate. Critics of the reform question the rationale for the so-called nine-year integrated curriculum. They argue that there are differences between elementary and junior high education in terms of students' needs in learning and in their psychological development. The pressure junior high students face in having to sit for the senior high school entrance examination marks a further difference between junior high and elementary (Chang, 1999). The new curriculum ignores the special needs of students at each educational level. Second, it is argued that one of the tasks for junior high education is to prepare students for senior high school life. The new nine-year curriculum not only fails to fulfil this task but also creates a big gap and inconsistency between junior and senior high education (Liu & Doong, 2002). Third, since 1996, the MOE has been encouraging and helping local governments to establish a six-year combined high school system which includes junior and senior high school students within a unified school government, educating students from the age of 12 to 18. There were 61 combined public high schools established as of the school year 2000, and a number of junior high schools are in the process of transforming into combined high schools (Ministry of Education, 2001d). Thus, critics of the reform argue that a six-year integrated curriculum for junior and senior high education is more appropriate than one that combines the elementary and junior high levels.

Americanised direction of the curriculum. There are a lot of similarities between the *National Standards for Social Studies* of the United States and Taiwan's *Grade 1-9 Curriculum Guidelines* (Liu, 2003; Liu & Doong, 2002). Both disciplinary scholars and teacher educators in Taiwan criticised the new curriculum as "Americanised." They argued that the curriculum guidelines mimicked American thematic standards without considerations of divergent cultural, social and educational contexts between Taiwan and America (Chang, 1999; Liu & Doong, 2002). Thus critics have addressed the need to investigate what is taken to be worthwhile knowledge in Taiwan's society, so as to establish more appropriate curriculum guidelines for Taiwan's social, cultural and educational context (Doong, 2003).

Vagueness of the curriculum guidelines. Scholars and teachers questioned the possibility of implementing those guidelines given the fact that they are overwhelmingly vague in nature. The curriculum standards have created difficulties on account of their alleged vagueness when used by scholars as guidelines for writing textbooks (Liu & Doong, 2002). As a result, different versions of textbooks present completely different and often widely divergent knowledge. Many teachers have reported that students have difficulties adapting to the de-standardised textbooks ("Education Reforms," 2003).

Decline in teaching time. The teaching time for social studies in the new curriculum has been reduced drastically. According to the curriculum guidelines, the learning periods of social studies account for 10%-15% of the total area learning periods. The reality is that most schools assign only 10% of the total area learning periods to social studies, and that alternative learning periods are only assigned to "high status" subjects, such as English and Mathematics. The teaching time for social studies has been cut down approximately from six periods to three periods per week. The "status" of citizenship-related subjects is even lower than it was already since the so-called curriculum reform. Table 3.2 compares the teaching times between the old and the new citizenship curriculum.

Avoidance of national identity issues. Some social groups criticised the new citizenship curriculum for failing to deal with the issues of national identity. They argued that citizenship curriculum should aim at promoting pupils' appreciation of "Taiwanese subjectivity." The curriculum should be designed with a view that Taiwan is an independent entity; that "our" history is Taiwan's history; that "our" geography is Taiwan's geography; and that Chinese history and geography should be studied as foreign history and geography (Southern Taiwan Society, Eastern Taiwan Society, & PEN Taiwan, 2003). They also argued that the history of the ROC before 1949 should be included in Chinese ancient history, not the history of Taiwan. From their point of view, Dr Sun Yatsen is not the "Father of the Nation," but a "foreigner" ("Gov't Plans," 2004). Moreover, in one interview by a journalist, the Minister of Education, Tu Chengsheng,[ix] claimed that Taiwan's education system needs to teach children and teenagers to recognise the history and culture of their land. He believes "elements" of Taiwan play an important part in the development of children's personality and knowledge, and that these can be conveyed through coursework in the humanities and social sciences, including the subjects language, literature, history, geography and civics. He indicated that the Ministry of Education will write a new curriculum that clearly demonstrates how the local elements could be compiled into the nine-year integrated curriculum (Huang, 2004). The debate about national identity issues created by the citizenship curriculum is heating up, indeed.

Table 3.2 Comparison of Teaching Time of the Old and New Citizenship Curriculum

Year/Version	Title of Subject	Periods per Week		
		Year 1	Year 2	Year 3
1994 Curriculum Standard for Junior High School	Understanding Taiwan	3	0	0
	Civics and Morality	0	2	2
	History	0	2	2
	Geography	0	2	2
	Total	3	6	6
2000 Grade 1-9 Curriculum Guidelines	Social Studies	3	3	3
	Total	3	3	3

Constraints on School-Based Curriculum Development

In two recent studies (Chen & Chung, 2002; Doong, 2003), some implementation difficulties and constraints were identified in the development of school-based curriculum. First, most school administrators and teachers were frustrated because the vagueness of the curriculum guidelines failed to provide a clear enough picture for them to set the goals and directions for school curriculum.

Second, teachers in Taiwan have become highly dependent on national standards and uniform textbooks. As a result, most are not sufficiently motivated or have the necessary experience and ability to develop and design their own curriculum. Many teachers claimed that they had never been trained to do curriculum design and evaluation so they did not possess the knowledge and skills required to develop school-based curriculum. Some teachers gave as the main reason for their participation in the school-based curriculum development pressure from their principals and directors of Academic Affairs.

Third, while some teachers did express interest in and have tried some curriculum innovation at classroom level, they felt, however, that they did not get enough administrative support in providing necessary reference materials, working space, in-service training courses or workshops, and external help from advisory specialists. They also indicated that the shortage of time was a major problem standing in the way of doing curriculum design. Besides, teachers thought that the necessary partnership of teachers working as a team to develop school-based curriculum was lacking. Problems frequently arose in the partnerships and it was rather difficult for them to reach consensus as to what should be included in or excluded from the curriculum.

Finally, Taiwan is a society in which a fanatical belief in the value of education has long existed. To some extent, this belief includes a corrupted form of so-called "school promotionism" – the phenomenon of focusing on climbing up the school ladder to reach university and college as the preferred route to success. Most school administrators and teachers were afraid that the school-based curriculum would increase "unnecessary" study burdens on students and even lower their competence level in the senior high school entrance examination. As a result, some teachers indicated that school-based curriculum was only good for a "curriculum design contest", but was never a realistic and useful school practice at the junior high level.

Issues of Interdisciplinary Instruction

In implementing the nine-year integrated curriculum, teachers need to be able to design and develop curriculum utilizing an interdisciplinary approach. However, there are gaps between the ideal and the reality, particularly at the junior high school level. In the past, the teaching of citizenship education at the junior high schools was mainly covered in one subject, "Civics and Morality." Both "History" and "Geography," which shoulder tremendous responsibility in terms of citizenship education in the United States, had never been considered a part of citizenship education in Taiwan. "History," "Geography" and "Civics and Morality" were isolated subjects at the junior high level. There are different teacher education departments at normal universities for history, geography, and civics and morality. Social Studies has never been an integrated field in Taiwan.

Additionally, history and geography are more academically-oriented than citizenship-oriented in the standard teacher education programmes. Teachers of "Civics and Morality" have never been trained to teach history and geography. Similarly, political science, law and economics, and social sciences are not required courses and are not even offered in history and geography teacher education programmes. Nor have teacher education programmes ever offered courses on how to integrate knowledge of those disciplines in their curriculum and teaching. In other words, teachers of "History," "Geography" and "Civics and Morality" at the junior high school have not been trained to teach integrated social studies.

Unfortunately, the MOE and local governments offered very limited opportunities for workshops providing in-service teacher training in this regard. Neither has any long-term effective teacher re-education plan been proposed to date. As a result, teachers at the junior high schools feel very anxious about the new curriculum due to their lack of professional knowledge and teaching skills for other subjects (Liu & Doong, 2002). In a survey reported in January 2003, 90% of teachers polled admitted that they are having problems teaching the new curriculum. In addition, a large number of frustrated teachers who have found it hard to keep up with the new curriculum have been submitting requests for early retirement ("Education Reform," 2003). Therefore, the sweeping and radical changes from the discipline-based curriculum to the integrated curriculum have resulted in a deep gap between ideal and reality.

Problems of Textbook Writing

Problems also arose from the decentralisation of textbook control. There are no longer standardised versions of textbooks for all school levels. Different privately published textbooks vary in content, scope and sequence. As a result, students are forced to read as many versions of textbooks as they can so as to get a high score in the senior high school entrance examination (Hsu, 2001). Research also found that most publishers do their best to design the integrative social studies textbooks, but it is still difficult for them to reach the goal of real curriculum integration. Besides, the textbook editors fail to thoroughly deal with interdisciplinary knowledge and issues. Therefore, curriculum integration never happened in the writing of textbooks (Wu, 2002).

Conclusion

A significant curriculum reform such as Taiwan's nine-year integrated curriculum requires no less than the restructuring of education. Fundamentally, it involves the reallocation of societal authorities and values. In practice, it also involves a series of compromises among diverse groups and efforts to reach an accord with the public priorities of society. By its very nature, curriculum reform is a political activity, with the process of developing Taiwan's citizenship curriculum clearly demonstrating the political nature of curriculum reform. Taiwan's citizenship curriculum was once, under the leadership of Chiang Kaishek, a means of "de-Taiwanisation," aimed at "recovering the Mainland." It is now regarded as an instrument of "de-Sinicisation" by Chen Shuibian's administration to push for Taiwan's independence. Interestingly, although Chiang and Chen took very different stands on the issue of Taiwan's national identity, they both used citizenship curriculum as a battlefield in fighting against communist China. The citizenship curriculum in Taiwan was and still is a very party-political issue and driven by ideology.

Furthermore, no matter how comprehensively or carefully a curriculum has been developed, the ultimate test of the curriculum is the way it is implemented and experienced by teachers and pupils in the classroom. Taiwan's new curriculum reform has been criticised for lacking sufficient dialogue with those directly involved in education, such as teachers, students and parents, as well as putting too much emphasis on easing controls on the curriculum without feasible implementation strategies. Moreover, the citizenship curriculum guidelines were also criticised for their Americanised direction, which obviously followed in the footsteps of U.S. curriculum standards.

Taiwan's citizenship curriculum is at a crossroads. Having had only a relatively short time for its implementation, it is hard to tell whether the new reform policies will survive the challenges. However, there will be no future for Taiwan's citizenship education if Taiwan's educational policy-makers remain in favour of imported Americanised knowledge, or are getting stuck in the mud of the unification-independence battle. The sooner they wake up to the gravity of the flaws in the curriculum reform policies, the better the curriculum will be able to cultivate good citizenship among the pupils. Therefore, it might be necessary for all educational policy-makers, particularly the MOE, to quickly establish an effective mechanism for diagnosing flaws in policies, testing the results of curriculum reform, mapping out implementation strategies, and, most importantly, for investigating what is considered worthwhile knowledge in Taiwan. The latter is clearly needed if a consensus is to be reached by concerned groups for more appropriate curriculum guidelines in Taiwan's context. It is the author's sincere hope that these steps will be seen in the very near future.

Notes

[i]   The indigenous people are comprised of 12 tribes: Amis, Atayal, Paiwan, Bunun, Rukai, Pu-yuma, Tsou, Saisiyat, Yami, Thao, Kavalan and Truku. They are Malayo-Polynesian and speak various Austronesian languages. Collectively, they comprise less than 2% of Taiwan's total population (Council of Indigenous Peoples, 2004).

[ii] These two groups comprise about 85% of the Han population, with Fujianese outnumbering Hakka by about three to one.

[iii] As of 2004, Mainlanders account for less than 15% of the Han population.

[iv] During the immediate postwar period, the KMT administration of Taiwan was repressive and corrupt, leading to local discontent. As a result, tensions between the local Taiwanese and the new arrivals from the Mainland increased in the intervening years. Anti-Mainlander violence flared on February 28, 1947, prompted by an incident in which a cigarette seller was injured and a passer-by was shot dead by KMT authorities. For several weeks after the February 28 Incident, the rebels held control of much of the island. The KMT then assembled a large military force that attacked Taiwan, killing many Taiwanese and imprisoning thousands of others. (Retrieved November 11, 2004, from The Free Dictionary Com Website, http://encyclopedia.thefreedictionary. com/228%20Massacre).

[v]   President Chiang Kaishek and his son, President Chiang Chingkuo, had governed Taiwan from 1949-1988, a total of 40 years.

[vi] Lee Tenghui was born in Taiwan and educated in the public school system during the Japanese colonial period; he later studied in Japan and then in the United States. Although he was once a member and the leader of the KMT, he has a strong sense of Taiwanese consciousness and advocates the independence of Taiwan. Lee was in power for twelve years, from 1988-2000.

[vii] The role of the competence indicators in the Grade 1-9 Curriculum reform is similar to those found in academic standards in the standards-based education reform in the U.S.A. Both seek to establish clear and challenging academic standards for all students, to help all students to achieve standards and to prepare them for success in the 21st century.

[viii] The total learning periods for each grade vary. For example, the total learning periods for Grade 7 are 32-34, which comprise 28 area learning periods and 4-6 alternative learning periods.

[ix] Tu became the Minister of Education in May 2004. He is a historian who has been advocating reforms in Taiwan's history education. The subject "Understanding Taiwan" is based upon his "concentric circle theory", in which "elements of Taiwan" predominate. He also proposed a new Taiwan map layout, which turns the current map 90 degrees counter-clockwise, with Taiwan on top of China instead of on its right.

4

Citizenship Curriculum in China: A Shifting Discourse towards Chinese Democracy, Law Education and Psychological Health

Minghua ZHONG and Wing On LEE

Introduction: Democracy in the Chinese Context

According to the Director of the 21ˢᵗ Century Education Development Research Academy in China, civic education is in its infancy in mainland China. The Director points out that "the term only surfaced in public in the past couple of years. It was very sensitive and couldn't be talked about before" (Liu, 2005). However, Zhou Hongling, Director of the Beijing New Era Citizen Education Centre, argues that "for the transformation of China from a traditional autocratic society into a modern democratic nation instruction in civic education is a necessity." Zhou further alleges that providing civic education, promoting "citizen action," and eventually establishing a civil society could lead to a peaceful and gradual transition (cited in Liu, 2005, p.A6).

This is not likely to be a rapid transition. In a recent white paper issued by the China State Council Information Office entitled "Building of Political Democracy in China," China's leaders argue that China's democratic system has been continuously improved, and varied forms of democracy have been introduced. However, it should be understood that in China political democracy is not the same as Western liberal democracy. Rather it is "socialist democracy with Chinese characteristics" in which the Communist Party of China (CPC) remains the paramount source of power and leadership. The white paper vigorously defends China's right to pursue its own path in perfecting its democracy:

> The history and reality of human political civilization have proved that there is no one single and absolute democratic mode in the world that is universally applicable. To say whether a political system is democratic or not, the key is to see whether the will of the overwhelming majority of the people is fully reflected, whether their rights as masters of the country are fully realized, and whether their legitimate rights and interests are fully guaranteed.

The arduous explorations and struggles made by the Chinese people over the past 100 years and more in order to realize democracy, and especially China's success in building a socialist political democracy, have made the CPC and the Chinese people realize that China must base the building of political democracy on is own reality, review its own experience gained in practice, treasure its own achievements, and learn from the experience and achievements of the political civilization of other countries.

But, it must not copy any model of other countries. (State Council Information Office, 2005)

While citing shortcomings such as the abuse of power, corruption and failure to enforce laws, the white paper also notes that there is still a long way to go in building political democracy, and that a complete model of democracy cannot be built overnight. What is required is an orderly step-by-step process towards the objective of developing a socialist political democracy in the Chinese context. At the same time the white paper states that the concept of democracy and legal awareness of the whole society need to be enhanced. It is in this context that Zhou Hongling and others publicly argue that the need for public instruction in civic education is urgent.

The appearance of a white paper defending the state of democracy in China is reflective of widespread changes in China over the last three decades. Since 1978, China has experienced dramatic changes in many aspects of life. The adoption of the open door policy and the modernisation policy has led to significant changes in the social and economic fabric of Chinese society. One remarkable change was the shift from a planned economy to a market-oriented economy (called 'socialist market economy' in China). The rise of a socialist market economy has led to new demands for citizenship qualities, such as a global perspective, an orientation towards achievement, open-mindedness, democratic awareness, etc. Such changes in political circumstances (i.e., the adoption of the open door policy) and social and economic circumstances (i.e., the rise of the socialist market economy) underscore the recent directions of citizenship curriculum development in China.

This chapter attempts to track the change of emphases in the citizenship curriculum in light of the changes in political, social and economic circumstances during this period. In this context we should note that the term "citizenship (or civic) education" is in general not used in the literature in China, or adopted in the official curriculum, as it has been perceived that the term is a Western political concept alleging democratic citizenship. The closest terms to citizenship education in China would include political education, ideological education and moral education. A Chinese dictionary of moral education suggests that the three terms are actually three-in-one in connotation, and can be used interchangeably (Liu, 1998, p.120). These concepts are so interrelated that they merge variably into ideopolitical education (*sixiang zhengzhi jiaoyu*) and ideomoral education (*sixiang pinde jiaoyu*). It is only in the past few years that the term civic education has surfaced in public (Liu, 2005, p.A6).

This chapter will first outline the historical development of the citizenship curriculum in China, with special reference to three stages of orientation shifts: (1) political orientation, (2) political and moral orientation, and (3) moral orientation. The chapter will further discuss recent developments of three themes of citizenship curriculum, namely nationalistic education, democracy education and psychological health education.

The Politically-Oriented Citizenship Curriculum (1949-1978)

The early years of citizenship education in the People's Republic of China were essentially political education based on Marxist-Leninist ideology or ideopolitical education. After the founding of the Peoples' Republic in 1949, the task of moral education in China was mainly "to destroy feudalist, bourgeois, and fascist ideologies, and to nurture such national virtues as loving the country, loving the people, loving labour, loving science and loving public property" (Communist Party of China [CPC], 1949a, 1949b). In 1951, the government adopted the *Social Science Basic Knowledge Course* as a text for ideopolitical education in senior secondary schools (Wei, 1951), and *Chinese Revolution Studies* in junior secondary schools. The teaching of current issues was flavoured by anti-American imperialism. At that time, the primary function of ideopolitical education was to strengthen socialist ideologies, develop a dialectic materialistic world view, and nurture communist moral qualities among students (Hu, 1951). In 1958, *Political Literacy* and *Socialist Foundations* were introduced to the curriculum, requiring schools to provide ideopolitical education that advocated Marxist-Leninism, and develop among teachers and students the view points of the proletariat, the masses, the collectivity, of labour (including both mental and physical labour) and dialectical materialism. In sum, the foci of citizenship curriculum in this period were to serve national goals, support the nationally promulgated ideologies, criticise those ideologies disapproved of by the government and cultivate such citizenship values as collectivism, patriotism, nationalism and self-sacrifice.

The Politically- and Morally-Oriented Citizenship Curriculum (1978-1993)

1978 was a turning point in China's political development which had far-reaching impact upon the country's social and economic development, and subsequently the citizenship curriculum. The Third Plenum of the CPC Central Committee decided to adopt an open door policy, and this marked the beginning of the modernisation period in China. In the same year, the government reinstated the *Behavioural Code for Primary and Secondary Students* (Ministry of Education, 1979). According to the code, the task of moral education was to cultivate students' ideals, morality, culture, and discipline; affectivity towards the socialist motherland and the socialist enterprise; dedication to the country's development; thirst for new knowledge; willingness to think and the courage to be creative. In 1988, a radical revision of the political education curriculum took place. At junior secondary level, "Civics" was introduced in Year 7, "Social History" in Year 8, and "Construction of Chinese Socialism" in Year 9. At senior secondary level, "Scientific View of Life" was introduced in Year 10, "Economics" in Year 11, and "Politics" in Year 12. Although politics was still very much an emphasis of citizenship education in school, "Civics" began to be introduced as a separate subject, focusing on students' behaviour. In the same year, the government issued the *Outline of Moral Education in Secondary School* (China Education Yearbook, Various Years), which was fully implemented in 1991. The significance of this document is that "moral education" was used independently, without being prefixed by "ideology." Moral education began to emerge as a single focus in the citizenship curriculum. The *Outline* provided detailed deliberations on teaching contents and approaches, as well as the values, attitudes and behaviours to be espoused. In the main, the syllabus advocated the teaching of:

- Socialism and collectivism based upon patriotism;
- Students' moral standards and behaviours; and
- Using a motivational approach to develop self-esteem, self-reliance (independence) and self-strengthening in students.

Moreover, the *Outline* called for the building of a campus culture that would support moral education in school.

The change in the orientation of citizenship education was subtle. During this period there were several waves of government movements to combat the emergence of capitalist liberalisation and peaceful revolution, which were seen to be jeopardising the status of socialist ideologies. However, at the same time, the emergence of the modernisation policy soon after the adoption of the open door policy also triggered needs to develop the kind of citizenship qualities that would support modernisation. It was in this context that the theory of the primary stage of socialism emerged (Lee & Postiglione, 1994). According to the theory, China was in the primary stage of socialism that involved the development of production forces and wealth accumulation. These would be achieved through the introduction of markets and opening to the outside world (BBC, 2003). Even though ideological control became more stringent after the June 4 Tianmen incident in 1989, the theory was not officially denounced.

In 1993, a government document entitled *Opinions on Strengthening and Improving the Party and Ideopolitical Works in Higher Institutes in New Circumstances* (Ministry of Education, 1994b) was published. The document launched the idea of "two lessons (*liangke*)" education, meaning that ideopolitical education was defined as a combination of Marxist theory lessons and ideopolitical education lessons. Such a distinction in the two kinds of lessons in citizenship education conferred an official status on ideopolitical education while maintaining the significance of Marxism in the school curriculum. The term ideopolitical education in this context actually refers to "the cultivation of ideo-moral quality (*sixiang daode xiuyang*)," which is comprised of the teaching of ideologies and life philosophies (Zhang, 1995, p.202). Such a distinction is significant in its recognition of the official status of moral education in the curriculum. It also initiated further development of moral education towards psychological health, virtues and life philosophies which were unrelated to politics. In this sense, the 1993 document officially demarcated a new era for citizenship education, with moral education being formally depoliticised.

Citizenship Education as Moral Education (since 1993)

The adoption of the "two lessons" policy marked the identification of moral education as a subject in its own right. However, rather than being simply a recognition of the independent status of moral education by the government, it also reflected the policies developed towards this direction in the community. Since the adoption of the modernisation policy, an increasing need was felt to teach young citizens, and even adults, to develop personal qualities that would match features of the market economy. For example, massive discussions on self-image, self-management, personality development and meanings of life have emerged since the early nineties, in relation to building among the young the capacity to make independent moral judgements (State Education Commission, 1990; Lee, 2002b). However, the policy contributed to legitimizing moral education as disassociated from politics. While the collective and social dimension was still very much upheld, the significance of the personal dimension of citizenship became increasingly explicit in the citizenship literature.

In 1996, the Ministry of Education issued the *Curriculum Standards for Whole-day General Senior Secondary School Ideopolitical Education* (Ministry of Education, 1996). In 2001, the Ministry of Education further issued the *Curriculum Standards for Nine-year Compulsory Ideomoral Education in Primary School and Ideopolitical Education in Junior Secondary School* (Ministry of Education, 2001a). The two curriculum documents placed obvious emphasis on the development of the psychological health of individual students and their ability to make moral judgements. The curriculum content and the proposed pedagogy concurred with the thrusts of citizenship education in many other societies, emphasising the development of self-esteem and related citizenship skills, such as critical thinking, problem solving, etc. We conclude that the citizenship curriculum developed in this period was designed to address the needs of Chinese society in the process of its modernisation and opening up to the world, and resulted in a shift in the citizenship curriculum to focus more on individual growth rather than ideopolitical socialisation.

Current Themes in the Citizenship Curriculum

The above section aimed to depict a macro picture of the trend of the citizenship curriculum over the last few decades from a historical perspective. Below, we will further analyse the latest development of the three themes of citizenship, namely nationalistic education, democracy education, and psychological health education. These themes are key components of the current citizenship curriculum, and changes in emphases and contents of each theme can illustrate changes in the citizenship curriculum in general.

Nationalistic Education

Nationalistic education is always a key agenda of citizenship education in China. The notion of nationalistic education is rather broad-based, as according to the 1988 *Outline of Moral Education in Secondary School* (State Education Commission, 1988), junior secondary students have to be taught concepts of the country, respect towards other ethnicities, love of peace, love of the country (patriotism) and international understanding. The senior secondary students have to be taught a higher level of patriotism, which places the interests of the country over individual interests. The 1995 revised *Secondary School Moral Education Syllabus* (Ministry of Education, 1995) further enriched the content on patriotism, including such topics as Chinese culture, revolutionary heroes, contemporary achievements and national unity. In 2001, the government issued *Revised Curriculum Standards for the Primary Ideomoral and Junior Secondary Ideopolitical Curriculum of the Nine-year Universal Education* (Ministry of Education, 2001b). The document has provided more detailed guidelines on nationalistic education, which cover three major aspects, namely patriotism, nationalism and international perspectives.

Education for patriotism refers to the cultivation of affectivity towards the motherland so that the nation state's dignity may be sustained through students' good behaviour (Ministry of Education, 2001b, Chapter 9, Year 7). This aspect of education covers Chinese socialist culture so that students can inherit the good traditions and culture of China. Particular emphasis is placed on fostering students' cultural identity by teaching how an individual is inseparable from the nation's culture and the country's fate (Ministry of Education, 2001b, Chapter 5, Year 10). Education for nationalism refers to concepts of the nation state, the composition of ethnic groups in China and the government's policies towards the various ethnic groups in China. Religious education is also taught in the context of learning about other nations so that students will respect various nations' religions, and understand the government's policy towards religious freedom (Ministry of Education, 2001b, Chapter 4, Year 10). Nationalism has to be understood in an international context, thus the development of an international perspective has recently been emphasised in the citizenship curriculum. This aspect of education covers the formation and constitution of an international society, the nation's sovereignty and international organisations. China's position in the international society is also taught in order to cultivate the pride of being a Chinese citizen (Ministry of Education, 2001b, Chapter 5, Year 10).

Education for Democracy

Education for democracy was rather neglected during the period of the planned economy in China prior to 1978. However, it has become increasingly emphasised since the reforms initiated by the open door policy, particularly as the Chinese economy has further opened up and become marketised with the adoption of the modernisation policy. In the then Premier of the State Council Zhu Rongji's (2001) *Report on the Outline of the Tenth*

Five-year Plan for National Economic and Social Development (2001-2005), a section is devoted to the establishment of democracy in China, entitled "Promoting Spiritual Civilisation, Improving Democracy and the Legal System, and Strengthening National Defence." He says:

> We need to work hard and foster ideas and ethics appropriate for a socialist market economy. We need to administer the country in accordance with moral principles as well as the law.
>
> Energetically improving socialist democracy and the legal system, we need to develop a socialist democratic political system, govern the country according to the law, and make China a socialist country ruled by law. We need to press ahead with reform of the political system; implement democratic elections, decision-making, management and supervision; protect the extensive rights and freedoms of the people as prescribed by law; and respect and guarantee human rights. We need to continue to strengthen the legislative and supervisory role of the People's Congress, and expand the role of the Chinese People's Political Consultative Conference in political consultation, democratic supervision, and administration and deliberation of state affairs. We need to bring the legal system into line with a socialist market economy.

Zhu's speech captured the major features of education for democracy as a key development in the citizenship education curriculum in the last ten years. The 1988 *Outline of Moral Education in Secondary School* aimed to develop a basic understanding of the concepts of democracy and jurisprudence (such as constitutional and criminal law), citizen rights, and responsibility for junior secondary students and socialist democracy education for senior secondary students (State Education Commission, 1988). The 1995 revised *Outline* added understanding and observing laws, and education about laws for protecting individuals, human rights and maintaining social harmony (State Education Commission, 1995). Below are listed the three major areas of development in the context of education for democracy:

Enhance Understanding of Law. This refers to an understanding of China's constitution, government institutions, social organisations and the functions of the constitution as the supreme guide to people's behaviour (Ministry of Education, 2001b, Chapter 8, Year 9). It stresses the significance of law in maintaining public life and the public order of the socialist market economy. It also stresses the significance of the constitution and the law to governance. For example, the law for protecting juveniles is taught to enhance students' ability to protect themselves against exploitation. Students are taught the law against violating peace and order to learn how to maintain public order. In addition, moral attitudes is emphasised on top of behavioural regulation, such as politeness, honesty, frugality, dedication to work and to the country (Ministry of Education, 2001b, Chapter 8, Year 9)

Enhance Understanding of Democracy. This refers to understanding the nature of people's democracy in China, including:

- The role and function of People's Congress as people's representatives in exercising the country's sovereignty (Ministry of Education, 2001b, Chapter 3, Year 10);

- China's election system, e.g., students of senior secondary 3 can vote and are encouraged to exercise their voting rights (Ministry of Education, 2001b, Chapter 1, Year 10); and

- China's political system of negotiated democracy (Ministry of Education, 2001b, Chapter 3, Year 10).

To support a democratic system, students are taught citizen rights and responsibilities, not only in political participation, but also in familial relationships, as well as in education and economic activities. With respect to education, the Compulsory Education Law is taught so that students are aware of their educational rights and responsibilities. In respect of economic participation, students are taught knowledge of the economic system of China, such as concepts of the socialist market economy and the responsibility to pay tax.

In respect of political rights, in addition to the electoral system students are taught the significance of national unity and their various citizen rights and political freedoms, such as freedom of speech (to make criticisms and suggestions), freedom of gathering, and freedom of demonstrations and protests (Ministry of Education, 2001b, Chapters 9-12, 13, 14, 16, Year 10) as provided in the Constitution and the laws. The revised curriculum standards regard the teaching of political rights and responsibilities as a significant component of citizenship education. For example, in the junior secondary curriculum, students are taught to exercise their legal rights in daily life and fulfil various citizen responsibilities, such as participating in elections and political decisions, and "supervising" the government. The Constitution and laws related to these rights are covered in greater detail in the Senior Secondary Curriculum (Ministry of Education, 2001b), such as political rights and freedoms in Articles 33-37, the rights of election in Article 34, and the right to supervise the government in Article 41 ('Constitution', 1982). The Chapter "Citizens and the Country" in the Year 10 textbook says:

Political freedom is the foundation of democratic politics. It allows people to fully express their wishes, participate in political life, dare to speak up and speak the truth. The assurance of these rights is significant for people to exercise their political rights, and is a concrete realisation of socialist democracy. Of course, political freedom is not without constraints, nor does it imply that people can do whatever they want. Freedom is relative, and this applies to political freedom. There is no freedom that can be exempted from the boundary of the law. The law both realises and protects freedom, and therefore law and freedom are unified. Thus, all citizens are subject to the boundary of law in exercising their freedom.

Exercising the right of supervision is important to correct bureaucratic and corruption practices, improve the practices of state organisations, and protect the country's interests and people's interests. (Ministry of Education, 2001b)

The above analysis shows that, although democracy education used to be a weaker component of the citizenship curriculum in China, it has become increasingly important in the revised curriculum. There is a significant directional change in its emphasis on freedom and rights, as well as action and participation. Although the mention of rights and freedom is always balanced by responsibilities and limits to the law, the deliberate emphasis on rights and freedoms is a remarkable sign for a new era of citizenship education to appear. In this new era, responsibilities are not mentioned as an obligation to fulfil, but as a balance of rights and freedoms. The manner in which rights and responsibilities are discussed has shown significant conceptual change towards the endorsement of the rights of individual citizens. This is a major departure from the overarching emphasis on collectivism over individualism in conventional moral education textbooks in China.

Emphasise Psychological Health and Moral Quality. It used to be thought that modernisation and democratisation are unachievable without a populace of good moral quality. Therefore a major trend in the development of citizenship education is an emphasis on the development of the moral quality of individuals. In 2000, the State Council published a white paper entitled *China's Population and Development in the 21st Century*. The white paper made specific comment on the need to strengthen the moral quality of individuals:

> In order to raise the people's ideological and moral standards, it is necessary to enhance the people's sense of law and concept of rule by law. Outmoded regulations and bad habits as well as old backward ideology should be changed and superstitions discarded. At the same time, healthy values, moral standards, good public opinions on culture and social practices are to be encouraged. Great importance should be attached to the healthy development of youngsters by providing them with colourful and meaningful cultural and educational activities. The young people's understanding of morality should be strengthened so that improper behaviour can be avoided. (para. 19)

In the same year, the then CPC General Secretary Jiang Zemin delivered a speech in the Ideological and Political Work Conference of the CPC Central Committee. He stressed the importance of spreading socialist ethics and raising the moral standards of the Chinese people at a time when the nation is developing a socialist market economy and to ensure the success of the country's modernisation. He regarded both law and ethics as necessary for regulating people's behaviours (Jiang, 2000).

In 2001, Jiang issued a document entitled *Implementation Outline on Ethic Building for Citizens*. The 10,000-character document pointed out the emergence of moral anomies, such as moneyism, hedonism, extreme individualism, corruption, dishonesty and power abuse, occurring in the process of modernisation. These anomalies are described as "social pollution." The building of civic virtues and socialist ethics is thus regarded as essential in supporting the socialist market economy. Jiang stressed that the country should not only be ruled by law but also by morality. It is, therefore, imperative that the overall moral quality of the citizens be improved (Xinhua News Agency, 2001a; 2001b).

In November 2002, in the Report presented to the Sixteenth National Congress of the Communist Party, Jiang reiterated the significance of enhancing the moral quality of the people:

> The ideological and ethical standards, the scientific and cultural qualities, and the health of the whole people will be enhanced notably. ... A learning society in which all the people will learn or even pursue lifelong education will emerge to boost their all-round development. (Jiang, 2002)

The last decade has witnessed significant change in the citizenship curriculum towards an emphasis on psychological health as a new component in moral education. The 1995 revised *Secondary School Moral Education Syllabus* added new components in moral education, such as traditional Chinese ethics, environmental ethics and psychological health. In November 1999, the Ministry of Education issued a document entitled *Several Suggestions on Reinforcing Psychological Health Education in Primary and Secondary Education* (Ministry of Education, 1999a), suggesting that schools integrate moral education and psychological health education to develop students' self-esteem and the ability to cope with frustrations and social changes. The document advised schools to develop guidance and counselling to support psychological health education. In September 2002, the Department of Basic Education issued the *Outline of Psychological Health Education in Primary and Secondary Schools* (Ministry of Education, 2002d). The *Outline* stressed that the aim of psychological health education should be improving students' psychological quality, optimizing their potential, cultivating optimistic and ambitious character, improving self-education abilities and strengthening adaptation abilities. The task of psychological health education was to create a new generation with creative and practical skills, ideals and good moral quality (Ministry of Education, 2002a).

The newly developed civic and moral education curriculum guides and syllabi also show an increasing flavour of psychological health education. In 2001, the government's *Circular on the Revised Nine-year Compulsory Primary Ideomoral and Secondary Ideopolitical Curriculum Standards* (Ministry of Education, 2001c) introduced major revisions in the revised curriculum standards, and the focus on psychological health education was salient. Topics added to the curriculum include enhancing learning through exchanging of ideas with teachers and communicating with people and learning to be self-confident.

The teaching contents of Junior Secondary 1 have been revised to integrate psychological quality, moral education and healthy character education in order to strengthen the moral quality of students. The chapter titles have been revised from a single emphasis to a dual emphasis. For example, "The Cultivation of Psychological Quality" has been changed to "The Cultivation of Psychological Quality and the

Enhancement of Moral Quality," and "Be Good at Emotional Adjustment" has been changed to "Be Good at Emotional Adjustment and being Optimistic." Corresponding adjustments have also been made to the chapter contents. For example, the chapter "The Cultivation of Psychological Quality" has added "Characters Needed for Healthy Growth of Young People; Good Psychological Quality Needed for Moral Character Development, …"

In June 2002, the Basic Education Department of the Ministry of Education announced new syllabi of civic and moral education for primary schools, namely *Morality and Living Curriculum Standards* (for junior primary) and *Morality and Society Curriculum Standards* (for senior primary) (Ministry of Education, 2002b, 2002c). The two syllabi were announced as trial versions, being piloted by 33 regions. The announcement says:

> … compared to the [old] ideomoral and social studies, the new curriculum is outstanding in its emphasis on (1) the person as the foundation of education. The new curriculum is focused on cultivating civilised behaviours and habits, good moral quality and healthy social development, so that they will love their lives and enjoy making enquiries, and become students with good moral quality and healthy social characters; and (2) students' lives as the foundation of education, closely linking children's life experience and social experience to their learning experience; (3) encouraging students to actively participate in learning, and under the guidance of teachers to develop moral affection, establish value judgements, and avoid simple lectures; and (4) integrative and activity related learning. (Ministry of Education, 2002b, pp.1-2)

There are fundamental changes in the new citizenship education syllabi. First, the prefix "ideo-" is removed from the title, which clearly signifies that the role and functions of citizenship education are disassociated from politics. Second, whereas the emphasis on collectivism and the negation of individualism always preceded almost any citizenship syllabus or textbook in the past, these emphases no longer exist in the new syllabi. Patriotism and collectivism are still mentioned in the preface but followed by the "Basic Concepts" section, which focuses on the significance of child development, such as the child's inner world, personality and character. Whereas the "self" was more or less equated with individualism in the past, in the new syllabi the self was seen rather positively and became the centre of citizenship education. For example, in the *Morality and Society Curriculum Standards*, the series of topics to be taught are "I Am Growing," "Me and My Family," "Me and My School," "Me and My Home Town (Community)," "Me and My country," "Facing the World" (Ministry of Education, 2002c). The sequence was almost identical to those proposed in the Hong Kong *Guidelines on Civic Education in Schools* (Curriculum Development Council, 1996). In fact, the teachers' manual developed by Shanghai Normal University made specific reference to the Hong Kong Civic Education Guidelines, which covers areas ranging from the self and family, to the country and the world (Zhang, 2004).

In a lesson plan developed to implement the syllabi, Li and her associates have caught the spirit of the syllabi, suggesting the need for on affective education. They say:

> Affectivity is a heart journey that everyone is experiencing in life. Therefore it plays a significant role in the formation of a person's character, personality, moral quality, life perspectives and value systems. … In every lesson, we try to integrate "knowledge and skills," "process and methods" and "affections and values" in our teaching, and "affections and values" is a catalyst for the other two. Therefore, when we succeed in affective education, students will … naturally build up their value systems. Then we can attain the goal of moral education. (Li, Chen & Chen, 2003)

Conclusions

This chapter shows a clear change in the orientations of citizenship curriculum over the last twenty years in China, since the adoption of the open door policy in 1978. The policy has had a far-reaching impact on the social and political circumstances in the country. With the launch of the modernisation policy, which is associated with the emergence of a market economy, society has become increasingly open. Despite continuing complaints from the Western world that China has neglected human rights and that the Communist Party still monopolises political control, the Chinese leadership would argue that internally on the whole the country is moving on a democratisation track. The emphasis on democratisation in the various reports and speeches presented at the People's Congress along with calls for the rule of law and law education would be cited as evidence in support of the overall trend towards a more open and democratic system and less emphasis on socialist ideology. This has been reflected in recent changes in textbooks. For example, in August 2006 the *New York Times* described the emergence of "a less ideological Chinese text" in Shanghai. According to Kahn (2006), in this revised senior history textbook,

> Socialism has been reduced to a single, short chapter in the senior high school history course. Chinese communism prior to economic reform in 1979 is covered in a sentence. The text mentions Mao only once, in a chapter on etiquette. . . . The changes passed high-level scrutiny, the authors say, and are part of a broader effort to promote a more stable, less violent view of Chinese history that serves today's economic and political goals. . . . It is better if people think more about the future than the past. (http://www.iht.com/articles/2006/08/31/news/china.php)

The impact of these political, social and economic changes has been obvious in education. Our historical review suggests that the historical development of the citizenship curriculum can be classified into three major periods: from political orientation, to both political and moral orientations in parallel, to moral orientation. Examining the themes of the current citizenship curriculum, we have found that nationalistic education, which used to be the dominant theme, is now just one of the three major themes of the curriculum. The emerging significant themes are democracy education and psychological health education. In terms of education for democracy, there are many reiterations of the significance of law education. The call for the country to be governed by law has been clear and strong, and is something which is also included in the newly revised citizenship curriculum.

Another significant theme that has emerged in the citizenship curriculum is psychological health education. The call for psychological health is to correct the anomalies that have emerged in the process of modernisation and marketisation. However, the call for the need to build up individuals' moral quality has also paved the way for new perspectives in citizenship education. Rather than negating the self as equivalent to individualism, the new citizenship curriculum emphasises the significance of self-esteem, character building and self-management. The development of the self has become the centre of the themes (e.g., My Growth, Me and My Family, My School, My Home Town and My Country) in the latest curriculum *Morality and Social Studies*.

The growing emphasis on democratisation and psychological health education in the citizenship curriculum has paved way for the emerging independent status of moral education in the citizenship curriculum. Of course, democratisation is always a political agenda, but in China the emergence of education for democracy has been facilitated by a depoliticised citizenship curriculum. The new mode of citizenship education is characterised by the disassociation of moral education from politics, and an emphasis on personal moral quality as well as on psychological health. Also, the democracy mindset is closely associated with modernisation and the development of the market economy, which is also a departure from traditional political emphases. Part of the traditional emphasis was characterised by anti-Western (anti-imperialist or anti-capitalist) sentiments, but these sentiments have become diluted, if not extinguished, by the growing modernisation and marketisation of the economy.

5

Citizenship Education Curriculum in Japan

Kazuko Otsu

Introduction

Three Japanese citizens were freed in April 2004 after they had been threatened with execution by militants in Iraq. The Prime Minister criticised the three, who returned to Japan, stating that they had been imprudent to go to Iraq at that time. Conservative members of parliament insisted that those who had been captured in Iraq were anti-Japanese. Some media conducted a campaign criticizing the three, claiming that "It was you who went to Iraq. Why are you asking the government to rescue you when you were kidnapped? You were told not to go. Your loss of your life is your own responsibility" ("Your own responsibility," 2004). According to a survey,[i] more than half of the first-year students at a university supported this opinion, and more than half of the rest responded, "I feel sympathetic to the three returnees, but they should not have gone to Iraq." A small number of the students argued that the three returnees should not be criticised. Most of the students had no idea whether the government had a duty to protect its citizens and whether citizens have the right to ask the government for protection. Thus, the students were shocked by the following article, and in particular, its concept of citizen.

> The three returnees had stayed as individuals for their own goals, to help street children in Baghdad, to do research on raising awareness about the health effects of depleted uranium munitions, and to report on Iraq for a weekly news magazine. The militants who captured the three civilians tried to negotiate with the Japanese government; therefore, it is right for the families of the three to ask the government to negotiate with the militants. It was the Japanese government that endangered the three returnees by sending troops to Iraq. The three returnees are citizens, not representatives of the state. The militants freed the hostages because they distinguished citizens from the government. The three should not apologise because they are victims. We are very proud of them as courageous citizens. (Ueno, 2004, p.10)

All of the students had taken social studies classes, including civics in junior and senior high school. It is also supposed that they had had opportunities to learn about being citizens and citizenship through various school activities, as well as in other classes. Why do most of the students have no concept of what being a citizen means?

This chapter examines educational policies, citizenship curriculum development, implementation, and the major challenges for citizenship education in Japan. The first section begins with a historical and educational background and argues for current educational reform, focusing on the *Report of the Central Council for Education*. The second section examines the citizenship curriculum, gaps between the prescribed objectives of subjects and activities related to citizenship education, and their implementation at the junior high school level. The third section discusses controversies and challenges confronting citizenship education in Japan. In order to "develop [the true meaning of] the basic civic qualities essential to the shapers of a democratic and peaceful nation and society" (Ministry of Education, Culture, Sports, Science, and Technology, 1998, p.16), the final section proposes an alternative structured framework for citizenship education.

Historical and Educational Background

Japan is an island nation off the east coast of the Asian continent. The total land area is roughly 378,000 square kilometres. Population statistics show approximately 128 million residents (2004), including all foreigners living in Japan. The defeat of Japan in 1945 under atomic clouds brought the Allied Occupation, demilitarisation, dissolution of the old industrial combines (*zaibatsu*), renunciation of divinity by the emperor, a new constitution, democratisation and a new educational system under the Fundamental Law of Education (Ministry of Education, Culture, Sports, Science, and Technology, 2005a). After a painful period of postwar rehabilitation, the Japanese economy began to surge ahead in the 1960s and 1970s, after which Japan became the number two economic power in the world. However, Japan's economy has been stagnant since the bubble economy burst in the 1990s. Since 1945, a conservative party, the Liberal Democratic Party (LDP), has dominated the government of Japan.

The Ministry of Education, Culture, Sports, Science, and Technology (MEXT)[ii] has the power to control national educational activities. All textbooks used in elementary, junior high and senior high schools are authorised by MEXT. To maintain and improve the national standard of school education, the approved Courses of Study and authorisation of textbooks are effective to some extent. However, they have been strongly influenced by conservative trends. For example, in sections concerning the history of the Second World War, some writers of textbooks were asked by MEXT to replace the term "invading" with "entering" other Asian countries during wartime. In 1965 Professor Ienaga instituted a lawsuit against the textbook authorisation system, and, thirty-two years later, the Supreme Court ruled that the authorisation was constitutional (Tokutake, 1999). Writers tend to voluntarily censor what they write in the textbooks so that their books pass the authorisation process.

Definitions of Citizen and Citizenship

The term citizen can be translated into Japanese in two different ways: *shimin* and *kohmin*. On the one hand, "shimin" has been used by the mass media in contexts referring to civil society. On the other hand, MEXT has never used shimin and translates "citizen" as "kohmin". Courses of Studies have used kohmin as a key concept in the objectives of social studies, defining it in two ways: an authorised member of the state (kokumin), and a member of a civil society (shimin) (Ministry of Education, Culture, Sports, Science, and Technology, 1970). In addition, kohmin refers to both the name of a subject in senior high school, "civics," and the name of a field of social studies in junior high school. However, the mass media and ordinary people never use kohmin in daily conversation. The two definitions of "citizen" lead to confusion.

Since September 11, 2001, the tension between the use of kokumin versus shimin has appeared to have increased even more. The Koizumi Administration, which has been cooperating with the Bush Administration, sent vessels to the Indian Ocean to support the U.S. troops bombing Afghanistan under the name of "the war against terrorism." It also gave unconditional support to the Iraq war and promised to spend about US$5 billion for the "reconstruction" of Iraq, led by the allied forces of the U.S./U.K. Furthermore, it sent Self-Defense Force troops to Iraq in 2004. Some LDP members insist that those who are against the government's policies are *hi-kokumin* (anti-Japanese).

Many people are worried about the precedent. Some criticise the enactment of laws for wartime, as well as sending troops overseas, claiming such actions are against the Constitution. Non-governmental organisations and people who are involved in peace actions call themselves shimin. Numbers of shimin have organised rallies and demonstrations against wars, the amendments of the Fundamental Law of Education and of the Constitution, and the enforced use of the *Kimigayo* (the national anthem) and the *Hinomaru* (the national flag). Educational reform, including the amendment of the Fundamental Law of Education, reflects the current political situation.

Educational Reform

Report of Central Council for Education

In 2003, the Central Council for Education submitted its final report, which is regarded as a baseline of educational policies, to MEXT. The report analyses the current educational situation in Japanese society as follows:

> Japanese society has been facing an enormous crisis. It seems that most people lack self-confidence, ethics, and a sense of social responsibility. Japanese society has had less vitality due to the aging population and economic stagnation, and people themselves feel as if they were living in a stifling straitjacket. Education in Japan has also confronted a serious crisis. It seems difficult for the youth to have dreams

for the future. Children and young people appear to be less conscious of morals and less autonomous. Many schools are still faced with the problems of bullying, dropouts, skipping school, and *gakkyu hohkai* (classroom disorder). The number of vicious crimes has increased dramatically. It seems difficult for the youth to cultivate a love for their parents and friends, and to foster good relations with them. (Ministry of Education, Culture, Sports, Science, and Technology, 2003, p.2)

First, based on this analysis, with the aim of "cultivating the spirit of Japanese people to carve out the 21st century with richness in mind," the report set forth the following five objectives:

1. Cultivate people who are independent-minded and seek personal development.
2. Cultivate people who are warm-hearted and enjoy physical well-being.
3. Cultivate people to become creative leaders of a Century of Knowledge.
4. Cultivate Japanese who are civic-minded and who will actively participate in the formation of a state and society befitting the 21st century.
5. Cultivate Japanese people based on the traditions and culture of Japan to live in a globalised world. (official translation)

It is notable that Japanese tradition and culture are emphasised in the objectives, a point which will be discussed later.

Second, the report recommends an amendment to the law entitled the Fundamental Law of Education, which was designed as the basis for postwar education in Japan and enacted in 1947. The law stipulated the basic principles of education, specifying equal opportunity for education, and compulsory education to be provided free of charge for a period of nine years. It is this law that forms the basis of all education-related laws, including the School Education Law and the Social Education Law. Education in Japan has been carried out in accordance with the spirit of the Fundamental Law of Education.

The report, however, insists that "the law has remained unchanged for over half a century, during which time great changes have taken place in society and various issues have arisen in education as a whole. Given the situation today, and under the concept that it is now necessary to revise the modalities for education, the report of the Central Council for Education has given rise to much controversy."

Controversy over the Fundamental Law of Education

For years the government has tried to amend the Fundamental Law of Education and has requested the Central Council for Education to discuss it. Corresponding to the report, many controversies have arisen in various ways. For example, the Japan Federation of Bar Associations (2002) made a strong protest against the recommendation for an amendment. The Federation's major points are as follows:

1. The report aims to instruct people to be useful for the state rather than to seek personal development. It endangers the human right to an education guaranteed by the Constitution.
2. The report aims to force "love of the nation" on people through public education. This could violate Article 19 of the Constitution, which guarantees freedom of thought and conscience.
3. The report describes the provision of new regulations for parents' roles and responsibilities in the near future. This means state intervention in family education which, therefore, could violate parents' right to educate their children.
4. The report aims to cut Article 5 from the Constitution, which guarantees co-education. This is problematic from a perspective of gender equality because there still remains gender bias in the educational system and curricula.
5. The report regards state intervention in the content of education as guaranteed. This is against the decision by the Supreme Court; "It is necessary that state intervention in the content of education be restrained as much as possible." (Japan Federation of Bar Associations, 2002)

Many organisations and NGOs have argued against the recommendation for an amendment to the Fundamental Law of Education. The Association for Developing Japanese Education and Culture toward the World (2003), consisting of professors, novelists, actors, journalists, medical doctors, activists and others added the following:

1. It is too irrational and groundless to amend the Fundamental Law of Education. It is impossible to solve the problems in both society and schools by amending the Fundamental Law of Education.
2. The procedure for submitting the recommendation to amend the Fundamental Law of Education is too abnormal and inappropriate. Based on the report from a private advisory body of the Prime Minister, the National Commission on Education Reform, MEXT inquired into the amendment of the Fundamental Law of Education to the Central Council for Education. MEXT officials made up the interim report without enough discussion. Then, MEXT chose supportive persons as members of the public for the hearings and added a MEXT bureaucrat.

Some critical issues have emerged from the controversy. First of all, what are the major causes of the current social problems? Hayama (2003) argues that it is too one-sided to attribute social problems to educational failures. He insists that economic policies based on neoliberalism, such as deregulation and privatisation, have increasingly caused income differentials, resulting in a stratified society. As a result, communities and family structures have tended to collapse, and a tide of individualism has appeared. At one time people believed that the children of blue-collar workers could become white-collar workers if they were educated. Most Japanese had thought they belonged to the middle class. Being conscious of belonging to the middle class generated a feeling of unity in society and in the state. However, nowadays it is difficult for members of the "junior class" to get a better job because the social strata tend to be fixed.

Sato explains that the concept has changed from "people in society can get a better job somehow if they make an effort" to "people in society make an effort in vain" (2000, p.19). He argues that this trend began in the 1980s and has almost run its course. What may come next is that "people in society are not willing to make an effort." Unexpected and terrible crimes, such as the murder committed by a man at an elementary school in Osaka,[iii] can happen repeatedly in a society without a sense of solidarity and centripetal culture.

Secondly, what is the major aim of education? The Fundamental Law of Education declares that:

> Education shall aim at the full development of personality, striving for the rearing of people, sound in mind and body, who shall love truth and justice, esteem individual value, respect labour, have a deep sense of responsibility, and be imbued with an independent spirit, as builders of a peaceful state and society. (Article 1, p.1)

On the contrary, the report of the Central Council for Education recommends replacing these aims with "education shall cultivate Japanese who receive an education based on Japanese tradition and culture in order to live in an international society" (Ministry of Education, Culture, Sports, Science, and Technology, 2003, p.11). It emphasises fostering people who are suitable for the state rather than enabling personal development. The report also recommends making a new regulation which forces love of the nation in the arena of public education. This does not seem like an amendment but rather a mutilation of the Fundamental Law of Education.

Citizenship Education in the Current Curriculum Reform

Revised Courses of Study. MEXT revised the Courses of Study in 1998, and these have been implemented since 2002. The purpose of the new Courses of Study under the comprehensive five-day school week system is to foster "zest for living" (*ikiruchikara*) in children. The Courses of Study seek to "foster the qualities and abilities necessary to acquire steadily the rudimentary basics of education, such as reading, writing, and arithmetic; and to learn, think, and act for oneself, as well as develop problem-solving skills" (Ministry of Education, Culture, Sports, Science, and Technology, 1998, p.25).

In the formal curriculum, the major subjects and activities related to citizenship education are integrated study, social studies, moral education and special activities.

The introduction of integrated study is one of the major strategies of the revised Courses of Study. More than two hours a week are allocated to this new interdisciplinary subject from Grade 3 in elementary school through senior high school. It aims "to help pupils develop their skills with regard to learning, reasoning, problem solving, and inquiry / investigation as well as help them develop independent and creative thinking, and deepen their understanding of their own way of life" (Ministry of Education, Culture, Sports, Science, and Technology, 1999a, p.3).

Table 5.1   Prescribed Subjects and the Number of School Hours at Junior High School

Compulsory / Selective	Subjects	Grade 1	Grade 2	Grade 3
Compulsory	Japanese	140	105	105
	Social Studies	105	105	85
	Mathematics	105	105	105
	Science	105	105	80
	Music	45	35	35
	Arts	45	35	35
	Physics	90	90	90
	Home Economics	70	70	35
	Foreign Language	105	105	105
	Integrated Studies	70-100	70-105	70-130
	Moral Education	35	35	35
	Special Activities	35	35	35
Selective		0-30	50-85	105-165
Total		980	980	980

Integrated Study. The introduction of integrated study marks the first time MEXT has permitted individual schools to create individual classes. Moreover, it is the first time there are classes with no required textbooks or examinations.

The Courses of Study recommends that teachers deal with the following in the period for integrated study:

- Interdisciplinary themes including international understanding, information technology studies, environmental education and education on welfare.
- Themes children are interested in.
- Themes corresponding to particular characteristics of the school or community. (Ministry of Education, Culture, Sports, Science, and Technology, 1999a, p.56)

For integrated studies the Courses of Studies require that teachers attempt the following:

- To introduce activities such as natural experiences, volunteer activities, observation, experiments, visitations, research, presentations, discussion, productive activities and problem-solving learning.
- To devise group learning for different-aged children, cooperative teaching with people in the community as well as all school staff, and learning materials and the environment of the community.

The implementation of integrated study varies from school to school. Each school is expected to create its own curriculum for integrated study. Some schools set up "welfare" for the first grade students, "international understanding" for the second grade and "environmental issues" for the third grade. Some schools have created outstanding lessons. In other schools, teachers merely make students do research on topics in the community, invite foreigners to their classrooms, or send students to nursing homes for volunteer activities without any clear idea of a curriculum for integrated study. At the moment, it seems that few teachers have ideas for creating lessons for integrated study.

Social Studies. The social studies curriculum is set from Grade 3 of elementary school through senior high school. At the junior high level, social studies consists of three fields: geography, history and civics. The goals of civics are, as described in the Courses of Study, "to be interested in society, to consider events from various perspectives based on references or data, to deepen students' understanding and love of their nation and history, to cultivate the foundation of knowledge necessary for them to achieve a broad perspective as citizens, and to develop basic civic qualities essential to the shapers of a democratic and peaceful nation and society" (Ministry of Education, Culture, Sports, Science, and Technology, 1998, p.16).

Although the overall objective of civics is to help students develop into responsible citizens, the current approaches do not appear to fully address that need. The textbooks tend to use a social science-based approach, full of abstract concepts and difficult explanations of political and economic systems. Very few teachers try to discuss contemporary or controversial issues in their classes. Therefore, students have few opportunities to develop critical thinking skills.

Moral Education. The major objectives of moral education in junior high school, according to the Courses of Study, are as follows:

1. Help students cultivate respect for human beings and nurture a feeling of awe towards life.
2. Help students nurture a richness of the heart.
3. Encourage students to succeed in developing traditional culture and creating a rich culture.
4. Foster students committed to building a democratic society and the nation as a whole.
5. Develop students who can contribute to a peaceful international community.
6. Foster members of Japanese society who can think, judge, act and be responsible for their own behavior.
7. Foster morality.

(Ministry of Education, Culture, Sports, Science, and Technology, 1999b, pp.25-29)

MEXT distributed *Kokoro no Note* (Notebook of My Mind) to all elementary and junior high schools, which cost 85% of the budget for moral education in 2002. *Kokoro no Note*, filled with beautiful coloured illustrations, recommends that children and students write their reflections, feelings and ideas in the notebook. MEXT explains that *Kokoro no Note* is neither a textbook nor a complementary reader. According to the explanation given by MEXT, *Kokoro no Note* cannot be a textbook because it is not legally authorised and MEXT has no legal power to distribute any complementary reader. MEXT announced that it is not compulsory for schools to use the notebook. However, MEXT ordered educational boards to investigate how *Kokoro no Note* was being used in schools. According to a statistical survey by MEXT (2005b), more than 93% of junior high schools and 97% of elementary schools use it in moral education.

Kokoro no Note emphasises love of family, hometown and the nation, saying, "love of the hometown is naturally connected with love of the nation" and "it is natural for us to love our nation." Noda (2004) criticises this concept, saying that there exists a logical gap between love of one's hometown and love of the nation. Love of the nation tends to develop in those who have benefited directly from the nation, whereas people naturally have some emotional feelings about their hometown. The nation might be an abstract concept for many people. Thus, the love of one's nation is not necessarily one that develops naturally. Furthermore, *Kokoro no Note* encourages young people to substitute personal psychological issues for critical interests in society. *Kokoro no Note* does not allow young people to think critically about what defines the nation (Noda, 2004).

Special Activities. Special activities include classroom activities, and involvement in the student council, club activities and school events (ceremonies, school festivals, excursions, sports day, etc.). The objectives of special activities are as follows:

1. Encourage students to participate in desirable group activities.
2. Help students develop individuality, well-balanced between mind and body.
3. Help students develop social characteristics as a member of groups and society.
4. Help students develop an independent and practical attitude.
5. Help students be aware of a way of living as a human being and cultivate an ability to realize one's self.

In most schools, school festivals are designed particularly to support the learning of civic values. Both students and teachers work hard together for several weeks prior to the events. Teachers and students plan class events, make decorations or set up shops for a bazaar. Parents and local residents visit the school to enjoy the festival. Students compete for a prize for the best class chorus. Students are expected to learn how to associate and cooperate with others through preparing for these events.

Every school has a student council which simulates the Diet and is a symbol of democracy. According to the student handbook, which every student must bring on every school day, the student council aims at fostering "co-operation and independence," and advancing school life. All students are members of the student council, and there are a number of functional committees including health, welfare, library, broadcasting and editing committees. A formal general meeting of the student council is held twice a year; all students are required to attend and sit in rows in roll call order; teachers also attend to keep order. General meetings tend to be largely ceremonial with only a few questions and proposals from the participants.

All schools assign students daily cleaning responsibilities. Students clean the classrooms, halls, toilets, laboratories and other areas. Groups of students take turns; each group is usually in charge of cleaning for one week every month. Teachers stay with students while they are cleaning to check on them or to instruct them in how to perform their duties.

Students are encouraged to join clubs. Most sports clubs employ a seniority system under which junior students have to obey senior students. Some athletes remark that through belonging to clubs they learned the significance of perseverance and making an effort. Many students seem to enjoy and value the club activities more than they do their classes.

Issues Confronting Citizenship Education

Citizenship education is closely related to political and social issues. One of the most significant controversies regarding citizenship education is the issue of the *Hinomaru*, the national flag, and the *Kimigayo*, the national anthem. The following article illustrates an aspect of the issue.

School term starts under *Kimigayo* cloud

Enrollment ceremonies were held on Tuesday at public schools in Tokyo, where the board of education issued a controversial order in October that the national flag must be flown and the anthem sung at such ceremonies. Also on Tuesday, the education board punished 20 more teachers for disobeying the order to stand and sing the *Kimigayo* at graduation ceremonies in March at schools run by the metropolitan government. The move brought the total number of teachers punished since the ordinance was issued to 196.

The board is sending officials to the ceremonies for the new school year at all schools run by the metropolitan government to check whether the order is being followed, board officials said. On Tuesday, 1,326 elementary schools, 25 junior high schools and 12 senior high schools and evening high schools held enrollment ceremonies, according to the board. Ceremonies for junior high and senior high schools will peak on Wednesday.

Last Wednesday, the board reprimanded 171 teachers for disobeying principals' orders to stand and sing the *Kimigayo* at ceremonies in March at Tokyo-run high schools. It also refused to renew the contracts of five teachers who had been re-employed as part-timers after retirement. The teachers punished on Tuesday were from elementary, junior high and other Tokyo government-run schools, including one teacher who received a 10 per cent pay cut for a month.

> The board on Oct. 23 issued the order requiring schools to fly the *Hinomaru* flag on the stage and teachers to stand and sing the anthem while facing the flag. Many teachers refused, calling the order a violation of their freedom of expression. The order stipulates that teachers who refuse will be punished. ("School Term," 2004, p.12)

There has long been controversy over the use of the *Hinomaru* and the *Kimigayo*. MEXT has rationalised that the *Hinomaru* and the *Kimigayo* are needed to foster a sense of national identity through schools and to make young people proud and aware of their identity as Japanese (Ministry of Education, Culture, Sports, Science, and Technology, 2001b). However, opponents reason that the *Hinomaru* and the *Kimigayo* are not worthy of the peaceful and democratic postwar Japan because they are symbols of imperialism and Japanese militarism, aggression and brutality (Sakamoto, 1999). Actually, *Kimigayo* means the Age of the Emperor, and the words of the song are ones of praise: "May the reign of the Emperor continue for thousands of years." Opponents argue that these are undesirable symbols for encouraging young people to respect their nation, especially at a time when the nation is trying very hard to improve its image in East Asia and around the world. They also claim that to force Japanese citizens to honour and respect the *Hinomaru* and the *Kimigayo* is a violation of the UN Human Rights Charter, which, along with the Japanese Constitution, guarantees "freedom of thought, belief, and conscience" to all people (Tanaka, 1999).

Since the government passed legislation making the *Hinomaru* the official national flag and the *Kimigayo* the official national anthem in 1999, MEXT has required that these symbols be recognised and honoured at all official school ceremonies and events. A number of teachers, who have not stood up while *Kimigayo* was being sung at school ceremonies, have been punished by educational boards every year. In the case of some students who do not stand while *Kimigayo* is being sung, the classroom teacher can be punished.

The issue of the *Hinomaru* and the *Kimigayo* is closely related to the proposed amendment to the Fundamental Law of Education. MEXT has strongly pushed nationalism into education. According to the Citizenship Education Policy Study (Cogan & Derricott, 1998, p.108), "loyalty to one's nation" was rated the lowest of the 20 characteristics of a good citizen by expert policy-makers and scholars in nine countries including Japan. On the contrary, the characteristics of a good citizen which got the highest score were the "ability to look at and approach problems as a member of a global society," "capacity to think in a critical and systemic way," and the "ability to work with others in a cooperative way and to take responsibility for one's roles/duties within society" (ibid., p.97). The differences among these characteristics will be discussed in the next section.

Challenges in Citizenship Education

As described above, special activities, including school festivals, classroom activities, cleaning activities and club activities, are intended to encourage students to work with others in a cooperative way and to take responsibility for their roles and duties within the school. This refers to the fact that most junior high schools have the school precepts of "working hard together" and "caring for others."

At the same time, citizenship education in Japan is beset by several problems. First, civics textbooks are basically compendia of facts and use a social science-based approach as described above.

Second, lecture-based instructional approaches in civics provide little opportunity for discussion. Although students memorise a great deal of information about political and economic systems, they rarely learn how those systems work in an actual context. Because of this, it is difficult for students to think about problems in a critical and systemic way.

Third, the student council, which is supposed to be a democratic body in school society, does not fulfil its function. Although students may learn something about the implementation of the democratic process through the operation of the student council, they get no opportunity to learn about the essence or spirit of democracy as a political process or concept. Students are not regarded as members of a democratic school society since teachers maintain tight control over student councils, which have very limited powers.

Thus, related to the problems above, citizenship education in Japan has emphasised social initiation rather than social reformation. Case and Clark (1997) argue:

> Citizenship education as social initiation, on the one hand, aims at passing on the understandings, abilities and values that students require if they are to fit into and be productive members of the society. On the other hand, citizenship education as social reformation aims at empowering students with the understandings, abilities and values necessary to critique and ultimately improve their society. (p.18)

The emphasis on social initiation refers to the fact that MEXT has tried to promote community service. The Educational Reform Plan, which MEXT published in 2001, based on the recommendations of a private advisory committee of the Prime Minister, the National Commission on Education Reform, recommends that all students participate in community service for two weeks in elementary and junior high schools, one month in senior high schools, and one year for all youth over 18 (Ministry of Education, Culture, Sports, Science, and Technology, 2001a). This has resulted in another dispute, although the Metropolitan Board of Education decided to make community service a compulsory subject at all senior high schools run by the metropolitan government in 2004. Such service may give students opportunities for civic learning while working in the community. However, community service is different from voluntary activities. Community service is equivalent to forced labour. This might be inconsistent with democratic principles and even with the MEXT policy of assigning importance to the individuality of children. Community service in and of itself does not provide students with opportunities to develop their critical thinking skills and may only place more emphasis on citizenship education as social initiation.

Lastly, MEXT has emphasised national identity in its educational policy. Based on the report of the Central Council emphasising "Japanese tradition and culture," the Course of Study for social studies describes how teachers should help students understand the significance of the national flag and the national anthem, and have respect for them. In addition, the Course of Study for moral education stresses "Japanese tradition and culture" (Ministry of Education, Culture, Sports, Science, and Technology, 1998).

Regarding citizenship education, the tension between nationalism and globalism has been discussed at great length. "People need gradually to become world citizens without losing their roots and while continuing to play an active part in the life of their nation and their local community." (United Nations Educational, Scientific and Cultural Organization [UNESCO], 1996, p.17) In an interconnected and global age, citizenship should be defined in a much broader context. Identity as a citizen should include a global identity as well as local and national identities.

The next section discusses international education as a means of alternative citizenship education.

Citizenship Education for the 21st Century

International Education[iv]

International education in Japan had been implemented experimentally at UNESCO associated schools from the 1950s to the 1970s. However, this implementation has spread to hardly any other schools. Since the 1980s, responding to calls for the internationalisation of Japanese society, MEXT has promoted international education. However, MEXT has put an emphasis on teaching communicative English, educating returnees from foreign countries, and understanding different cultures, particularly Western cultures, rather than global interdependence and issues. At the same time, MEXT has stressed developing national identity by using the rationale that it is necessary to understand one's own traditional culture first, in order to understand other cultures. This is in reference to the controversy regarding the *Hinomaru* and the *Kimigayo*, as mentioned above.

On the other hand, since the 1990s some teachers and educators who are interested in development education have tried to teach global issues as well as cultural issues in social studies. They insist that international education should be fundamentally based on the UNESCO recommendation, although some contemporary concepts should be added. They regard international education, in a broad sense, as an umbrella concept of education which includes understanding different cultures, global interdependence and issues (Otsu, 1992). The author believes that international education is most essential to promote citizenship education in Japan.

Goals and Objectives for International Education

What should be the key goals for citizenship education in a global age? The Citizenship

Education Policy Study proposed a multidimensional citizenship model which includes personal development and social commitment to thinking and acting in ways that take account of local, national, and global communities and their concerns. It is a concept based on dimensions of time, that is, it takes into account current problems in ways that respect the heritage of the past while also protecting the interests of the future. It is also spatial in nature in that it acknowledges the different levels of community which must be taken into account as we face and attempt to resolve global problems and issues which are manifested in regional, state, provincial, and most certainly, local circumstances (Cogan & Derricott, 1998, p.2).

Corresponding to the present state of citizenship education in Japan discussed above, the author proposes objectives for international education, in four dimensions (personal, social, spatial and temporal) and three aspects (knowledge, skills, and attitudes). Considering that lessons in the period for integrated study have sometimes been implemented in combination with various subjects including social studies, Japanese, English, music and computer science, the objectives for international education in the four interrelated dimensions can be described as follows:

Personal dimension
- The ability to be sensitive towards and to defend human rights.
- The ability to understand, appreciate, accept and tolerate cultural differences.
- The ability to understand global interdependence and approach problems as a member of a global society.
- The ability to collect, select and analyse information from various sources.
- The ability to think in a critical and systemic way in order to solve problems.
- The ability to communicate with people with different cultures and values.

Social dimension
- The willingness to work with others in a cooperative way and to take responsibility for one's roles/duties within society.

Spatial dimension
- The capacity to understand citizenship identity in an interconnected global world including at local, state and national levels.

Temporal dimension
- The willingness to look at the present while reflecting on both the past and the future.

The objectives of international education can be operationally described in three aspects—knowledge, skills, and attitudes—which are equivalent to the three aspects of the objectives in the Courses of Study. Responding to the current situation in Japan, the author proposes objectives for international education, as shown in Table 5.2.

Table 5.2a   Objectives for Knowledge

Cultural diversity	• There are many different ways of behaving, but everyone has a similar nature, similar physical needs, and similar wishes and hopes. • Cultures have always been created and changed through exchanges between different cultures. • It is important to appreciate and try to live together in the world, although it may be difficult to understand different cultures.
Interdependence	• Our lives are connected in various ways with those of other people in the world. • Our lives are influenced by the world; at the same time, our lives can have an impact upon other people in the world. • It is essential to collect, select and analyse information in our information society.
Safety/peace	• There exist those who are threatened by direct violence or structural violence (e.g., poverty, oppression and the destruction of the environment) around the world. • Various efforts have been made in order to create a better world where everyone is respected as a human being and can pursue a safe and happy life.

Table 5.2b   Objectives for Skills

Communication	The ability to communicate in a variety of ways with people from different cultures and with different values.
Media literacy	The ability to collect, select and analyse information from various sources.
Critical thinking and problem solving	The ability to think in a critical and systemic way in order to solve problems.

Table 5.2c   Objectives for Attitudes

Respect for human rights	The willingness to accept the unique value of each individual human being, and to defend human rights.
Tolerance/sympathy	The willingness to understand, appreciate and accept or at least tolerate cultural differences.
Participation/cooperation	The willingness to work with others in a cooperative way and to take responsibility for one's roles/duties within society.

Curriculum for International Education

Since the ad hoc Council for Education emphasised the importance of international education in 1987, a number of lessons have been implemented in integrated studies, although the extent of such implementation depends on the schools and areas. Those lessons include a variety of topics and themes. However, in many cases it is not clear how interrelated each lesson is with other lessons, or how the placement of each lesson relates to the whole curriculum. As a result, it sometimes happens that teachers tend to give lessons that are only about a specific theme, unrelated to others. The areas of international education are so broad and interdisciplinary that teachers can hardly ever plan well-balanced lessons. It is much easier to plan lessons if teachers have a clear picture of a framework of international education, although, in practice, the curricula planned are not always achieved in the way expected.

In order to construct a curriculum for international education, the author divides international education into four major areas of learning, namely, multicultural society, global society, global issues and toward the future (Otsu, 1994). There can be key concepts in each area of learning, which are extracted from academic disciplines including economics, politics, sociology, peace studies, international development studies and so on. Responding to the level of the learners, the key concepts are organised as in Table 5.3.

In international education, learners are expected to develop their knowledge and ideas into actions described in the area "(D) toward the future" after or in the process of learning the area "(A) multicultural society," "(B) global society," or "(C) global issues" as shown in Figure 5.1. Some lessons can be integrated with two, three or four areas into one.

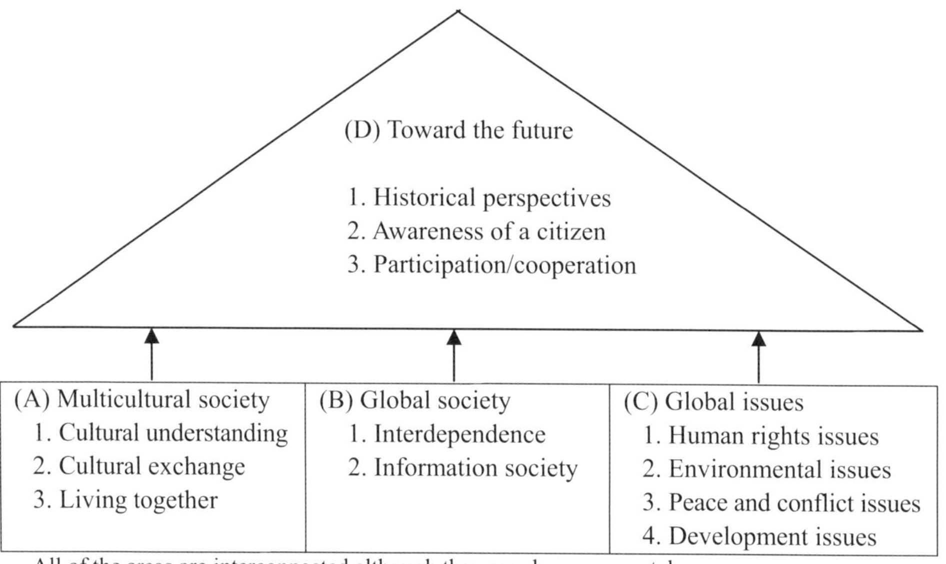

Figure 5.1 Structure of the Learning Areas

Table 5.3 Curricular Framework for International Education

Areas of learning	Contents	Key concepts		
		Grade 1-4 at elementary school and higher	**Grade 5-6 at elementary and lower secondary school and higher**	**Upper secondary school I and higher level**
A. Multi-cultural society	1. Cultural understanding	· There are a variety of songs or games for children, which most children like singing or playing. · Most children live with their family and go to school, but the types/patterns of family can be different.	· There are a variety of ways of daily life, but everyone has a similar nature, physical needs and similar wishes and hopes. · People have different views about what is important. · Finding out about the values and beliefs of other people can help us to understand them, and ourselves, better.	· There are different levels of culture including sub-cultures. · Countercultures such as youth culture can raise an objection to conventional cultures. · We should develop and create our cultures, as well as protect the legacy of the past.
	2. Cultural exchange	· There may be exchange programmes with foreign cities/towns in the community.	· Traditional cultures have been formed through the process of exchange with other cultures. · We should be culturally tolerant. · We can understand our culture and develop it much more through exchanging information and ideas with other cultures	· We should be broad-minded rather than ethnocentric. · There have been cultural friction, conflicts, changes and oppression throughout history.
	3. Living together	· There are some people with different cultures in the community.	· There may be minority people including the Ainu, Japanese Korean and workers from abroad in the community. · Minority people tend to be sensitive to their own identity while the majority are not. · It is important to try to understand and accept different cultures although it is sometimes not easy to understand them.	· Connected with various interests, some cultural values are opposed to other cultural values. We are sometimes caught in a dilemma in a multicultural society.

(Continue on next page)

Areas of learning	Contents	Key concepts		
		Grade 1-4 at elementary school and higher	Grade 5-6 at elementary and lower secondary school and higher	Upper secondary school I and higher level
B. Global society	1. Interdependence	· We are connected with the world through imported foods, clothes and other commodities. · Our city/town is connected with the world through ports and airports.	· Industrial products are exported from Japan to many countries. · People enjoy sports and music beyond their borders. · The number of foreign travellers, immigrants and mixed marriages has increased.	· Our lives are affected by global problems including terrorism, war, SARS and the greenhouse effect. · At the same time our life style can affect people in other parts of the world. · Globalisation has negative aspects as well as positive aspects.
	2. Information society	· We can get information immediately about the events in the world through TV or newspapers.	· Different media can report on the same events in different ways. · It is essential to gather, choose and analyse information and judge it fairly in the information society.	· Information gaps which can affect the economy, politics and military aspects have increased in the world. · Information tends to be controlled by those who have power.
C. Global issues	1. Human rights issues	· We should respect both ourselves and others since no one can be replaced. · Each of us has different ideas in the same way as each has a different face. · We tend to be biased or judge improperly when we hold stereotypical views.	· The Convention on the Rights of the Child has been ratified to help children whose human rights are not protected. · There are minority people, including indigenous people and Korean Japanese, who have been discriminated against in Japan for a long time.	· There are a minority people in the world who have been discriminated against because of their ethnicity, race, gender or sexuality. · A minority of people have struggled against discrimination.
	2. Environmental issues	· The amount of rubbish has increased in the community. · It is important to save finite resources in our daily lives.	· Deforestation causes serious environmental problems including disruption of the ozone layer. · We should know about measures being taken to protect the environment locally and globally.	· Conflicts of interest between developing and developed countries have increased due to environmental deterioration.

(Continue on next page)

Areas of learning	Contents	Key concepts		
		Grade 1-4 at elementary school and higher	**Grade 5-6 at elementary and lower secondary school and higher**	**Upper secondary school I and higher level**
	3. Peace and conflict issues	· Conflicts in everyday life can be analysed and resolved in various ways.	· Many children are affected by wars and ethnic conflicts in the world. · The UN and civil societies have made efforts for disarmament and peace.	· We should pursue not only negative peace but also positive peace without structural violence, including poverty or oppression. · It is essential to realise human security as well as national security. · It is up to ourselves to create a "culture of peace" (UNESCO).
	4. Development issues	· There are some children who cannot go to school and have to work.	· The economic gap between developing and developed countries has increased. · UN organisations, the ODA and NGOs have promoted international cooperation.	· It is critical to pursue not only economic development but also human development including health care and education. · It is important to pursue sustainable development.
D. Toward the future	1. Historical perspective	· We are part of our community's history.	· We are part of Asian history and are members of the Asian community.	· We should look at our history, integrated with Asian and world history.
	2. Membership of society	· We are members of our families and our community.	· We are members of a global society.	· We are member of a democratic society. · Social justice
	3. Participation and cooperation	· We can contribute to our community in some ways which can be specified.	· We can participate in voluntary activities of community development and international cooperation.	· We can act to influence the future of the community and the world. · We can join in a variety of ways to promote international cooperation.

1. Broken lines between areas of learning and levels of schooling show that each of them is not fixed but changeable, responding to the learners, the school and the community.
2. The area "toward the future" can be learnt either in the process of learning other areas or after learning other areas.

The curriculum framework and some examples of topics, taking into consideration the levels of the learners, as shown in Table 5.3, can help teachers develop both theoretical and practical lesson plans.

This curriculum framework was adopted as the basic one after discussion at project meetings for curriculum development for international education, organised by the Japan Association for International Education (JAIE). Based on the framework, the project team has created a format, which is helpful to teachers in searching for lesson plans for international education in the database as well as for their analysis of their lessons. In order to collect lessons for the database, the project team presented both the curriculum framework and the format at its annual conference in 2004. JAIE has encouraged teachers nationwide to mould their lessons so they can analyse the lessons they have planned, as well as create lessons based on the format and the framework. The final report was published in March 2006.

Conclusion

Citizenship education has been implemented in various ways. On the one hand, special activities such as school festivals and classroom activities are planned to encourage students to work with others in a cooperative way and to take responsibility for their roles and duties within the school. Such activities appear to have been successful at many schools. On the other hand, social studies, the major subject in citizenship education, aims to help students develop basic civic qualities essential to the shapers of a democratic and peaceful nation and society. However, students tend to regard social studies as a subject that merely requires them to memorise a list of facts.

The new subject, "integrated study," which is allocated more than two hours a week in the curriculum, can be a significant one for citizenship education. In order to promote citizenship education vigorously in the context of integrated study, the author proposes an alternative curriculum for international education. It could play a critical role in empowering students with the understanding, abilities and values necessary for a critique of their society and ultimately the ability to contribute to improving it. Students who will be the shapers of a democratic, peaceful nation and society in a global age need an education for citizenship that is much broader than what they can get in the curriculum prescribed by MEXT.

Notes

[i] The author surveyed one hundred students at Hokkaido University of Education in April 2004.

[ii] The Ministry of Education was renamed the Ministry of Education, Culture, Sports, Science, and Technology (MEXT) in 2000.

[iii] A 37-year-old man killed eight children at Ikeda University Elementary School on June 8, 2001.

[iv] International education is a broad concept and sometimes considered the same as global education or development education in Japan, although their origins and histories differ from each other. The reason why the author uses the term "international education" in this chapter is that MEXT never uses "development education" or "global education." Teachers are familiar with the term international education but not with the others.

South/Southeast Asia

6

The Anatomy of an Islamic Model: Citizenship Education in Pakistan

Iftikhar AHMAD

Introduction

Pakistan was carved out of India in 1947. The main purpose of its creation as an autonomous state was to protect the political rights of the Muslim population in South Asia. Since the founders of Pakistan were a Western educated elite, they envisaged that the new state would uphold the values of individual liberty, civic equality and religious diversity. They did not aspire to Islamic theocracy (Aziz, 1993; Jalal, 1994; Munir, 1979). However, for five decades a confluence of domestic and global forces and events has impinged upon the social, political and cultural ethos of Pakistan, catapulting the religious parties to political power.

Religious parties and their conservative allies in the nation's military have been playing a decisive role in promoting their Islamic ideology in Pakistan's national citizenship education curriculum policy (Haque, 1987). Their purpose in presenting Islam as an ideology of the state has been to: (a) sanctify their political role in society, (b) weaken their opponents, (c) galvanise social forces in Pakistan against India and the West, and (d) protect their political gains. In this effort, conservative forces, such as military regimes, the feudal class, government bureaucrats and religious extremists have coalesced and worked symbiotically towards a common goal of Islamizing the social order (Jalal, 1995, Alavi, 2002). To accomplish their goals, they have revised history, constructed official knowledge and manufactured a synthetic story about the heritage of the state of Pakistan. Thus, citizenship education became the first focus of their enterprise: An Islamic paradigm of citizenship education curriculum was promoted in the nation's schools. However, due to American pressure on Pakistan in recent years, the citizenship education pendulum has also begun to oscillate in a liberal-democratic direction. Hence the government has initiated a review of the existing paradigm of the national curriculum. But the government's decision has ruffled the feathers of entrenched conservative groups, triggering a new ideological debate on citizenship education (Mustafa, 2004).

Simply put, the current national policy debate on citizenship education curriculum in Pakistan epitomises the tempestuous character of that nation's polity itself. Therefore, a dispassionate examination of the status of citizenship education warrants understanding the ideological perspectives of the competing interest groups that have been in the vortex of this struggle. Essentially, these groups seek to foster their visions of what a good citizen needs to know, what knowledge is of most worth, what kind of society is desirable, and what curriculum policies are to be implemented in the nation's schools. Thus, this paper focuses on three themes. First, it examines the contemporary ideological debate on citizenship education in Pakistan. Second, it analyses the goals of Pakistan's national policy on citizenship education curriculum. Third, it reviews the Pakistani school textbooks on civics and history to evaluate how the national curriculum guidelines are being followed.

Religion and State in Citizenship Education: Competing Visions

At the outset, it would be fair to say that in contemporary Pakistan the basic controversy in citizenship education curriculum surrounds the relationship between religion and the state. Nowhere else, except perhaps in Israel, may the question of the separation of religion and state be as central to a nation's raison d'être as in today's Pakistan. It appears that in the public and academic discourses on citizenship education curriculum in Pakistan two competing perspectives, or visions, on the relationship between religion and state emerge, which may be characterised as theocratic and liberal-democratic respectively. The main disagreement between the two perspectives relates to the question of the role of religion in the affairs of the state and, indeed, the nature and function of the state itself.

Proponents of the theocratic approach seek to promote their agenda of an Islamic state by defining good citizenship in strictly religious terms. From their perspective, only an orthodox Muslim is a good citizen (Government of Pakistan, 2002a). In contrast, the liberal-democratic view draws a line between the affairs of the state and religion. The liberal-democrats define good citizenship in pluralist terms, emphasising that citizenship is merely a secular concept, and the acquisition of religious knowledge is neither necessary nor sufficient for good citizenship (Nayyar, 2003). Moreover, proponents of the liberal-democratic perspective support their premise with the pronouncements of Mohammad Ali Jinnah, Pakistan's liberal founding father.

Conversely, the adherents of the theocratic approach justify their claim by referring to the "ideology of Pakistan," a contrived and an exclusivist phrase which connotes that the essence of Pakistan was an Islamic state (Hoodbhoy & Nayyar, 1985). In other words, the two competing perspectives on the relationship between religion and the state also represent two competing visions of a good citizen. In the theocratic vision, a good citizen is a Muslim who follows the Islamic religious teachings in both public and private domains and, through his theocratic orientation, seeks to strengthen the Muslim *ummah* or Muslim community (Government of Pakistan, 2002a; Munir, 1979; Sheikh, 1995). According to this doctrine, the national citizenship education curriculum should include content knowledge from the *Quran* and *Hadith* (sayings of the prophet Mohammad) and teach Islamic moral values to build the students' Islamic character (Maududi, 1979; Nayyar, 2003).

By creating a compliant Muslim citizenry, the theocratic vision seeks to create a theocracy or a monolithic Islamic state, a mission that is conceptually at odds with the notion of a modern nation state. The theocratic vision categorically rejects the secular vision of citizenship by declaring it *ladiniyyat* or paganism. More importantly, the theocratic vision is premodern and defines the Islamic state in atavistic terms: The Islamic state is conceived as an entity that is transnational in orientation, transcending the sovereignty of a nation state. That is to say, by definition the Islamic state is action-oriented, expansionist and designed to export Islam as a political ideology to other nations (Ahmed, 1987; Brown, 2000).

On the other hand, the liberal-democratic vision of a good Pakistani citizen is, by and large, comparable to the Western philosophical vision: It conceives the good citizen as a rational and democratic person who lives by democratic ideals. The hallmark of a Pakistani model of the liberal-democratic vision is pluralism (Ahmed, 2003; Nayyar, 2003). The pluralist vision rejects the theocratic prescription of building a medieval form of Islamic state in Pakistan, contending that such an enterprise not only impedes human progress, it also excludes the non-Muslim citizens and women from equal civic participation (Nayyar, 2003; Saigol, 1995).

The two competing visions may also be viewed as forms of Islamic nationalism and Pakistani nationalism. Islamic nationalism is essentially radical Islamism seeking to achieve political unity among members of the worldwide Muslim *ummah* or Muslim community. Islamic nationalists propose a dualist and bifurcated worldview dividing the world into *Dar-al-Islam* or the land of peace and *Dar-al-harb* or the land of war (Brown, 2000; Jones, 2002; Kepel, 2002). They assert that waging *jihad* or holy war against the infidels or non-Muslim nations is one of the central tenets of Islam. This theocratic worldview has found a permanent beachhead in the national citizenship education curriculum and is being transmitted to school children through the social studies textbooks (Saleem, 2003).

On the other hand, as noted above, the scope and purpose of Pakistani nationalism is limited to the preservation of the identity of Pakistan as a modern nation state: It views Pakistan as a multi-faith, multi-cultural and multi-ethnic state, with equal rights for every citizen regardless of one's communal affiliation, faith or gender. The Pakistani nationalist or liberal-democratic approach is consistent with the secular vision of Quide-e-Azam Mohammad Ali Jinnah, the founding father of Pakistan who declared in his legendary speech to the Constituent Assembly on August 11, 1947:

> You are free; you are free to go to your temples, you are free to go to your mosques or to any other place of worship in this State of Pakistan. You may belong to any religion or caste or creed—that has nothing to do with the business of the State. (Quid-e-Azam Mohammad Ali Jinnah, 2000)

However, the Islamic nationalists reject the liberal-democratic vision as Western and un-Islamic, hence inappropriate for citizenship education curriculum in Pakistan (Pakistan Press International, 2004).

The citizenship education curriculum has thus become a special arena where the proponents of the theocratic and liberal-democratic visions clash. Considering the deleterious influence of religious extremism on Pakistani society, which has fostered sectarian violence across the country, General Musharraf (Musharraf, 2004, 2006) launched a liberal social reform agenda, calling it "enlightened moderation." Musharraf's agenda seeks to promote a gentler and more peaceful image of Islam, both inside and outside Pakistan. The primary focus of the proposed reform agenda is citizenship education curriculum.

When the government expressed its intention to review the social studies curriculum, it triggered frenzied opposition from the conservative Islamists, who rejected the idea as an American conspiracy. They launched nationwide street protests, demanding non-interference in the national curriculum (Gillani, 2004). Islamists accused the proponents of the liberal-democratic approach, especially President General Musharraf, as promoters of Western secularism (Pakistan Press International, 2004; Sarwar, 2004). Considering that for more than twenty years the Islamists played a key role in national curriculum policy-making, it is unlikely that they will surrender their ideological mission. Therefore, one could envisage an escalation of the struggle between the two ideological camps for the control of the citizenship education curriculum. The following section examines the goals of the current national citizenship education curriculum policy and how those policy goals find expression in the social studies textbooks.

National Citizenship Education Curriculum Policy

In Pakistan the major responsibility for citizenship education lies with social studies, which includes, in the main, the capstone courses of civics, Pakistan studies and *muasherati uloom* (social studies). Whereas the civics curriculum is an assortment of rudimentary political science, the history of Pakistan and sociology, the main thrust of Pakistan studies and *muasherati uloom* is the history, economy and geography of Pakistan. Nonetheless, the subject matters in civics, Pakistan studies and *muasherati uloom* overlap. These courses offer a formulaic narration of the story of Pakistan, which is explained within the theoretical framework of "Islamic ideology." These courses are taught at the lower as well as higher grade levels in schools. The aims, objectives, contents and methods of teaching these courses are explicitly delineated in the national curriculum policy statements disseminated by the Ministry of Education.

The policy statements lay down certain teleological guidelines in the national curriculum. It is mandatory for the authors of textbooks to adhere to the prescribed guidelines. Those guidelines provide a state-sanctioned standardised account of the nation's heritage. Through the textbooks, which play a pivotal role in adolescents' first encounter with citizenship education, the Pakistani government seeks to inculcate a specific political worldview. Therefore, like most other nations where textbooks contain an official narrative that transmits the nation's priorities, in Pakistan also "textbooks deliver packaged, homogenised knowledge to students" (Schubert, 1997, p.326). In addition, because education in Pakistan is essentially a provincial matter, the authority for adopting and endorsing textbooks lies with four Provincial Textbook Boards, one in each province, and is administered respectively by the governments of North West Frontier Province, Punjab, Sindh and Baluchistan. Within their own jurisdictions, Provincial Textbook Boards sanction the publication and distribution of textbooks that are generally authored by local subject specialists. Nonetheless, in selecting and organizing the material, authors enjoy limited autonomy and must follow the conceptual framework of the national curriculum. For example, in its introduction to the National Curriculum, the Ministry of Education highlights the following points as the conceptual framework for civics:

1. The ideology of Pakistan should permeate the thinking of the young generation.
2. The underlying philosophy of the National Curriculum is Islam and Ideology of Pakistan.
3. The curriculum is more representative and responsive to the Ideology of Pakistan and societal needs.
4. The purpose of the subject is to impart knowledge to the students through the successive stages and help them to discover the world around them. It would sharpen them regarding self-awareness while living in the contemporary world of Hi-Tech.
5. It is activity oriented, which has the capacity to develop in students the skills to think, comprehend, apply, evaluate, and synthesise a phenomenon.
6. The curriculum is mainly focused on applied aspects of the discipline to develop the research culture in Pakistan.
7. The curriculum is modernised in a way that it is very much equivalent to those of the developed world in content and approach.
8. The purpose of civics is to encourage critical thinking in the context of our own culture, society, and Islamic heritage reflected in the code of personal and social life.
9. The curriculum is designed in a way that it will inculcate among the students the sense of gratitude to Almighty Allah, the feelings of national integrity, cohesion and self-reliance and also the sense of patronising behaviour patterns of national character. (Government of Pakistan, 2002a, p.4)

The National Curriculum mentions the following five aims of civics:

1. To transmit the traditional values in consonance with modernity.
2. To develop for critical appraisal of alien culture and ideology.
3. To comprehend evil consequences of imperialism, colonialism and the significance of independence.
4. To promote the unity of Muslim Ummah in the world.
5. To develop and practice the spirit of ideology of Pakistan and Islam. (Government of Pakistan, 2002a, p.5)

The National Curriculum also presents the following as objectives of civics:

1. To develop understanding of the social nature and significance of civics, its key concepts and civic life.
2. To emphasise learning of related themes in a way that it encourages creativity, curiosity, observation, exploration, and questioning.
3. To create awareness about the nature of civic life and relationship between civics and other social sciences.
4. To inculcate a strong sense of gratitude to Almighty Allah for his blessings providing us an independent state.
5. To promote understanding about the Ideology of Pakistan and the struggle of Muslims for an Independent Islamic State.
6. To inculcate the behaviour patterns of National Character, and qualities of a good citizen, self reliance, patriotism and leadership.
7. To create a strong sense of national unity, integration and cohesion.
8. To prepare students as future citizens, conscious of their positive role in an Islamic society and the world at large. (Government of Pakistan, 2002a, p.5)

In essence, the conceptual framework, aims and objectives signify four kinds of national aspirations: (a) to integrate and balance religious and secular themes in citizenship education, (b) to inculcate an Islamic worldview in children, (c) to present Islamic ideology as the foundation for national unity, and (d) to seek congruence between belief in the religion of Islam and the exigencies of the modern age.

Indeed, by referring to Benjamin S. Bloom's (1956) taxonomy, the conceptual framework reflects the government's desire to project Pakistan as a forward-looking nation that seeks to benefit from the pedagogical approaches practised in the advanced nations, and also to demonstrate the compatibility of modernity and Islamic ideology. Perhaps that is why the conceptual framework claims that the national civics curriculum is as modern in content and approach as those used in the advanced nations (Government of Pakistan, 2002a; Government of Pakistan, 2002b). Embedded in this claim is the assumption that, as an approach to citizenship education, Islamic ideology is as central to the Pakistani cultural, political and historical context as democracy is to the Western cultural context.

Although the national curriculum is a comprehensive document, it contains inchoate ideas about democratic citizenship. Basic terms, such as "democracy," "citizenship" or "democratic values," which generally constitute the core of citizenship education curriculum in democratic societies, are certainly mentioned, but appear to be tangential to the main goals of the national curriculum. Textbooks for civics and *muasherati uloom* follow the same schema: Democracy is mentioned with caveats. However, the term "Islamic democracy" is frequently used, which connotes that curriculum policymakers do not entirely reject the concept of democracy as long as it conforms to the overarching framework of Islam. Indeed, this conceptualisation of democracy is deliberate. Perhaps Pakistani curriculum policy-makers relate the values of individual liberty, religious freedom, gender equality and equal rights—concepts that are pivotal to citizenship theory—to Western secularism and thus deem them inappropriate for an Islamic polity.

More importantly, because as a mode of socialisation citizenship education generally takes place in the affective domain, the national curriculum emphasises the Islamic approach in its affective objectives for the themes of government, the state, citizenship, rights and responsibilities. The following is an example of the curriculum objectives in the affective domain for 9-12 grade civics:

1. To create a sense of love for Islamic teachings (p.10);
2. To develop an Islamic civic sense about the state being the primary requisite Islamic state (p.10);
3. To develop an urge to make our country an Islamic welfare state (p.11);
4. To promote an urge to practice the teachings of Islam in its real spirit (p.11);
5. To demonstrate love for the Islamic way of life (p.12);
6. To demonstrate with reference to government a love for Islamic values (p.12);
7. To develop a sense of love for the ideology of Pakistan (p.13);
8. To enhance love and respect for the supreme law of Almighty Allah (p.13);
9. To demonstrate faith in the ideology of Pakistan (p.14); and
10. To promote a sense of respect for the Islamic code of life (p.15). (Government of Pakistan, 2002a, 2002b)

The purpose of an overemphasis on Islam in the course on civics suggests that the Pakistani curriculum makes no distinction between religious education and citizenship education. In essence, the Pakistani curriculum seeks to create devout Muslims. Moreover, it seeks to create Muslim citizens who are loyal to an Islamic state. Although an Islamic state is a romanticised idea, the curriculum is unequivocal in promoting it. However, considering the educational needs of all students, especially the non-Muslim students in public schools, these curricular objectives become problematic.

The following section reviews the textbooks on civics, Pakistan studies and *muasherati uloom*. It also chronicles the findings of two recent reports on the Islamic model of citizenship education in Pakistan. The first report was prepared by A.H. Nayyar and Ahmed Salim (2003), and the second by Yvette Claire Rosser. (2004)

Citizenship Education and Islamic Ideology

Citizenship education is a normative activity. Historically, the main purpose of the citizenship education component of the school curriculum has essentially been the inculcation of allegiance to national ideals and nation-building and the preparation of patriotic citizens (Gibson, 1971). Patriotism conjures up the feeling of belonging to a political community and the preservation of its ethos. In contemporary democratic theory, patriotism is defined in the context of civic unity and sharing common democratic ideals, including equality, justice, human rights, individual liberty and pluralism (Banks, 2004;

Gutmann, 2004). In the case of Pakistan, however, for about three decades there has been a conscious and consistent effort on the part of successive governments of different ideological stripes to shy away from the liberal-democratic paradigm of citizenship and citizenship education.

Considering the historical, cultural and geo-strategic milieu of Pakistan, like everything else in that nation, citizenship education has also been Islamised. Why did the Pakistani policy-makers decide to switch from a liberal model, which existed prior to 1979, to an Islamic model is a question that can be explained in the context of the historical developments in and around Pakistan. Veteran civic educator and education historian R. Freeman Butts (1977) theorised that citizenship education draws relatively greater attention during a period of national crisis because a nation needs unity and patriotic citizens to defend it against external threats, real or imaginary. In the same vein, both Susan Douglas Franzosa (1996) and Carole L. Hahn (2003) observe that the content and nature of citizenship education is context-specific. In other words, different nations have different needs and aspirations at different stages of their historical trajectory. Hahn goes a step further by positing that "because educational practices are deeply embedded in and reflective of particular cultural contexts, they cannot be simply borrowed" (p.78). To some extent these three observations offer insights into the Pakistani model in the sense that, as a postcolonial nation state, Pakistan has been in a perpetual crisis of religious and ethnic conflicts. It fought three wars against India, suffered humiliating defeats, and ultimately disintegrated in 1971.

Moreover, in the late 1970s, when the democratic experiment failed, Pakistan's military ruler, General Zia-ul-Haq, adopted Islamic ideology to control the state apparatus, unify a diverse population, raise the morale of a vanquished nation and defend Pakistan against external threats. But the use of Islamic ideology as a national motto and worldview boomeranged: It triggered sectarian violence and polarised the nation. Critics of Islamic ideology note that the conservative Islamist rulers used it as a device to coerce political opponents (Alavi, n.d.; Rashid, 1987). Also, it helped create a culture of religious intolerance and marginalised women and non-Muslim citizens from civic participation.

Thus it is evident from the national curriculum guidelines that the overarching theme of the curriculum on citizenship education in Pakistan is Islamic ideology. Further, the central goal of citizenship education is not the preparation of merely good citizens, as conceived in liberal-democratic theory, but the kind of citizens who are fundamentally *momin* or devout practitioners of Islam. Mobin Shorish (1988) characterised such citizens as "Homo Islamicus" (p.3). Indeed, a remarkable distinction exists between the characteristics of the two types of citizenship: Whereas a citizen of a modern nation state has always been associated with the Western notion of *civitas*, a momin, on the other hand, is a member of an *ummah* or Muslim political community governed by Islamic law or the *Sharia*. The Sharia derives from the Quran, a revealed book, and includes the rules by which a Muslim society is organised and governed. Ishtiaq Ahmed (1987) notes that the scope of Sharia is greater than enforceable law, and provides guidance about how to perform prayers, lead a proper matrimonial life and treat children and elders (p.40). An

Islamic state is required to implement the Sharia. Therefore, a momin is more than a political status; it requires allegiance to *tawhid*. Samira Haj (2002) posits that tawhid is a belief system and is performative in character in that this belief can only be realised through the enactment of a set of authorised practices and virtues (p.339).

In brief, religion reigns supreme in citizenship education curriculum in Pakistan. Teaching and learning about liberal-democratic values or the building of a liberal-democratic culture is extraneous to the mission of the Islamic model of citizenship education. Indeed, a particular version of Islam, *Wahabism*, pervades the pages of the textbooks for civics, Pakistan studies and *muasherati uloom* (social studies). Wahabism is a radical school of thought that was founded by Muhammad ibn 'Abdul Wahab in the eighteenth century at Najd (Ottoman central Arabia) and was imported into Pakistan by extremist clerics. In the late 1970s and early 1980s, President General Zia-ul-Haq adopted Wahabism as a state policy (Kepel, 2002). Once in place, the *Wahabi* version of Islam was canonised in 1991 by the Commission on Islamization of Education, which "ensured that the educational system of Pakistan was based on Islamic values of learning, teaching, and character building" (Ghafoor & Farooq, 1994, p.4264).

Islamic Ideology and Textbooks

The scope and sequence of material in several school textbooks on civics, Pakistan studies and *muasherati uloom* (social studies) confirm the salient status of Wahabi Islam, which is emphasised as more than a citizen's personal faith: It is presented as a complete way of life, a political ideology and a national enterprise. For example, my review of three high school textbooks shows that the first chapter in each of the two textbooks on Pakistan studies begins with "the Ideological Foundation of Pakistan," identified as Islam (Ahmad, Javed, & Saeed, n.d.; Kakakhel, Ahmad, Khan, & Abbas, n.d.). To put it plainly, the first chapter in each of the said books begins with an explicit declaration that Pakistan is an ideological state and that its ideology is Islam. The textbooks assert that Pakistan was created to establish an Islamic state, modelled after the city of Medina, which Mohammad, the Prophet of Islam, established in Arabia in the seventh century AD.

Describing the characteristics of an Islamic state, each textbook claims that its guiding principle is the tawhid. More importantly, the textbooks draw a clear distinction between Islam and democracy by asserting that the Islamic political system and Western democracy are two diametrically opposed concepts. Nothing more is mentioned about democracy except for the declarations that the Islamic system is superior. The textbooks enumerate the benefits of recognizing the primacy of the sovereignty of God in citizens' public and private affairs. Justice, equality, the rule of law and unity among the believers are also mentioned as features of an Islamic state.

A government-approved textbook, *Civics*, by M. Hasan Sheikh (1995) integrates political science and history. Sheikh compares the Western concept of nation with the Islamic concept of *millat* and explains that Islam rejects nation and nationalism. He argues that whereas the Western notion of nationalism is based on ethnicity and territoriality, millat is based on the ideology of Islam, transcending the boundaries of region, race, colour, language and culture. Hence, the textbook asserts there is no place for nation and nationalism in Islam (p.19). On the question of the rights and duties of citizens in an Islamic state, Sheikh offers two separate and comprehensive descriptions: one for the Muslim citizens and the other for non-Muslim citizens (pp.72-77). For the Muslim citizens, he identifies three kinds of rights: social, economic and political. According to Sheikh, in an Islamic state a Muslim citizen has a different set of rights and duties from those of a non-Muslim.

In the section "Duties of Muslim Citizens," Sheikh provides a detailed list. The first item proclaims: "It is the duty of every citizen not only to follow the teachings of the *Quran* and *Sunnah* but also to promote them in society" (p.75). The same list mentions that "it is the duty of every citizen to observe the five pillars of Islam: pray regularly, observe fast, be charitable, perform pilgrimage, and participate in *Jihad*" (p.75). The section on the rights and duties of Muslim citizens is followed by a small section on the "Rights and Duties of Non-Muslim Citizens," which classifies a non-Muslim citizen as a *zimmi*. Pakistani historian K.K. Aziz (1993) defines zimmi as "a non-Muslim citizen of an Islamic state whom the state undertakes to protect in the profession and practice of his religion in exchange for a special poll tax or *jizya*" (p.425). According to Sheikh's (1995) list of rights, in an Islamic state the non-Muslim citizens are allowed to practise their religion, build their places of worship, get educated and seek employment. He further explains that non-Muslims are forbidden from holding key political positions in government, such as president or prime minister (p.76). This point is highlighted also by Kakakhel et al. (n.d.) in the textbook *Pakistan Studies* for Grade 10, which goes a step further and defines Muslim (p.37). Referring to the constitution of Pakistan, Kakakhel et al. suggest that a person is recognised as Muslim who holds two basic beliefs: the unity or oneness of *Allah* (God) and the finality of prophethood (that Mohammad was God's last messenger).

Paradoxically, Sheikh's list of duties for the non-Muslim citizens is half the size of what he proposes for Muslim citizens. This short list includes five items: "loyalty to the Islamic state," "pay *jizya*" (*jizya* is a special tax on non-Muslim citizens), "worship only at separate and officially-approved locations," "abstaining from creating discord and civil strife in the Islamic state," and "playing an active role in strengthening the Islamic state" (p.77). Since these duties are prescribed for the non-Muslim citizens, one may conclude that Muslim citizens may be excluded from observing them.

An officially-approved textbook for the seventh grade course *muasherati uloom* is entirely focused on one theme: pan-Islamism. Authored by three college professors, *muasherati uloom* is adopted for the schools in the North West Frontier Province. There are eleven chapters in this textbook and ten of them describe the geography, culture, population, history and economy of the Muslim countries. The title of the first chapter is "Pakistan and the Muslim World," which provides a conceptual foundation for the succeeding chapters; it also provides a short description of each Muslim country in the contemporary world. Other chapters discuss the sub-themes, such as features of an Islamic society, the geo-strategic significance of the economic resources of the Muslim world, the history of the expansion of Islam, the history of Western domination over the Muslim world and revolutionary movements in Islam. Unlike other textbooks on *muasherati uloom*, this textbook has a unique feature in that its first chapter begins with the following three sentences: "Pakistan is a sovereign Islamic nation. A majority of the people in Pakistan are Muslims. In addition to the Muslims, Hindus, Sikhs, Parsis and Buddhists also live here" (Nazir, Khan, & Khan, n.d., p.1). One would expect that since the main thrust of the textbook is pan-Islamism, it would acknowledge only the Muslim citizens in Pakistan. However, in addition to this brief factual statement, there is hardly any discussion of the status of non-Muslims elsewhere in the textbook except in the context of the ancient conflicts between Muslims and non-Muslims.

Textbooks in other provinces contain more or less similar content and themes and follow the official guidelines. For example, a report *The Subtle Subversion: The State of Curricula and Textbooks in Pakistan* (Nayyar & Salim, 2003), demonstrates that the social studies textbooks contain material that can be characterised as insensitive towards non-Muslims and women. The report shows how school history books have fostered a militant Islamic sensibility and warns that this would have profound consequences for Pakistan's civic life. The main goal of the report was to understand how citizenship education was contributing to creating a culture of religious intolerance in Pakistan. A.H. Nayyar, one of the authors of the study, described the purpose of their report as follows:

> Our report used the official curriculum and the contents of the officially sanctioned textbooks actually in use, to show, instead of values of mutual respect, equality, justice and peace that can contribute towards a just, peaceful and democratic Pakistan, day after day, year after year, our children are taught to despise and hate peoples of other faiths and nations, to accept bias against women and minorities, to glorify violence and to celebrate jehad and shahadat. (Nayyar, 2004, p.3)

The report concludes that the school textbooks on civics and Pakistan studies contain "factual inaccuracy and omissions for ideological ends, encourage religious, national and ethnic prejudice, foster gender stereotypes and intolerance, and glorify war" (Nayyar & Salim, 2003, p.6). It also concludes that the social studies textbooks define citizenship in a manner that excludes non-Muslim Pakistanis from either being Pakistani citizens or from even being good human beings. For example, the report suggests that the textbooks equate patriotism with Islamic zeal and describe good people as those "who read the Quran and teach the Quran to others" (ibid., p.12).

One of the authors of *The Subtle Subversion*, Hajra Ahmed (2003), reviewed the social studies textbooks and noted that material on history "narrowly focused on the Muslim world" and that "religious prejudices pervade the books" (p.127). In Ahmed's view, the social studies textbooks made historical omissions to rationalise Islamic ideology. Similarly, Rosser (2004) analysed textbooks for Pakistan studies, a required course, and concluded that "Pakistani textbooks condone and even welcome the military's involvement in politics." (p.284) Rosser's research demonstrates that the textbooks on Pakistan studies eulogise the Islamist military ruler, General Zia-ul-Haq and his regime, for

Islamising Pakistani society. Rosser's work also validates the findings and conclusions of *The Subtle Subversion* that Pakistani history textbooks contain what she calls "hagiographies of Muslim heroes, and polemics about the superiority of Islamic principles over Hinduism" (p.267). Rosser avers that Pakistani textbooks seek to produce "patriotic Pakistanis who are also practicing orthodox Islam" (p.273). Rosser holds General Zia's curriculum policies responsible for institutionalizing Islamization in citizenship education and, thereby, fostering a culture of sectarianism, intolerance and global violence.

In brief, four specific themes emerge from the above empirical analyses of the social studies textbooks in Pakistan. First, the thematic structure and organisation of the textbooks echo the national curriculum policy goals mandated by the government of Pakistan, which underscore Islamic ideology as a grand unifying theory. Second, to sanctify Islamic ideology as an article of faith, the textbooks conveniently twist historical facts about the nation's cultural and political heritage. Third, the textbooks offer a biased treatment of women, non-Muslim citizens and nationalities in Pakistan. Finally, the main objective of the social studies textbooks, especially textbooks on Pakistan studies, civics and *muasherati uloom*, is to indoctrinate children for a romanticised Islamic state, as conceptualised by Islamic nationalists. Indeed, overwhelming evidence demonstrates that it is not the goal of these textbooks to prepare democratic and tolerant citizens or to foster cultural pluralism in Pakistan.

Conclusion

In their effort to Islamise Pakistani society, in the early 1980s the Islamist military rulers canonised Islamic ideology in the citizenship education curriculum. However, in response to recent American pressure, the current government of Pakistan is curtailing the Islamic paradigm of citizenship education. This has led to a vociferous national debate. Two issues are at the centre of this debate: the separation of religion and state, and the definition of a good citizen. Proponents of the liberal-democratic agenda argue that Pakistan should be a constitutional democracy based on the principles of religious freedom. Also, they define the good citizen as a tolerant human being. Hence, in their view the citizenship education curriculum policy of Pakistan should foster liberal-democratic values.

Conversely, Islamic theocrats contend that Pakistan was created on the basis of Islamic ideology, which calls for the creation of an Islamic state. They also argue that, since Pakistan is a homeland for Muslims, Islamic law must be implemented there. They reject the notion of liberal democracy. Moreover, in the theocratic vision, the good citizen is a Muslim who should enjoy more rights in Pakistan than a non-Muslim citizen. This perspective has found a beachhead in the citizenship education curriculum of Pakistan.

It must be argued that the Islamic model of citizenship education does not reflect the sentiments of a majority of the people because it is not the product of a national democratic debate: It was imposed upon the people by a state *diktat*. Indeed, it represents a parochial, sectarian and conformist view of a praetorian group that used the coercive power of the state to indoctrinate the nation's children (Haque, 1987; Nayyar, 2003). Moreover, the Islamic model has neither taken into consideration the needs of a developing society, nor has it presented Islamic civilisation as a progressive alternative.

Therefore, curriculum policy-makers in Pakistan would have to recognise that citizenship education is not theology. The goals of the citizenship education curriculum are temporal, not otherworldly: Good citizenship is a civic virtue, not a religious virtue. In addition, it is impossible for a nation state to provide religious guidance to citizens. More importantly, because Pakistan is home to numerous sects of Islam, the government cannot grant official endorsement to one sect or another. Hence, the central goal for a successful social studies curriculum must be one that seeks to create a strong *Unum* from *Pluribus*. It would be able to do so if it underscored teaching and learning about democratic civic ideals as proposed by Mohammad Ali Jinnah, the founding father of Pakistan, who was a Muslim and a liberal-democrat; he did not see a contradiction between his Islamic faith and his democratic values (Wolpert, 1984).

In sum, as the people of Pakistan face the challenges of the 21st century, one would expect that, in their own cultural context, they would like to keep pace with the global transformations in social, political and economic spheres. Because contemporary worldwide trends of reforms in citizenship education curricula are also a part of the global transformation, it would be beneficial if Pakistani curriculum policy-makers learned from the experiences of other nations, especially Muslim nations, so that they may be able to serve adequately the needs of their children and society.

7

Citizenship Discourse in the Context of Decentralisation: The Case of Indonesia

Mary FEARNLEY-SANDER and Ella YULAELAWATI

Introduction: Citizenship Education and Democracy

The Preamble to Indonesia's 1945 Constitution sets out the philosophy of the state. That philosophy is known as *Pancasila*, meaning five principles. They are:

1. Belief in the One and Only God.
2. Just and Civilised Humanity.
3. Unity of Indonesia.
4. Sovereignty of the People Led by the Inner Wisdom of Deliberation amongst Representatives.
5. Social Justice for the Whole of the People of Indonesia.[i]

These principles still constitute the formulation of the principles of national life. Each principle was designed to hold together competing religious, political and ethnic aspirations for the political identity of the new Indonesia within a unitary state. Because of their breadth of statement, these principles have been subjected to interpretations in support of the prevailing political agenda over the course of Indonesia's national history. These interpretations, though never without contestation, intended to preserve both elements in the formulation *unity in diversity*. By definition, any discussion of the formal curriculum for citizenship in Indonesia must be based on these principles of citizenship. No matter how potent other identities for social and political activism—religious identities, for example—their civic mission and meaning is conferred on them by the terms of their inclusion in the constitutional definition of citizenship.

The principles of *Pancasila* underpin the national education project itself. The new Education Act, *Sisdiknas* (*Undang-Undang Republik Indonesia Nomor 20 Tahun 2003 Tentang Sistem Pendidikan Nasional*) stipulates the function and aim of education in Chapter II, Article 3:

National education functions to develop the capability, character, and civilization of the nation by enhancing its intellectual capacity, and is aimed at developing learners' potential so that they become persons imbued with human values who are faithful and pious to the one and only God; who possess good morals and noble character, who are healthy, knowledgeable, competent, creative, independent; and as citizens, are democratic and responsible.

All schools in Indonesia which provide a general education, state and private schools, and *madrasah* (Islamic Schools), constitute the arena of formal schooling, and as such are subject to the Education Law. While private schools and madrasah are entitled to reflect the characteristics and values of the community they serve, national regulations and specifications regarding graduation, accreditation and curriculum apply equally to them, including the domain of citizenship education.[ii] The discussion in this chapter thus encompasses all schools in the formal sector of education. It presents an account of the contemporary citizenship curriculum as it is framed by the philosophy of the state, and looks at how the curriculum has accommodated significant political change during the transition to democratisation at the end of Soeharto's rule in 1998.

In the transition from the New Order, as Soeharto's thirty-two-year rule is known, the national government of Indonesia launched democratising policies in the areas of electoral politics, governance and education. Politically, these included the decentralisation laws. Law No. 22 (*Undang-Undang Republik Indonesia Nomor No. 22 Tahun 1999 Tentang Pemerintahan Daerah*) on Local Governance is the legal basis for the decentralisation of authorities in eleven out of sixteen major government sectors, including that of education. This law is articulated in Government Regulation No. 25, 1999, which sets out the sharing of authority between central and district government. According to this regulation, operational and technical arrangements in educational implementation now belong to the district or municipal government. Authorities left in the central government in education are those related to the setting of national policies for competency standards, the national curriculum, the education calendar and evaluation. In respect of national policies, the national programme has mandated participative school-based management and a new curriculum framework based on competency attainment in all school subjects, including citizenship.

The reforms in both governance and curriculum describe their objectives in terms of democratisation. Decentralisation is justified in the policy rhetoric as building community capacity for democracy through localisation of government. And the logic of decentralisation that legitimates local government marches right on to the school, requiring authority and resources transfer from the district departments of education to school communities in the interests of plurality and participative governance. The new curriculum for citizenship is explicit in its orientation to participatory citizenship. The competency curriculum is advocated as fulfilling the localisation objectives of decentralisation, through local empowerment and reinforcement of local say in educational provision.

In this chapter we trace the conceptual commitments of national educationists to democratic citizenship in the formulation of key new policy and curriculum texts. We limit our attention to the level of policy discourse. A study of take-up in the field is premature, given the recency of the specifically educational policy changes, still in the process of socialisation.[iii] In our inquiry, we have in mind the question of the interaction of these changes with Indonesia's democratisation. Some theorists studying Indonesia's transition question the value of taking such policy change as evidence of democratisation. Their argument is that these "technical solutions" are only mistaken for democratisation by neo-institutionalists eliding the factor of power from political change. Democratisation in their terms is defined by a sustainable shift in political power from elites to organised mass movements (Hadiz, 2003; Priyono, Prasetyo & Tornquist, 2003).

However, in its concern with class-based dynamics, this version of democratisation theory does not give enough attention to governance in the relationship between decentralisation and democratisation. It does not take account of the conduciveness of small units of governance to political participation. Nor does it take enough account of the potential for participation in self-governance in Indonesia's long tradition of communitarian citizenship, once freed from authoritarian centralism and in the conducive environment of decentralisation. Rather, the problematic nature of decentralisation as a strategy for civic activation consists in the historical weakness of civic agency or instrumentality in Indonesia.

In the view of Muhammad Hikam (1999, p.59), an historian of Indonesian citizenship, this weakness is a result of the overstrong state brought into being by the integration of the executive and the legislative functions in the 1945 Constitution, and exploited in the New Order bureaucratic authoritarianism. In his view, this political history has obscured the very idea of the politics of citizenship, and has meant that there is little in the way of a civic tradition to build on.

The argument in this chapter is that, in the post-New Order era, civic agency has been foregrounded in the citizenship curriculum through its organisation around competencies for citizenship, and that it is decentralisation that is steering the communitarian traditions of Indonesian citizenship in the direction of democratic citizenship. In terms of models of citizenship, this reorientation is defined in this chapter as a move away from communitarian citizenship, characterised by self-identification with the state, towards a republican model of citizenship. The concept of citizenship is still strongly organised around the collective pursuit of a common goal, but the goal is defined as the democratic goal of citizens' self-government. Civic identity is no longer seen as the integration of citizens' wills in a supreme, personified state.[iv]

The impetus towards this reorientation derives not necessarily from the democratic ideal of decentralisation alone. It is also impelled by the sense of risk in decentralisation—the risk of that decentralisation resulting not in community self-management but rather in "small despots" at the level of the district. This is a risk from the perspective of central governments of any persuasion, and thus is to some extent independent of democratising motivations. In the conditions of decentralisation, civic participation need no longer be about unity of will between citizen and state but about bridling unaccountable and undemocratic local power. The new policy discourse of citizenship legitimises the project of self-governance; and the reorganisation of citizenship education around the production of citizens with the competencies for political participation is a prerequisite—no less significant for being "technical"—for grassroots mobilisation for democracy.

The following discussion is divided into two sections. In the first section we look at the models of citizenship on which the new curriculum is based. Our interest is in tracking the emergence of a new orientation towards civic autonomy in thinking about citizenship, and its reconciliation with the communitarianism of Indonesia's civic tradition. In the second section we look at the relationship of the new curriculum to decentralisation to see what congruence there is between the discourse of making citizens and the new conditions of governance in decentralised Indonesia.

Section I: The New Curriculum for Citizenship in Indonesia

Models of Citizenship and their Influence on the Genesis of the New Curriculum

Hikam's view cited above, about the weakness of agency in Indonesian civic tradition, is supported by the history of the goals that citizenship education, and education more generally, has served in Indonesia, from the period after Independence to the present transition era. Educational reforms in Indonesia from 1947 up to 1975 were closely linked to the inculcation of national ideology and beliefs in the service of social and political rationales. The first educational planning (1947-1952) was aimed at meeting the need of a newly independent country and a rural society. Developing patriotism became a priority. Eradication of superstition through explanation of natural phenomena, eradication of violence and cultivation of a national aesthetics were among the goals of primary education, at the expense of the development of science and technology.

The emphasis on national ideology was even more concentrated in the sixties, as can be seen from the 1964 education plan. Political disturbances at that time explained why development of citizenship ideals was in keeping with the values of the national philosophy of *Pancasila*, then interpreted in a way that supported Indonesian socialism (Yulaelawati, 2002, p.56). The development of *Bahasa Indonesia* as a national language and at the same time the preservation of Indonesian heterocultures were also emphasised. Four years later, at the start of the "New-Order" government, the emphasis on ideology was yet more significant. Developing *"Pancasila* identity" became the priority in the curriculum of 1968. The 1968 Curriculum is articulated around an understanding of the rights and duties of the *"Pancasila* Man." *Pancasila* Man is the citizen whose daily conduct reflects the integrity of *Pancasila*'s five principles (Government of Indonesia, 1988, p.73).

A new curriculum came into operation in 1975. This curriculum emphasised "good citizenship," meaning citizens that are healthy and have mastered skills, knowledge and values sufficiently to become lifelong learners. In 1975, curriculum reform placed considerable emphasis on science and technological development in support of national development goals. This reform resulted in a much overloaded curriculum, heavy in content. It was accompanied by a positivistic instructional design paradigm, relying on objectives, instructional design and evaluation, and was particularly oriented to the "objective" assessment of exams.

The 1984 reform attempted to simplify all of these, and was taken further in the reform of 1994 which incorporated science and technology through problem-solving, critical thinking and inquiry skills into classroom practice. In this reform, nine years compulsory basic education was mandatory and the importance of human resource development—citizens as economic actors—was further emphasised. However, the 1994 centralised national curriculum did not cater sufficiently to the diversity of the Indonesian societies in spite of the fact that, alongside more generalised cultural influences transmitted through the educational system, local Indonesians have strong traditional values and norms (*adat*).

Despite advancements from the eighties in terms of content and methodologies, it is clear that the management of the national curriculum from 1947 up to 1994 remained highly centralised and was heavily content-based. It is against this background that we need to assess the achievement of the educational reforms accompanying decentralisation, which was ushered in by the 1999 Law of Regional Autonomy.

In 1998, in the euphoric sense of possibilities at the end of thirty-two years of authoritarian rule, the scope of citizenship education for supporting democracy was quickly seen. One of the first changes was designing a citizenship curriculum in the form of "Citizenship Education" (*Pendidikan Kewarganegaraan*). This was a reframing of "*Pancasila* and Citizenship Education" (*Pendidikan Pancasila dan Kewarganegaraan* [PPKn]). The change was made because of the view that, while *Pancasila* should be the philosophical underpinning of citizenship education, citizenship education should not try to turn *Pancasila* itself into a curriculum. The New Order administration had imposed an integral interpretation on *Pancasila*, with too much emphasis on communalism through a consensus-seeking deliberation of problems and issues in the community *(mufakat or musyawarah)*. There was little room in such prescribed identity of interest between the state and citizen for notions of civic rights and opposition which counterpoised the citizen to the state (Ubaidillah, 2004).

During 1999, groups from various tertiary institutions prominent for citizenship education lobbied for replacements models (Winataputra, 2000, pp.44-45). The model that had the highest profile in the curriculum debate during 1999-2000 was a liberal-democratic model, for which there was little precedent in Indonesian political culture up to that point.[v] It took a "civic education" approach to citizenship education, focusing on conceptual understanding of democratic systems and the rule of law, and on civil society values, such as active citizenship, tolerance, human rights civility, equity, cultural diversity and social justice.

By the end of 2000, the Centre for Curriculum (PUSKUR) in the National Department of Education had drawn on other sources for citizenship education and had developed its own curriculum framework for citizenship. The framework incorporated most features of the civic model, but also re-emphasised *Pancasila* as the source of Indonesian state philosophy, civic values and national identity.

Over the next two years, the citizenship curriculum was worked into a competency-based framework, along with all other school subjects. This entailed further changes to the model of citizenship. Inherent in the competency-based curriculum framework is the aim of developing agency. (This is in contrast to "civic education," in which the political agency of the citizen is largely confined to the act of voting.) The competency framework is organised around civic competencies: civic knowledge, civic skills, civic values, and national identity (Departemen Pendidikan Nasional, 2001a). In addition, the competency curriculum framework in Indonesia is infused with constructivism in its presentation of "civic knowledge." Constructivism could be described as a democratic epistemology, insofar as it dislodges the authority of received accounts of things and focuses on the constructive role of the learner in the production of knowledge.

In 2001, the competency-based curriculum was trialled in a limited number of schools and in 2003 it was widely adopted in schools, thus ready for staged take-up in the 2004-5 teaching year.

Organisation and Content: How the New Curriculum Constructs the Citizen

As a result of these origins, the new curriculum incorporates three kinds of political values in its structure and content: (a) a commitment to *Pancasila* as the source of national identity, (b) a commitment to civic competency, and (c) a rights-oriented view of citizenship. For reasons which have to do with the developmental organisation of the Indonesian curriculum, these three values in the curriculum will be discussed in the order below.

Commitment to Pancasila as the Source of National Identity

As befits a preamble to a curriculum for citizenship, the formal description of its rationale, goals and function leave no doubt as to the state's interest in its outcomes. The preamble opens with a quotation from the Preparatory Committee for Indonesia's Independence (PPKI) in 1945 concerning the formation of a unitary state-based community varying in religion and ethnicity through a shared nationalism (Departemen Pendidikan Nasional, 2001a, p.1). Further quotations from the Preamble to the 1945 Constitution characterise the nation in terms of the five principles of *Pancasila*. The stated intent of the curriculum evokes the nationalist project of shaping subjectivities that vary in respect of religion, culture, language, age and ethnicity into Indonesian citizens whose character is mandated by *Pancasila* and the Constitution of 1945 (p.2).

However, the introduction to the curriculum also goes on to include respect for rights as its other political ideal—respect for rights in the dispositions of the community, as well as in the institutions of state and society. In the body of the curriculum, these two sets of ideals—the traditional political identity of *Pancasila* and the new commitment to democratic rights—are frequently associated. At every level of schooling, rights are mentioned in the vicinity of *Pancasila*.

There is, however, a contrast in the presentation of learning approaches to *Pancasila* values on the one hand, and on the other, to the rest of Indonesia's political institutions that bear on the quality of democracy and human rights. The material on *Pancasila* requires an unquestioning commitment to it as the foundation of the state along with the constitution of 1945. Thus in the junior secondary curriculum students are expected to be able to show why *Pancasila* is a superior philosophy for the state and to identify behaviour that shows loyalty to the principles of *Pancasila* (Departemen Pendidikan Nasional, 2001b, p.8). By contrast, most of the other topics require a critical, evaluative approach by the student which includes identification of weaknesses as well as strengths in the history and structuring of political and legal institutions.

The Pancasilaist content of the curriculum (*Pancasila*, the 1945 constitution and the unitariness of the Indonesian state), however, is surprisingly small, far outweighed by other topics concerned with political institutions and life. Entirely gone from the treatment of *Pancasila* is any attempt to define students' personal or even civic identities in terms of it, which was so marked in the curriculum of the New Order.

Commitment to Civic Competency

> It's about time the world of education played a role as a critical force in relation to the manipulative tendencies of power. The arrival of the competency-based curriculum … fulfils that promise and needs to be supported. … Citizenship education rather than just being education in general values that we should uphold should be a multi-dimensional character education that includes several elements that every citizen needs: civic knowledge, civic dispositions, civic skills, civic competencies, civic confidence and civic commitments. (Ubaidillah, 2004)

This comment by an Indonesian educationist shows how the competency-based curriculum lends itself to being seen as a means for civic agency; and agency in the context of the protection of citizens vis-à-vis state power. We will now look at the degree to which such a purpose can be traced in the construction of the citizenship curriculum itself.

In the new competency-based curriculum, the competency framework extends from the beginning of primary to the end of senior secondary school: The statement of rationale, goals and functions are the same at each level and the same competencies are targeted, developmentally, throughout schooling. Curriculum scope differs by level; in primary, the focus is more local to the student; in junior secondary, the content is more about the constituent features of the political community of contemporary Indonesia; and in senior secondary, the concern is on an understanding Indonesia's institutions of government in a comparative framework.

In spite of the unitary objectives, there is a major difference between the primary school preparation for citizenship and that for secondary school. In primary, education for citizenship is incorporated into the social knowledge area of the curriculum without its own identity as a subject, while in the senior secondary it is a distinct subject area called Citizenship Education. This disappearance of the subject name in the first stage of schooling is more significant than a change of nomenclature. Compared with the consecrated position of the New Order's *Pancasila* citizenship programme in the curriculum, it seems to mark the withdrawal of the state from the project of shaping children for the state. Instead, children are being prepared for their own autonomous exercise of citizenship.

The strongest evidence for the orientation of the Indonesian citizenship curriculum to the idea of civic competency is the extent of the similarity with the organisation of the Australian social curriculum, which also encompasses citizenship education. In the Indonesian curriculum there are five standard competencies derived from the constituent subject areas of citizenship education: "the ability to understand and apply facts, concepts and generalisations" about (1) social and cultural systems; (2) people, place and environment; (3) economic behaviour; (4) time, continuity and change; (5) national and state systems." (Curriculum Corporation, 2000) The Australian social curriculum for primary/junior secondary is also organised in the same way, as can be seen in Table 7.1:

Table 7.1   The Social Knowledge Organisation of the Indonesian and the Australian Curriculum

	Indonesia	*Australia*
Subject name:	Social Knowledge	Studies of Society and Environment
Strands: 1. 2. 3. 4. 5. 6.	Social system and culture People, Place and Environment Economic behaviour and prosperity Time, continuity and change National and state systems	Culture Place and space Resources Time, continuity and change Natural and social systems Investigation, communication and participation

Source: Curriculum Corporation, 2000

The framing of the competencies around "facts, concepts and generalisations" in the Indonesian curriculum still resonates with the positivistic social science paradigm of social learning. But those formulations are also internally at odds with a constructivist approach in this area of the curriculum, which certainly seems to organise the approach to learning more systematically.

The standard competencies in the two disciplinary areas of the social curriculum most potent for citizen formation, social anthropology and history are imbued with constructivism. The competence entailed in "understanding society," for example, puts considerable emphasis on the competence of understanding difference, so that students can:

- Develop critical attitudes in regard to social situations that arise as a result of differences in the communities

- Respect the varieties of social and cultural systems in a multicultural community (Departemen Pendidikan Nasional, 2001b, p.2)

The preparation of students for responding to difference is taken further than treating difference with respect, which was how difference was handled in the old curriculum, in the interests of preventing social disruptions produced by intolerance of group differences. Much is added by the specification of *critically looking at the role of difference in social situations.* When understanding the *historical production of difference* is added further to this aim, there is the potential in this learning area for developing political insights into social situations. One of the rationales of the history strand is an understanding of the historically situated formation of difference, as this specification indicates:

> Respecting social, cultural, religious, ethnic and political differences in the community as a result of studying history. (Departemen Pendidikan Nasional, 2001b, p.9)

The typology of history in the curriculum is "time, continuity and change" (Curriculum Corporation, 2000). It is a typology which invites an understanding of the ways things are as the contingent outcomes of historical processes. It assumes changeability. That is very different from a reading of Indonesian history as a manifestation of immanent and ahistorical attributes of the communities, which was how Indonesian history was presented in the New Order citizenship curriculum (Fearnley-Sander, 2000).

The construction of identity, individual, community and nation is another assumption made about the competence of historical understanding. Students are called on to "*reconstruct* the past, make meaning out of the present and predict the future" (Departemen Pendidikan Nasional, 2001b, p.3). Indeed, the whole area of the curriculum is described in the preamble statement in these terms:

> Essentially, Social Knowledge is a subject area which is a discourse and an instrument for answering questions, including these, amongst others: Who am I? What community am I part of? What requirements do I have to fulfil to become a member of a community and a nation? What does it mean to become a member of a national and a world community? How does the life of people and communities change over time? (Departemen Pendidikan Nasional, 2003, p.2)

In this statement, the young Indonesian has plural identities. National identity is presented as transaction between a citizen and a country, rather than a metaphysical unity of soul. In this transaction, knowledge of the historical and contemporary experience of the nation is not a disclosure of personal identity but a guide to the implications of membership, which are always interim.

The supporting guidelines for the Indonesian competency curriculum indicate a systematic understanding of the methodological implications of this approach. Besides the discipline-based competencies, there are also cross-curricular ones, such as critical,

creative and inquiring thinking, finding and using information, problem solving, enterprise and social skills, which include awareness of social values further specified as the
capacity to work together within a community and a world characterised by difference
(p.7). The indicators for these competencies are framed in ways that exercise students in
these skills. The assessment guidelines make a feature of application, demonstration and
performance. Sometimes these are "real world" applications. Thus the senior secondary
level includes practical inquiry with real world problems as part of the course (Departemen Pendidikan Nasional, 2001c, p.13). Teachers' guides to the syllabus development
specify assessment instruments that track students' competence development, such as
portfolios. Schools and teachers face an enormous challenge in mastering such procedures that are so radically different from the transmission teaching of the past, but the
cautious and staged introduction of the syllabus at least shows that educationalists are
aware of the scale of learning required by teachers and students alike.

Rights-oriented Views of Citizenship

The preamble to the competency-based curriculum states that:

> It is hoped that Indonesia in the future will never again incur authoritarian govern-
> ment which stifles the rights of citizens to implement democratic principles in the
> life of the community, the nation and the state. Democracy in daily life, in the envi-
> ronment of the family, school, community, government and non-government or-
> ganisations needs to become familiar, to start occurring, be internalised and be ap-
> plied for the nation and state of Indonesia to succeed. (Departemen Pendidikan
> Nasional, 2001b, p.1)

Rights are included in the curriculum. Particularly prominent are human rights and aspects which occur at every level of schooling, such as the study of their chequered history.
Civil and political rights are more indistinct. Political rights are mainly implied through
the emphasis on personal competencies. There is an emphasis on the capacity and the
responsibility of expressing opinions; including the competence to evaluate politicians.
(Departemen Pendidikan Nasional, 2001b, p.6; 2001c, p.7). Though such skills are
highly relevant to the voting role of citizens in a representative democracy, it is worthy of
note that there is comparatively very little in the curriculum to *technically* equip students
to maximise their vote.[vi] This is surprising given Indonesia's electoral reforms and particularly the introduction of direct election of the president and of district heads in 2004.
The country has embarked on extensive community education programmes to support
these electoral changes, but there is almost no reflection of them in the school curriculum,
in spite of the fact that senior secondary students are of voting age in their last year of
schooling.[vii]

   Overall, the orientation on rights is towards the securing of freedom from oppression through the shaping of dispositions and aptitudes in the individual and in the

community to uphold democracy (Departemen Pendidikan Nasional, 2001a, p.v). The competency statement in the senior secondary curriculum sums up this orientation:

> Participate in the shaping of a community and governance that is democratic, that upholds, implements and respects human rights. (Departemen Pendidikan Nasional, 2001c, p.4)

This is an appropriate point to return to the discussion of the model of citizenship influencing this curriculum and the significance of the rights focus that was especially strong at the start of the era of *reformasi*. The treatment of rights appears to be in the service of a republican, rather than a liberal model of citizenship where the focus is on *individual* liberties vis-à-vis government. What is at stake in the republican citizenship is the people's sovereignty and freedom from the abuse of power, which necessitates the development of the robust civic subjectivities that will ensure participation. The first of the competencies for the junior secondary curriculum, for example, seises the opportunity for participation provided by decentralisation: the capacity to participate in the era of autonomy. The indicators for the competency relating to political participation include:

- Explain the importance of community participation in the development of public policies at the district level.
- Analyse the consequences of the community not taking an active part in the development of public policies at the district level. (Departemen Pendidikan Nasional, 2001b, p.5)

This orientation towards citizens with the capacity for self-government helps make sense of the strong focus on the more communally-oriented human rights, as compared, for example, with civil rights, which are aimed at enhancing individuality and marking off the civil sphere from the state.

Section II: Public Discourse and the New Citizenship Curriculum

Curriculum Change and Political Response

A salient feature of the momentous changes to the curriculum for citizenship since 1999 is that there has been next to no contestation or discussion in the educational world or the wider public about their implications for the civic identity of Indonesia's future citizens.

What is the reason for this lack of contention? Is there a disconnection between educational discourse and real political life? Or a disconnection between the rhetoric of citizenship and agency—is citizenship a "floating" concept in reformasi? Or does it reflect broad public endorsement of the changes in civic identity?

A case can be made for the last of these alternatives. The overturning of the old order helped to legitimise the inclusion of rights because the transition was about repudiating the institutionalisation of asymmetrical relations between the state and the citizen. In the area of civic identity, this has been done by a reconciliation of a strongly collectivist tradition of civic identity with a concept of popular sovereignty that is not coterminous with the state. In this, Indonesia has to strike a careful balance between republican ideals of government by the people and the preservation of national unity which, as we saw in the discussion of the Pancasilaist content of the new curriculum, emphatically remains a commitment of Indonesian citizens. Perhaps more surprising is the lack of any public or even any educationists' response to the historicist, contingent view of human societies and values in the social curriculum, which undercuts the idea of an immanent national identity. This acceptance of a historicist view of Indonesian culture and society is particularly interesting in view of the long prevailing *ahistorical* idea of an intrinsic national character manifesting itself through the history of the archipelago, and of which Sukarno's *Pancasila* formulation was the inspired expression. Overall, however, lack of reaction to these changes is of a piece with the weakening of the normative role of *Pancasila* in public and political debate, which has been insufficiently remarked as the ending of an era in the history of Indonesia's political culture.[viii]

We have looked so far at policy effecting citizen education. Now we turn to the policy role of decentralisation in the promotion of participatory citizenship, particularly as it regards education.

Decentralisation, Education and Citizenship

The strongest argument for the potential of policy to effect change in political cultures comes from the policies and regulations governing Indonesia's implementation of regional autonomy since 1999 (*Undang-Undang Republik Indonesia Nomor No. 22 Tahun 1999 Tentang Pemerintahan Daerah; Undang-Undang Republik Indonesia Nomor No. 25 Tahun 1999 Tentang Perimbangan Keuangan Antara Pemerintah Pusat dan Daerah*), particularly in relation to education. Regional autonomy was motivated reputedly by concerns about national disintegration. The ideas governing the legislation concerned redressing the imbalance between the centre and the regions. The units of governance chosen were too small to threaten the growth of movements for independence, being district rather than province. This account of the politics of decentralisation makes it appear less concerned with the democratic consequences of moving government closer to the people than with the enduring Indonesian preoccupation with national integrity. However, in a way that shows the limitations of a simple dichotomy between the powerful state and powerless citizenry, the implementation of decentralisation has also been assisted by the reassertion of the national government as the watchdog of democratisation vis-à-vis district power.

In education, furthermore, decentralisation has developed a very close relationship with democratisation through its interaction with two of the reforms that were contemporary with regional autonomy: the competency-based curriculum and school-based management. We have already looked at the contribution of the curriculum to the reactivation of citizen agency, but not yet at how the context of decentralised governance enhances its effectiveness.

The opening words of the competency standards for the primary school social knowledge curriculum stress the context of decentralisation as one of the contextual factors in response to which the new curriculum has been developed.

> The development of the social curriculum responds positively to several developments … including decentralisation. This is done through increasing the relevance of the social learning to local conditions and needs. (Departemen Pendidikan Nasional, 2003, p.2)

A key purpose of the competency-based curriculum is to empower the school community locally, through relating what is learnt to local situations. This empowerment is intended to work not only at the level of constructing students' subjectivities as agents in their own world, as we have already explored. It is also meant to alter the working lives of others involved in schools, for example teachers. The Indonesian competency-based curriculum is a framework intended to standardise educational outcomes. It will liberate teachers to develop their own ways of helping students to attain those outcomes, requiring teachers to generate their own materials, lessons and assessments. Gone are national examinations below the level of the final year of school and even end-of-semester exams are no longer mandated. Thus localisation is also an instrument of teacher professionalism.

In providing more scope for locally developed curriculum, the competency-based curriculum will contribute to the formation of cultural identity in the direction of plurality because the "local" itself is not singular. Diversity in Indonesian heterocultures can be seen in their local languages, norms, values, traditions and *adat* (customary laws). But at the same time the competency-based curriculum also helps to keep the balance between the local and the nation. Local curricula must also fit national standards and priorities. These national standards provide a framework that gives overall unity to the curriculum. It is expected that through national standards parents will know how well their children perform by comparing them with others across the nation. Schools will be able to evaluate and report on their efforts in reaching the standards. A dynamic balance, then, must continuously be sought between "similarities" and "differences" for the realisation of *Bhinneka Tunggal Ika* (Unity in Diversity).

In the years since decentralisation began, decentralisation in education has progressively become associated with capacity building for professionalism. The role of the centre in this activity is clarified in an extended statement on educational decentralisation issued by the National Department of Education in 2003. In this statement, the meaning of decentralisation is subtly altered from meaning the decentralisation of power to meaning the decentralisation of service.

> Autonomy in the development of the education sector is understood as the giving of a wide, real and professionally responsible authorisation for taking the initiative in

participative and coordinated educational planning while at the same time empowering all relevant potential [human] resources available. (Unit Fasilitasi Desentralisasi Pendidikan [UFDP], 2003, p.1)

Another key instrument in the idea of service of the community is the institutions supporting school-based management.

The formation of school committees at the school level and the Education Council at the district level represent the logical consequence of the paradigmatic change from centralism to district autonomy.... Because of this the formation of the Education Council and the school committee represent the real implementation of community-based participation. (p.7)

The educational rhetoric is insistent that the point of educational decentralisation is to support community say in the schools. Community say in school management supports democracy in two ways. A school taking its policy cues from its community (via the school committee) guarantees that the school reflects community needs and priorities, and, through the committee's involvement in planning and budgeting, is accountable to the school community. Also entailed in community involvement in the school is a required change on the part of school principals to democratic participatory leadership, educating the community in open management (p.29). Secondly, the intention of the district Education Councils is expressly to provide a counterweight educational institution in civil society to government. The district council will act as a source of independent advice to the local executive and parliament on education policy. Part of its function is to articulate community participation through the "grassroots" school committees. Potentially such articulation is a powerful institutionalisation of citizen agency in public life. The policy statement itself identifies this link between decentralisation and democracy:

The aim is to make educational planning work for the principles of democracy, community participation and the strengthening of the human resources that are available in the Education Office. ... Decentralisation is intended to increase professionalism, transparency and accountability—without these there will be no increase of democracy in education. (p.28)

Conclusion

Undoubtedly the statement explored above is policy rhetoric at its best. But one of the strengths of this example of the potential of policy change for democratisation is its *realpolitik*. Support for democracy through strengthening civic participation is not dependent on rhetoric. The conjunction of national and civic interest vis-à-vis district power is what gives it promise. Interpreting decentralisation to mean service provision is also a way of retaining power at the centre, but to the advantage of the citizen. When educational decentralisation is looked at closely, there does not seem to be much scope for local autonomy as initiative-taking. The idea of service has guided the national department into a quality assurance role in the context of decentralisation. It has focused since 2000 on developing ways to standardise quality: through minimum service standards for schools, competency standards for students, for teacher recruitment, accreditation of schools and universities, and standardised guidelines for budgetary practice in local offices of education. Standards setting means that policy formulation is retained at the centre. The insistence is that the role of the district government is to operationalise education policy, not invent it.

However limited policy changes are in effecting transitions to democracy, it is hard to resist the fact of the coherence of all educational policy change around citizen activism; hard not to think that what has been put in place through decentralizing the responsibilities of government, the competency-based curriculum and the institutions of school-based management are the means of restructuring civic identity and opportunity at the grassroots level. It is particularly tempting to think that all of this might add up to a deliberate democraticizing objective on the part of policy-makers when one sees the fit between this restructuring of citizenship and the new emphasis in the national ideology on elements of democracy that promote a rights-regarding sovereignty of the people, rather than the state.

Acknowledgement

The authors would like to acknowledge the assistance given by Ibu Lili Nurlaeli from the Citizenship Education section of the Curriculum Centre of the National Department of Education in Indonesia in providing information on changes to the citizenship curriculum since 1999 and updates on the 2004 curriculum.

Notes

[i] All translations from the Indonesian in this chapter are those of the authors.

[ii] *Madrasah* are one of the two principal institutions providing an Islamic education in Indonesia. The other is *Pesantren*. Madrasah are more numerous than Pesantren, accounting for 13.6% of the total 169,147 primary schools, one-third of the 32,322 junior secondary schools and a quarter of the senior secondary schools (United Nations Common Country Assessment, 2004, p. 15). Madrasah are required to provide 100% of the national curriculum in addition to their full Islamic curriculum (five religious subject areas). Religion, because of its scope in Madrasah education, is the only subject area in which Madrasah depart from the Ministry of Education's curricular guidelines, which in state schools cover Islamic religion in a single subject (for Muslim children). Pesantren, which continues the precolonial form of Islamic education, comes under the non-formal sector of education in the Indonesian system. Some do and some do not provide a general education in addition to religious training, which is more akin to seminarian training than the religious education provided in Madrasah.

[iii] For an analysis of how Indonesia's educational goals are to be achieved in the context of decentralisation, see the World Bank (2004) funded Government of Indonesia-donor community.

[iv] See the discussion of republican citizenship in Mouritsen (2001).

[v] This model was associated with a group of academics centred in Bandung that had formed the

Centre for Indonesian Civic Education (CICED). It had affiliations with U.S. centres for citizenship education (Interview with Dra. Lili Nurlaeli, 2000 March).

[vi] In the senior high school curriculum, there is only one reference to electoral politics in the topics for learning. It is related to the competency of appreciating democratic principles. Details (indicators) of that include two points: demonstrate democratic principles in the process of general elections, and indicate behaviours which support the upholding of democratic principles.

[vii] Provision for voter education became one of the tasks of the Commission for the General Election (Komisi Pemilihan Umum_KPU) (Keputusan komisi pemilihan umum Nomor 623 tahun 2003 Tentang Pedoman pelaksanaan Informasi pemilihan umum dan pendidikan pemilih).

[viii] See Ramage (1995) for a study of the use of *Pancasila* to legitimate both regime and opposition philosophies since the 1970s.

8

The Building of a Nation and Ideas of Nationhood: Citizenship Education in Malaysia

Ibrahim Ahmad BAJUNID

Introduction

At the birth of the Malaysian state in 1957 it had more than 60 ethnic groups of various sizes. Each group had its own languages, religions, customs, traditions, culture and leaders. The new state had an unsettled territorial configuration and untested democratic political processes. Political institutions were unformed and political culture undeveloped; democratic institutions were not set in motion. In the early years of Independence, there was the threat of a communist insurgency, causing racial tensions, and peoples from various origins did not have the experience of working together as an independent united entity. The state had a very large immigrant population, which in the early years did not share a common history and had no shared vision of a common future destiny. The various ethnic groups lived apart in ethnic enclaves marking cultural and economic cleavages, disparities in education and various other kinds of status divides (Khoo, 2001; Mahathir, 1970; Means, 1991; Purcell, 1967; Ratnam, 1965; Roff, 1967).

Five decades after independence this profile of Malaysia has changed dramatically. In November 2003 Malaysia conducted its eleventh General Elections. The country has developed a relatively peaceful working democracy that is politically stable and economically vibrant. In 2004 the population of Malaysia was 25.6 million: The Malays constituted about 54% of the population, the Chinese 25%, the Indians 8% and other indigenous groups 12%. While retaining their ethnic identities, Malaysians have begun to confront common problems. By developing a collective national memory of 50 years of shared history and common worldview experiences, they have begun to share common visions of the future. The national education system has fostered a common national consciousness that typically transcends ethnic, linguistic, religious and parochial identities. The educational system has also attempted to foster the internalisation of values, attitudes and behaviours that support a healthy multicultural society, fostering mutual understanding, mutual respect, a democratic culture and regard for fundamental human rights (Malaysia, 2003a).

The country has not been completely successful in its journey towards societal integration and harmony. One of the most tragic incidents remembered in the country were the May 13, 1969 racial riots which took the lives of so many people and shattered the complacency of the nation (Tunku, 1969). It was after the racial riots that the state formulated the *Rukunegara*. The Rukunegara was, at the time of its formulation, seen as a creative all-party and national solution to the problems of racial and ideological divides and the basis for citizenship education and development. If the formulation of the Malaysian Constitution and the practice of democracy provided the legitimate foundation for nationhood, then the formulation and implementation of the National Education Policy was the first turning point in the nation-building agenda. The Rukunegara—the National Ideology—was the next turning point in the definition of nationhood. It expressed the pledge of united efforts in nation-building and citizenship education, guided by the principles of Belief in God, Loyalty to King and Country, Upholding the Constitution, respecting the Rule of Law, and inculcating Good Behaviours and Morality. Vision 2020 articulated in 1991 was yet another turning point in the conceptualisation of a nation state determined to become a successful, developed nation. Currently, the promotion of the idea of *Islam Hadhari* helps to define the role of Islam in the nation within the context of the new world order where the definitive reality is the power of knowledge and knowledge as power (Department of Islamic Development, Malaysia, 2004). Within this context Malaysian society continues to seek creative, politically feasible and just ways of development based on multicultural national unity and patriotism. However, the path to a more just society is not without its setbacks, struggles and controversies.

Alternative Notions of State and Citizenship

The debate about the nature of Malaysian society and the form of government for a multi-racial society continues (Harper, 2001). At the core of the debate is whether Malaysia is an Islamic state or otherwise. The majority of Muslims uphold and cherish the idea of the democratic state (Ahmad Sarji, 1994; Kua, 2002; Malaysia, 1988; Senu, 1971). The current solution to conflictual issues of religious, linguistic or ethnic differences which make the country vulnerable to conflicts is encapsulated in the idea of the "social contract." The notion of social contract is expressed thus by Abdullah (2004):

> … any society and especially diverse multicultural societies will benefit from a social contract. It provides a framework for political, social and economic intercourse that is agreed upon by all communities. It reduces misunderstandings and conflicts of interest, and allows people to focus upon improving their lives in peace and harmony. The failure to put in place viable social contracts is at the root of many conflicts afflicting nation states around the world. … Malaysia's experience is that a strategy of inclusion, participation and respect for the legitimate rights of all ethnic, religious and cultural groups, and just recognition of the special position due to the indigenous peoples is the best formula to manage its diversity. (p.5)

It is noted that such ideas of a social contract are discussed publicly in mass media forums and under various topics in the school curriculum. The idea is, of course, one of the topics in citizenship education at all levels of education.

In the multi-racial Malaysian context, with differentiated constitutional functions of the State and Federal Governments, the concept of citizenship creates various kinds of tensions (Abdul Aziz, 2002; Lee, 1995; Mohamed Suffian; Wan Arfah & Ramy, 2003). Beyond local and national duties as citizens, there are international duties of global citizenship within the contents of civil, political and social rights and responsibilities.

The Quest to Understand the Role and Impact of Citizenship Education in Malaysia

To scholars, policy-makers and comparative educationists, the study of citizenship education in Malaysia is a dynamic area of study as this multi-racial nation continues to define and redefine the constitutional, legal, political, religious and social possibilities of the meaning of citizenship (Anuar, 2004). In this changing sociopolitical environment, teaching and learning about citizenship can be both exciting and complex. It is exciting because of the possibilities of fostering social and civic responsibilities. It is perplexing because of the complexity inherent in the relationship between the individual and the community at local, regional, national and international levels, as well as at the levels of civilisation and the human species. Learning about citizenship has a cognitive factual dimension and also an experiential dimension, including vicarious experiences. Learning about and experiencing citizenship are about dealing with issues, values and valuing, and decision-making or problem-solving processes. These various processes are considered to be the tools of thoughts for active and effective citizenship and for an enabled and empowered democracy (Jones & Jones, 1992). There is much more going on in the cocurricular domains and in the wider society regarding citizenship education than in the formal educational system (Malaysia, 2001). This is because the formal educational system with its final public examinations is so academically oriented that legitimacy is given primarily to those academic subjects which will give students an advantage of entry into higher institutions of education. Citizenship education is not such an academic subject.

The search by the author for an understanding of citizenship education in Malaysia is a search across five decades of the development of an education system and across many domains of formal and non-formal education. It is also a search for an understanding of the debates and agendas of politicians, intellectuals and the definers of nationhood and citizenship. The search is historical, constitutional, legal, political, civil and social. It involves the government, the private sector and non-governmental leadership. Though leaders from various backgrounds play very significant roles in the arena of the dominant conceptualisations of the meaning of citizenship education, it is political and societal thought that ultimately become the contents of citizenship education in the school curriculum (Bajunid, 1980).

As a subject, citizenship education is broad-based. In Malaysia, however, before 2005 there was not a subject designated Citizenship Education. The contents of what was considered Citizenship Education were mainly discussed in other school subjects. Over the years, in Malaysian educational history, the core ideas and ideals of citizenship education were located and embedded in such subjects as Moral Studies, Malaysian Studies, Islamic Studies, Social Studies, Civics and History (Kementerian Pendidikan Malaysia, 1994, 2002a, 2002b, 2002c). The battle for space in the overcrowded curriculum has pushed out various topics in citizenship education to become topics in other school subjects. Throughout the period of the battle for time and priority in the curriculum, citizenship education, with its broad-based notions and concepts, has always found a niche in cocurricular or extracurricular activities in schools. This aspect of the embedded knowledge, skills and attitudes of citizenship education and cocurricular activities will be discussed later in this chapter.

A few years ago a new curriculum entitled "Civics Education and Citizenship" was formulated by the Curriculum Development Center, Ministry of Education, Malaysia. Typically, members of Curriculum Committees are educationists, subject matter experts, academicians, representatives from teachers' unions and professional bodies, non-governmental organisations, community leaders and even private sector representatives. Implementation began in 2005 for the 4th year of primary education through the 6th year and beginning with the 1st year of secondary education to the 5th year. Teaching-learning materials and resources for the curriculum are still being generated. By 2009 it is expected that all students will have gone through the full curriculum cycle of the newly introduced syllabi for eight years. The objectives and contents of Civics Education and Citizenship curriculum as identified by teachers, educationists and opinion leaders reinforce the goals of civil society, Malaysian nationhood and patriotism. The curriculum was framed within the ideals articulated in UNESCO's *Learning to Be*, emphasising the four pillars of learning, specifically learning to know, learning to do, learning to live with others and learning to be, with emphasis on Civics knowledge, skills and values (Delors, 1996).

The contents and themes for the primary level are care and love of self, loving the family, living together in school and society, knowing Malaysian culture, Malaysia My Homeland, readiness to face challenges, and a Citizenship Project Portfolio of at least ten hours a year. The contents for the secondary level are self-achievement/attainment, family relationships, community living, multicultural heritage of Malaysia, Malaysia as a sovereign nation, future challenges and a Social Service Project of at least ten hours a year.

As teachers are required to use various teaching strategies to arouse and sustain the interest of students, they are also required to use appropriate and multiple methods of evaluation including observation, behavioural checklists, tests, assignments and reports. Meta-analysis of the contents of many of the topics and themes of activities of various school subjects reveal that there are overlaps which can be used for reinforcement, but there is a need to ensure that students learn new knowledge and skills at higher levels of understanding and insights. If teachers fail to make wise use of the various overlaps for learning reinforcement, boredom among students may raise the issue of curricular relevance, teaching effectiveness and efficiency of the use of precious time and lost opportunities for meaningful education when students are captive learners in the school system (Kementerian Pendidikan Malaysia, 2005a, 2005b).

With the on-going curriculum review and reform over the years, one of the major compulsory subjects left with the task of exploring the various goals of citizenship education is History. Therefore, in order to understand the substance and direction of citizenship education in Malaysia, it is pertinent to analyse and review the History curriculum in schools. In addition to the History curriculum, an understanding of citizenship education can also be developed by an analysis of the Islamic Studies and the Moral Education syllabi in the school and university curricula. The fact that citizenship education is considered central, but that there are difficulties in finding a place for it to be accorded meaning and value, create both conceptual challenges in curriculum formulation and logistical problems in the timetable. Typically, subjects which do not stand on their own do not have strong champions, including institutionalised champions such as professional associations and teachers' trade unions. In national educational reform initiatives, the pressure groups which draw champions from the political, cultural, social and professional sectors are strongest in the areas of language and religion.

Historical Background of Citizenship Education

In the past, citizenship education was located in a subject known as Civics. In 1968, the Malaysian Education Association held a National Seminar in Civics Education and contributed to the early championing of citizenship education (Malaysian Association for Education, 1968). In 1973, the Teacher Education Division of the Ministry of Education also conducted a National Seminar on Civic Education. Such continuing interest showed the importance placed by educators and other leaders on the notion of citizenship education. Throughout the nation's history, national and educational leaders have referred to various ideas and ideals of civics education, citizenship education and civil society. In terms of practical detail, such sustained attention to civic education has fostered the sharing of a body of knowledge and created intergenerational groups of educators who are aware of and even become the champions of citizenship education and related subject matters and processes.

The subject of citizenship education includes political literacy, human rights, consumer rights, and workers' and citizens' rights. It also encompasses personal, social and community hygiene, habits and courtesies. Educators, national leaders and the citizenry as a whole have always been supportive of a broad and balanced curriculum providing opportunities for personal growth and the understanding of ideas about modernisation, growth, progress and development in the intellectual, social and civil, political, economic and cultural fields. The reality is that the vastness of the subject allows for dilution and lack of academic rigour and uncertain and unsatisfactory resolutions of controversies regarding citizenship issues and challenges.

In 1975, the new Civics syllabus was implemented in the Malaysian education system. Textbook writers contributed by preparing the series on Civics for Secondary

Schools from Year 1 to Year 5 (Goon, Naidu & Lee, 1977; Ruslan, 1975a, 1975b). While educators contributed positively to the implementation of the civics curriculum, simultaneously there was also the preparation of a National History syllabus that presented serious competition for the Civics subject. A specially appointed Syllabus Committee was established in 1973 to review the History syllabi from primary school up to sixth form. This Committee was the first curriculum committee which was totally comprised of Malaysian citizens and curriculum developers, teacher educators, historians and teachers. In fact, lobbying by historians and educators who saw history as more fundamental to nation building led to the replacement of Civics with History as a compulsory school subject.

History as the Basis for Citizenship Education

In the 1970s, while various subject syllabi were being formulated and implemented, there was the simultaneous review and reform of the primary and secondary school curriculum. The curriculum reform was initiated by the then Minister of Education (1978-1981), Musa Hitam, who eventually became Deputy Prime Minister (1981-1986). The curriculum reform led to the development and implementation of the New Primary and Secondary School Curriculum. The implementation of the New Primary School Curriculum, which began in 1982, gave emphases to a new subject entitled "Man and the Environment" (Shahril @ Charil & Habib, 1999). This new subject includes History, Geography and Civics as an integrated subject. The idea of values, language and thinking across the curriculum began to become part of educational thought and policy around the time of the curriculum reforms in the 1970s.

In the new Integrated Secondary School Curriculum, implemented in 1988, History is a core subject which must be studied for five years, from Form 1 to Form 5. The History curriculum integrates three related threads, specifically, the overall notion of patriotism, the contents of History, and the structure of the discipline of History. The history syllabus contains concepts such as family, community, local community, affiliative community, school community, state community, regional community and world community. Key citizenship concepts in the curriculum which involve political and historical literacy simultaneously include ideas of citizen's national and international rights, duties, obligations, entitlements and privileges. Within the contents of the history curriculum there are ample opportunities to discuss the key citizenship concepts of justice and fairness; rights and responsibilities; gender equality and individual liberty; laws, rules and regulations; charters, power, authority and ruling elites; interest and pressure groups; democracy and community; conflict and cooperation; dialogue, discourse and negotiation; diversity and independence; and freedom and constraints. The patriotic component emphasises the development of a citizen who is proud to be a Malaysian; who is loyal to the country; who has the spirit of belongingness; and who is disciplined, industrious and economically and culturally productive. The study of foreign nations and international organisations is to enable an understanding of the evolution of human civilisation and to locate Malaysia's place in the sweep of world history.

The component of the structure of the discipline focuses on historical thinking that encompasses the skills of inquiry in history, the collection of primary and secondary resources, the skills of critical thinking, historical explanation, historical understanding and empathy. Historical thinking includes critical and imaginative thinking, exploration of complex and abstract ideas, and the skills of specific thinking in the historical construction of past realities. Critical thinking is fostered by mastery of the skills of understanding chronology, the exploration of evidence, the skills of historical interpretation and historical imagination, rational decision making, historical explanation and historical understanding. The study of history as an aspect of citizenship education is not just limited to academic study but is also to be applied. In this sense, the stimulus for the application of the lessons and skills of history is to be encapsulated under the concept of empathy. Historical empathy is defined as follows:

> Historical empathy means the attainment of thinking which enables the understanding of continuity and change as to why people did what they did and why present circumstances and realities are as they are today. This understanding of Historical Empathy is supposed to be from multiple perspectives. The student who looks at history from the perspective of historical empathy is actually building an open pattern of thought which is tolerant and mature. History education is regarded as the "tool" which will produce citizens who are more responsible. (Kementerian Pendidikan Malaysia, 2002b, p.8)

Besides generic thinking skills, the two categories of thinking skills considered essential to history and citizenship education include critical thinking and creative thinking skills, which are to be used for decision making and problem solving (Kementerian Pendidikan Malaysia, 2002b).

The new history syllabus has taken the objectives of history teaching and learning to a different but more elaborated level than the former history syllabus. If history teaching for five secondary years of schooling is successful, then this will mean the creation of a community familiar with critical and creative thinking skills which can be applied to decision making and problem solving in everyday national life or people's personal lives. Also, if the current 5.6 million primary and secondary students and every generation of school students were to master the subject History with its diverse political, civil and social contents, then the level of education of the citizenry should be at a more enlightened level than it is now. Such a citizenry should be more active and engaged in the political and democratic processes, specifically in social and civil processes. In this respect, what has been pointed out regarding Dahrendorf's (1990) definition of the precise concepts of rights—civil, political and social—is pertinent.

> Civil rights entail equality before the law, the due process of justice, and the right to conclude contracts as equals—that is, the rule of law in its widest sense. Political rights include the right to vote and to express one's views. Social rights in part embrace civil and political rights—they liberate people from insecurity, and in-

clude the right to an education and the right not to fall below a certain level of income.

The uses of History for citizenship education in Malaysia encompass history for moral and patriotic citizenship education, social education and international citizenship. The Malaysian experience in the use of history for citizenship education is in many significant ways similar to the British experience (Wong, 1997). The similarity can be ascribed to the colonial experience leaving behind the British political, administrative and educational legacy and fostering some shared policies and practices among the nations of the former British Commonwealth. The Malaysian Studies Curriculum is closely related to the History, Geography and Civics syllabi and is offered in the Civil Service training programmes; it is a compulsory subject taught in universities, particularly in the private ones. Typically, evaluation studies are conducted to assess whether the various official school subject syllabi are implemented in the classrooms as expected. Among such studies is the study of the implementation of the school history curriculum which noted that the contents, objectives and ideals of the national curriculum are not necessarily translated with integrity and effectively in classroom contexts (Nagendralingan, Rajendra, Sophia, Lim, Norshah, & Idris, 2005).

Citizenship Education across the Curriculum: Thinking Skills and Citizenship Education

Interestingly, whether formally articulated or otherwise, it would seem that aspects of citizenship education, such as human rights, civic consciousness, values clarification, and straight and crooked thinking are, in some significant ways, also located in the subject termed "Thinking Skills" (Rajendran, 2001). While some public and private universities and university colleges have begun to introduce "Entrepreneurship" as a university-wide subject, almost all universities and teachers' colleges have introduced "Thinking Skills" as a subject. It is assumed that the quality of active and enlightened citizenship will be better when more citizens are able to think better. Malaysian educators and scholars have continued to focus on the nurturing of the reading culture and the identification of new literacy which contributes to citizenship education in some direct and indirect ways (Ambigapathy, 1997; Ambigapathy & Chakravarthy, 2003). While there is the articulated and elaborate notion of language across the curriculum and thinking across the curriculum in schools, citizenship education across the curriculum has not been formally articulated. Notwithstanding its non-articulation, the significant components of citizenship education are nevertheless embedded in other subjects. However, citizenship education across cocurriculum activities and across the lifespan of citizens is actually put into practice. Evidence of this is found in such initiatives as the Vision School Projects where students from schools from various language streams sharing common facilities, such as school hall, playing fields and school canteens, are encouraged to play and socialise together. Other occasions where students from different backgrounds come together are found during the Malaysian Schools Sports Council meets. Beyond the secondary school years, the National Service Programme provides opportunities for interracial, interreligious sharing of collective experiences of character building and fostering of patriotism. Most of the cocurricular activities, whether competitive or participative, foster socialisation among students, teachers and parents from different ethnic, religious and socioeconomic backgrounds to organise events together, play together and celebrate sportsmanship and citizenship together. To ensure a more effective formulation and implementation of the citizenship education agenda, there has to be clear and coherent articulation of the various critical conceptualisations of citizenship education.

Values across the School Curriculum and Beyond Schooling

During the last two decades the Malaysian education system has focused on values education (Barone & Bajunid, 2001). Values education was directly related to the government's emphasis on such policies as the Inculcation of Universal Islamic Values in government administration and in society. In the public service, universal humanistic values were identified with a focus on the Twelve Pillars. Within this context of an emphasis on values, the education system identified 16 core values across the curriculum. The Islamic Education Division itself identified 47 Islamic values in the Islamic Studies curriculum. The notions of accountability and good governance and the corporate-civil service-community interface continue to be clarified and further enhanced. (Bajunid, 1995; Malaysia, 1993, 1997, 1998; Samsudin, Zulkurnain, & Sarojini, 2000). Comparative insights into the values considered important in Malaysian society and in the civil service, and the values considered important to be inculcated in studies across the curriculum can be elicited and analysed by meticulous study of the universe of values identified and are presented in the Appendix.

These values are in many direct and indirect ways related and central to the values, principles, ideas and ideals of citizenship education. At the teaching level, these values can be used for values-based strategic thinking, strategic planning, decision making and problem solving in the daily lives of citizens or in the professional lives of citizens as employees, whether semi-skilled or highly skilled knowledge workers. The search for Asian values is an ongoing theme in Asian and Malaysian national development history (Cummings, Tatto, & Hawkins, 2001; Richter & Mar, 2002; Roff, 1974; Sheridan, 1999), and intersects with the development of citizenship education.

Islamic Education and Citizenship Education in Schools

The philosophy of Islamic Education in Malaysian schools is articulated as follows:

> Islamic education is a continuous effort to acquire knowledge, develop skills and internalise positive attitudes based on the Quran and the Traditions of the Prophet, towards building attitudes, skills, identity and world views as God's servants who have the responsibility to develop the self, the community, the environment and the

nation in order to achieve success in this world and eternal harmony in the hereafter. (Kementerian Pendidikan Malaysia, 2002c, p.3)

The objectives of Islamic Education for the primary and secondary schools are complementary, based on the principle of progressively more profound and deeper understanding of the faith and of greater religious proficiency as follows:

1. To read the Quranic verses accurately, proficiently and to reinforce the practice of reading the Quran.
2. To memorise the verses of the Quran in order to increase Quranic recitation in daily prayers and other daily blessings.
3. To understand the various Quranic verses as well as the Prophetic Traditions and to internalise the lessons and injunctions as the sources of God's Commandments and guidance to Believers.
4. To reinforce the Islamic Faith and awaken the concept of *Tauhid* (Oneness) consciously in all actions and practices as the citadel of Belief and Piety.
5. To reinforce and uplift the practices of Obligatory Practices of Islam (the *Fardhu Ain*) and to understand the Optional Practices (*Fardhu Kifayah*) as the imperative for Muslims to contribute towards the advancement of the *umma* (the Islamic community) in this world and in the hereafter.
6. To understand and to draw lessons from the life histories of Prophets and Messengers, Khulafa'al-Rasyidin and Islamic luminaries as the bases for the shaping and development of the person who loves and contributes to the development of the civilisation of the race and the nation.
7. To develop virtuous character and to practice positive values as the pillars of a race culture with dignity.
8. To read and write Jawi through its use in Islamic teaching and learning as a cultural heritage which is preserved and sustained. (Kementerian Pendidikan Malaysia, 2002d, p.2)

The Islamic Education Curriculum for the primary school is divided into four components: (a) the practice and reading of the verses of the Quran, (b) the Foundations of the Faith and the Commandments, (c) the Foundations of Islamic Morality, and (d) the learning of the Jawi script. There is always an "execution gap" between the ideals of the formal curriculum and classroom level realities. Whether teachers internalise and uphold the ideals of the curriculum to the letter or whether instead there is the "hidden curriculum" in play, fostering elements of teaching as a subversive activity and unleashing the pedagogy of the oppressed remains a relatively open question. It has not been well studied in the Malaysian context, although elsewhere there has been a relatively strong tradition of educational criticism along these lines (Freire, 1970; Goodman, 1973; Illich, 1970; Reimer, 1974; Weingartner & Postman, 1969). While there is study of "Contesting Malayness," there is no corresponding study of "Contesting Islamness" which might shed light on varieties of formal and non-formal religious learning experiences (Ikeda &

Tehranian, 2003; Livingstone, 1989; Mottahedeh, 1985; Satha-Anand, 2005). There are, however, stances and positions taken based on such notions as "secular" and "religious education" (Al-Afendi & Baloch, 1980; Al-Attas, 1979; Hunter, 1988; Huntington, 1996).

Islam in Society

Islam as a way of life covers all conceivable activities of man and provides guidance on ways and means to deal with emerging issues. In its philosophy, the oneness of the Islamic curriculum fosters citizenship education in all contexts. Muslims are guided on how to live in contexts where Muslims are in the majority, in the minority or in pluralistic or balanced demographic circumstances. Besides the articles of Faith, Islamic education covers the whole range of etiquette and Islamic morality. There is etiquette in daily living, including personal hygiene and self-management. There is etiquette towards parents and family, and etiquette in social relations. There is also etiquette in the quest for knowledge, in prayer and in the pursuit of faith. For each of the broad categories of Islamic etiquette, there are detailed subcategories. For instance, in social relations there is etiquette in hosting guests, whether Muslims or non-Muslims; etiquette at work; etiquette in public spaces, in buying and selling, in giving and receiving gifts, in looking after the environment, in dealing with prisoners of war, and in relations with neighbours (Badr, 1993; Omar, 2003; Thanwi, 1992). The Islamic education curriculum actually provides complete guidance to citizenship education. If there is a failure of the outcomes of education, it is the failure of the implementation of the curriculum when teaching-learning may be focused more on the rituals of beliefs than on the practices of etiquette of citizenship and Islamic morality. The weaknesses of Islamic education may actually be the weaknesses of teachers and learners, misinterpretations and deviationist ideologies rather than of the virtues and idealistic living demanded by the Faith of this universal religion (Bakri, 2003, 2004; Barnard, 2004; Mahayudin, 2001; *Report of the Malay Education Congress*, 2001).

In the wider society, there is a large body of literature on all dimensions of Islam at different levels and degrees of simplicity and complexity. At school level the focus of much of the literature is on the fundamentals of the faith, the acquisition and mastery of the pillars and commandments of the religion, and the memorisation of verses for prayers and *doa*. The criticisms of Islamic Studies and Moral Education have been that the focus is always on the personal mastery of religious rituals and dogma with no appropriate transfer to the practices of good civic-minded conduct in the chores of daily life. Somehow there has not been due emphasis on personal etiquette and personal responsibility towards social development, social etiquette and citizenship roles. However, outside the school through the print and electronic media there is much discussion of the roles of citizens based on a deeper and more profound understanding of the faith. This divide may be because the learning of religion in school focuses on the mastery of the essentials for the foundations and pillars of the religion, including the payments of tithes, the faithful mastery of religious rituals and practices of the faith which is examined in schools and public examinations. Assessments of religious knowledge and practices focused more in terms of intrapersonal cognition and affect do not, as yet, adequately address behaviours and citizenship and civic roles in interpersonal relations (Khairul & Faizal, 2001). In talk shows, letters to the editor and other public forums Muslim leaders and lay persons sometimes self-critically observe that the best Islamic religious practices (e.g., regarding ablutions, cleanliness and prayers) are not necessarily transferred to the best civic practices in other domains of life. Such non-transfer of the best habits from one domain or dimension of life to other domains or dimensions con-stitutes a serious challenge to the efforts of building a knowledge and virtues-based society with exemplary critical mass of "good character and towering personalities" which are able to change the mindset of a "third world mentality" to a "first world men-tality."

Moral Education in Malaysian Schools

Over the last five decades, many overarching ideas have been introduced and experi-mented with in nation building by the ruling government coalitions, agencies of gov-ernment, professional and non-governmental organisations and local communities. In the early years of independence, one such powerful idea was nationalism. During the last years of the 20th century and into the 21st century, nationalism is no longer an idea in cur-rency, but has ceded its place of dominance to patriotism. The idea of patriotism is itself finding a relationship to the notion of global citizenry as the idea of national "social contract" among the races and political groups finds its ties to the ideas of a "universal declaration of rights" in diverse domains, including international laws of the sea and of cyber space, and rights such as intellectual property rights. The effectiveness of the ideas of citizenship education will be determined by the clarity of the ideas of educators and other intellectuals and leaders who define, drive and shape national aspirations and in the process influence the education received by the students and the citizenry (Bajunid 2002b, 2002c).

In the Malaysian education system, Moral Education is a programme which allows "the child to become a moral person or a noble person with virtues which emphasise the development of moral thinking/thought, moral affect/feelings/sensitivity/empathy and moral action" (Kementerian Pendidikan Malaysia, 2000 p.1). The Moral Education syllabi focus on four components, namely values, academic contents, learning outcomes and learning activities. Moral Education from Year 1 to Year 6 of primary school and Form 1 to Form 5 of secondary school maintain the same basic principles of moral education (Kementerian Pendidikan Malaysia, 2000). The principles of moral education at all levels of schooling are as follows:

- Taking responsibility for the self, the family and other people.
- To be faithful to religious teachings.
- To be concerned with the environment and ecological issues.
- To sustain peaceful and harmonious living.

- To foster the spirit of patriotism.
- To respect basic human rights.
- To practise the principles of democracy in life.

In all, seven fields of study were identified and moral values were to be transmitted and learned from these fields. For the six years in primary schools, the five fields of study focused on are values related to:

1. Personal Development
2. Self and the Family
3. Self and Society
4. Self and the Environment
5. Self and the Nation

For the five years of secondary schools, the seven fields of study focused on are values related to:

1. Personal Development
2. Family Life
3. Environment
4. Patriotism
5. Basic Human Rights
6. Democracy
7. Peace and Harmony

(Kementerian Pendidikan Malaysia, 2003a, p.1, 2003b, p.1)

While the ethos of personal discipline, good habits and behaviours are studied by Muslim and non-Muslim students, much of the content of what is studied is different. The major difference is the religious perspective as differentiated from the secular liberal-democratic perspective. Generally, the emphasis of the Islamic studies curriculum is on worship and personal mastery of religious ideology and foundations of faith and belief. The Islamic Studies curriculum focuses on man's relationship with God and to some extent with man's relationship to man. The Moral Education curriculum does give emphasis to the relation between man and man, and man and the environment (Kementerian Pendidikan Malaysia, 2003c). Curriculum ideals are not always translated into practice as the formal curriculum is interpreted by the teacher and becomes the instructional curriculum. The instructional curriculum itself undergoes transformation and becomes the operational curriculum because of such practical realities as classroom facilities, class schedules, teacher expertise and attitude differences, availability or otherwise of learning resources. Finally, what really matters is "the experiential curriculum" that is experienced by the learner in the final learning contexts and processes and which constitutes the outcomes of learning (Chew, 1980).

Cocurricular Activities and Citizenship Education

Malaysian educators have always been dealing with "the knowledge worth knowing" (Hussein Ahmad, 1993, p.403) and how such tacit and explicit knowledge is captured and organised in syllabi and curriculum. Typically knowledge considered valuable is encapsulated in the traditional subjects in the humanities, social sciences and physical and natural sciences. Components of citizenship education considered all important and which require different pedagogical approaches and emphasis, because such knowledge and skills sets are embedded in various other subjects, are promoted as knowledge, skills, values and attitudes across the curriculum. The importance of knowledge, values and attitudes across the curriculum is expressed thus:

> It is the teachers' and the schools' responsibility to give balanced focus on the knowledge, values and attitudes and skills and physical/practical focus of education to ensure a balanced and holistic development of students. In our school system, besides religious studies and civics, other subjects also tacitly and explicitly espouse positive values which can all contribute to the development of positive attitude, discipline and good character among students. It is the school's responsibility through teachers to foster and enhance positive living values in the teaching-learning processes, whether in formal or informal conditions or situations and through in-class and out-of-class activities. (Kementerian Pelajaran Malaysia, 1981, pp.15-16)

> Positive values, and good habits which are explicit and implicit in subject lessons and school activities cannot be fostered among students if schools only transmit information and focus on success in examinations. Therefore, a balance between academic knowledge, the inculcation of values and physical development must be practiced in schools. (Kementerian Pelajaran Malaysia, 1981, p.23)

A little book on discipline delineates in tables positive values, characteristics, qualities and best habits that are explicitly and tacitly found in the school curriculum. Explicit and tacit behaviours / characteristics were identified in Civics, Islamic Studies, Malay Language, Integrated Sciences, General Science, Chemistry, Physics and Biology, Agricultural Science, Geography, History, Mathematics, Music, Art and Crafts, Health Science, Commercial Studies, Domestic / Home Science and Physical Education.

Examples of out-of-class activities which promote good character and good citizenship were explained as follows:

Table 8.1 Explicit and Implicit Values, Characteristics and Good Habits

Out-of-Class Activities	Explicit	Implicit
Uniformed Units (Scouts, Girl Guides, Red Cross/Crescent, St. Johns Ambulance)	a) To foster interest, talents and aptitudes beyond academic studies b) To foster discipline and respect for the law c) To foster belongingness and togetherness d) To foster self-reliance and cooperation e) To foster the spirit of volunteerism	a) To build good and useful citizenship b) To eliminate discrimination between groups c) To use leisure time productively
Sports	a) To foster discipline b) To foster cooperation c) To foster healthy competition d) To develop skills and competencies	a) To foster meaningful leisure b) To foster the quality of risk-taking and trials c) To foster the spirit of togetherness and oneness
Associations and Clubs	a) To foster cooperation b) To build mutual respect c) To inculcate the respect for the laws d) To develop responsibility e) To develop leadership skills	To inculcate the spirit of: a) Unity b) Togetherness and belongingness c) Tolerance

Source: Kementerian Pelajaran Malaysia, 1981, pp.15-23

The importance of co-curricular activities as an integral aspect of education has been emphasised again and again over the years. The educational values to be derived from cocurricular activities include the following: Belief in God, culture and personal refinements, loyalty, responsibility, sincerity, self-control, helpfulness and cooperation, personal cleanliness, love, forgiveness, open-mindedness, positive ambition, courage, intellectual character, rationality and logic, self-reliance and creativity and imagination. For instance, the guidebook on the management of cocurricular activities in secondary schools emphasised that, besides the educational values in cocurricular activities, such activities will enable students to "reinforce leadership qualities, the taking of responsibility for self improvement, democratic qualities, the sporting spirit and the mastery of skills in the fields of interests." (Kementerian Pelajaran Malaysia, 1985, p.3) The series of Guidebooks and Professional Circulars from the Ministry of Education constitute an immensely rich compendium of resources for education, a corpus of mature educational knowledge of philosophies, ideas and practices which could be drawn upon in educational practice. The notions of knowledge, skills and values continue to be promoted as language, thinking, values and management across the curriculum. In the wider society, the Ministry of Youth and Sports continues to address the issue of citizenship education by following through on the skills acquired by students in schools. For instance, the

Ministry established the National Research Institute on Youth in 2004. Among the various research interests are concerns for citizenship education and also a concern that many youths are not involved in youth associations and, particularly, concern at apathy concerning volunteerism, which is considered to be an important aspect of active, caring and responsible citizenship (Syed Arabi, 2005; Teoh, 2005).

The Notion of Patriotism as a Central Concept in Citizenship Education in Malaysia

Education in schools takes place not only in the classrooms in academic learning but also through the planned as well as unplanned and incidental curriculum in school grounds and on sites outside the classroom. Instructions to take advantage of various learning activities are always contained in the Professional Circulars sent to all educational leaders in the education system and in its institutions. One such circular pertaining to citizenship education explains the importance of patriotism and citizenship education:

> The spirit of Patriotism is the essence of national strength and the citizens' happiness. To foster the feeling/spirit of patriotism is one aspect of comprehensive and integrated education. As Malaysian citizens, all school administrators, teachers and students come together to show their serious attitude regarding loyalty and undivided love for the nation. The ceremonies of raising the Malaysian flag, singing the national anthem, and taking the pledge should be ideally conducted during daily or weekly assemblies. If the ceremony cannot be conducted in weekly or daily group assemblies, the ceremony should be conducted simultaneously in the respective classrooms at the discretion of the school. Schools which have a good public address system should ensure that the ceremony takes place simultaneously for the whole school. (Kementerian Pendidikan Malaysia, 1994, p.7)

The Future of Citizenship Education: Towards a Lifelong Learning and Knowledge Society

To foster collective values, a collective memory, a sense of community and oneness among Malaysians, the school system has adopted a standardised approach in the process of education with its policy of a common curriculum and cocurriculum for all: a common medium of instruction from the secondary level onwards; common textbooks, software and other resource materials; common public examinations; common teacher education; common school rituals and ceremonies; and common school uniforms. In practical terms, such communal imperatives have happened because education in Malaysia is the responsibility of the Federal Government, and the Malaysian administrative system itself is a centralised system. While there are distinctive advantages in the centralisation of fostering national "commonality and collective belongingness experiences," there are also disadvantages when an overcentralised and overregulated system demotivates and prevents local and institutional initiatives. There has always been an argument for more decentralisation and empowerment, particularly in the realm of professional matters, if not in financial and legal matters. To this end, the Ministry of Education has made the policy decision to reduce bureaucratic red-tape and allow for greater autonomy at institutional levels. School principals have been invited to take institution-level leadership initiatives without waiting for the approval from the District Education Office, the State Education Department and the respective Division of the Federal Ministry of Education and other authorities (Hishammuddin, 2005).

Within the overall framework of the citizenship building agenda, each individual student has the opportunity to develop his or her talents, intelligence and opportunities to the fullest. As a national philosophy, the principle of "unity in diversity" has been adopted in almost all activities, in and out of school. School-based efforts to promote citizenship education are reinforced, in content and spirit, through principles, programmes and practices in teacher education in colleges and universities and in the wider society. The Philosophy of Teacher Education and the Code of Ethics of the Teaching Profession celebrate the values of professionalism as a citizenship value (Teacher Education Division, 1982). At university level, citizenship education is located in the compulsory core subjects for all university students known as *Tamadun Islam dan Tamadun Asia (TITAS)* – Islamic Civilisation and Asian Civilisation (Mardiana & Hasnah, 2004; Penerbit Universiti Malaya, 2001). The founding of the Human Rights Commission, the formulation of the National Social Policy, the establishment of the National Integrity Institute and National Integrity Master Plan, the establishment of such institutes as the Institute for the Study of History and Patriotism, as well as the Institute of Research on Youth Matters and the implementation of the National Service Programmes are continuing initiatives by the Federal and State Governments to promote national unity and foster citizenship education (Institut Kajian Sejarah dan Patriotisme Malaysia, 2004; Malaysia, 1988, 2003b; SUHAKAM, 2004).

The challenge of creating a civil and knowledge society with a participative citizenry is a complex and continuing one. While there are possibilities for the achievement of the next level of development of citizenry, there are also possibilities for societal regress if there is neglect and complacency regarding human rights and citizenship education. The precondition for progress is the provision of good education to all citizens across their lifespan. The Malaysian story of educational progress, with its rubs as well as smooth elegance, is closely related to the story of the development of an enlightened citizenry. Since Independence, many different initiatives have been taken to create opportunities for the education of school-going children, as well as young adults and others throughout their lives. Besides using its technological advantages in the transformation of society, Malaysia focuses on its human resources and develops its social capital through citizenship education (Bajunid, 2001; Ghosh, 1998). While the overarching ideas and ideals of nationhood and nation building are rational, and even inspirational, there are always forces, groups, organisations and individuals having alternative worldviews and models of desired futures, who become "little Napoleons" subverting mainstream ideas and ideals of national unity and national development.

"Little Napoleons" is a derogatory term used by the Prime Minister of Malaysia criticizing a small group of civil servants who created their own bureaucratic empires and lorded over the citizenry. It was observed that these abrasive individuals in power, who have forgotten the meaning of being civil, act arrogantly to show their power by delaying the implementation of the country's development projects (Bernama, 2006).

The philosophy, principles, policies and agenda of lifelong learning are articulated and gain inspiration both from international and indigenous contributions to the field. With the acceptance of the notion of lifelong learning, citizenship education begins to find itself in the abode of life-wide learning and learning across the lifespan of its citizens (Amer Hamzah, Hassan, Bajunid, Shaharil, & Shansulbahriah, 2002; Field, 2001; Longworth & Davies, 1996). With the implementation of the lifelong learning agenda which could help realise the vision of creating and developing a knowledge and virtues-based society, there are various curricular possibilities for enhancing citizenship education (Bajunid, 2003a, 2004a, 2004b, 2004c).

The citizenship education curriculum in Malaysia has drawn its contents from diverse sources, including History and Civics, Islamic Education, Moral Education, co-curriculum activities and also from the broad notions of values education, thinking and communication across the curriculum and from the character education curriculum existing in indigenous educational traditions. More recently, the citizenship education curriculum has drawn philosophy, principles, framework, objectives and contents from the germinal ideals in the UNESCO Reports on education, specifically *Learning to Be* and *Learning: The Treasure Within* (Delors, 1996). The central ideas in the reports and the lifelong learning agenda have become the cornerstones of the ideals of education, incorporating the notions of "learning" as learning to learn, unlearn and relearn, learning to know and understand, learning to do, learning to live with others, learning for employment and re-employment, learning to become active citizens in participatory democracies, learning to be committed to ensure social inclusion, of all the citizenry, and learning for personal development to achieve the goal of the character of "becoming" better persons through the lifespan (Awang Had S., 2002; Bajunid 2002a; Delors, 1996; Faure, 1972). In sum, citizenship education teachers in Malaysia are asked by the government and expected by the people as a whole to undertake the development of future citizens into all they can be, with talents, potentials, civic, social and moral responsibilities, personal accountability and social conscience, and right social action for the general good in a civil society.

Appendix   Values Across the School Curriculum and Beyond Schooling

Upholding The Integrity of the Malaysian Civil Service-Universal Values and Twelve Pillars	Sixteen Values Across the Malaysian School Curriculum	List of Islamic Virtues in Schools		The Family Virtues Guide (Popov, 1997)	
The Inculcation of consciousness of high Moral Principles and Universal Humanistic values of Service leadership fostered: • Trustworthiness • Responsibility • Sincerity • Dedication • Moderation • Diligence • Clean Conduct • Co-operativeness • Honourable • Gratitude	1. Good-heartedness 2. Independent-Self-reliant 3. High Consideration 4. Mutual Respect 5. Love and Care 6. Justice 7. Freedom 8. Courage 9. Mental and Physical Cleanliness 10. Honesty 11. Diligence 12. Cooperation 13. Moderation 14. Gratitude 15. Rational 16. Community-spiritedness	1. Blessing 2. Rational 3. Insightful 4. Goodness 5. Truthful 6. Gratitude 7. Diligence 8. Concern 9. Competence 10. Confident in Knowledge 11. Good Judgement 12. Fear of God 13. Sensitive 14. Firm 15. Love and Caring 16. Good Relations 17. Thankful 18. Good Judgement 19. Tolerance 20. Forgiving	28. Civic consciousness 29. Sense of Community 30. Self-confidence 31. Shame 32. Respect/Politeness/Courtesy 33. Patience 34. Good Heartedness 35. Generous 36. Liberty 37. Qaraah 38. Perseverance 39. Discipline 40. Initiative 41. Peaceful 42. Pious 43. Religious 44. Cleanliness	1. Caring 2. Compassion 3. Consideration 4. Excellence 5. Generosity 6. Helpfulness 7. Humility 8. Justice 9. Kindness 10. Modesty 11. Respect 12. Self-discipline 13. Tact 14. Tolerance 15. Trust 16. Unity 17. Assertiveness 18. Cleanliness 19. Confidence 20. Courage 21. Courtesy	30. Honesty 31. Honour 32. Idealism 33. Joyfulness 34. Love 35. Loyalty 36. Mercy 37. Moderation 38. Obedience 39. Orderliness 40. Patience 41. Peacefulness 42. Prayerfulness 43. Purposefulness 44. Reliability 45. Responsibility 46. Reverence 47. Service 48. Steadfastness 49. Thankfulness 50. Trustworthiness

Upholding The Integrity of the Malaysian Civil Service-Universal Values and Twelve Pillars	Sixteen Values Across the Malaysian School Curriculum	List of Islamic Virtues in Schools		The Family Virtues Guide (Popov, 1997)	
The Twelve Pillars or Core Values of the Civil Service : 1. Value of Time 2. Perseverance towards Success 3. Job Satisfaction 4. Moderation 5. Personal Excellence 6. Good Heartedness 7. Role Model 8. Job Responsibility 9. Wise Consideration 10. Patience 11. Competence Improvement 12. Joy of Innovation		21. Dignity 22. Prayer 23. Sensitivity 24. Justice 25. Honesty 26. Cooperation 27. Self-Reliance	45. Self-cleanliness 46. Environmental Cleanliness 47. Mental Cleanliness 48. Spiritual Cleanliness 49. Punctuality 50. Good Use of Time 51. Dedication 52. High Considera-tion 53. Big-heartedness	22. Creativity 23. Detachment 24. Determination 25. Enthusiasm 26. Faithfulness 27. Self-Confidence 28. Risk Taking 29. Mutual Advice In the Abrahamic Tradition of Judaism, Christianity and Islam, the Spiritual Teachings for Citizenship Education are founded on the Disciplines of Grace: iv. Thou shall have no other Gods before me. v. Thou shall not make for thyself an idol in the form of anything. vi. Thou shall not misuse the name of the Lord thy God.	51. Truthfulness 52. Gentlefulness 53. Friendliness 54. Forgiveness 55. Flexibility 56. High Morale 57. Resilience iv. Remember the Sabbath by keeping it Holy. v. Honour thy father and thy mother. vi. Thou shall not murder vii. Thou shall not commit adultery. viii. Thou shall not steal. ix. Thou shall not give false testimony against thy neighbour x. Thou shall not covet. (see Hughes, 1993)

Note: Because of the nuances and connotations of cultural meaning differences in religious and historical traditions, the translations of values may not be exact but are approximate.

9

Political Pragmatism and Citizenship Training in Singapore

Tai Wei TAN and Lee Chin CHEW

Political involvement in education has been inevitable from the start of Singapore's nationhood. Her independent statehood was undesired, fraught as she was with the twin perils of economic and social disintegration. An island of only about 600 square kilometres with no hinterland and natural resources, and dependent mainly on entrepot trading, she was, her population being predominantly ethnic Chinese, alienated racially from the predominantly Malay neighbouring countries she depended on for her trade. Internally, there was the danger of racial conflict between the minority Malays and the majority Chinese, which would impede the social cohesion deemed to be essential for economic survival. She was a former British colony with a predominantly migrant Chinese population, infiltrated with Marxist ideology and looking towards communist China for inspiration and salvation. She was granted independence from Britain as a state within the newly constituted Federation of Malaysia in August 1963, along with Sabah and Sarawak, and the previous Federated Malay States of Malaya. Joining her with Malaysia was to neutralise her Marxist inclination (see Lee, 1998, Chapter 21). Taking her predominantly Chinese population (70% of the populace) into Malaysia was granted by Malayan leaders only on condition that Sabah and Sarawak, which had predominantly Malay populations, also joined, in order that the previous political dominance of the indigenous Malays would be preserved in the new federation (see Lee, 1998, Chapter 22). Lee Kuan Yew, who subsequently became a prominent opposition leader in the Malaysian parliament, soon led a united front of Chinese, Indians and others, including some "moderate" Malays, to campaign for a "Malaysian Malaysia" rather than a "Malay Malaysia" (Lee, 1965a, 1965b, 1965c). The reaction was intensified racist friction and even riots initiated by Malays against the Chinese, culminating in the expulsion of Singapore from Malaysia in August 1965 and the establishment of independent Singapore, with a population of 70% Chinese, 20% Malays and 10% Indians and others, such as Eurasians.

So, independent Singapore began with a divided populace, Malays being fearful of a government seen as Chinese as they looked towards Malay Malaysia in loyalty and hope, and the Chinese, and Indians also (some of them had supported the Chinese in the racial conflict), resentful against Malays as they waited to see what Lee Kuan Yew and his People's Action Party (PAP) could do to deliver on their electioneering promises. Meanwhile, many cast a dreamy eye towards China or India, at least for identity and belonging. This orientation towards a motherland located elsewhere was the continuation of a "migrant mentality," as the Chinese and Indians were descendents of working class people who had come to Singapore just to make money to take home. So the stage was set from the start for direct political manipulation by a government driven by exigencies to exert exclusive pragmatic leadership over the training of a divided, disorientated, fearful and therefore easy-to-rule populace. Confinement of the people within a tiny geographical entity rendered communication, and surveillance of compliance, easy and effective. Therefore, a survey of what passes as citizenship education in Singapore must go beyond considering school curricular programmes to involve government social policies, including school structuring and administration designed to implement them. Where people are regarded as mentally children, leaders act as schoolmasters and the entire country becomes a school.

Government Initiatives

Lee Kuan Yew had, at the start of Singapore's nationhood, personally told school principals in a speech (Lee, 1966) to cultivate school environments conducive to pupils' social bonding. He illustrated the selfish individualism of Singaporeans by reference to incidents "when the Japanese were coming in" during the World War Two Japanese invasion of Singapore. People were "quickly setting up flags with a red ball in the centre (i.e., the Japanese flag), quickly pushing them out through window-holes, closed the windows tight and peeped through the window holes. ... That was personal survival" (ibid., p.2). The speech was the blueprint, complete with design and rationale, of the various measures that his government has institutionalised through the years, to condition people in "the reflexes of group thinking ... in order to ensure the survival of the community, not the survival of the individual" (ibid., p.9). Singapore was to be a "tightly-knit society" with the talented few identified early and streamed into elite schools for leadership training. The minority would-be implementers of policies and schemes, and business managers were to be similarly identified and taught in better schools. The vast majority of people were to be trained to be good followers.

We must have qualities of leadership at the top, and qualities of cohesion on the ground (ibid., p.9). This was a clear declaration that the social cohesion citizenship "education" was to forge is not a virtue itself that measures the quality of human life, but only what is ingrained in order that people would be appeased by it, and be skilled at following the commandant. Lee's concept of education was clear in his speech. He was "extremely anxious about the generation that is growing up literate but uneducated. They can read ... write . . . pass examinations. But they are not really educated ... formed ... developed." Now, we might expect a climactic pronouncement on the ultimate virtues of an educated person. What we get is an anticlimax: The generation growing-up is not educated because "they are not effective digits for the community" (ibid., p.19).

Lee commented on several measures already then in place—which have since been intensified in their implementation—which would foster the social cohesion deemed to be fundamental for Singaporeans' training to be effective digits in their destined roles in the tightly-knit society. He referred to the daily school ritual of singing the national anthem before the national flag, followed by the saying of a pledge of loyalty and commitment, and regretted that, unlike countries which had traditions to be proud of and sing about, Singaporeans lacked the inspiration of national songs. He also regretted the anonymity of the average government school with its "listless" teachers and principals, and applauded some Christian and Chinese clan schools which still preserved some of their traditions and identity, and therefore were more effective as training grounds for social bonding. Government has through the years sustained the ritual practice in schools and nation, and preserved and developed those traditional schools.

School and State Rituals

The daily flag-raising ceremony held at the beginning of every school day (in afternoon session schools, a flag-lowering ceremony at the close), conducted in military formation, could inspire a feeling of pride and collective involvement even when the full meaning of the pledge and the national anthem were not grasped (the diction is not simplified for primary pupils). To combat inter-race suspicion and fear, pupils pledge "as one united people, regardless of race, language or religion." To orientate them towards nation build-ing, rather than absorbing the sentiments of some parents or grandparents in looking towards their racial motherlands, they begin their pledge repeating the phrase "we the citizens of Singapore." They pledge "to build a democratic society, based on justice and equality." Had this been all, the pledge would satisfy the requirements of citizenship *education*. For justice and equality and democratic values such as respect for personal dignity and autonomy, social cohesion, love and compassion, are intrinsic values of good citizens. However, the pledge goes on to say that all those virtues are worthy "so as to achieve happiness, prosperity and progress for our nation." So pupils are required to say, by implication, that those virtues are valid only when they work towards national pros-perity and progress. The pledge has in recent years been rendered into a national song sung annually at the National Day parade, for which schools train many months to par-ticipate. The tune begins low-keyed, but rises in a high pitch crescendo where the pledge culminates in declaring the ultimate aim to achieve national prosperity and progress. And true to this spirit, Lee has often, in response to appeals for more tolerance and freedom, said he stood only for "democracy that works." Indeed, he has proclaimed he is not "anticommunist" but only "noncommunist." He is noncommunist only because Singa-pore depends upon the free world for business and trade, and not because of a particular preference for democratic values. In fact, he has in the recent past toyed with the idea of revising "the one-man-one-vote system." In recent years he declared in several reports in the national newspaper, "We have not yet found it necessary to do so," but "should it become necessary, we will."

Similar sentiments are enshrined in the words of the national anthem. It makes no mention of justice, equality and democracy. "Come, fellow Singaporeans," it urges, "let us progress together towards happiness and success … let us unite in a new spirit, let our voices soar.…" The impact of this daily indoctrination has been limited for the Chinese and Indians, as the anthem is in Malay (which was initially the nominal national language chosen for political expediency; in latter years, four "official languages" have been declared, i.e., Chinese, Malay and Tamil, with English as the common language). Even where schools explain the anthem, pupils would miss the sentiments that accompany words sung and meant directly from the heart and mind, such as words sung in a familiar language.

Lee's complaint that Singaporeans lacked songs they could feel and identify with is one he has tried to address throughout the years by requiring the writing of national songs. The number of such songs has grown steadily, and are sung repeatedly in schools and over the media, especially during periods leading towards the annual National Day parade. In latter years the parade has been transformed into a party and show in order to reach an electorate that is getting younger. The National Stadium would be packed to capacity with the rest of Singapore viewing it live on all TV channels. A crowd 60,000 strong would sing national songs led by a combined schools choir and television performers. The quality of much of the music and lyrics, however, does not match the passion. Many songs are more like advertisement jingles. One goes "We are Singapore, we are Singapore; we will stand together, hear the lion roar." (Singapore is known as the lion city; legend has it that a lion-like beast was once spotted on its shore. But the inspiration of this song probably came from the days when Singaporeans who came to an MGM film late would have to stand together behind the theatre and hear the MGM lion roar, as they waited for the usher to show them to their seats.) Artistic standards *per se* are, however, not the concerns of pragmatists, who would say that it is songs "that work" they stood for, even if sung at the expense of value and education.

Preserving and Building School Identity

Another move Lee's speech envisaged has been to preserve a sense of cultural identity and bonding within schools. In order to create in all schools the familial and clannish continuity he observed existed in Christian and Chinese-clan schools, priority of enrolment of pupils in schools has largely been accorded to siblings and children of former students, and to people living in the immediate school neighbourhood. In the case of Christian schools, church membership is an important criterion for the admission of pupils. Associations of school alumni have been formed or preserved, and advisory committees at schools set up to involve neighbourhoods, former students and parents of pupils.

The situation has been more complicated in Chinese clan schools. On the one hand, Lee thought it important to combat racist exclusiveness by converting them into English medium schools with a curriculum common to all schools. On the other hand, he wanted to preserve the cultural bonds peculiar to them. The result has been to treat them as Special Assistance Plan Schools, where the previous "Chinese-ness," in terms of manners and etiquette such as bowing to teachers is preserved, and where students can study both Chinese and English up to first language standard, unlike other schools where the mother tongue (Chinese, Malay or Tamil) is taught only as second or third language.

In recent years, there has been a move to allow several selected schools to go "independent" and a few more to become "autonomous," with the aim, among others, to let them develop distinct characters and identities. However, it is arguable how effective such freedom can be when only those schools that are perceived to have excelled at implementing prescribed policies are entrusted with independence or autonomy, and where government still wields power through its representatives sitting on school management councils, and through principals appointed on the basis of their track record at school administration under the Ministry of Education.

Language and Social Bonding

The learning of languages in the school curriculum has been prescribed for social bonding, besides vocational training. English has been made compulsory as "first language" to facilitate participation in global commerce and industry, and for its neutrality as regards racial affiliation among the three dominant racial groups. However, language comes with cultural orientations. The fear has been that pupils will learn "irresponsible Western individualism and liberalism" whilst learning English. To reduce this risk, all pupils have been required to learn their mother tongue, although at a lower second language standard (except for many in "independent" and "special assistance plan" schools). The standard is lowered in order not to overload pupils' learning; so it does not indicate lesser importance accorded to the language. It was unquestioningly assumed that Chinese, Malay and Tamil, being Asian languages, would come with common Asian values of social cohesion, and therefore learning them would counterbalance the morally decadent influence of English. To secure this perceived benefit, pupils are to get instruction in an Asian language in their most formative years, and so values education at primary school has been taught in their mother tongue, their lack of proficiency in the language notwithstanding. It is thought that learning the mother tongue would also help pupils to preserve or restore a Singaporean identity that Lee feared the learning of English would dilute. Lee thinks that Singaporeans should be Chinese, Malay and Indian Singaporeans, rather than English-educated and rootless.

The usefulness of Chinese, and to some extent Tamil, has recently been extended, in official thinking, to include facilitating commerce with China and India. Chinese means Mandarin, the common language of China: Lee has since the late seventies abolished the use of Chinese dialects at official functions and broadcasting, and discouraged their transmission among the Chinese in order that they, not being distracted by the learning of a dialect, could learn Mandarin better.

Didactic National Campaigns and Special Days

We said that Singapore has been like a school campus. She has had a tough headmaster, who worries over all details of her pupils' lives. Singaporeans have become accustomed to admonishment by government ministers and members of parliament, who have spoken repeatedly on the need for team spirit and intercommunal harmony at important social and school functions where it has been the practice for them to be invited guests of honour. Media reports invariably highlight, mostly exclusively, such speeches in covering the functions. And Lee has initiated the practice, which his successor Goh Chok Tong, and now Goh's successor, Lee's son, Lee Hsien Loong, have continued, of addressing the nation at an annual May Day rally, where the prime minister appears live on all television channels for some three hours lecturing on national concerns. These addresses invariably concern the economy and the need for national commitment and discipline.

Singapore celebrates annually Mother's Day, Father's Day and Children's Day, but with her own agenda of national bonding. In addition, she has her own Racial Harmony Day and Total Defence Day. Schools are the main target of such special "days," for the commemoration of which pupils and teachers organise didactic activities such as fashion parades, where multi-racial costumes and dresses are modelled to symbolise racial harmony. Annual national campaigns, such as courtesy and "speak Mandarin" campaigns, are also held, with school children being similarly targeted. In all this, ruling politicians play leading roles, both at functions in the constituencies they represent, and heading national committees that coordinate such activities. The anti-littering campaign illustrates the schoolmaster's concern even with pupils' toilet training. Singaporeans must flush their toilets or pay a $300 fine. And, as is well known, the school canteen cannot sell chewing gum, so that pupils could not stick it on the hinges of their desks.

National Service and School Uniform Groups

All male citizens register for National Service on reaching eighteen, and train full-time for two-and-a-half years, with subsequent annual refresher training, in order to provide recruits for a citizens army. State scholarship holders and medical students get their training deferred until after university graduation. (The scholars are the "elite" earmarked for leadership, whose education cannot be postponed, and requiring would-be doctors to serve their national service only after graduation ensures a free supply of medical personnel for the army.) The vast majority of male secondary school leavers, therefore, train for warfare for two-and-a-half years before proceeding to a job or tertiary education. So, National Service is an extension of school training for most school students. Besides, much importance is placed on military foot drill at school functions, especially at the flag raising and lowering ceremony (where students stand at attention with their fists clenched against their chests) and school-based National Day parades. The armed forces have their school counterpart in the form of the National Cadet Corps and the National Police Cadet Corps, which are school "uniformed groups" established for training pupils in army and police work. At school functions, students in police and army uniform direct traffic and control crowds. The training includes arms drill and live-firing of arms. At one stage, other school uniform groups, even those whose motto is to save lives, such as the Christian Boys' Brigade and Red Cross, were required to do rifle drill. The aim is to maintain continuity between school and National Service. And ministerial speeches delivered, within parliament and without, boast of the efficacy of army training for character and values inculcation. Military cohesion and loyalty is being upheld as the exemplar of the commitment within the tightly-knit society Lee envisioned. Officers who excel in the armed forces are systematically recruited into Lee's ruling party, presented to the electorate and then promoted to be government ministers, and these retain their military rank and title. Just recently, Goh handed over the prime ministership to Brigadier General Lee Hsien Loong, Lee's eldest son. It is significant that in all this, no bifurcation between military training and cultivating the gentler and freer virtues of educated living in peace time, has been acknowledged. Singapore is to be as tightly-knit as a military outfit, and citizenship "education" is army-like training.

Tightly-knit Society and its Cost to Social Cohesion

The tightly-knit society has come with tough laws and sanctions that have their rationale in pragmatism rather than justice, equality, familial bonds and compassion. There is no awareness that the uncompassionate inflicting of legal sanctions, even when required by justice, would detract from the tempering of justice with mercy, often called for when people are bonded. Efficacy at deterring crimes is Singapore's measure of the appropriateness of her legal sanctions, rather than the justice and equality the national pledge vouches for. So, whipping foreigners who overstay is cavalierly defended with the claim that mere imprisonment, with its free lodging, feeds and daily exercise, would be welcomed by offenders coming in, desperate for a job. Whipping, on the other hand, would be excruciatingly painful and scar them for life, and so, being an effective deterrent, could be inflicted without moral qualms. House owners and housing rental agents suffer mandatory imprisonment for "harbouring illegal immigrants," even where they are only victims of their tenants' producing fraudulent immigration documents. Whipping, "strokes of the rotan," originally meant for convicts of violent crimes, has come to be used mandatorily on "vandals," such as the American boy who only smeared some paint on somebody's Mercedes. A dog owner, who similarly "vandalised" his neighbour's car after the neighbour kicked his dog, was sentenced to jail and caned. Lee, when pressed about hanging for drug traffickers, has habitually defended it, more on grounds of expediency rather than justice. Being an international airport with drug traffickers constantly coming through, Singapore would have to build and maintain many more prisons if the traffickers were not hanged, Lee opined when interviewed on the BBC television programme Hard Talk several years ago.

The tight control has included restricting publication, speech and assembly, and the monitoring of all movements deemed subversive of state interest by, among other measures, recourse to the *Internal Security Act* that allows for imprisonment without trial. And Lee has admitted that coercive measures have to be used during interrogation of those imprisoned under the Act. What these measures are has never been explained, and those few Singaporeans who care to know have recourse only to a couple of books published in America (not sold in Singapore) by a former political activist who was imprisoned under the Act, and who now lives in America as a political refugee. Singaporeans can only hope the information there is inaccurate. There have been a few aspirants to political opposition, and several of these have been monitored, the Act having been used against them. Several others have been sued by Lee and his associates and ordered by the courts to pay many hundreds of thousands of dollars for saying questionable things during the heat of electioneering. A couple of persons who stood for election, and were able to garner a significant proportion of votes, found it necessary subsequently to leave the country. The cost of such perceptions of state "persecution of the opposition," to the state's effort to instil courtesy and forge familial bonds, has never been counted. Family values accord priority to compassion and forgiveness. What family would let its "black sheep" feel constrained to leave home?

There has been a shift in recent years to soften things and increase welfare aid, even in the form of "give-aways" of money, and shares of government-owned businesses, to the people. This was in sharp contrast to what Lee had maintained all along, that "nobody owes you a living." The softening is welcome. Indications are that things will be softened further with Lee Hsien Loong as prime minister. In his first National Day speech after taking the baton from Goh in August 2004, he appealed for more participation in leadership and repealed a long-standing rule that even indoor public meetings must be licensed. Such softening coheres better with the attempt to cultivate social bonding. What family would cease to support its member should he be unable to fend for himself? What parent would muffle his talkative child? The shift is commonly associated, in the public's mind, with the gentler style of Goh, who succeeded Lee as prime minister in 1990 (but with Lee still remaining as the only Senior Minister in Singapore; with the new Premier Lee, both Goh and Lee Kuan Yew remain, as Senior Minister and Mentor Minister, respectively). Part, at least, of the truth lies elsewhere, unacknowledged. It was the opposition leader, J.B. Jeyaretnam, who campaigned for years, at election after election, for a more compassionate and freer society at a time when Lee was still maintaining that nobody owed anyone a living. Jeyaretnam eventually won a by-election, and, thereafter, continued to win at several general elections. Since then, the few opposition parties that exist have increased their vote counts at most parliamentary elections, and two or three of their candidates have even made it into parliament. It was evident that the opposition's call for a more gracious, freer and compassionate society was appealing. Goh's gentler rule should in part be credited to Jeyaretnam's effectiveness at political opposition. This would mean also that the softening under Goh, and now Lee Hsien Loong, is yet another pragmatic strategy adopted for Singapore's survival. Lee Kuan Yew and company have always identified their political party's survival with Singapore's survival.

However, the tough legal sanctions instituted for pragmatic reasons, which we mentioned above, have remained intact under Goh. Indeed, he initiated some of them. There is no evidence of any chance of their being softened, even under the younger Lee's leadership. So Singapore's citizenship "education" in the area of cultivating a national familial bond will continue to be undermined by legal toughness.

School Citizenship "Education"

School citizenship education has been only a part of total citizenship training in tightly-knit Singapore. It might be the political leadership's confidence in the effectiveness of their direct influence on all Singaporeans that explains their leaving values education in school, from the beginning years of independent statehood in 1965 to the late seventies, to educationists to develop and administer. Schools were left much to their own devices to organise the teaching of two periods per week on ethics and civics, with the then Ministry of Education continuing the practice inherited from colonial days of providing only a syllabus guide of topic headings. Christian schools integrated ethics / civics with the teaching of Bible knowledge. There was, therefore, a greater chance, then, depending on the quality of the interpreters of the syllabi, for breadth and depth of values, coupled with true values motivation to be taught, and true moral education achieved. Eventually, a broad-based and comprehensive values education programme was developed by the Ministry's curriculum planners, its comprehensiveness denoted by its title, Education for Living. Although the programme, which came complete with pupils' textbooks and teachers' guides also stressed national consciousness and duty, it went beyond this to cover the wide arena of living. Along with this more pedagogically defensible programme, there was an older syllabus which provided more traditional-styled textbooks, which Education for Living was meant to replace. This older syllabus had also been written by curriculum planners without direct instructions from politicians, but the writers were themselves obviously very nationalistically inclined. The syllabus was entitled Good Citizens, and in this we see already the trend, which was to be followed subsequently, of political concerns being given priority in values teaching in schools.

Lee not infrequently intervened to get things done at short notice in reaction to perceived urgent needs. So it was that, in the late seventies, it suddenly hit him that a national ideology based upon Confucian family values was needed. Those years were the heyday of Japanese economic excellence, before the Asian financial crisis of the nineties. Lee often hailed Japanese familial bonding and team spirit, which he ascribed to the influence of Confucian morality, to explain the driving force behind its success. In Singapore, however, there had been a growing number of cases of "criminal breach of trust," committed by professionals. This was viewed to be detrimental to Singapore's image as a safe place for foreign investment. Lee had embarked with remarkable success on changing Singapore, from being solely dependent on entrepot trading to becoming industrialised. Multinational companies were needed to base their operations in the country, contribute their expertise and create jobs. He therefore became concerned that values teaching by schools had failed. He suddenly required that Confucian ethics be taught in school, and instructed his former deputy prime minister and latterly minister of defence—a notably strong man in government, whom he had lately made education minister—to implement the requirement. He was Dr Goh Keng Swee.

Despite the popular thesis that Confucianism was a system of secular morality, it was seen as a religion by many people. It was also Chinese in origin. The Malays were Muslims. So, teaching Confucianism exclusively could become a racist issue. And there were other religions. So Dr Goh made religious studies, and not just Confucian studies, compulsory at secondary three and four, to crown a values education curriculum taught from primary one to secondary two. Students were to opt for Confucianism, Buddhism, Islam, Hinduism, Sikhism or Christianity. Despite the fact that Confucianism was only one option, it could be expected that a good proportion of Chinese would choose it, and that would mean a good representation of the population, since over 70% of it was Chinese. Religion was not taught for its intrinsic value, but only as instrumental for producing Singaporeans who would cohere well, like the Japanese. "If you believe in God, good luck to you," Dr Goh said. He was teaching religion because he had noticed that those professionals who had committed criminal breaches of trust did not have their secondary schooling in Christian schools.

Dr Goh had been moved, in the late seventies, to the education ministry to overhaul the whole education system, and tighten it further in order to meet the needs of state and industry. Singapore was getting expensive, and could not compete with other Asian countries with their cheaper labour and lower cost of living. Better skilled workers were needed as Singapore moved into higher technical "knowledge-based" industries where she could maintain a monopoly among Asian economies. "Educational wastage," in the form of a high dropout rate among pupils after completing primary or lower secondary school, had to be prevented because even the least academically inclined had to acquire industrial skills, and few unskilled jobs would remain available.

Dr Goh revamped the education system and instituted an attempt at a more discriminative and definitive system of streaming pupils according to their aptitude and national vocational needs. At primary three, it was already to be decided who would follow the academic streams that led eventually to "white collar" professions, and who would follow a "technical stream" leading towards manual "blue collar" jobs. His ministry adamantly defended the policy in response to criticisms that the streaming was being done too early. However, under a new education minister, the streaming was subsequently delayed until primary four, and the nature of the streaming further fine-tuned. Streaming at primary four is, of course, still too early. The impatience to decide so soon shows the narrowly pragmatic agenda of government. "Education" must contribute to the state's manpower needs if it is not to be "educational wastage." The earlier differing abilities are identified, the less the "wastage."

It was not surprising, therefore, that Education for Living was thought by Goh's officials to be too broad and not focused on "relevant" objectives. Dr Goh required a new values education curriculum to be developed for pupils from primary one to secondary two. Meanwhile, schools were to use the Good Citizens programme up to secondary two, before teaching religious studies as a continuation of values teaching in secondary three and four. A new programme entitled Being and Becoming began to be available in stages. Like Education for Living, it went beyond the narrow confines of straight values teaching and focused on human relations that are coterminous with the being and becoming that comes with living. It required experiential learning in real life encounters beyond the classroom, and even within the classroom learning was activity-orientated. Thus, pupils wore name cards with personal information of themselves written behind, and they had to reveal the back of the cards only when they felt comfortable with those they befriended, as an indication of familiarity and depth of the social bonds they gradually forged. Only a teachers' manual was provided to suggest such activities, much being left to individual teachers' imagination and initiative. While the new programme was being introduced in stages, Good Citizens remained an option for schools to adopt, and it became the more popular option because it came with students' textbooks and, therefore, was easier to teach.

The teaching of religion at secondary three and four began rubbing up against inter-religious and inter-racial sensitivities. What was surprising was the consequent sudden doing away with religious teaching. A government, proud of its systematic forward planning, must have anticipated the problems that arose, and would have decided to brave the risks for the conceived benefits of religious studies. The preparation of the several religious curricula was done at great public expense, involving foreign consultants and some three years of full-time curriculum planning and writing. Anyhow, change was yet again directed by the political leadership to replace all previous values teaching, including religious studies, with a common Civics and Moral Education (CME) programme. Confucian virtues were to be taught within CME, along with other desired values culled from the previous religious and other moral studies, even though this aim was not explicitly stated. Simultaneously, the then minister-of-state for community development was appointed to identify afresh Singapore Shared Values, which the CME was to incorporate. This renewed emphasis on forging consensus was a pragmatic response, not only to inter-ethnic and religious friction that was perceived to be threatening again with the revival of Muslim fundamentalism elsewhere and in Singapore, but also to the increasing globalisation of nations and industries. Well-educated Singaporean cosmopolitans, who could move on to greener pastures elsewhere, had to be instilled with loyalty to the soil and remain rooted. Foreign talent were being readily granted permanent residency with the view to offering them citizenship in order that they would contribute economically to "talent scarce" Singapore, and so their children had to be imbued with Singapore values. So, everything done in the name of education, even religious and moral teaching, has been aimed instrumentally towards "nation-building" perceived largely in economic terms. In other areas of education, the response to industrial globalisation has included the promotion of thinking and creativity and lifelong learning, in order to prepare students for the knowledge-based economy of the 21st century. The implication is that without the economy, humans would not need values, morality, religion, thinking, creativity and learning.

Civics and Moral Education

What remains to be discussed is the common CME programme eventually produced and currently used. The renewed search for Singapore "shared values" resulted in five being identified:

- Nation before community and society before self
- Community support and respect for the individual
- Family as the basic unit of society
- Consensus in place of conflict
- Racial and religious harmony

These values are more prescriptive of what Singaporeans should share rather than descriptive of what they shared, for they are merely another variant of the values that have been officially campaigned for over the years. The question of their justification was never raised during the "search." They are seemingly to be upheld just because they are shared. But they had to be at most only a selection of what Singaporeans in fact shared, their selection being made by the pragmatic criteria of "prosperity and progress for our nation."

Besides the shared values, CME is also to incorporate "national education messages." National Education was another citizenship training programme initiated "top-down" quite suddenly. There had been diplomatic friction between Malaysia and Singapore, which Singapore leaders viewed as hangovers of the events that led to Singapore's expulsion from Malaysia. Speaking with some school students, Premier Goh was appalled at their ignorance of even the fact that Singapore was once part of Malaysia. A top civil servant was appointed to plan a compulsory national education programme for all schools, focused on the teaching of recent political history. This knowledge was thought to be important for enabling young Singaporeans to appreciate the dangers of inter-communal friction, arising from racial and religious sensitivities that had much of their roots in recent history. National Education is, therefore, part of an ongoing politicised campaign of "total defence," that involves physical and ideological training of Singaporeans of all levels and professional sectors, and not only of young citizens drafted into "national service." It is assumed that history will indisputably show who were at fault in past racial conflicts, and where similar dangers lurk today, and thereby motivate the young where to place their loyalty. National Education is clearly not a separate subject but only an aspect of CME focused on understanding relevant history for the appraisal of values. Rightly, it is not implemented as a new curriculum but integrated into the teaching of existing subjects, especially CME, and school cocurricular activities.

With such objectives, the specific policies and content of CME would have a decided leaning towards meeting practical needs. Under the heading "Rationale," the primary CME syllabus (Singapore Ministry of Education, 2000c, p.4) states that "the alignment of CME content with national and societal needs is vital" because of "the fragility of our country … with its vulnerabilities and constraints." This requires the cultivation of "good habits … that enable students to work efficiently with others and cope well in times of change and uncertainties." It also requires cultivating "one's loyalty and commitment to the nation" because of "the impact of globalisation" which "poses a constant challenge" to national loyalty. Also, under "Knowledge Objectives," understanding of "teamwork" and "concerns of the community and … the ways they could contribute to the community" and "being aware of the ideals of the nation" loom large (p.5). At the culmination of a list of skills for training are those that "contribute to total defence." Students are to cultivate attitudes which "show a sense of belonging and love for Singapore as their homeland" (p.6). In all this, due consideration was not given to the need, in moral and citizenship education, for "ideals of the nation" to be morally appraised, and for students to accept such ideals as autonomously understood and morally defensible principles. The yardstick of moral worth is only what the nation in fact desires for the meeting of practical needs.

Five themes are identified for the teaching of CME, beginning with "self" and culminating with "nation," with "family," "school" and "society" intervening, in that order. "Within the parameters of relationships extending from Self to Nation, pupils are equipped with knowledge, skills and attitudes that reflect the values and principles deemed important and good, and upheld by society, which include Our Shared Values, Singapore Family Values and the Desired Outcomes of Education." (p.6) That pupils should be educated to autonomously appraise Singapore's shared or desired values, which would be done with the risk that they might not find all such desired values desirable, is not reflected in CME.

This pragmatic orientation is emphasised even more in the secondary school syllabus, which aims (Singapore Ministry of Education, 2000d, p.2) to "incorporate more concepts and contents … to meet the changing needs and future challenges of the nation." "National Education messages have been infused," specifically "values and attitudes of responsible citizenship" and "issues that concern the nation." The rationale is "the need to enhance our pupils' sense of emotional bonding and commitment to the community and the nation in the midst of increasing globalisation and a borderless world." They "need to know and appreciate the uniqueness of Singapore, the struggles and vulnerabilities and the achievements of our nation … to heighten our pupils' confidence in our nation's future and security … to be provided with opportunities that help them develop instincts for survival." "The overarching goal of CME is to nurture a person of integrity who acts responsibly with the welfare and interests of others and the nation in mind. This is to mould the people who will determine the future of the nation."

The themes follow the same order as those of the primary syllabus, starting with self and proceeding through family and community, and culminating with "our nation, our heritage" and the "challenges ahead." The latter themes usher pupils into a postsecondary civics module taught during the two-year pre-university schooling for students reading for the advanced-level Cambridge school certificate. This is a continuation of citizenship education beyond secondary school CME. Its content and objectives, however, appear more like a national leadership training course. Although labelled Civics (the term moral is significantly dropped from CME), its aims render it only one specific aspect of civics, relevant only to those citizens identified for national leadership (Singapore Ministry of Education, 2000b). This is frankly admitted in its sub-title Challenge of Leadership. The aims are "to equip our students with the requisite knowledge and skills as future leaders to make sound decisions for the nation," and to "develop the willingness to take on the responsibility to contribute to shaping the future of our nation" (p.2).

The slant towards "statecraft" becomes very decided in the secondary school CME knowledge objectives (Singapore Ministry of Education, 2000d, p.3). The values to be taught are only those "essential to the well-being of our nation." Pupils are to "know the people and the events of our nation's past, and their links with the present, the factors that contribute to nation-building, our nation's constraints and vulnerabilities, and how to overcome these constraints, our system of government, the impact and issues of a fast changing world on our nation's survival and success." In the pupils' books, where these objectives are translated into curricular content and activities, the pragmatic interest has evidently motivated the inclusion or exclusion of historical persons, events, concepts and values. For instance, in the Pupils' Book for Secondary Four (for 16 year-old pupils; Singapore Ministry of Education, Curriculum Planning & Development Division, 2000-2002), where "our system of government" is featured, there is no attempt to teach a critical awareness of democratic values with which to help pupils appraise the actual system of governance being practised. Only a description of the features of the system in practice is given, detailing the functions of each.

This is especially telling when some of those features are peculiar to democracy in Singapore, such as the provision for government-approved, non-elected *nominated members of parliament* and the election of *grouped members of parliament* representing grouped constituencies. These are contentious issues, with detractors claiming that they are really strategies meant to offset the swing of votes in recent elections towards the opposition. The perception is that voters have lately supported opposition candidates only in order to have alternative viewpoints in parliament. Providing for nominated members in parliament would render it unnecessary to elect opposition candidates in order to fulfil that function. And requiring some electoral constituencies to elect a team of at least three election candidates, each of a different race to represent one of the three dominant racial groups in Singapore, has the effect of making it difficult for poorly staffed and resourced opposition political parties to compete. Another observation is that a significant number of previously single-candidate constituencies that had supported opposition candidates strongly at previous elections have been subsequently merged with other constituencies under this grouping scheme in order to neutralise the support. Whatever the merit of such views, the "depoliticised" teaching of governance should surely not present such debatable and debated features as parts of the normal and ac-cepted process of democracy.

Another example is the teaching of the people and the events of our nation's past. Political personages deemed worthy for inclusion as national heroes and paragons of virtue are all PAP personnel. It could not possibly be the case that none of the political leaders in office during those tumultuous years of struggling for independent statehood, before Lee's party took the reigns of government, deserve to surface. For instance, David Marshall, Singapore's first Chief Minister during the years when Singapore was ac-corded internal self-government, and when the fledgling PAP was in the opposition in the then Legislative Assembly, is not mentioned, despite that Lee, in later years, had thought Marshall virtuous and able enough to appoint him as ambassador to France. Yet another example is the teaching of students to appreciate, as an important responsibility of citi-zenship, only political leaders of ability and integrity. In the context of present-day Singapore party politics, pupils are wont to believe that good leaders are by and large those in the PAP, since Singaporeans are constantly told that the party has searched "high and low" to identify and rope in persons of ability and integrity in talent-scarce Singa-pore. And its standard response to political opposition has been to attack the integrity and competence of its aspirants.

The syllabus's themes, recycled several times yearly through primary and secondary schooling, of self, family, community and nation, seem to be disinterested moral and civics education. But that they subserve national interests, too, is evident when we examine them in relation to social facts. The theme of Self seems to be important in the light of one of the shared values—respect of the community for the individual. Topics such as the worth of responsible individualism should then be featured, with due warnings given, say, of not to overly stress collective interests at the expense of individual development and autonomy. As the syllabus has it, however, self is "character development." Now, a person's character is formed in practice as one relates to others within family, community and nation. Therefore, self, as CME has it, is only the start, focusing more on the development of personal attributes, of teaching the themes of family, community and nation.

The themes of Family and Community, as they are understood in Singapore, are not free of a political and pragmatic tinge either. "Singapore family values" have been officially pronounced as counterpoints to undesirable Western individualism. So, another of the shared values is "consensus, not conflict," rather than Western "confrontational" democracy. In addition, there is the pragmatic interest of enabling the young to feel Confucian filial piety and, therefore, support their old parents in a population a large segment of which are fast ageing. Also, under family values, marriage and the obligation to have children, and some sex education, are featured in CME. Even such personal concerns are not unconnected with political expediency. The government has been concerned that better educated citizens are not marrying and reproducing themselves and their talents in a country where humans are the only natural resource. There has been the additional worry that the racial composition of the nation—"the formula that works"—would be upset with the Chinese and Indians not reproducing themselves proportionally to the Malays, whose Islamic values forbid contraception.

With regard to the political significance of the theme Community, every electoral constituency in Singapore has a community centre, which comes under the direct purview of a People's Association, an extension of the Prime Minister's Office. Advisors of the centres are PAP members of parliament. In the one or two constituencies which elected opposition members of parliament, failed PAP election candidates continue to advise the centres. There are also community projects, such as PAP-run kindergartens, and community self-help organisations established under the purview of government. Housing estates are served by residents' committees, advised by PAP members of parliament, which organise social functions for residents. So, CME's teaching of the theme of responsibility to the community in terms of participation and contribution would, of course, include advocating volunteering one's services to such politicised social services.

CME is, therefore, another instance of Singapore citizenship training crafted to fit a people for a nationhood conceived narrowly in terms of economic survival and progress.

Pacific Rim

10

Democracy at a Crossroads:
Political Tensions Concerning Educating
for Citizenship in the United States

Thomas SCOTT and John J. COGAN

Citizenship Education and Local Control

The debate concerning what constitutes an acceptable curriculum that best serves the economic, social, political and cultural concerns of educating for citizenship has a long and controversial history in the United States. Never has this debate been more contentious than at present. The stakes in the outcome of the debate are significant: It will determine the groups that benefit from citizenship, who is excluded, and how citizenship is defined and practised in the United States.

Any attempt to describe this debate is rendered more complex by the decentralised nature of the U.S. educational system and the diverse stakeholders connected to it. The structure of the American public education system in itself poses significant challenges for the analyst examining the citizenship education curriculum in the United States. First, there is the practical challenge of finding suitable content and pedagogical approaches for citizenship education among the fifty states (Pederson & Cogan, 2000). Unlike the majority of nations profiled in this book, the United States does not have a centralised ministry of education responsible for administering top-down policies and reform initiatives. Instead, individual states are given the constitutional power to create and administer systems of public education. The result is a highly decentralised system characterised by disparate policy approaches that often conform to local educational needs and political realities. Further complicating matters is the existence of nearly 15,000 independent and locally controlled school districts that are responsible for implementing state policy. More than 90,000 public schools attempt to align district curriculum mandates with each school's curriculum, where a teaching corps that has an established tradition of autonomy and pedagogical isolation then delivers the curriculum in their classrooms. Despite aggressive attempts currently underway by the federal government to standardise the public school curriculum, variation and fragmentation still characterise the citizenship education curricula in the United States (Pederson & Cogan, 2000).

Second, analysts are also confronted by a philosophical challenge related to the lack of acceptance regarding the epistemology of citizenship. In a pluralistic nation such as the United States, citizenship has a multiplicity of meanings that are closely dependent upon class identity, the historical experience of cultural groups, gender differences and racial identities. Establishing an acceptable definition of citizenship in a milieu of fluid and often conflicting identity politics proves problematic. Complicating this definition is how citizenship is measured. Should it be measured solely by birth, the recognition of specific rights, or by civic agency? For example, do we measure active citizenship through voting, working in a soup kitchen, dutifully paying taxes, or a combination of all of these?

In this chapter we examine the history of this debate in the context of the citizenship education curriculum, offer an analysis of civic disengagement occurring among many students in the United States today, and describe the current controversy between liberals and neo-conservatives over what constitutes the most appropriate citizenship curriculum for the 21st century. We then examine a host of tensions teachers, curriculum designers, policy-makers and citizens face as they struggle to define American citizenship. Finally, we offer a curricular synthesis that attempts to transcend these controversies and provides classroom teachers with a practical approach to what Parker (1996) calls an "advanced" citizenship education curriculum.

History of Civic Education Curriculum in the United States

Modern civic education in the United States dates back to the year 1916. Before this date, civics was taught mainly through the history curriculum. Indeed, the discipline of history dominates the social subjects taught in American schools to this very day. The "Civics Study Group," formed under the Commission on the Reorganization of Secondary Education (National Education Association [NEA], 1916) proposed two major changes that would have a long-term impact upon the teaching of civics and government in U.S. schools.

First, they proposed the development of a new course at the 9th grade level to be called "Community Civics." This was to be a foundational course since many students left school for the workplace after Grade 9. Second, at Grade 12, the final year of high school for those who went on to a complete secondary education, there was to be a "Problems of Democracy" course. This was to build upon the foundational concepts and principles of the Grade 9 "civics" course but was to focus more specifically upon the problems, issues and conditions which students would face in their daily lives upon leaving formal schooling. The Civic Study Group designed the course to help young people develop the skills necessary to examine civic problems and issues and fulfil their roles and responsibilities as citizens living in a democratic society. The goal here was to develop *participatory* citizenship. In practice, very little participation has ever been achieved in most U.S. civics or government courses. Instead, this 12th grade course is for the most part a content knowledge course that overviews the structure, organisation, function and symbols of American government. There have been attempts over the years to modify these offerings, but in the main these have been *the* two courses designed to educate for citizenship in the secondary school curriculum over the last century.

However, the 1990s saw a new era in civic education curriculum development. The publication in 1991 of a new framework for civic education called *CIVITAS* (Centre for Civic Education), followed in 1994 with the *National Standards for Civics and Government* (Centre for Civic Education), signalled major changes to the 1916 recommendations. The *CIVITAS* document was used as the theoretical framework in the development of the *National Standards for Civics and Government*. This document along with *Expectations of Excellence* (National Council for the Social Studies, 1994), set curriculum standards for the social studies in general in the United States, renewed the *debate* about the role of civics and government in the curriculum regarding the development of citizen knowledge, skills and behaviours. The major change was that the *National Standards for Civics and Government* focused on the *entire* K-12 curriculum, a departure from the focus upon the two courses offerings in the past at Grades 9 and 12. Participants in the debate over the civics and government curriculum standards included social studies educators, government officials, representatives from the major political parties, fundamentalist Christians and other special interest groups.

In the policy arena, the *National Standards for Civics and Government* (Centre for Civic Education, 1994) comes the closest to anything the nation has ever had in terms of "citizenship education policy." The historically decentralised system of schooling in the United States has only recently begun to focus more upon what might be termed a "national" curriculum. This has evolved through the development of national "curriculum standards" documents in the various subject areas, including civics and government. A recent survey by Pederson and Cogan (2000; see also Galston, 2004; Ross, 2004; Westheimer & Kahne, 2004) of the 50 states revealed no real unified policy on civics education. Rather an eclectic approach prevails, with most states having simply adopted the *National Standards for Civics and Government* document and/or the *Expectations of Excellence* standards of the National Council for the Social Studies (NCSS) and made them their de facto policy statement in this curriculum area.

The *National Standards for Civics and Government* published by the Centre for Civic Education (1994) suggests that a civic education curriculum must revolve around five essential questions:

1. What are civic life, politics, and government?
2. What are the foundations of the American political system?
3. How does the government established by the Constitution embody the purposes, values, and principles of American democracy?
4. What is the relationship of the United States to other nations and to world affairs?
5. What are the roles of citizens in American democracy? (p.1)

The NCSS identifies "Civic Ideals and Practices" as one of its ten themes for curriculum standards in the social studies. Associated with this theme is the following standard:

"Social studies programs should include experiences that provide for the study of *the ideals, principles, and practices of citizenship in a democratic republic*" (*Expectations of Excellence*, National Council for the Social Studies, 1994, p.139). A set of "performance expectations" related to the standard allows students to "exhibit the knowledge, skills, scholarly perspectives, and commitments to American democratic ideals" (ibid., p.14). These performance expectations require students to explain, interpret, analyse, evaluate and synthesise a variety of skills and civic-related content that is critical to effective citizenship. The expectations include:

- Key ideals of the democratic republican experiment
- Citizens' rights and responsibilities
- Knowledge of selected public issues
- Civic discussion and participation
- Citizen action on public policy
- Analysis of public policies and issues
- Effectiveness of public opinion in influencing and shaping public policy
- Citizen behaviour and how it fosters the ideals of democratic republican form of government
- Constructing policy statements and action plans
- Participating in activities to strengthen the "common good" (ibid., p.139)

Defining the Curriculum: The Neo-conservative and Liberal Schism

In many respects the historical development of citizenship education is rooted in conflicting ideologies that are part of a larger debate over the definition of the social studies that has characterised the field for the last century (Evans, 2004). In particular, the past two decades have seen a hardening of conflicting ideologies regarding the structure, aims and content of the civic education curriculum. The National Commission on Excellence in Education's (1983) report, *A Nation at Risk*, identified a "rising tide of mediocrity" in America's schools and suggested the United States was engaged in an "act of unilateral educational disarmament." Commissioned by President Ronald Reagan, the report examined what many conservatives felt was a failing public education system. It proclaimed the United States was losing the international race for educational excellence from economic competitors, such as Germany and Japan, threatening the United States' economic pre-eminence in the world. In its call for reform of the public education system, the Report received significant ideological support from political conservatives and corporate interests, laying the foundation for standards-based reforms which emerged from the *America 2000 Excellence in Education Act* policy of George W. Bush and the *Goals 2000 Educate America Act* policy of Bill Clinton.

Although these two reform movements devoted substantial rhetoric to civic education and the positive impact that civic-minded youth could have on their local communities, the curricular framework of citizenship education increasingly came under the control of "back to basics" conservatives who equated curricular reform with rote memorisation of factual information, aligned to a set of quantifiably measured standards. Such standards were designed to advance a neo-liberal economic agenda with one overarching goal: The creation of a skilled, compliant workforce that could compete with America's economic rivals. With the standards movement, the epistemological nature of the social studies in general, and of citizenship education in particular, was reversed from the progressive emphasis on inquiry into the human condition and the examination of local, national and global problems, to a human resource model rooted in econometric objectives designed to help the United States adjust to the economic imperatives of 21st century globalisation. Thus, during the decade of the 1990's corporate leaders and many elected officials at both the state and national levels associated a good citizen with being a skilled, obedient worker. This human resource approach to civic education has accelerated under George W. Bush's *No Child Left Behind Act of 2001* (NCLB, 2002).

The Bush education initiatives are consistent with the neo-conservative approach to civic education that, since September 11th, has emphasised American patriotism, respect for the flag, the moral force of prayer, a Christian national identity and a messianic duty of the United States to transfer the benefits of democracy, free markets and American values around the world. Global awareness is viewed from an "America First" perspective that sees the U.S. as a global hegemonic power which has the right to dominate the world because of its spiritual and political exceptionalism. Controversial content and the critical deliberation of sensitive political issues have been eliminated through the writing of standards which promote an ideologically-driven curriculum that ignores the historical contributions of dissent and social movements that retaliated against the shortcomings of American democracy. Political dissent against U.S. policies in schools and universities is under attack throughout the United States (Lapham, 2004), constraining academic freedom and critical inquiry.

Many teachers are hesitant to create curricular activities that discuss controversial issues related to education for citizenship because they fear criticism from parents and others (Avery, 2002; Kahne, Rodriquez, Smith, & Thiede, 2000; Marciano, 2001; Pederson & Cogan, 2000; Torney-Purta, 2002). Curricula designed to discuss controversial issues are considered negative and unpatriotic. Neo-conservative "Contrarians" claim that secondary students cannot learn from such discussions because they do not possess the cognitive capabilities required of curricula that develop higher order thinking (Leming, 2003). They further argue that values associated with progressive views of citizenship taught in public schools "differ from those of many parents" (Finn, 2004, p.20). Those teachers who engage in such "subversive" activities do so at their own risk (see Westheimer, 2004). After the 2004 election of George W. Bush to a second term, the neo-conservative viewpoint continued to infiltrate the citizenship education curriculum. Loyalty to a narrow set of social values and allegiance to the state emerged as the prevailing norms of citizenship education. This narrow vision of citizenship, however, is facing resistance by many progressive teachers throughout the United States (see *Four More Years of Resistance*, editorial, 2004-05, p.4; Giroux, 2004). Joel Westheimer (2006) in a recent edition of the American education journal *Phi Delta Kappan*, profiles a variety of teachers who have created lessons since Sept 11th questioning the prevailing political climate. For example, in New Mexico a teacher designed lessons questioning United States involvement in Iraq. In Florida a teacher critically examined the constitutionality of the Patriot Act. In Oregon a teacher engaged in discussions involving the relationship between patriotism and the First Amendment. In Wisconsin a 5th grade teacher had students engage in reflective writing about threats of terrorism, the meaning of the Pledge of Allegiance, and what students thought about ordinary citizens of Afghanistan (pp.612-618). Several of the teachers above were disciplined or suspended for their teaching methods. As the examples above illustrate, progressive teachers continue to see their classrooms as spaces for deliberative political discourse. They continue to use constructivist teaching methods rather than succumb to rote test preparation, and they continue to view citizenship with a broad lens, actively preparing students to become engaged actors in the social, cultural and political life of the nation.

Whither Democracy? The Dilemma of Political Participation

In many respects it is not surprising that the neo-conservative educational reform movement should focus on the development of human capital as a means of coping with the economic challenges of globalisation. A commensurate challenge exists with civic agency among a large percentage of young people in the United States; however, the neo-conservative response has been tepid at best. There is significant concern that young people are consciously becoming disengaged from political activity in the United States (Branson, 2003; Albert Shanker Institute, 2003; Gagnon, 2003; Scott, 2004). Voting records reinforce this concern. Less than 30% of registered voters aged 18-20 voted in the 2000 presidential election, a percentage that has continuously declined over the last decade (United States Census Bureau, 2001). On an encouraging note, during the recent 2004 presidential election it has been estimated that the percentage of young people aged 18-24 who voted was over 42% (Centre for Information & Research on Civic Learning & Engagement [CIRCLE], 2004). Despite this positive outcome of the youth vote, a "civic deficit" similar to that described by Kerry Kennedy in his chapter on Australia also exists in the United States. A recent national report on civic education stated:

> Surveys have shown that they [students] are not as interested in political discussion and public issues as past generations were at the same point in their lives. In addition, there are gaps in young people's knowledge of fundamental democratic principles and processes. As a result, many young Americans are not prepared to participate fully in our democracy now and when they become adults. (CIRCLE, 2003, p.8)

Research by Putnam (2002) illustrates the complex nature of the political disengagement among youth in the United States. Putnam notes that since the September 11th terrorist attacks, interest in public affairs grew by 27% among those aged 35 and less and trust in community-based political figures increased by 19%. However, Putnam acknowledged that this spike in greater interest in public affairs has not necessarily led to a behavioural shift leading to more political action on the part of the young.

Putnam's findings are significant because they illustrate a serious dichotomy between students' understanding of politics and its application in a democratic society. It is not civic engagement or necessarily citizenship education that turns students off. In the recent Second IEA civic education study, the percentage of 9th grade students volunteering in their local community was the highest of the 28 countries participating in the study (Torney-Purta, Lehmann, Oswald, & Schulz, 2001). Students seem enthusiastic and willing to volunteer and work to better their local communities. However, they are also rejecting the political process as being out of touch with their needs and lacking connection to issues they feel have a direct impact on their lives. They are increasingly sceptical of the exclusivity of political decision-making and feel ignored by political power brokers (see Re-Generation, 2003).

A significant question emerges from the dichotomous perspective many young people have of citizenship: How can civic agency be maintained among large percentages of citizens who choose not to exercise the rights and responsibilities of citizenship?

This question is confounded by a corresponding problem: the delivery of citizenship education curricula in many public schools in the United States. Incongruities exist in the alignment of the curriculum, teaching methodology, and the creation of classroom and school climates that are conducive to democratic practices. These incongruities may explain why many students in the United States appear to have a limited knowledge base when it comes to understanding concepts related to citizenship. For example, knowledge of civic content as measured by the 2000 National Assessment of Educational Progress (NAEP) suggest that three fourths of 4th, 8th and 12th graders scored below the proficiency level, 35% of high school seniors tested below basic level and 39% were at the basic level (Galston, 2003). In a study of high school students' enrolment in government classes, Niemi and Smith (2001) found that only 50% of high school seniors took a year course in American government, only about 2% of graduating seniors took an Advanced Placement (AP) course in American government, and that the content of government classes placed little emphasis on developing citizenship skills, analysing contemporary political activities or the processes associated with political systems.

Further, observations of 135 social studies classrooms in Chicago (Kahne, Rodriquez, Smith & Thiede, 2000) found only 12% of the classrooms engaged students in higher order thinking activities for substantial portions of the class period; less than 8% of the classrooms developed deep disciplined inquiry; less than 8% of the classrooms provided opportunities for students to engage in democratic practices; and only 1.5% of the classrooms engaged students in a consideration of the complex issues regarding living in a diverse society.

Finally, according to findings from the recent Second IEA Civic Education study, nearly 90% of the students in the United States identified reading textbooks, completing worksheets and other types of rote learning activities as the most common instructional methods for studying civic-related topics (Torney-Purta, 2002).

Historian David Tyack (2003) points out that in "periods of sharp demographic change, or war, or ethno-religious conflict, or economic challenge" the principles associated with civic education become increasingly acute and Americans become "especially self-conscious about the civic values that schools should teach" (p.12). The United States is currently confronting a variety of political, sociocultural and economic challenges that are testing the adaptability and sustainability of democracy: A polarised electorate sharply divided over nearly all aspects of public policy; dramatic demographic shifts in age, race and regional identity; a perpetual postmodern war on terrorism which has led to an assault on civil liberties in the name of national security; a war in Iraq started under false pretences; and an alarming gap that has emerged between the rich and the poor. Creating a national commitment to the development and implementation of effective citizenship education curricula throughout the United States is of critical importance if we are to reinvigorate civil society in these times of political, social and economic uncertainty.

Implementing Citizenship Education: Enduring Tensions

A variety of challenges exist in the United States regarding the creation of an acceptable curricular framework for civic education and its implementation in schools. Ideology, standardised testing, developing coherent curriculum standards and the traditional school structure have all contributed to tension in developing and delivering the citizenship education curriculum.

Ideology and Educational Reform

A raging ideological debate has emerged in American society pitting those who promote the progressive and constructionist traditions of John Dewey, with its student-centred, pragmatic and reality-based curriculum, against those who wish to return to a more factually-based, teacher-centred approach that measures academic success through standardised high-stakes tests. Educational policy creation has now become a battleground with ideological principles becoming more influential than sound empirical research (Apple, 1996; Aronowitz & Giroux, 1985; Spies, 2004).

Ideological tensions have been exacerbated by massive Federal intrusion in elementary and secondary education through the *No Child Left Behind Act of 2001* (NCLB, 2002) that has forced school districts throughout the United States to rewrite curriculum in the hopes of aligning it with externally mandated high-stakes tests. Critics of NCLB claim it has opened the door for a national curriculum, destroying traditional local control of educational decision-making (Kohn, 2004). Proponents contend that it is simply making schools and the teachers in them more accountable (Finn, 2004).

The prospect that public schools will continue to experience eroding public support due to the failure of many schools meeting the Adequate Yearly Progress (AYP) guidelines of NCLB offers a scenario in which privatisation through various school choice options will become a more prominent alternative for many parents who will choose private schools over a perceived failing public system. This scenario has serious implications for citizenship education. For example, an increasingly privatised school system destroys the historic mandate of public schools as an arena of political socialisation that transcends class, race, ethnicity, gender and religious affiliation. As Paterson (2000) has found, sectarian schools, especially religious schools, often use textbooks that are highly ideological in nature, and label various groups and individuals in American society in religious and political terms. Seen in this light, privatisation has the potential to erode an essential purpose of citizenship education: to inculcate a shared commitment to citizenship among students from diverse backgrounds. Rather than promoting national unity, increasing privatisation may have a "Balkanizing" effect on American society.

Testing and Citizenship

Mastery of factual knowledge in order to pass externally mandated standardised tests has become the end-all of educational reform under the current Bush administration. The econometrics of testing has taken precedence over critical inquiry and civic deliberation. In the final Presidential debate leading up to the 2004 election, George W. Bush referred to NCLB as a "work program." Likewise, in an October 2004 article in *Phi Delta Kappan*, Bush (2004) emphasised the economic prerogatives of NCLB when he stated in his "Presidential Statement" the debate about education reform "is about jobs, opportunities, economic and national security, and the prosperity of our families" (p.121). Bush devoted only one sentence in his "Statement" to citizenship.

Because of the AYP provisions of NCLB, reading and mathematics assessments are mandatory in all states, while it has been recommended that the assessment of 12th grade civics be placed below the "highly desirable" subjects of writing and science in future NAEP tests. NAEP assessments are now focused on 12th grade readiness for college, training for employment, and entrance into the military (National Commission on NAEP 12th Grade Assessment and Reporting, 2004), while civic education is given short shrift. The historic mandate of the public school to prepare students for their role as citizens in a democratic society has been completely overshadowed by the demands of test preparation in reading and mathematics. Narrow economic goals have triumphed over educating for citizenship.

Moreover, federally mandated tests have created a Darwinian struggle over what subjects will enhance American economic competitiveness in the 21st century. The result of this struggle has been a significant narrowing of the curriculum in which subjects like art, music, civics and geography are viewed as superfluous to increasing student test scores (Bartlett & von Zastrow, 2004). Social studies instruction, although seen as valuable for students after September 11th, is increasingly being cut out of the core curriculum, particularly in elementary classrooms throughout the United States (ibid.).

Can Coherent Standards be Created?

Quigley (2003) has argued that "one of the major reasons why civics is not taught adequately is that most of our states and school districts do not have sufficient requirements for instruction in civics and government" (p.3). Tolo (1999) concurs, stressing that no coherent approach has been taken by state departments of education and local school districts to implement a serious and continuous K-12 curricular approach to civics instruction in the schools. Instead, Tolo notes, there is an assumption that students will acquire civic content knowledge and the necessary dispositions of citizenship through the existing curriculum, the general process of attending school, or through community-based organisations. Tolo presents a broad agenda to solve the coherency problem.

> What is needed in each state are explicit, comprehensive, and complementary state civic education policies that provide the foundation for effective civic education for all students throughout the K-12 grades; that are communicated to and understood by district and school administrators and teachers, as well as by the general public; that foster greater attention to civic education practices, curricula, and course content at the district and school level; and that effectively involve enthusiastic and knowledgeable teachers. (p.220)

To effectively implement coherent standards, quality education of teachers is crucial. Currently, many pre-service teachers have little preparation to teach courses in civics and government as the focus continues to be upon history; this must change. Quigley (2000) estimates that less than 15% of in-service social studies teachers in the United States have adequate preparation to provide effective civics and government instruction. One approach to address these shortcomings would be to develop a required course of all pre-service social studies education majors in civic pedagogy.

Constraints of the Traditional School Structure

Generally, citizenship education curricula do not transcend the school building. Most schools in the United States still adhere to a rigid, segmented structure in which control is valued over flexibility. However, effective education for citizenship requires participatory citizens. Kahne and Westheimer (2003) state that, "academic study does not guarantee our humanity, and it will not sustain our democracy. If we care about educating democratic citizens, we must enlarge and enrich both our educational priorities and our practices (p.64)." Thus, there is a significant need for a structure that can accommodate the community becoming an extension of the school and an arena for experimentation and application of curricular outcomes. Students need to be allowed the capacity to study community-related problems, and then immerse themselves in that community in the search for solutions to those problems. The school must be viewed as part of this community to be studied.

Exposure to an effective civic education curriculum is related to socioeconomic levels (Torney-Purta, 2002). Students who live in low-income communities are *less* likely to discuss relevant social or political issues in their local neighbourhoods and communities. They often do not have teachers who have adequate training in teaching content related to civic education. As a result, students from communities with high concentrations of poverty are increasingly marginalised; they are not being exposed to a curriculum that will prepare them to engage in political action whereby they can address the economic and political inequities they face as citizens. Ironically, Putnam (2001) notes that revitalising American community life may in turn revitalise American schools. Until students in poor neighbourhoods are taught effective citizenship skills, this revitalisation is unlikely to occur.

Citizenship Education: A Curricular Framework for the 21st Century

It is clear that in the United States a new curricular framework must be introduced in the teaching of citizenship, a framework that establishes enhanced relevance between civic agency and the daily experiences of students. When identifying the constructs of citizenship education two questions arise that present serious curricular challenges reflecting the complexity and ephemeral nature of life in the 21st century. What specific parameters exist in developing a suitable and adaptable curricular approach that affirms the expansive nature of life in the Information Age? What constitutes the appropriate content that does justice to the complexity of citizens' rights and responsibilities in an interdependent global society?

One primary goal of citizenship education in the United States is to create "informed, responsible participation in political life by competent citizens committed to the fundamental values and principles of American constitutional democracy" (Quigley, 2003, p.2). In an interdependent global age students must also become cognisant of citizenship applied on a planetary basis. According to Barber (2003),

> Citizenship has always been attached to activities and attitudes associated with the neighbourhood: this means that imagining what global citizenship actually entails is a daunting task. Still, it is absolutely necessary, because while participation is local, power is global: unless local citizens can become globally engaged, the true levers of power will remain beyond their grasp. (p.205)

Theorists have suggested American students be taught "multidimensional citizenship"; the personal, social, spatial and temporal attitudes, behaviours and skills necessary for citizens to adapt and confront significant global issues of the 21st century across national borders (Cogan & Derricott, 1998, 2000; Parker, Ninomiya & Cogan, 1999). Likewise, Banks (2002) has called for a new conception of citizenship education that takes into account increasing global immigration and the rise of racism and discrimination occurring throughout the world. Scott (2004) contends that an essential aspect of 21st century citizenship involves students developing personal responses to the impact of American foreign policy and its impact on other countries.

As Deborah Meier (2002) has noted, schools play an important role in instilling "democratic habits" among students. Citizenship education in the United States must once again focus on the specific types of skills students can employ as participants in the democratic process. Patrick (1997) observes that "civic skills" include both cognitive capacities, such as understanding, explaining, comparing and evaluating governmental processes and the requirements of citizenship, as well as participatory skills that include citizen action in political decision making. Some of the participatory skills that relate to effective citizenship include working in groups, speaking in public, developing coalitions, and engaging in protest or writing petitions to foster change (Kahne & Westheimer, 2003), the development of listening skills (Battistoni, 1997), cross-cultural literacy skills (Banks, 2002), the ability to compromise (Ehrlich, 1999), critical thinking and co-operative learning or work skills (Cogan & Derricott, 1998, 2000), and collective deliberation, setting agendas, conducting meetings, collecting and analysing data (Scott, 2004).

The analysis, evaluation and assessment of information in traditional print form, as well as electronic sources such as the Internet are increasingly associated with citizenship education in the United States. Students are being taught to identify and expose sources of misinformation, information that has been purposely circulated to deceive or misrepresent political positions, ideas or policy statements. Roszak (1994) suggests that students must become aware of the power of computer technology to potentially "concentrate and control information" (p.205), thus subverting true democratic discourse. In addition, skills such as collective problem solving, scenario building and evaluating the implications of decisions that affect various groups locally, nationally and globally must be seen as critical to understanding participatory democracy.

To accomplish the stated expectations of civic education standards such as those created by the NCSS and the Centre for Civic Education, the curriculum must emphasise the use of primary and secondary sources and have students engage in lively discussion about current political issues in the United States and the world that are crucial to citizenship in the United States. Hahn (1999) observed that, "when the school curriculum includes political education, students tend to be more interested in public affairs" (p.246). As a means of enhancing this "political education" we propose expanding the civic education curriculum so that it includes the study of historical and contemporary figures who have demonstrated the normative dispositions of citizenship, acted upon them, and expanded and strengthened democracy through their agency.

Neil Postman (1995) sees the story of the United States "as a great experiment and as a canter of continuous argument" (p.132). An examination of marginalised groups that engaged in continuous struggle to acquire the constitutional rights associated with citizenship must become an integral part of any study of the foundations of American democracy. In the story of marginalised groups, students examine the expansion of democracy and how certain individuals helped mobilise disenfranchised groups toward having their political, economic, cultural and gender rights recognised. Howard Zinn's

(1990) perspective on social movements is worth noting here as teachers construct curriculum for citizenship education:

> As a result of omitting, or downplaying, the importance of social movements in our history—the actions of abolitionists, labour leaders, radicals, feminists, and pacifists—a fundamental principle of democracy is undermined: the principle that it is the citizenry, rather than the government, that is the ultimate source of power and the locomotive that pulls the train of government in the direction of equality and justice. (p.62)

Thus, slave narratives, such as Frederick Douglass' (1967) *Narrative Of The Life Of Frederick Douglass*, the abolitionist William Lloyd Garrison's *Prospectus For the Liberator* and Abraham Lincoln's *The Gettysburg Address* (Ravitch, 1990), help students understand the nature of slavery, its affect on the human spirit, and the resultant civil discontent it created that eventually split the nation. Chief Seattle's impassioned plea to the United States government for the recognition of Native American's cultural rights and just treatment in their relocation to the reservation system (see Safire, 1992), the *Seneca Falls Declaration* (Ravitch, 1990) outlining the pursuit of human rights based on gender, and the *Selected Writings of Alice Paul* (Jenkins McElroy, 1997) provide students with models of individual strength and courage in the face of oppression. Samuel Gompers's *What Does the Working Man Want?* and Eugene Debs's *Statement to the Court* (Ravitch, 1990) illustrate the struggle to achieve economic justice and chronicle the long fight by workers to end oppressive working conditions throughout the United States. Justice John Marshall Harlan's critique (Harrison & Gilbert, 1994) of the Plessy versus Ferguson Supreme Court decision, which legalised racial segregation in the United States, examines the poignant voice of dissent in democracy, suggesting the application of justice should not be bound by race.

Martin Luther King's *I Have A Dream* (Loque, 1997) speech recognised the need for vision to enable society to achieve social and economic justice, while his *Letter from Birmingham Jail* (Carson, 1998) not only provided the moral imperative to resist and disobey laws that perpetuated injustice, it laid out an organisational methodology for engaging in nonviolent, civil disobedience.

The interdependent nature of life in the 21st century requires that citizenship education instils global awareness among citizens in the United States. As Patrick (2003) states: "By teaching democracy comparatively, we direct the attention of students to alternatives and the consequences of making particular decisions. And we enable students to understand the common or generic political and civic choices confronted by people across the cultures and civilisations of the world" (p.8).

There exist a variety of curricular approaches to convey the cross-cultural dimensions of democracy and its relationship to citizenship on a global basis. For example, Mahatma Gandhi's (1958) concept of *swaraj*, a vedic word that refers to self-rule and self-restraint, played an important role in India's anticolonial movement against Britain.

Gandhi believed that, "civil disobedience is the inherent right of a citizen" and to try to crush it by force was an "attempt to imprison conscience" (p.138).

Speeches by the former President of the Czech Republic Vaclav Havel, who helped mobilise the Czech citizenry against de facto Soviet rule in Czechoslovakia, have significant application to the study of global democracy and citizenship. In one of his speeches Havel calls for the "creation of a new model of coexistence among various cultures, peoples, races and religious spheres within a single interconnected civilisation" (*Vital Speeches of the Day*, 1994, July).

Likewise an example of mass mobilisation against oppression and the struggle for democracy can be found in the works of Nelson Mandela. Mandela emphasises a new reality for South Africa, one that will build "peace, prosperity, nonsexism, nonracialism, and democracy" (*Vital Speeches of the Day*, 1994, May).

The writings of Aung San Suu Kyi (1999), illustrate the global appeal of democracy in the face of oppression. In her address on the 9th anniversary of the Burmese general elections in which her party, the National League for Democracy, was denied its rightful place as the ruling party by the Burmese military junta, Aung discusses the importance of political parties to the democratic process and argues that participation in elections is an affirmation of a voter's belief in democracy.

The individuals we have profiled led movements to expand democratic ideals and enhanced the collective imagination with regard to the realisation of democratic systems throughout the world. Their historical experiences demonstrate that individuals do have the power to change society and proves to students that democracy is a system of continuous experimentation and refinement. Indeed, it is the responsibility of *every* citizen in a democracy, ordinary or extraordinary, to work for these same ideals and practices.

Conclusion

As the title of this chapter notes, educating for citizenship in the United States at present is a story of tensions in curriculum policies and practices that are mirror images of the tensions that exist in the society at large in the early 21st century. The United States is more divided today than at any time in our history since the American Civil War; even more so than in the Vietnam War era in the late 1960s and early 1970s. The events of 11th September 2001 are often cited in contemporary media as the genesis of this great divide. However, we believe that the nation has been moving in this direction for most of the last half century. It is first and foremost a clash of views since the Vietnam War era about what it means to be a "citizen" in the United States. 9/11 crystallised this tension with two polar views about what constitutes a "patriot", i.e., citizen. One view is that you defend and support the actions of your nation without question; the other perspective is that in a democracy it is one's responsibility to ask questions, critique policies and decisions taken by politicians, and debate critical issues facing society in order to clarify views, impact governance and improve the society.

The invasion of Iraq in early 2003 only served to harden these positions. It is our view that, in part, these tensions will be played out in social studies courses, including civics and government. Current civics curricula, textbooks and other instructional materials available to school districts and teachers across the land also reflect the polarised points of view we outlined above. American schools are likely to be at the centre of this controversy for some time and how they respond may well dictate the future direction of the entire society.

United States Senator Paul Wellstone of Minnesota, now deceased, commented often about what it meant to be a politician. We use his words to conclude this chapter because we believe they apply equally well to citizens and emphasise the enormous challenge facing the U.S. public schools and teachers in them as outlined above.

> Politics is not about left, right, or centre. It is about speaking to the concerns and circumstances of people's lives. (2001, p.29)

If schools, through their civic education curricula, could instil this belief in young citizens in their classrooms, the nation and the world would be a much better place.

11

More Civics, Less Democracy: Competing Discourses for Citizenship Education in Australia

Kerry J. KENNEDY

Introduction

It has been common in the last decade to read about the "renaissance" in civics and citizenship education in Australia (Print, 1997). This is an allusion to a deliberate revival of civics and citizenship education that has had bilateral support from the major political parties and at all levels of government. Yet if "renaissance" refers to "a revival of learning and culture," then such a claim for civics and citizenship education in Australia has been somewhat premature. Australian politics in the 1990s was subject to successive waves of disparate ideological influences, and these influences fundamentally altered the contexts in which the revival of civics took place. What may have started as a "renaissance" was short-lived, thus emphasising the importance of understanding how different contexts in Australia have shaped an emerging civics and citizenship education.

In the early 1990s, under the influence of a young Labor Prime Minister, Paul Keating, Australia appeared to be embracing the need to become an independent republic, sought engagement with Asia, acknowledged the need for reconciliation with indigenous people and in general sought a new role for itself in the global community (Kennedy & Howard, 2004). Yet the excitement created by this "big picture" politics was short-lived. In 1996 Paul Keating's government was replaced by a conservative coalition under John Howard. His government looked back to the 1950s to derive images of Australia that were safe and secure, while also making a concerted effort to place much greater reliance on Australia's British and European heritage.

The revival of civics and citizenship education may have been conceived in a renaissance-like environment created by the second Keating government, but it was delivered in an environment more akin to that of the "dark ages" where the future was created by looking backwards. Yet, in retrospect, this kind of conservatism may seem benign and even welcome. The events of September 11, 2001, in New York and October 12, 2002, in Bali ushered in a new and more destructive kind of conservatism that has sought systematically to undermine the very institutions of democracy that even traditional conservatives have come to value. The Australian story in the new century became one of escalating involvement in international conflicts. Australia has been engaged in two wars (Afghanistan and Iraq) and several United Nations (UN) peace keeping operations (East Timor and Solomon Islands). What is more, there has been the vexed and shameful issue of the imprisonment of refugees seeking asylum in the country. Australia's official civic discourse post-September 11, 2001, is more akin to what some writers have referred to as neo-conservatism—not just a longing to return to the past and its assumed safety, but an active opposition to universal human rights and the kind of freedoms we have come to associate with liberal democracy. Neo-conservatism, or at least its Australian equivalent, has fundamentally changed the Australian political and social landscape and this landscape was inherited by the newly elected Rudd Labor government in November 2007.

There may well be more civics and citizenship in Australian schools than there was in the early 1990s. Yet this has not created a renaissance! The key issues are the ends to which civics and citizenship education have been directed and its effectiveness in combating new and destructive forces in the Australian polity. These are the issues to be addressed in this chapter, for they are issues about the nature and function of Australian democracy in the 21st century and civic and citizenship's support for it.

The purposes of this chapter, therefore, are to:

- investigate the nature of the changes in the Australian social and political landscape, since they have significant implications for programmes of civics and citizenship education;
- assess the extent to which these changes are reflected in civics and citizenship programmes in Australia; and
- suggest ways in which civics and citizenship can contribute to the education of an intelligent citizenry in these troubling and uncertain times.

Australia's Changing Social and Political Landscape: Contexts for Civics and Citizenship Education

The so called "civics renaissance" initiated under Paul Keating was abruptly brought to a halt once the Howard government came to power (Kennedy & Howard, 2004). It took just over a year before the Howard government's version of civics was announced. The Hon. David Kemp, Minister for Employment, Education and Training, used the opening of the Curriculum Corporation's Annual Conference to make the public announcement (Kemp, 1997). Unlike the previous version, this one was not preceded by any consultation with educators or the community although it did seek to retain a bipartisan approach and it did retain a commitment to a similar level of funding. Yet it most definitely signalled a change in direction.

The only written text available for analysis is Minister Kemp's speech, subsequently turned into a Ministerial Statement (Kemp, 1997). It remains the only extant statement of the Howard government's position on civic education. The speech looked back to and valorised the development of democratic institutions in Australia consequent upon British taking possession of the land and its existing peoples. It highlighted the advances and achievements that were seen to have been made to the present time and signalled a fundamental commitment to the teaching of Australian history. It announced that the civics and citizenship education programme, to be called *Discovering Democracy*, would refocus its efforts on ensuring that young people were aware of and appreciative of the institutions of the past that have shaped present-day Australia. Knowledge of the growth of democracy in Great Britain and Europe was seen as a fundamental prerequisite for young Australians entering the 21st century.

This kind of conservatism was quite consistent with the Minister's personal and political views enunciated long before he was on the government front bench. He had an academic background as Professor of Politics at Monash University. Yet more than this, he had thought deeply about issues of Australian national identity and heritage. For Kemp, it was liberalism rather than trade unions or the Labor Party that had been responsible for Australian development since Federation and this tradition, he argued, was best expressed in the Liberal Party. He confronted Keating directly on issues such as the Australian flag, the Constitution and, perhaps most importantly, Keating's direct attack on the "British core of its (i.e., Australia's) historical achievement" (Kemp, 1994, p.56). He accused the former Prime Minister of promoting disunity at the expense of national cohesion. In the end, Kemp believed that it was the Liberal Party rather than Keating's Labor Party that could act as the party of national cohesion:

> There is a strong cultural element to Liberalism. In a broad sense Liberalism aims to develop the civic culture which underpins a democratic society and fosters the attitudes of trust, tolerance, reciprocity, fairness and restraint, on which democratic political and market institutions depend. (Kemp, 1994, p.61)

Given that Kemp was writing several years prior to the election of the Howard government his broad vision as it relates to civics and citizenship education is an important one. In the end, he saw that the task for a re-elected Liberal Party was one of "reshaping the grand vision of our founders, an equal democratic state without parallel in the world" (Kemp, 1994, p.62). He could have added that this Australian democracy, in his view at least, had been forged in the traditions of Great Britain and Europe and it was these traditions that would inform his version of the new civics.

The views expressed here by Minister Kemp were not marginal comments or mere academic preference. They soon became typical of the views being expressed by the Howard government in support of retaining Australia's status as a constitutional monarchy linked to the British throne rather than as an independent republic. The momentum on the republican issue, initiated by the second Keating government, had been too strong for the incoming government to ignore so it had little option but to support a referendum. Yet, the incoming Prime Minister, John Howard, had made his views clear: He was a staunch monarchist who did not want to sever the links to Great Britain. During the referendum, he campaigned on that position, but more importantly he had the responsibility for defining the referendum questions. He did it in such a way that it was bound to fail. He ensured that, as Australia approached the new century, its citizens would reject the questions about new forms of constitutional arrangements. The republican debate was lost at the ballot box as the majority of Australians and a large majority of the States/ Territories rejected the form of republican government that was on offer. By default, the electorate opted to maintain a constitutional monarchy, with the Queen of England as the Head of State. Conservatism triumphed and the Keating vision vanished. Australia looked backwards for its vision of the new century.

This outcome, of course, was disappointing for social progressives in Australia and especially for the Australian Labor Party that had campaigned so vigorously for a new republic. Yet this loss paled into insignificance when compared to the impact of the events of September 2001 and October 2002, the attacks on the World Trade Centre in New York and the Bali bombings. These events ushered in a new era so that the "war on terrorism" became the new mantra for politicians of all kinds. Yet it was more than a mantra—it was an indicator of a new way to conceive of democracy. It led to a new Western alliance that displaced multilateralism and the United Nations with unilatera- lism and "the coalition of the willing"; it supported pre-emptive strikes against perceived enemies and expressed no concern when it was shown that the reasons for war did not exist; and it raised national security issues to the top of the domestic political agenda. In pursuing these objectives, governments were willing to sacrifice the civil liberties of individual citizens in the name of the "war on terror." Democracy thus suffered not only from the external threat of terrorism but also from internal threats posed by a democratic government seeking to respond to terrorism.

Following September 11, 2001, the Howard government presented twenty-four pieces of legislation aimed at the "war on terrorism" (Attorney General's Department, 2004). A number of legal commentators highlighted the extent to which aspects of this legislation have sought to limit the civil liberties of individual Australians (Hocking, 2003, 2004; Michaelsen, 2003; Williams, 2003, 2004; Zaman, 2003). Speaking of the *Australian Security Intelligence Organisation Legislation Amendment (Terrorism) Act 2003*, Zaman (2003, p.41) commented that "it is a harsh piece of legislation. It clearly constitutes a drastic aberration from inalienable civil libertarian tenets that have formed the bedrock of Australian laws dealing with security and public order." The passing of the *Security Legislation Amendment (Terrorism) Act 2002* led one newspaper columnist, Margot Kingston, to comment:

> It's the climate of fear since September 11 that's letting the government do this to us, but it's running the mood for all it's worth to get itself incredible, unaccountable power which in the wrong hands could virtually destroy our democracy. (Kingston, 2002)

and:

> Is it really about changing the law to help it stamp out terrorism, or is it in part using the present climate of fear as a cover for a massive extension of its powers to con-

trol citizen's political freedoms? (Kingston, 2002)

At times, the Senate, Australia's upper house of parliament, prevented even more draconian forms of legislation from being passed. Yet, after the re-election of the fourth Howard Government in late 2004 when for the first time in many years the government controlled both houses of parliament, the Attorney General was reported to be "prepared to reintroduce controversial powers blocked by the Senate that include powers to detain and strip-search children as young as 12, if they are needed" (Walker, 2004). The continuation of this antiliberal stance remained a feature of Australia's political landscape at least until the end of 2007 when a new Labor government was elected.

While it is possible to link this antiliberalism directly to post-September 11, 2001, it is also important to see it as part of a broader political agenda, with its roots in the United States, that has come to be called neo-conservatism (Blecher, 2003; Drury, 2003; Gleason, 2003). The "war on terror" provided neo-conservatives in the U.S. with the opportunity to pursue an imperial foreign policy and a domestic policy characterised by "no gay rights, no liberated women, no uppity blacks, lots of prayer in the schools, a strong commitment to the death penalty, and the re-criminalisation of abortion" (Drury, 2003). An Australian academic commented that "it is not clear that Australians would generally embrace the neo-conservatism and Christian fundamentalism which permeates the Bush Administration—even if John Howard, Peter Costello and Michael Jeffery do" (Burchill, 2003).

Despite this assertion, the jury is still out on whether the American brand of neo-conservatism that appears to drive the Bush administration was also apparent in the Howard government. Jay (2004) argued that it was, both domestically and internationally, but Hywood (2003) and Norton (2003) argue against. What is clear, however, is that the "revolt against liberalism" that Gleason (2003) claims characterised American neo-conservatism, was also characteristic of the Howard government. It was most obvious in the "war on terror" response, but was also apparent in the government's attitudes to refugees, and in particular mandatory detention policies, the inability to apologise to indigenous Australians for the "stolen generation," and the proposal to seek constitutional reform in order to prevent gay marriages. Such anti-liberalism was obvious, too, in the phenomenon of Pauline Hanson[i] who continued to contest even the 2007 election on an anti-immigration policy. The electoral appeal of anti-liberalism worked initially for her and it subsequently worked for the Howard government. On its own, anti-liberalism may not be full-blown neo-conservatism. Yet once it was linked to an aggressive foreign policy and unquestioning obedience to U.S. triumphalism, it became a new kind of conservatism not previously seen in Australia. It was the most significant influence on Australian politics during the first decade of the new century and it remains to be seen how it will be ameliorated by the new Rudd Labor government. What is known, however, is that civics and citizenship education became embedded in the school curriculum during these years. Yet to what extent did it confront the issues referred to above? This question will be addressed in the following section.

More Civics – The Formal Curriculum

Australia's *National Goals for Schooling* made it clear that the development of citizens was a key educational objective. Students are expected to:

> ... be active and informed citizens with an understanding and appreciation of Australia's system of government and civic life. (goal 1.4) ... have the capacity to exercise judgement and responsibility in matters of morality, ethics and social justice, and the capacity to make sense of their world, to think about how things got to be the way they are, to make rational and informed decisions about their lives and to accept responsibility for their own actions. (goal 1.3) (Ministerial Council on Education, Employment, Training and Youth Affairs, 1999)

Yet the constitutional responsibility for such education does not rest with a single educational authority[ii] but rather with eight separate authorities in the Australian States/ Territories. In addition, the Federal government, while having no constitutional authority in the area of education, nevertheless seeks to influence policy and directions through its financial powers. It did this in the area of civics and citizenship education from 1997-2004 by providing $32 million to support a curriculum resources and professional development programme called *Discovering Democracy*. Yet to be successful the Federal government must also have the support of subnational governments. Such support has not always come easily for centrally determined initiatives in education but in the case of civics and citizenship education there has been unanimous support at State/Territory levels.

In New South Wales, for example, when the Minister for Education and Training introduced the second reading of the *Education Reform Further Amendment Bill 1997*, he referred to a programme of state-wide testing in, among other things, Australian history, geography and civics. The purpose of this testing programme was "to ensure that the study of Australian social and political institutions forms part of the experience of every school student" (Aquilina, 1997, p.4). The Minister went on to say that:

> The government sees much of this knowledge and understanding being achieved in the context of learning about Australian Geography and History. We do not envisage Civics as an additional subject within the curriculum. Placing the external examinations at the end of Year 10 will help to ensure these subjects are treated more seriously. (Aquilina, 1997, p.4)

In another state, Victoria, civics and citizenship education was made a curriculum priority in the *Curriculum Standards Framework (CSF 11)*[iii]:

> The CSF aims to help students to become active and informed citizens. This requires them to develop understanding about key elements of Australia's legal, economic and political systems. It requires an understanding of the history of the

country and its people. It requires an understanding of the values that the community shares and an awareness of the rights and responsibilities of citizens. (Victorian Curriculum and Assessment Authority, 2002)

The Victorian CSF identified the Key Learning Area (KLA) of Studies of Society and Environment as the natural home for civics and citizenship, although the point is made that "opportunities to explore elements of the attitudes and values associated with developing active citizenship occur across key learning areas" (Victorian Curriculum and Assessment Authority, 2002).

This kind of support for civics and citizenship education has been translated into syllabus design in all States and Territories. The design framework, however, is not always the same. In New South Wales, for example, the focus is on single academic disciplines rather than an integrated area of study as in the case of Victoria above:

Civics and Citizenship is integrated in the History and Geography syllabuses to ensure that all students develop the knowledge, understanding, skills, values and attitudes necessary for personal competence and responsible participation in Australian society. Aspects of Civics and Citizenship flow from the study of key features of Australia's physical and human geography, and the study of Australia's political, social and cultural history. (Board of Studies NSW, 2001)

In Queensland, as in most other States/Territories, civics and citizenship is integrated into the strands of the Key Learning Area (KLA), Studies of Society and the Environment:

Civics as a field of study within the Studies of Society and Environment key learning area relates strongly to the Culture and Identity strand and the Systems, Resources and Power strand. Culture and Identity covers the dynamic nature of contemporary societies. It includes the primacy of culture and the construction of various identities and provides ways by which these are understood. The Systems, Resources and Power strand complements this by providing opportunities for studying what has been the traditional focus of Civics and citizenship education, namely public institutions, economic, legal and governmental systems, the use of public power and the values of justice, sustainability and social cohesion inherent in these concepts. The origins of many contemporary practices and ideas associated with Civics and citizenship education are covered within the Time, Continuity and Change strand. In the Place and Space strand, Civics education emphasises the importance of location and spatial relationships in the structure and functions of society including public policy, environmental issues and the processes of social, natural and built environments. (Queensland School Curriculum Council, 2000, p.52)

There will always be debates about disciplines versus integrated approaches to social education and how civics and citizenship can best be related to whatever approach is adopted. What seems clear is that there is an equal commitment to civics and citizenship irrespective of the curriculum design model that is used. A more important question now seems to be that, given the presence of civics and citizenship education in the formal curriculum, to what extent is it capable of addressing the new conservatism and geo-political realities referred to in the previous section?

To answer this question, the following section will examine the nature of civics and citizenship in Australian schools, the national assessment of students' civics and citizenship understandings, including the implications for future curriculum provision, and how these issues might contribute to the real world needs of students confronted by an uncertain and at times horrifying political landscape.

The Formal Curriculum in Practice—Constructing Civics and Citizenship Education in Schools

It is clear that there is more civics and citizenship education in the formal curriculum in Australian schools than there was a decade ago. Yet it is not clear exactly what form this curriculum takes. A recent report attempted to summarise the commonalities in the formal curriculum across States/Territories along the following lines:

- Australia's democratic heritage and the current operation of the Australian system of government and law
- Australian national identity as it has changed over time and now encompasses cultural diversity and social cohesion
- The skills and values necessary for informed and active participation in civic life (Ministerial Council on Education, Employment, Training and Youth Affairs, 2003)

This summary of common themes masks a tension that the report itself refers to as the "debate about the extent to which the content and pedagogy of civics and citizenship education should be informed by historical awareness, and the extent to which it should foster the development of participatory skills and values" (Ministerial Council on Education, Employment, Training and Youth Affairs, 2003). Yet it appears that this is no longer a debate. The national assessment of civics and citizenship included two assessment domains: "Knowledge & Understanding of Civic Institutions & Processes" and "Citizenship: Dispositions & Skills for Participation." These two domains were equated with "civics" and "citizenship" education respectively, the former based on "civic knowledge" and the latter being largely "dispositional" (attitudes, values dispositions and skills). Mellor (2004) saw the domains as closely related:

> Without civic knowledge and a disposition to engage, a person cannot effectively practise citizenship.

The distinction between "civics" and "citizenship" is an important one to make, especially in relation to the situation in Australian schools. There is considerable evidence to suggest that Australian teachers are influenced by this distinction in quite practical ways. In the IEA Civic Education Study, for example, Australian teachers indicated that, in their schools, the greatest emphasis was placed on "student participation in community and political activities (80%), and also student independent (critical) thinking (72%)" with only 30% indicating that knowledge about society was a priority (Mellor, Kennedy & Greenwood, 2002, p.117). Yet when asked where the emphasis should lie, over 80% of teachers felt it should rest with "knowledge of society"—almost the reverse of the current situation. It follows that fewer teachers felt that "participation in the community" and "critical thinking" should be as important as they currently are. Thus, based on the IEA data at least, there seems to be a tension between civics and citizenship education for Australian teachers—too much of the latter and not enough of the former.

Other studies also support the existence of this tension, although it is not always expressed in the same way as it was in the IEA Study. Sets of case studies conducted by different teams of researchers have shown that teachers have an overwhelming preference for citizenship education (Kennedy, Jimenez, Mayer, Mellor, & Smith, 2003). When interviewed on site in their own schools, teachers tended to argue for the importance of citizenship activities rather than the teaching of civic knowledge. Teachers thought it was more relevant and more engaging for students than the dull recitation of "civic facts." In a sense, this was the argument for the status quo as indicated by the IEA Study—the dominance of citizenship rather than civics. The teaching of formal courses of civics was advocated by initiatives like the *Discovering Democracy Program* and while reports of its general usage are very encouraging (Cole, 2003; Zbar, 2004), it clearly faces an uphill battle.

There is little doubt that the *Discovering Democracy Program* has played a significant role influencing the directions of civics and citizenship education in Australian schools. It could hardly have been otherwise: The Federal government spent $32 million dollars over a seven-year period to develop curriculum materials and support teacher professional development. A summary of the scope of the curriculum materials, drawn from Kennedy (2005b, p.314), is shown in Table 11.1.

These materials are in every school in Australia—primary and secondary. The issue is: What happens to them? How do teachers use them? What does civics and citizenship education look like on the ground? This is a difficult question to answer in any comprehensive way, but one of the features of the *Discovering Democracy Program* has been the use of web-based technology to advertise and promote "best practice" in civics and citizenship education. Thus, on an official site called School Show Case, 2003, civics and citizenship education programmes from six schools in different States/Territories are featured. The theme is community participation, and the site demonstrates in a practical way how the *Discovering Democracy* materials can be used from junior primary through to secondary to assist students understand important civic concepts (e.g., "participation," "collaboration," "civic action"), to involve them in school-based and community-based projects and to provide them with a sense of agency so that they learn how to make a difference (Curriculum Corporation, 2004a). This kind of usage supports the citizenship rather than the civics side of the continuum and is consistent with what we know to be teacher preferences, but it is of some interest to note that schools are using the materials in this way.

Table 11.1 Discovering Democracy Curriculum Materials at a Glance

Themes*	Primary	Secondary		
		Units[iv]		
	Middle	*Upper*	*Lower*	*Middle*
1. Who rules?	• Stories of the People and Rulers	• Parliament versus Monarch	• Should the People Rule?	• Parties Control Parliament
2. Laws and Rights	• Rules and Laws	• The Law Rules	• Law	• Human Rights
				• Democracy Destroyed (+ Theme 1)
3. The Australian Nation	• We Remember	• The People Make a Nation	• Democratic Struggles	• Making a Nation
4. Citizens and Public Life	• Joining	• People Power	• Men and Women in Public Life	• Getting Things Done
				• What Sort of Nation
* Each theme is linked to State and Territory curriculum requirements				
* Teachers' Guides for Units and Readers				
		Australian Readers[v]		
* Videos and CD-ROMS for selected units * Posters * *A Guide to Law and Government in Australia* for teachers.	• Good Rulers and Bad Rulers • Living with Rules and Laws • We Are Australian • Lest We Forget • Good Neighbours	• Liberty, Equality, Fraternity • This is My Country • True Patriots • From Little Things Big Things Grow • Juice	• Who Should Rule • When Law Breaks Down • Stories We Tell About Ourselves	• Political People • Law and Justice • Equality and Difference

Another perspective on school-based approaches to civics and citizenship can be gained through a review of projects that were funded in the States/Territories by the *Discovery Democracy Program*. In New South Wales, for example, thirty primary school projects were featured. There were three broad characteristics of these projects. The *Discovering Democracy Materials* appear to have acted as much as resources for teacher professional development as they do as student resources. Almost without exception, schools reported that, after their projects had been completed, teachers felt much more confident about teaching civics and citizenship than they had been previously. This is an important point given teachers' lack of formal training in the area (Mellor, Kennedy, & Greenwood, 2002). Most schools were not content with conservative approaches to pedagogy and there were concerted efforts to make the content relevant by linking themes to local community and activities that would involve students in taking some kind of civic action. In all projects, efforts were made to link *Discovering Democracy Materials* to local curriculum requirements so that local standards could be met (NSW Department of Education and Training, 2000). This is an important issue if civics and citizenship is not to be sidelined as an "add on." The approach of linking local priorities to the nationally developed materials has been taken up in other jurisdictions such as Queensland (Kennedy, 2005b, p.311). His analysis of the way this has worked is shown in Table 11.2:

Table 11.2   Support Materials for Civics and Citizenship Linked to Strands and Levels of Schooling for Queensland Schools

Modules	Strand(s)	Level of Schooling
*Ready, set, go: Rights and responsibilities	Culture and Identity Systems, Resources and Power	One
*Read all about it: Participating	Culture and Identity Systems, Resources and Power Time Continuity and Change	Two
*Citizens then and now: beginnings of democracy	Culture and Identity Systems, Resources and Power	Three
*Everyone can have a say: Local decision making	Place and Space Systems, Resources and Power Time Continuity and Change	Three
*Our rights: Origins of Australian democracy	Systems, Resources and Power Time Continuity and Change	Four
*Active citizens, Australian governments: Australia's democracy	Systems, Resources and Power	Four
*The Federation of Australia: Federation	Culture and Identity Systems, Resources and Power Time Continuity and Change	Four
*Law and the media: Civics and citizenship	Culture and Identity Systems, Resources and Power Time Continuity and Change	Five
*Governments and citizens: Independent study	Culture and Identity Place and Space Systems, Resources and Power Time Continuity and Change	Six
The global citizen: Ecology and economy		Six
*Potentials of democracy: Civics and citizenship	Culture and Identity Systems, Resources and Power Time Continuity and Change	Six

*Linked to the *Discovering Democracy* resource materials.

The question with which this section of the chapter started was: Given the presence of civics and citizenship education in the formal curriculum, to what extent is it capable of addressing the new conservatism and geo-political realities referred to in the previous section? A number of points can be made:

1. Despite the activity across States/Territories, civics and citizenship is still not a core requirement for all Australian students. This is a significant drawback to ensuring that all young Australians are equipped to both understand and respond to the new realities.
2. There is a reliance on schools to make decisions about what should and should not be included in civics and citizenship education programmes. As shown in the review above, schools seem to be very much aware of making civics and citizenship education relevant to the needs of local communities and to students. This is a positive trend that can help schools take into account new issues as they emerge to affect communities.
3. The content of civics and citizenship as revealed by Tables 11.1 and 11.2 is overwhelmingly Australian. This content is embedded in State/Territory curriculum requirements, as well as in the *Discovering Democracy Materials*. This is not entirely unexpected, except that the new geo-political realities are overwhelmingly global. A key issue for the future is how to blend local, national and global content in civics and citizenship education so that students will have the broadest perspectives on existing and emerging global issues.

This review suggests that there are both positives and negatives for civics and citizenship education in Australia. There may well be more civics in Australian schools but it does not necessarily mean that new issues and realities can be confronted. Local curriculum requirements and resource materials tie schools to the past and can prevent them from dealing with the present and the future. Teachers do make adaptations to materials and they do seek to make civics relevant, and this is positive. Thus, schools do have the capacity to deal with the new realities of Australia's geo-political context, but it will take deliberate and positive efforts on their part to do so. How they might be able to do this will be addressed in the final section of the chapter.

Constructing a Future for Civics and Citizenship Education in Australia

There are two ways to addressing this issue. One is to speculate what a new Labor government might do with this area of the school curriculum and the other is to make a judgement about the possible impact of the national assessment of civics and citizenship that is now a feature of the Australian educational landscape (Ministerial Advisory Council on Education, Employment, Training and Youth Affairs. (2006). As to the first, it appears, that there is a strong inclination on the part of the Rudd government to support Howard's reliance on the teaching of History rather than integrated approaches.

What this means for civics and citizenship education remains to be seen. The issue is the content of that history and whether it is inclusive enough to encompass the widely disparate views represented in the Australian community.

There was a wealth of information about the national testing programme well before it was administered (Curriculum Corporation, 2004b) and the public discussion was more widespread and informative than is often the case with national assessments (Zbar, 2004, pp.31-36). Having defined two assessment domains referred to above (broadly, these are "Civic Knowledge" and "Civic Dispositions"), it can be expected that they must influence what happens in schools. As Suzanne Mellor, the Australian Council of Educational Research's Manager for the national assessment of project, has said:

> The domain descriptors further explicate the kinds of knowledge, understanding, dispositions and skills students are expected to demonstrate in the assessment. The descriptors were the focus of the items as they were developed and constitute "the learning outcomes being tested in the assessment." The implication is, therefore, that they ought to be the focus of CCE teaching in the school. (Zbar, 2004, p.33)

The interesting point about the domain descriptors is that for the two domains at both Year 6 and 10 (the two age cohorts tested), the focus is on Australian political institutions and practices. Only domain descriptor 10.6—"Analyse Australia's role as a nation in the global community"—provided opportunities for teachers to engage students explicitly in international issues that might impact on civic life and civic action. This is not to say that there cannot be a more general preparation for civic action as students experience the range of opportunities envisaged in the "Civic Dispositions" domain throughout primary and secondary schooling. Yet teachers will have to work hard to focus students' attention not only on local and national issues, but also on global issues. Teachers themselves will need to see this as a priority and embed it in their practice. It is not an impossible task, but it is a demanding one.

Teachers can be assisted with this task if they have access to a broader conceptualisation of civics and citizenship education than that embedded in current curriculum and assessment requirements. A recently developed framework (Kennedy, 2005b, p.301) has been elaborated further in Table 11.3. It is one attempt to expand the key domains of civics and citizenship so that education can engage with current issues and priorities and remain relevant for both students and society. It is not a static framework but one that needs to be constantly revised and updated if it is to be a continuing guide to schools and teachers.

There are many ways to modify and adapt this framework. Its purpose is to provide a broader perspective and set of understandings for schools and teachers. These are necessary if schools are to prepare students for an uncertain and challenging world where the focus is on constructing and influencing the future, both in Australia and globally. Such an approach does not exclude current perspectives that focus on Australian civic institutions and practices. Rather, the framework builds on that focus by incorporating global and personal perspectives that will enable students to look both outwards towards a world beyond Australia and inwards at how they themselves construct the world around them. These multiple perspectives have the potential to equip students better for citizenship—a citizenship that is now as much global as it is national.

Table 11.3   Framework for a Broader Approach to Civics and Citizenship Education

Rationale	Description	Implications for Civics and Citizenship Education
New *geo-political realities* highlight the uncertainty of the global environment.	Global conflicts have intensified in recent times. Even though Australia is geographically isolated, her citizens cannot help but be affected by the increasing number of violent events and activities over which they have no control.	Global perspectives must be central to civics and citizenship education. Australia's contribution to global issues such as environmental protection, peace and social justice need to be regularly assessed.
The *deficit* in *civic knowledge* can put democracy in danger.	The community in general, but young people in particular, appear to know little about the formal structures of government and the constitutional arrangements that govern Australia as a democratic society.	If citizens are to defend democracy they must understand its basic structures and functions. This "knowledge building" process can be linked to civic involvement and action to ensure its relevance.
Civic megatrends define who Australians are and have fundamental implications for the Australian social landscape.	Within Australia issues such as multiculturalism, reconciliation with indigenous Australians, the role of women in Australian society, the constitutional debate concerning an Australian republic and contentious immigration issues related to refugees and so-called "illegal immigrants" have had serious social and political implications for all Australians. These issues have the potential to redefine Australian society, and not always in a positive way.	Civics and citizenship education must deal with those issues that are fundamental to defining Australian values, even when these issues are controversial. Some such issues may have an historical link but others will emerge as a result of government actions. In both cases students need to be aware of them and know what actions, if any, may need to be taken to defend Australian values.
Civic realities construct the world of young people – realities that may be hidden from parents and teachers.	The prevalence of youth cultures has been well-documented. These might be represented by rave parties, moshing, the availability of hard drugs and alcohol, homelessness, alienation, lack of employment opportunities or a general feeling of being "different." The fact is that young people inhabit a world that is as much structured by their own values and mores as those of their parents or the community.	If students are to develop as citizens then the starting point must be their own values. Students' own hopes, dreams and commitments have the potential to help or hinder them in their journeys to citizenship. They cannot be ignored in civics and citizenship education.

Conclusion

Australia can no longer remain isolated—a European outpost with an Asian geography. Future citizens must know themselves and others as well; they must know how and when to take civic action; and they must know how the institutions of democracy can help them in these tasks. Considerable progress has been made with civics and citizenship education in Australia over the past decade and many teachers have taken advantage of the government support that has been available. It is now time for teachers to look beyond that support to the development of sustainable and relevant programmes that will meet new needs and priorities. This is a great challenge for teachers, who are now in a better position to meet it than they were a decade ago. Their success in doing so may well determine the way future citizens both respond to and influence the world around them. There can be no more important curriculum priority for Australian schools in the years ahead.

Notes

[i] Pauline Hanson was an Independent member of the Australian Federal Parliament elected on an ultra-conservative platform that appeared to support racism and xenophobia.

[ii] Under the Australian Constitution the responsibilities of the central government are clearly set out and all other residual responsibilities, of which education is one, reside with the States/Territories.

[iii] Since this was written civics and citizenship has been designated a domain in the Physical, Personal and Social Learning strand of the Victorian P-10 Curriculum and Standards (Victorian Curriculum and Assessment Authority, 2006).

[iv] Online versions of these units can be found at http://www.curriculum.edu.au/democracy/ddunits/units.htm

[v] "*The Australian Readers* are collections of factual and fictional, historical and contemporary texts that deal with civic and citizenship themes" (Curriculum Corporation, 1999, *To the Teacher*).

12

"Creative and Innovative Citizenry": Exploring the Past, Present and Future of Citizenship Education in New Zealand

Carol MUTCH

Introduction

The reform of educational administration and the revision of the compulsory schooling curriculum in New Zealand throughout the 1980s and 1990s had many parallels with similar initiatives in other countries. Within the curriculum revisions, the tensions between the "new right," economically-driven agenda and New Zealand's liberal progressive educational traditions were very apparent. Citizenship education was used by proponents of both sides of the ideological debate as a panacea for New Zealand's social and economic ills. Although education for citizenship was to take a key position as an overarching aim in the revised national curriculum, there was little specific guidance on how to achieve this end. Unlike the majority of examples in this book, citizenship education in New Zealand did not become a compulsory curriculum area or even a content strand within other areas, but the author (Mutch, 2002, 2003) has argued that citizenship notions do underpin several key curriculum areas. More recently, the New Zealand Ministry of Education has conducted a "curriculum stocktake" and the results reveal that citizenship education has again become an area of intense interest and debate.

This chapter examines the relationship between educational policy and education for citizenship in New Zealand through three lenses—the past, the present and the future. The first section, focusing on the past, examines the political nature of the development of citizenship education in New Zealand. The next section, focusing on the present, outlines the current status of citizenship education and examines the nature of citizenship notions in New Zealand curriculum documents before describing a case study of citizenship education as implemented in one New Zealand school and enacted in one classroom within that school. The final section brings all these threads together to place citizenship education in its current context in relation to public and educational debates and raises questions about its present status and its possible future.

Themes threaded throughout the chapter include the contested and contextual nature of citizenship education, its relationship to New Zealand's search for its own unique identity, and the way citizenship education has been used as a political tool for both sides of the ideological debate. It will be argued that the foundation for sound citizenship education is already available in curriculum documents and classroom practices in New Zealand, but that any moves to make it more explicitly articulated and more actively implemented first need wide consultation and thoughtful consideration.

Definitions of Citizenship and Citizenship Education

In a report on citizenship education, Kerr (2000) defines the field of study as encompassing "the preparation of young people for their roles and responsibilities as citizens and, in particular, the role of education, (through schooling, teaching and learning) in that preparatory process." In Kerr's study, countries varied in their approaches and he lists the variety of guises under which such preparation occurs—"citizenship, civics, social sciences, social studies, world studies, society, studies of society, life skills and moral education." In the current New Zealand context, it could be argued that values, environmental and health education could be added to that list.

Gilbert (1996) views citizenship as a contested term: "Some definitions emphasise the nation state as an entity to which people should give allegiance and loyalty. Other definitions emphasise individual rights or a sense of shared loyalty. Others focus on citizen participation in government" (p.108). Gilbert outlines four major views of citizenship: (a) citizenship as a status implying formal rights and duties; (b) citizenship as an identity and a set of moral and social virtues based on the democratic ideal; (c) citizenship as a public practice conducted through legal and political processes; and (d) citizenship as participation in decision making in all aspects of life. Elsewhere the author of this chapter (Mutch, 2002, 2003) has adapted these categories as follows with the second one being separated into two to make a total of five: (i) citizenship as *status*; (ii) citizenship as *identity*; (iii) citizenship as the *democratic ideal*; (iv) citizenship as *public practice*; and (v) citizenship as *participation*. These categories are useful to bear in mind in later sections as citizenship education is explored in New Zealand's past, present and future.

The Past: The Development of Citizenship Education in New Zealand

Notions of citizenship in New Zealand have been tied to the development of the nation's identity and what it has meant to be a New Zealander. Although geographically remote, the South Pacific country of New Zealand has mirrored the debates and issues of other nations. Its formal education legacy is British and it is still a member of the British Commonwealth. A strong resurgence by its indigenous people, the Maori, has led to a stronger bicultural identity in the last few decades. Immigration in the second half of the twentieth century and changing trade and political alliances have also led to New Zealand having a more Pacific and Asian outlook.

Elsewhere the author (Mutch, 2000) has described New Zealand curriculum history as consisting of three eras, each characterised by tensions between key social and political forces of the time. The first era (pre-European contact to the early 1900s) is titled "indigenous versus colonial," the second era (1900-1070s) "traditional conservative versus liberal progressive," and the third era (1980s-the present) is "new right versus liberal left."

In the indigenous versus colonial era, the tensions were between a colonial government wishing "to bring an uninitiated but intelligent and high spirited people into line with our civilisation" (cited in Bailey, 1977, p.5) and an indigenous population who already had a "complex, efficient education system prior to the arrival of the Pakeha [European] colonisers" (Irwin, 1994, p.338).

Prior to European colonisation identity was related to ancestor, family and tribal affiliation. Physical and spiritual ties to the land were exemplified by the relationship to local geographical features. The Maori education system differed from the industrial model in Britain. It was more family and community-based, and followed a practical apprenticeship style, but the British model was quickly adopted.

In 1840, some Maori chiefs signed a treaty with representatives of the British Crown that set the parameters for the relationship between the cultures. Barr, Hunter and Keown (1999) describe this era as one of optimism:

> Maori hoped for the establishment of a "light" form of British "control" to establish order but wished to retain control over their lands and cultural treasures while at the same time gaining advantages from the trade and technology brought by European settlers. (p.1)

The first formal national curriculum was written after the *Education Act of 1877*, which had made schooling free, compulsory and secular for primary school-aged children. This curriculum gives an insight into what it meant to be a New Zealand citizen at that time. If you were a primary school-aged student, you studied English grammar and composition, reading, writing, arithmetic, science, geography, vocal music and drawing, with needlework and domestics available for girls, and history as an option (due to concerns about denominational bias). This curriculum was modelled on the schooling available in the homeland of the more recent arrivals. The Act also included the suggested syllabus for those able to go on to high school as "all the branches of a liberal education comprising Latin and Greek classics, French and other modern languages, mathematics and such other branches of science as the advancement of the colony and increase of population may from time to time require" (cited in Bailey, 1977, p.3). Education for Maori children was covered by the separate *Native Schools Act* with a more practical and vocational focus.

Citizenship ideals were taught through history, geography, civics and moral instruction. As McGee (1998) states, "The dominant themes of character training and moral content which were offered to the masses in eighteenth and nineteenth century England were brought to New Zealand by the early colonists" (p.47). Along with these moral principles was a new theme, that of loyalty to the British Empire.

Successive policies of assimilation of Maori into Pakeha culture were to follow. A society whose identity had been interwoven with the people and the land around them became fragmented and alienated. The Maori were eventually politically, economically and educationally marginalised, and by the end of the century were only 4% of the population (Simon, 1994).

The turn of the century saw the development and rise of secondary schools, again following the British model, this time in the nature of selecting students for academic or vocational courses. The school curriculum in the late 1920s included citizenship as a topic in the history curriculum. The two main ideological views of the time were those of the traditional conservatives and the liberal progressives. A traditional conservative view of what it meant to be a New Zealand citizen looked back to Britain, to a more stratified society, and was proud that New Zealand provided raw materials for her manufacturing and young men to fight for the Crown. Liberal progressives sought to establish a view of citizenship that focused on a more egalitarian society, on upholding democracy and on providing social and educational opportunities for all. The primary school curriculum was in the liberal progressive mould and was championed by the first Labour Prime Minister, Peter Fraser, and his Director General of Education, Clarence Beeby. For many years this statement (penned in the 1930s by Beeby but delivered by Fraser) was seen as the cornerstone of New Zealand education:

> The Government's objective, broadly expressed, is that every person whatever his level of academic ability, whether he be rich or poor, whether he live in town or country, has a right as a citizen, to a free education for which he is best fitted and to the fullest extent of his powers. (cited in Alcorn, 1999, p.99)

With the rise of liberal progressive ideology, ideas such as internationalism and democratic consensus were promoted. As Archer and Openshaw (1992) state:

> Alongside the strictures of the older citizenship ethic—obedience, loyalty and duty—were set the new imperatives of the liberal-progressive one—human brotherhood, international understanding, respect for other cultures. (p.22)

By 1942, secondary education was to come into line with this philosophy with a core compulsory curriculum promoted for the first two years of secondary schooling, which was to include social studies for the first time. Social studies was described as "an integrated course of history and civics, geography and some descriptive economics" (Shuker, 1992, p.36). McGee (1998) states that "rather than teaching morals it was intended that pupils, through the new subject, would learn to identify and solve social problems, and become immersed in the workings of society" (p.49).

Following the Second World War patriotic citizenship ideals were emphasised, as in the 1950s syllabus for social studies:

> Each part of the curriculum contributes to the preparation of children for life in our society; but history and geography by virtue of their content, are particularly rich in opportunities for the development of the attitudes, the abilities, and the various kinds of appreciation that are necessary in a democratic society such as ours.... Love of one's country, willingness to serve it, and faith in its future are a complex growth which should begin in the primary-school child's own emotional life. (Department of Education, 1954, p.1)

In the 1960s there was a shift from the postwar patriotic rhetoric to one with a focus on social justice and a more global view. The aim of social studies at this time was:

> ... to help children understand the world they live in and take their own place in it. In particular, social studies should help children to think clearly about social problems, to act responsibly and intelligently in social situations, and to take an intelligent and sympathetic interest in the various peoples, communities, and cultures of the world. (Department of Education, 1961, p.1)

At the end of the 1960s the New Zealand economy took a turn for the worse. "The welfare state bred new problems, inflation, and with it new inequalities and new anxieties" (Dunstall, 1981, p.398). Opposition to the Vietnam War, Maori cultural resurgence and a rising feminist movement created "a new wave of protest that brought a new hue to the social fabric" (Dunstall, 1981, p.428).

The 1970s heralded the third era in New Zealand's educational history in which calls for social justice competed with economic solutions. Trowler (1998) explains that there are two strands to new right ideology. Neo-conservative values include strong government, social authoritarianism, a disciplined society, hierarchy and subordination. Neo-liberal values focus on the individual, freedom of choice, a market society, a laissez-faire approach and minimal government intervention. The two forces within one ideological viewpoint were to lead to some contradictory decisions in educational policy at the time. The contesting ideology, dubbed by Barr (1997) as the "liberal left," has been described as "a fusion of earlier liberal progressive and more recent socially critical perspectives" (Mutch, 2005, p.194).

Nowhere were these tensions more apparent than in the curriculum reviews of the 1980s and 1990s. In 1985, a curriculum review was conducted with wide educational, academic and community consultation. It led to a proposed curriculum that departed in the main from traditional subject divisions. Instead of mathematics, science, English, social studies, physical education, and music and art, it suggested: culture and heritage; language; creative and aesthetic development; mathematics; practical abilities; living in society; science, technology and the environment; and health and well-being.

By 1991, with a change of government ideology, the Minister of Education was talking instead of a core curriculum based around English, mathematics, science, and technology. The curriculum had gone from an integrated and liberal document to one based in the neo-conservative rhetoric of the time. The final version was more centrist and was to become the formal policy document the *New Zealand Curriculum Framework* (Ministry of Education, 1993b). It was to underpin all the curriculum development that followed and education for citizenship became a key emphasis in the new framework. In the foreword, the Secretary for Education highlighted the government's view of what it meant to be a citizen of New Zealand and the world with the following statement (Ministry of Education, 1993b):

> Today, New Zealand faces many significant challenges. If we wish to progress as a nation, and to enjoy healthy prosperity in today's and tomorrow's competitive world economy, our education system must adapt to meet these challenges ... we need a workforce which is increasingly highly skilled and adaptable, and which has an international and multi-cultural perspective. (p.1)

During the 1980s and 1990s the view of a citizen as a skilled contributor to the economy was diffused through educational discourse. As the 1990s came to a close and the economic experiment was not bearing its anticipated fruit, other views of citizenship resurfaced. A change of government in 1999 also signalled a change of rhetoric as the centre-left coalition talked of "social cohesion" and "closing the gaps." These ideas could already be seen coming to the fore in the curriculum documents of the late 1990s. These documents included the curriculum documents for social studies, and health and physical education, and the guidelines for environmental education.

In summary, there has not been a single dominant view of what it means to be a New Zealand citizen, but rather competing views that might gain ascendancy at any one time due to political patronage. In the latter half of the twentieth century the focus can be seen as having shifted from one of citizenship as status and allegiance to one's nation and heritage to a broader view of one's position and participation in local, national and global affairs.

The Present: Citizenship Education in Current Curriculum Documents

As has already been stated, citizenship education in New Zealand is neither a curriculum area of its own nor an identified strand within other curriculum areas. The policy document which guided the development of the curriculum revisions, the *New Zealand Curriculum Framework*, did allude many times to citizenship ideals and even included a page on commonly recognised attitudes and values in New Zealand which were summarised as follows:

> The school curriculum, through its practices and procedures, will reinforce the commonly held values of individual and collective responsibility, which underpin New Zealand's democratic society. These values include honesty, reliability, respect for others, respect for the law, tolerance (*rangimarie*), fairness, caring or compassion (*aroha*), non-sexism, and non-racism. The school curriculum will help

students to develop and clarify their own values and beliefs, and to respect and be sensitive to the rights of individuals, families, and groups to hold attitudes and values which are different from their own. (Ministry of Education, 1993b, p.21)

Two of the curriculum documents prepared following the release of the framework strongly link to citizenship notions, especially in relation to identity, democracy and participation.

The social studies curriculum (Ministry of Education, 1997) states its main aim as follows:

Social studies education aims to enable students to participate in a changing society as informed, confident and responsible citizens. (p.8)

There are several ways in which the social studies document approaches this task. First, there are the concepts in the content strands that cover many concepts underpinning citizenship ideals. Examples of key concepts in the social organisation strand are understanding how and why groups are organised; how leadership is exercised; making and implementing laws; exercising rights and responsibilities; maintaining social justice and human rights; and the impacts of reform. The culture and heritage strand looks beyond the concepts in its title to consider interaction between groups, movement of peoples and ideas, and adapting to change. Place and environment also considers change, movement, interaction and resolving differences but within the context of the physical as well as the social environment. Time, continuity and change aims to help students to see patterns over time and to live in the future by learning from the past. Concepts other than those in the strand title include influences, causes and effects, points of view and interpretations. Resources and economic activities has students examine allocation and management of resources, participation in economic activities, the changing nature of work and the social consequences of economic change.

Second, the process strands provide the means for teaching skills in a relevant context. The inquiry process has students collecting, analysing and communicating information, and reflecting both on the "process" and the "product." It is important in the preparation for the role of citizen because it ensures that students collect relevant information on which to base their judgements and decisions. The values exploration process has students examining and clarifying their own values and those of others in relation to selected issues. The document states: When children explore values they are challenged to think about the nature of social justice, the welfare of others, acceptance of cultural diversity, and respect for the environment. The social decision making process has students take the next step and decide on appropriate courses of action, using the information and skills they have gained.

Third, the content and processes taught within any chosen topic are to reflect a range of perspectives. The importance of New Zealand's developing identity can be seen in the first three—bicultural, multicultural and gender perspectives. These ensure that teaching and learning look beyond the understandings and experiences of the dominant culture or groups. Perspectives on current issues ensure that an understanding of how and why issues have arisen locally, nationally and internationally is covered. The inclusion of perspectives on the future is a new and timely addition to social studies education. The purposes of this perspective are as follows and these are closely aligned to notions of citizenship, especially global citizenship. They are to:

> … encourage students to practise creative problem solving skills; develop in students the confidence that they can contribute to the future of their society and help shape it; examine the possible future impact of current global trends; develop understandings of how future changes in work patterns and in technology may affect society and individual people; [and] examine a range of perspectives on the future. (Ministry of Education, 1997, p.21)

Health and Physical Education in the New Zealand Curriculum (Ministry of Education, 1999b) promotes a very holistic view of identity and citizenship. Health education had previously focused on an approach where individuals had responsibility for their own health and physical well-being. Physical education had taken a very scientific approach in the secondary school teaching anatomy, exercise physiology, and bio-mechanics, while in the primary school it was very skills-based. The current approach integrates health and physical education and views them as socially constructed notions. The document states that the curriculum is underpinned by four concepts—well-being (*hauora*), health promotion, the socio-ecological perspective, and the importance of attitudes and values that promote *hauora*. The four strands expand upon these ideas and delineate the new areas of academic focus—personal health and physical development, movement concepts and motor skills, relationships with other people, and healthy communities and environments. The third and fourth strands, in particular, demonstrate key citizenship education concepts.

To summarise, it can be seen that within these two compulsory curriculum documents there are strong links to democratic values and citizenship ideals. What needs to happen next is for policy-makers, educators and the general public to be made aware that these threads already exist and only need to be more clearly articulated and more actively implemented. The next section takes up this challenge and examines how one school has interpreted the framework and various curriculum documents to implement citizenship education and how two teachers model the implied practices.

The Present: A Case Study of Citizenship Education in One New Zealand School

In writing about citizenship education in New Zealand, Barr (1998) states:

> So citizenship education in New Zealand is not based on a solid core of content. There are no generally used textbooks, and curriculum goals in citizenship are expressed in the most generic terms. There is, in fact, no formal programme of

citizenship education in New Zealand schools. If New Zealanders are good citizens it may be because they learn the knowledge, skills and values required of a good citizen outside the classroom, or it may be that factors other than information about social and political systems are more important in developing confident and informed and responsible citizens. (p.30)

The author (Mutch, 2003) undertook a qualitative case study to investigate elements of Barr's claim. The focus was on one school but used multiple sources of data and multiple methods to gather a detailed description. Excerpts from the study are detailed below.[i]

The case study school is a large state-funded urban primary school for Year 1-6 children (5-10 year-olds) set in an above average socioeconomic area but drawing students from pockets of state and council subsidised housing. It has a highly multicultural population with students representing over 30 ethnic groups.

The school's motto is "Celebrating Achievement; Celebrating Diversity" and exemplifies the vision that the principal holds for the school. She considers that each child, regardless of ability or background, should find acceptance and success in this school. Emphasis is given to children setting their own goals, taking responsibility for their own learning and behaviour, and respecting the rights of others. The school also prides itself on links with the community. Important school documents, notices and the school's weekly newsletter are translated into several languages by parent volunteers; conversation groups are held to support non-English speaking families; links with local *iwi* (Maori tribal groups) are established; and parents and community groups regularly support school outings, fundraising, sports and cultural activities.

The principal is able to show how the school sees itself as a democratic organisation modelling citizenship ideals. Notions such as "understanding and caring for others" permeated the school's documentation from the mission statement, through the strategic plan and the three-year developmental plan to the annual plan. These are expressed through goals such as "fostering good communication, rights, responsibilities and respect" which translate to specific objectives such as, "Principal will keep building staff relationships and teamwork through open door policy, visibility in school and seeking simplicity [in systems]." This is mirrored in the way the school's management structure is organised. Rather than a hierarchical system the school has a flattened management structure that is designed "to give as many people as possible the chance to take part in decision-making and develop leadership skills." Consultation is a key strategy in working democratically and one example sitting on the principal's desk is a survey about first aid procedures, which has been completed by school staff, a random selection of school families, and a group of senior students.

New Zealand school children are expected to participate in a range of school duties. At this school they issue library books, lunch orders and sports equipment, serve on the road patrol, and unpack the staff room dishwasher. They also act in more responsible roles, such as trained "peer mediators," where they help children in the playground effectively resolve disputes, or as class representatives on the student council. The student council's concerns, be they new rules for the adventure playground or more rubbish bins, are added to staff meeting agendas and treated with the same accord as staff issues.

As with all New Zealand schools, which are just emerging from years of reviews and reforms, there is a constant tension between meeting student and community needs in appropriate ways and yet meeting national curriculum, assessment and accountability requirements. This school through its open door policy, its consultation process and constant re-evaluation of procedures appears to be trying to successfully meet these expectations.

The case study classroom has 28 children at Year 6 (age range at January 2002, 9.7-10.3). (The class had been together since the beginning of the school year in late January and the research was conducted between March and May.) Excerpts from researcher field notes describe the classroom below:

> As I enter the classroom foyer I am met by a welcome sign and a series of coloured labels: "This is an inquiry classroom. Are you an independent learner? Are you excited by learning? Then this is the place for you. Your teachers are here to help you." The foyer is set out as an extension of the classroom containing posters and displays. A digital photo of every child is accompanied by a statement about what makes them a good friend. Examples of work from their rules and responsibilities unit, photos from their science trip and a written language unit, and a collage of children's personal symbols and mottoes are on display.

> On the whiteboard the teacher has outlined the objectives for the upcoming social studies unit, "During this study we will study other groups in society from the past, present and future to find out how values may differ/change because of different social organisation and beliefs."

Two teachers share the teaching of the class—Teacher A from Monday to Wednesday lunchtime and Teacher B for the rest of the week. They are released for part of each week to complete their wider school responsibilities. The teachers allowed the researcher to view relevant classroom documentation. Most instructive for this study were long-term plans, unit plans, weekly timetables and resource material. In term one, the major unit with citizenship themes was from the health curriculum. It was titled "Building positive relationships," and it included activities such as preparing and signing a set of class rules; displaying a trust collage in the foyer; being a good friend; becoming a better listener; understanding rights, rules and responsibilities; coping with criticism; and dealing with arguments. These ideas were supported in other curriculum areas, for example, trust games in physical education, cooperative writing activities in language and preparing a *mihi* (a formalised personal introduction in the Maori language).

In term two, the major unit with citizenship themes will be the social studies unit outlined on the whiteboard in the classroom description—social organisation. Within this unit the class will discuss their own society's values and then look at social organisation and values in a society in the past as a comparison and end with future scenarios.

Skills will focus on interviewing, listening to the opinions of others, determining fact and opinion, and justifying opinions.

The class attended a four-day camp during the data-gathering phase. Barr (1998) used school camps as an example of an integrated teaching and learning practice that promotes active citizenship, "almost every New Zealand primary school has an annual class camp. … Students stay in huts or dormitories and are expected to contribute to duties like preparing and cooking food or cleaning dormitories and bathrooms" (p.33).

It is also the case at this camp. The setting is several hours' drive from the city at the foot of the nearby mountains. The two teachers are supported by six parent volunteers. While the adults take ultimate responsibility, children set tables, help prepare meals, wash dishes, mop floors and clean showers. The duties are rostered to ensure all children participate in all duties. The teachers model further democratic practices by allowing children to help plan and select learning and recreational activities and to participate in a range of teacher and self-selected groups. When issues arise, the concerns are given back to the children to apply problem-solving skills or negotiate appropriate outcomes.

Informal and formal observations within the classroom and during the class camp show that the teachers try hard to "walk the talk." The ideals and values expressed in their classroom planning and displays, and reiterated in their interviews, are modelled in the ways they interact with the children, each other and other adults.

The teachers each define their own views of citizenship education:

Citizenship is when you belong to a group, country, school, culture. Citizenship education is about how you can enhance relationships … like a big family. It's about respect, values, interrelationships, how children are taught right and wrong. The ideal is paramount. (Teacher A)

It is to develop understanding and tolerance for fellow human beings to live in a world which accepts and celebrates differences yet moves forward together. (Teacher B)

Both teachers feel that the formal curriculum does not expressly outline citizenship ideals, with the exception of health and social studies. One teacher comments that it is hard not to be superficial and tokenistic when approaching such important and complex ideas. They both feel that what is most important is how individual teachers approach the curriculum and how they pick up on all the informal opportunities to reinforce these ideals. Both teachers think that showing respect for the children they teach—for them as individuals, for their cultures and beliefs—is the most important way they could enhance these ideals. From there they want to get children to feel good about themselves, to show respect and responsibility towards others and to celebrate difference "as the fabric of life."

Both teachers feel that citizenship ideals are influenced by the school and the practices it models, but more critical is an individual teacher's commitment and in-volvement. Both teachers talk of the importance of the home and the community in determining children's values and attitudes. Teacher A feels that, as schools have children for "a large part of the receptive day," they could be a "moderating influence" on inappropriate attitudes and behaviours and "provide other values from which to draw." Teacher B feels a more systemic approach is needed that strategically draws schools and communities closer together.

This case study supports Barr's (1998) claim regarding the importance of pedagogy in citizenship education, but would place the importance of pedagogical practices into a wider context. This context would include the school's vision for its students and its enacted interpretation, and the teachers' understandings of, and commitment to, citizenship ideals (even when they are not articulated as such). The importance of the school is supported, for example, by the IEA Civic Knowledge and Engagement Study (Torney-Purta, Lehmann, Oswald & Schultz, 2001) which states, "schools that model democratic values by promoting an open climate for discussing issues and inviting students to take part in shaping school life are effective in promoting both civic knowledge and engagement" (p.8).

The findings of the case study show the importance of a high degree of congruence between the school's vision, the practices and procedures in place, the teachers' stated beliefs and practices, the curriculum content selected, the pedagogical practices employed and the behaviours modelled.

What is now needed is that more schools examine their documents and practices in order to aim for a greater match between what they say and what they do.

The Future: Current Debates and Future Trends

As stated earlier, citizenship has again become a "hot topic," both in the media and in education circles. Two current issues are highlighted here and the interplay between the categories described above (citizenship as status, identity, democratic ideal, public practice and participation) can be clearly seen, as can the tension between neo-conservative and liberal democratic views.

In recent times fierce debate has raged in the media around citizenship entitlement in New Zealand. One of the issues to bring the debate to a head was a new bill, which has been proposed in an effort to tighten immigration and citizenship policies and practices, following terrorist scares and passport fraud. Currently, (under the *Citizenship Act, 1977*) the main rules to gain citizenship for non-New Zealanders are that the applicant has:

- completed a period of permanent residency for three years (or two years if married to a New Zealand citizen);
- the intention to continue to live in New Zealand;
- the ability to understand and speak English;
- knowledge of the responsibilities and privileges of New Zealand citizenship; and
- been certified to be of good character.[ii]

The *Identity (Citizenship and Travel Documents) Bill* was introduced into Parliament on June 17, 2004. It proposed to increase the residency period from three to five years, remove the provision of special treatment for spouses of New Zealand citizens and strengthen the vetting of applications.[iii] It included further measures that disclose travel arrangements and can lead to the prevention of current citizens travelling abroad. A supplementary order paper had also been discussed that reviewed the right of children born in New Zealand to automatically gain New Zealand citizenship.

The Government's reasons for the changes, as explained by the Hon. George Hawkins (Minister of Internal Affairs) were:

> The impact of September 11 and other terrorist incidents, together with increasing levels of international identity fraud, [have] highlighted international border security and travel document integrity ... New Zealanders could be proud of having one of the most secure and highly respected passports in the world. Our passport also includes visa free arrangements with 53 countries which has the effect of making it highly sought after by fraudsters and other criminals.[iv]

Comment on the bill has included:

> Are terrorists and criminals hiding in New Zealand or using its passport as cover abroad? A spate of scandals has Kiwis wondering—and worrying. The jailing of a refugee accused of terrorist ties, a citizenship ban on three New Zealand residents, passport fraud charges against two Israeli visitors and a local immigration agency, and a forgery scam that's compromised hundreds of Kiwi passports have made border security a topic nearly as talked-about as rugby. (Feizkhah, 2004, p.1)

> I fear this bill sends two clear messages. Under the citizenship provisions it says to every migrant: "We don't trust you," and so two more years will be added to your probationary period for citizenship. And in the passport provisions to every New Zealander it says: "We can deprive you of the right to travel even though you have committed no crime. ... This bill does not help us "to build together." This bill divides us. This bill places unnecessary and discriminatory hurdles in the paths of those who have made New Zealand their home by choice ... [and] introduces a dangerous anti-democratic practice into New Zealand.[v]

These debates go right to the heart of what it means to be a New Zealander (valuing freedom, trust, compassion and integrity) and what the status of being a New Zealander guarantees (for example, the right to publicly funded education and health care for all and to travel abroad at will). Concerns that such measures will produce a xenophobic and mistrusting society are very real. The speed of the progress of this bill, and the lack of broad public consultation, highlight the second issue—the fact that New Zealand does not have a formal written constitution.

As Henderson and Bellamy (2002, p.33) state, "Parliament is the supreme political body and can, with a majority vote, make changes to the constitution and laws as it sees fit." They explain further:

> Following the British tradition, New Zealand does not have an overriding formal written constitutional document. Its constitution is made up of the statutes of the New Zealand parliament, common law, constitutional convention, law and custom of parliament, and the heritage of British constitutional history. (p.19)

Concerns have been expressed from both sides of the political spectrum about the vulnerability of the public in such a system. Henderson and Bellamy (2002) express the conduct of New Zealand's political affairs as "genuinely democratic" with the exception of the economic reforms of the 1980s, which were to have far-reaching consequences still felt today. Consequences have included the widening gap between rich and poor and the increasing disadvantage of Maori and Pacific Islanders in New Zealand. Would the production of a formal written constitution provide more stability and equity? Or does the evidence from countries that do have such a document, not inspire confidence? The debate continues.

How have debates such as these impacted upon educational policy-makers? The Ministry of Education's Curriculum Stocktake (a review of the current compulsory curriculum) picked up on the notion of fostering citizenship as a means to redressing social ills. When talking about the purpose of curriculum, the Ministry informed the Minister: "Curricula help develop a creative and innovative citizenry, developing life-long learners and safeguarding and promoting social cohesion" (Ministry of Education, 2002f, p.3). The report recommends that local and global citizenship skills be added to the essential skills and suggests future-focused cross-curricular themes, such as social cohesion (including resilience and a sense of social connectedness), citizenship (local, national, global), and education for a sustainable future.

Educational policy-makers interviewed in a recent study on future scenarios in education (Mutch, 2004) were unanimous in their expression of the need for all stakeholders in New Zealand education to become involved in broad consultation and focused debate on the purpose and future of education in New Zealand. They stated that this was necessary so that New Zealanders could move forward with a shared vision that reflected their unique identity, protected their diversity, and aimed at high standards and equitable outcomes for all.

However, the use of the term citizenship, and its multiple connotations, are themselves matters of debate. In recent discussion documents relating to a review of the social studies curriculum[vi] concern was raised about citizenship education introducing a coercive and political tone. This was seen as being at odds with the spirit of critical inquiry that social studies seeks to promote.

And so, what of the place of citizenship education in New Zealand? In the immediate future, social studies (supported by health education) will continue to be the key vehicle for the promotion of citizenship content, even if it is not specifically stated as such. There are, however, indications that discussions around the formal inclusion of citizenship in the curriculum will be strengthened. As Sinnema (2004), a consultant investigating the future direction of social studies states, "Dialogue around the place of citizenship in New Zealand's curriculum has begun to, and will continue to occur" (p.13). At this point, however, it is interesting to return to Barr's (1998) earlier claim:

> If New Zealanders are good citizens it may be because they learn the knowledge, skills and values required of a good citizen outside the classroom, or it may be that factors other than information about social and political systems are more important in developing confident and informed and responsible citizens. (p.30)

Will the promotion of explicit citizenship education enhance or detract from the current situation? What lessons have we earned from the past? What present practices should we maintain? What is the best direction for the future? Because of the ideological nature of citizenship education, it is important that these questions be widely discussed and that any answers proposed are in the best interests of all sectors of society.

The debate is still open.

Notes

[i] Report in more detail in Mutch, C. (2003). Citizenship education in New Zealand: Inside or outside the curriculum? *Citizenship, Social and Economic Education*, 5(3), 164-179. Extracts reprinted here are done so with the permission of the publisher.

[ii] Department of Internal Affairs website. *Requirements for New Zealand Citizenship*. Retrieved September 8, 2004, from http://www.dia.govt.nz/diawebsite.nsf/wpg_URL/Services-Citizenship-Requirements-for-New-Zealand-Citizenship?OpenDocument.

[iii] Department of Internal Affairs website. *Identity (Citizenship and Travel Documents) Bill*. Retrieved September 8, 2004, from http://www.citizenship.govt.nz/diawebsite.nsf/wpg_URL/Whats-new-Citizenship-FAQs-Citizenship-Amendment-Act-2005?OpenDocument.

[iv] New Bill protects NZ passport and border security. (June 17, 2004). Media statement from Hon. George Hawkins, Minister of Internal Affairs. Retrieved September 8, 2004, from http://www.dia.govt.nz/web/press.nsf/d77da9b523f12931cc256ac5000d19b6/c5432c1b54f1bb39cc256eba000029e3!OpenDocument.

[v] Speech notes prepared for the Hon, Matt Robson's response in Parliament to the introduction of the Identity (Citizenship and Travel Documents) Bill (July 29, 2004).

[vi] These concerns are documented in an unpublished set of notes from the "Leaders in Social Sciences Hui," Wellington (May 25-26, 2004).

Reflective Analysis

13

Tensions and Contentions in Citizenship Curriculum in Asia and the Pacific

Wing On LEE

Introduction

This volume is a continuation of our efforts to explore features of citizenship and citizenship education in Asia-Pacific societies. The first volume, *Citizenship Education in Asia and the Pacific: Concepts and Issues* (Lee, Grossman, Kennedy & Fairbrother, 2004) tried to identify commonalities and differences in citizenship education across a number of Asia-Pacific societies, especially trying to identify what could be *Asian* in citizenship concepts and issues. In this volume, we move one step forward and analyse the curriculum aspect of citizenship education. Further, in the previous volume, in addition to identifying some citizenship features that are quite distinctively Asian, we also noted some tensions in citizenship education. For example, Liu (2004, pp.113-116) pointed out that in citizenship discourse in Taiwan, there are tensions between the individual and society, freedom and order, diversity and uniformity, Americanisation and localisation, rights and responsibilities, deliberation and civic virtues, universal citizenship and differentiated citizenship, and fixed citizenship and flexible citizenship.

In this second volume with its focus on citizenship curriculum, we have found further tensions and contentions in relation to what should be taught, how it is to be taught, whether the curriculum should be state-oriented or individual-oriented, and whether the citizenship curriculum should remain unchanged. We have also found that the focus on curriculum has given us an opportunity to look deeper into features related to citizenship education, particularly in identifying uncertainties in an area of education which is expected to provide certainties for the students in developing their national identity and support of their political systems. We thus note a lot of tensions and contentions in an area of education which is expected to bring about consensus, harmony and social cohesion. The identification of these tensions, contentions and uncertainties underscores the emphases of this chapter.

This chapter will firstly explain the approach towards curriculum we have adopted and the relationship between curriculum and citizenship education, and then discuss whether the Asia-Pacific cases included in this volume help understand these perspectives.

Curriculum: Broad Concept and Context-based

As noted in the introduction to this volume, curriculum is a broad concept, and there are varied approaches to defining its features. The first approach, which is most widely adopted, is to see curriculum as an organisation of study, defining curriculum in terms of planned teaching and learning experiences for students, prepared as a set of subjects; a set of materials; a sequence of courses; a course of study; and/or a set of performance objectives. At times it is referred to as syllabus, content outline, textbooks and sometimes even as teaching materials. As an organisation of study, curriculum is not restricted to teaching contents, but can also be viewed as a process, and in this way referring broadly to school activities as a series of learning experiences that involve academic, athletic, emotional and social experiences, and interpersonal relationships in the school context (Oliva, 1992; Marsh, 1997; Posner, 1998).

A second approach is to conceive curriculum as a learning orientation. From this perspective, Eisner and Vallance (1974) point out that there are five types of curriculum orientations: cognitive process orientation, self-actualisation orientation, technological orientation, academic-rationalist orientation and social reconstructionist orientation. From a different perspective, Longstreet and Shane (1993) identify four types of curriculum orientations, namely society-oriented curriculum, student-oriented curriculum, knowledge-oriented curriculum and eclectic curriculum. The latter looks at curriculum from the broadest possible perspective that involves various compromises related to the purpose and process of teaching and learning.

A third approach is to see curriculum in terms of school operation. From this perspective Eisner (1994) identifies three types of curriculum: official curriculum (or formal curriculum), operational curriculum (implemented curriculum) and hidden curriculum. The hidden curriculum, one that transmits implicit social norms and political expectations in an implicit way as a part of school life, is well known for its close relationship to citizenship education, particularly in respect to political socialisation. MacDonald (1977) suggests that the curriculum plays a mediation role between the individual and the societal order and the political order, through a process of internalisation developed from school experience.

The above discussion clearly shows that rather than being simply an organisation of study, curriculum has to be understood from broader perspectives, often in terms of the social and political context in which it is embedded. These broader perspectives are expressed sometimes in terms of the stakeholders (such as students) involved in the education system; sometimes in terms of the knowledge to be learned and how it is to be learned (such as seeing school subjects as disciplines but also valuing the technological aspect of learning); and sometimes in terms of the context of learning (such as the school, the society, and the political system within which the curriculum operates). When curriculum is discussed in contextual terms, its linkage to citizenship education becomes more salient, especially in its social reconstructionist functions. Further, curriculum is generally perceived as explicit, tangible and content specific in the course of learning, but it can also be invisible and intangible, subsumed in the school life and even the society's political atmosphere that both the teachers and students experience every day.

It is the study of the curriculum in terms of its social and political contexts that places the citizenship curriculum into tensions and contentions: tensions in terms of whether the curriculum should mainly focus on what kind of knowledge should be selected for transmission in a particular social and political context, and contentions in terms of whether curriculum should reflect, and how to reflect, the changing political orientations of the society. This makes the curriculum ever changing. As the cases in this volume have shown, curriculum policy decisions are always contentious when they govern who decides what to be taught and how it is to be taught. Curriculum development and reform in most societies tends to be contentious in general, and it is more contentious when it is linked to citizenship issues.

Citizenship Curriculum and Cultural Heritage

Curriculum and Culture

The school curriculum is never *ad hoc*, but a kind of selectivity, being coined as a selective tradition (Williams, 1976) or as selection from the larger culture (Giroux, 1981). The selectivity is an intentional activity, representing the way in which from a whole possible area of past and present, certain meanings and practices are chosen for emphasis, and certain other meanings and practices are neglected and excluded. In this way, school also becomes an agent of cultural incorporation, initiating the younger generation into selected cultural traditions (Williams, 1976). Giroux (1981, p.402, 1983, p.258) posits that school is reproductive in the cultural sense, functioning to distribute and legitimate forms of knowledge, values, languages and modes of style that constitute the dominant culture and its interests. How is this reflected in the case studies in this volume?

In the case of Taiwan, according to Doong (Chapter 3), its Chinese culture, based on Confucianism, serves as a significant context for the citizenship curriculum. A person's identity is built upon a complex web of social relationships, and one's moral behaviour is governed by relations and respect. Based on moral rules in human relations, such citizenship values as loyalty, obedience, filial piety and conformity are emphasised, with a social goal of maintaining harmony and peace.

In the case of Hong Kong, linking citizenship education to culture has been quite deliberate since its return to Chinese sovereignty in 1997. The government documents demonstrate a significant increase in China elements in the school curriculum. Chinese history and culture are designated as core elements of learning in the newly developed Personal, Social and Humanities Education (PSHE) key learning area. Moreover, extracurricular activities related to Chinese culture, such as Chinese orchestras, Chinese dance and kung fu classes have become intensified (Lee, Chapter 2).

We can find this linkage of citizenship education to culture in other Asian societies as well. In general, the Asian societies that have a Confucian past (such as China, Taiwan, Hong Kong, Japan, Korea and Singapore) still regard Confucianism as the core of cultural traditions. Many of the citizenship values promoted in these societies, such as filial piety, obedience, social responsibility and harmony are justified and legitimated by referring to Confucian teachings. These societies are often called post-Confucian societies, featuring the significance of upholding the Confucian traditions even in modern social contexts, to which the Confucian past may be no longer relevant.

Just as the post-Confucian societies make Confucian values central to citizenship education, Malaysia and Indonesia uphold Islam as the central cultural tradition to legitimate the choice of cultural values to be transmitted to the young. In Malaysia the citizenship curriculum is represented by History in school education and *Tamadun Islam dan Tamadun Asia* (TITAS), i.e., Islamic Civilization and Asian Civilization, in university education. The former aims to cultivate a kind of "historical empathy" that would allow students' understanding of citizenship to be anchored in the country's historical and cultural roots. The latter aims to foster citizenship upon the country's cultural context founded upon its religion and geographical roots (Bajunid, Chapter 8). Similarly, the citizenship curriculum in Indonesia stresses the need to develop the competency of historical understanding among students, so that they can "*reconstruct* the past, make meaning out of the present and predict the future" (Fearnley-Sander & Yulaelawati, Chapter 7).

However, the development of curriculum frameworks is far from a harmonious selection process. It reflects tensions and contentions within the society, as the curriculum "is produced out of the cultural, political, and economic conflicts, tensions, and compromises that organize and disorganize people" (Apple, 1996, pp.22-23). As expounded by Apple (1993), the idea of culture should not be used to celebrate an achieved or natural harmony. Culture is a constant and complex process, whereby meanings are made and shared. It does not grow out of a pre-given unity of a society. Rather, in many ways, it grows out of its divisions, and has to work to construct any unity that it has. Freire (1974) further points out that education is not only a political act and ideological choice, but also a means of cultural action. Schooling functions as a system of communicating a particular cultural message, but the cultural action is focused on instilling conformity that supports the existing order.

Various chapters in this volume show that the reference to cultural tradition (sometimes expressed in terms of historical tradition) was often made in the midst of ideological controversies, in order to justify a particular approach to citizenship education put forward by the state. For example, the significance of the Islamic culture in Indonesia and Malaysia was emphasised in the face of an increasingly diverse society, while the significance of Chinese culture was emphasised in Hong Kong in face of ideological uncertainties resulting from its political transition. Moreover, Confucian values were deployed in China, Taiwan and Singapore for different reasons. In the case of China, the process of modernisation and marketisation has made the society more susceptible to external influences on values. In the case of Taiwan, the various tensions mentioned at the beginning of this chapter necessitate a reinstatement of its cultural traditions. In the case of Singapore, there has also been a caution against the intrusion of

Western values. Confucianism forms a good foundation for Asian values, and is promoted as a state supported alternative for the younger generation.

The Close Relationship between Civic and Moral Education

One common cultural characteristic reflected in citizenship education in Asian societies is their emphasis on moral education in citizenship curriculum. We have identified this feature in our previous volume. Kennedy and Fairbrother (2004) pointed out that Asian citizenship education is characterised by conceptions of moral virtues and personal values. Lee (2004) identified this feature in terms of the "relationalistic" emphasis in citizenship. When analysing the development of citizenship curriculum in various societies in this volume, it is not difficult to find civics-and-moral education are basically a twin package being promoted in the Asian societies.

In China, citizenship education is a combination of civics education, moral education, political education and ideological education. Although there could be fine distinctions between them, they are also conceptually intertwined with one another, and often the terms are used interchangeably (Lee, 2002a; Lee & Ho, 2005). Zhong and Lee (Chapter 4) have identified a continuum between the politically-oriented civics and personally-oriented moral education in the development of citizenship curriculum in China over the last 50 years. Whereas citizenship education was almost equivalent to ideological and political education in the early years, the focus of citizenship education has become increasingly oriented towards personal moral qualities in recent years (although political elements are always present in China's history of citizenship education). Thus, the relationship between civics and moral education is a continuum in China, with the early period leaning towards civics but at present leaning towards moral education, and at no time without each other.

In Taiwan, the citizenship curriculum is represented by Life and Ethics, Morality and Health, and Civics and Morality. The former two emphasise moral education, teaching up to 18 key moral virtues. These virtues cover both a personal dimension (such as perseverance, frugality, honesty, bravery, diligence and a sense of shame) and a social dimension (such as cooperation, filial piety, justice, peace and observance of the law). The latter emphasises civics education, and is socially and politically oriented, touching upon politics, economics, law and culture (Doong, Chapter 3).

In most cases in Asia, civics is placed before moral education in nomenclature, even when the two concepts are culturally intertwined with each other. This suggests that national interests are also placed before the social and individual interests. This is most saliently manifested in the civics and moral curriculum in Singapore. In Singapore, the citizenship programme is officially called Civics and Moral Education (CME). The moral emphasis in the curriculum is manifested in two ways: the emphasis on Confucian virtues and the emphasis on Singapore's shared values. The moral emphasis, in the case of Singapore, is state-directed; and the moral dimension underscored by a civics agenda is socially oriented and politically driven. Thus, CME in Singapore has been perceived as "national education," and it is justified in terms of "the fragility of our country ... with its vulnerability and constraints." Henceforth, "the alignment of CME content with national and societal needs is vital," and the nation is put before the society and, likewise, society before the individual. The moral virtue to be advocated is responsible citizenship and the attitudes to be cultivated are loyalty and commitment to the nation for nation building, and "work efficiently" and "teamwork" for the economy (Tan & Chew, Chapter 9).

However, there is also an exception in the way civics and moral education are prioritised, e.g., in Hong Kong. Whereas CME is a rather common description of citizenship education in many Asian societies, Hong Kong reversely describes it as "Moral and Civic Education". The major task of MCE in Hong Kong, as described in the Hong Kong curriculum document, is "to help students establish their values and attitudes" and is focused on "students' personal and social development ... to meet the challenges of the 21st century" (Lee, Chapter 2). In this case, Hong Kong regards moral education as more important than civic education.

Whatever the priority in regard to civics or moral education, or at which point in the continuum between civics and moral education an Asian society finds its citizenship curriculum at a particular time in its history, any analysis of the citizenship curriculum has to be understood in terms of both elements. The twin relationship between civics and moral elements in citizenship education can be understood as a cultural trait in Asia and the Asian society cases in this volume explicitly adopt a position that emphasises both elements in their citizenship curriculum.

The Issue of Language and Citizenship

Another cultural feature that facilitates understanding of the distinctive feature of Asian citizenship is language. In our previous volume, *Citizenship Education in Asia and the Pacific: Concepts and Issues*, I argued that one problem with studying concepts of Asian citizenship is language (Lee, 2004). As "citizenship" is a rather Western term, when applying this Western terminology in the Asian contexts, there are likely to be two distinctively identifiable approaches. One approach is to simply transplant the Western concept into the Asian citizenship curriculum. In this way, the citizenship curriculum will appear, in a way, quite close to, or sometimes not different from, those developed in Western societies, including curriculum structure and contents, as well as curriculum expectations and evaluation. This kind of expression is found in many of the chapters in this volume. Another approach is to build the citizenship curriculum upon the country's traditional beliefs. Those curricula that have a stronger emphasis on the incorporation of traditional ideas and terminology would naturally show a fundamentally different understanding of citizenship.

The citizenship terminology in the Japanese curriculum is sensitively discussed from the language perspective in Otsu's chapter (Chapter 5). She points out that the term citizen can be translated into Japanese in two different ways: *shimin* and *kohmin*. The two terms have different connotations and, interestingly, as identified by Otsu, there are differential preferences between the government and the public in adopting the terminology when referring to citizenship. Otsu observes that the mass media tends to use *shimin* in contexts relating to civil society. However, the government has never used the term *shimin*, but, instead, uses the term *kohmin*. The term *kohmin* is used for the senior high school subject "civics" and also used as the name of a part of social studies in junior high school. The governmental Course of Study defines *kohmin* in two ways: both as *kokumin* and *shimin*, with the former referring to an authorised member of the state and the latter a member of a civil society. Otsu further points out that the adoption of different terms by the government and the public leads to confusion in concepts related to citizenship within Japanese society. The conceptual difference between the two terms creates tensions in society on citizenship issues, such as the attitude towards the issue of the rescue of the Japanese hostages.

Although only one chapter in this volume makes special reference to the use of language in relation to citizenship, it is illustrative enough to show the significance of the Asian languages used to describe citizenship. Otsu actually uses *kanji* (Chinese characters) in her discussion of the language of citizenship. These kanji do have some resemblance in meaning to equivalent Chinese words. The language reflects a cultural tradition and a unique conception adhering to that culture. The language of citizenship certainly deserves further investigation beyond what can be offered in this volume.

Curriculum and Politics

Curriculum and State Politics

Curriculum is always *political* by nature. As illustrated above, even when the cultural tradition is emphasised in curriculum development, the choice of cultural emphases is always underscored by a political purpose. The curriculum has, on the one hand, been seen as a tool to shape the beliefs and value orientations of its citizens (Westbury, 1985), and, on the other hand, seen to reflect the political ideals of the society (Wilson, 1970). The relationship between politics and education was made explicit when Plato tried to fashion the ideal state based on the notion of all-round education of free men, and when Durkheim pointed out that education reflected the ideal man of the society in a particular space and time (Bottcher, 1980; Durkheim, 1956). Altbach (1991) further points out that textbooks are one of the most political commodities:

> In a sense, textbooks define the nature of education. They embody legitimate knowledge. They are perceived as a powerful teaching tool and their content as one of the key determinants of what gets taught in schools. The content of textbooks is thus political and often a terrain for battles over the nature of education, and sometimes over important social issues or even how the nation, religion, or other sensitive issues are interpreted. (p.243)

Freire (1974, pp.18-19) argues that when we work on the content of the educational curriculum, when we discuss methods and processes, when we plan and when we draw up educational policies, we are engaged in political acts which imply an ideological choice; whether it is obscure or clear is not important.

In some cases the political intent of the citizenship curriculum is more explicit than in others. Referring to the citizenship curriculum in Singapore, Tan and Chew (Chapter 9) observe direct intervention of the state on the citizenship curriculum: "Political involvement in education has been inevitable from the start of Singapore's nationhood." "Education for Living" was adopted in the sixties. Although it was a values education programme, it stressed national consciousness and duty. In the seventies, the government suddenly developed a national ideology based upon Confucian "family values." This ideology was a means to promote Asian values against Western values; promote Confucian morality and team spirit as a driving force for economic success; rectify the failure of the previous values education programme (as manifested by the increase of professional crimes in the country); and promote Confucianism (by regarding it as a religion) as a balance to religious education in a multinational society. From 2000 onwards, the government introduced Civics and Moral Education. The syllabus clearly stipulates that national education messages have to be infused in the content of the syllabus. Moreover, what underpins the themes in the CME syllabus is the nation's ideology. Singapore's Shared Values are: nation before community and society above self (Singapore Ministry of Education, 2000a, pp.2-3). In response to these emphases, Tan and Chew comment that "National Education is, therefore, part of an ongoing politicized campaign of '"total defence,' that involves physical and ideological training of Singaporeans of all levels" (Chapter 9). Their conclusion is that they can only observe the sort of citizenship "education" which is more correctly described as citizenship training in Singapore:

> CME is, therefore, another instance of Singapore citizenship training crafted to fit a people for a nationhood conceived narrowly in terms of economic survival and progress (Chapter 9).

In the case of Japan, the government has made deliberate attempts to shape a curriculum that reflects the state's political intention. As Otsu (Chapter 5) comments, a case in point is that textbook authors were asked by the Ministry of Education, Culture, Sports, Science, and Technology (MEXT) to replace the term "invading" with "entering" other Asian countries. Otsu's chapter also mentions substantial opposition against the Central Council for Education's 2003 report. The report recommended the revision of Japan's Fundamental Law of Education to shape educational aims to suit the state's interests rather than personal development, in redefining the educational aim as cultivating Japanese tradition and culture, and forcing love of the nation in the arena of public education. The goals of civics, as described in the Courses of Study, are entirely state-oriented—"to be interested in society, ... to deepen students' understanding and love of their nation and history, to cultivate the foundation of knowledge necessary for them to achieve a broad perspective as citizens, and to develop basic civic qualities essential to the shapers of a democratic and peaceful society" (Chapter 5).

Curriculum and Ideological Contentions

Curriculum is also linked to politics in terms of ideology. According to Apple (1979, 1990, 1995, pp.21-22), schools distribute ideological knowledge and values, and the educational system constitutes a set of institutions that are fundamental to the production of knowledge. Johnson (1979, p.232) argues that it is not so much a question that schools are *ideologies*, but that they are *sites* where ideologies are produced. Further, according to Aronowitz and Giroux (1985, p.76), ideology has a material existence in the rituals, routines and social practices that both structure and mediate the day-to-day workings of schools. It is thus a set of material practices through which teachers and students live out their daily experiences. Althusser (1971) regards that such practices induce in teachers and students an imaginary relationship to their social existence.

While ideology seems to be a state apparatus, in the terms of Althusser (1971), and represents collective meanings, as a system of ideas, beliefs, fundamental commitments and values about social reality, ideology is also a system of meanings that justifies the interests of contending groups in society, and is, thus, contentious in nature. *Ideology* as a state apparatus is thus contentious, even though it appears to be consensual, and it represents a process of compromising contentious ideologies within the society, or the result of certain dominating ideologies overriding the others.

Ideological Dominance and Social Cohesion

Singapore's citizenship curriculum ideology aims to achieve social cohesion. However, the kind of social cohesion promoted in citizenship "education" is underscored by a state ideology that "we must have qualities of leadership at the top, and qualities of cohesion on the ground." The country needs a minority of elites who have to be trained as future leaders and would-be business managers and policy implementers. To sustain social cohesion, the majority has to receive citizenship training to become followers. As Tan and Chew remark, "the social cohesion citizenship 'education' was to forge is not a virtue itself … , but only what is ingrained in order that people would be appeased by it, and be skilled at following the commandant." The curriculum ideology described in Tan and Chew's chapter on Singapore closely manifests the kind of ideology domination mentioned above by Apple, Aronowitz and Giroux, and Althusser. Although there are no explicit contentions in ideology in Singapore, there are tensions, and the ideological tensions in Singapore are reflected in the domination of ideology by a particular social group.

Contentions between the Public and the State

Ideological contentions in Japan are expressed in the question "What is a good citizen?" or "What is an ideal citizen?" The way the question is asked is particularly *Asian*. Otsu's chapter (Chapter 5) starts with an interesting discussion on the issue of saving the Japanese hostages in Iraq in April 2004. The typical public response in Western countries would be that it is the responsibility of the government to protect and rescue their citizens. Of course, the government is not always successful and sometimes reluctant to take action based on all sorts of considerations, and then the government will generally be seen not to have tried its best to do its job and will always become a bit apologetic to the public. In the Japanese case, this is certainly the view of the media: "It was the Japanese government that endangered the three returnees by sending troops to Iraq. The three returnees are citizens … We are very proud of them as courageous citizens." However, interestingly, the public does not seem to have the same opinion, as half of the first-year students surveyed blamed the returnees: "It was you who went to Iraq. Why are you asking the government to rescue you when you were kidnapped? … Your loss of your life is your own responsibility" (Otsu, Chapter 5). The polarisation of views on this issue is interesting in its unveiling of ideological contentions, expressed in terms of the perception of ideal citizenry and the government's role towards its citizens in an Asian context. In both cases, polemical views are expressed. One extreme view is that it is the government's fault in sending troops to Iraq and it is the government's duty to protect its citizens, and those citizens taken hostage are courageous citizens. However, another extreme view is that the citizens have made a mistake in not supporting government policy and have put themselves at risk, and thus it is their mistake in the first place going to a risky country and thus should not expect the government to rescue them.

Ideological conflicts are most saliently illustrated in Otsu's chapter on Japan. The whole chapter explicates conflicts between state ideology and public ideology, to an extent that the state and the public are almost polarised in their view towards citizenship education. The government emphasises state-oriented civics, but the public prefers the kind of civics that is oriented towards the civil society. The state works hard to foster a more positive national image (of the government) by revising textbook expressions (replacing the word "invading" with "entering"), revising the Fundamental Law of Education so that educational aims reflect state expectations, such as tradition, culture and nationalism, and by enforcing *kimigayo* (raising national flag) and *hinomaru* (chanting national anthem). However, the public opposed all these, regarding it as more important for the Japanese citizens to know their historical past more accurately in order to avoid the revival of imperialism and militarism, to sustain democratisation of the country, and to maintain an education aim that would reflect personal development on the one hand and globalisation on the other (Otsu, Chapter 5).

De-ideologisation of the Citizenship Curriculum by the State

Interestingly, ideological tension in Taiwan takes place in a reverse manner. In the late 1990s, the Taiwan government introduced a new citizenship curriculum. The new curriculum is a flexible curriculum, school-based and deregulated from central control, in order to facilitate curriculum integration. By doing so, the government regards this as an alignment with the international trend of curriculum development. The curriculum ideology is individually oriented, emphasising critical thinking, knowledge integration, problem solving, individual abilities and disassociation from politics. In a way, it is de-ideologisation of the citizenship curriculum by the state. If this took place in Japan, it would have gained the public's applause, and this is what the educators have fought for. Ironically, in Taiwan the new curriculum is criticised for failing to deal with the national identity issue. They feel that the citizenship curriculum should have a political stand, which is to promote Taiwanese identity. Likewise, the citizenship curriculum should teach the young to know more about Taiwan's geography and history. Obviously, although Chen Shuibian's government is very much pro-Taiwan, the government feels it difficult to openly impose a de-sinicised and "Taiwanised" political stand in the citizenship curriculum. The government is at an ideological crossroads, but the public wants an ideological stand that suits their own interests (although the public may be divided on this point).

Complexities in Localisation, Nationalisation and Globalisation

Given the political context of having been a British colony for 150 years and then returned to Chinese sovereignty in 1997, ideological complications are most notable in Hong Kong. There is an obvious tension in terms of globalisation and localisation in citizenship education. However, even within localisation, there is further tension, as an emphasis on nationalisation can to some extent be viewed as "delocalised," thus, a delocalised local (national) emphasis and a localised local (Hong Kong) emphasis. Moreover, the localisation emphasis in Hong Kong can also become a kind of localised globalisation, when Hong Kong is identified as an international city. Further, the Hong Kong case shows that, while on the one hand there is an emphasis on nationalisation content in the citizenship curriculum, the citizenship skills advocated in the citizenship curriculum are globalised (Lee, Chapter 2).

Similar tensions are expressed in Bajunid's (Chapter 8) analysis of the Malaysian citizenship curriculum. He points out that:

> [T]he concept of citizenship creates various kinds of tensions. Beyond local and national duties as citizens, there are international duties of global citizenship within the contents of civil, political, and social rights and responsibilities.

Ideological Contentions between the "Church" Agenda, State Agenda and Human Rights

Of all the chapters in this volume, the Pakistan chapter (Ahmad, Chapter 6) is most explicitly related to ideology in its discussion of citizenship curriculum. It is also most illustrative of the ideological tensions and contentions in the country, as reflected in the way the citizenship curriculum is shaped. Ahmad in his chapter mentions "the Ideology of Pakistan" and "the Ideology of Islam" as guiding thought in Pakistan's citizenship curriculum construction. Moreover, Pakistan's National Curriculum explicitly mentions that one of the aims of civics is "to develop for critical appraisal of alien culture and ideology," and one of the curriculum objectives is "to promote understanding about the

Ideology of Pakistan and the struggle of Muslims for an Independent Islamic State." The imposition of *the* ideology (of Pakistan and Islam) in the citizenship curriculum in Pakistan clearly illustrates the state's domination in ideological control. The citizenship curriculum is designed to "deliver packaged, homogenized knowledge to students," "to promote a gentler and more peaceful image of Islam, both in and outside Pakistan," and "to export Islam as a political ideology to other nations."

However, despite these efforts, ideological contentions still emerge in the midst of ideological control. In the main, the ideology that the government promotes, according to Ahmad, "is conceptually at odds with the notion of a modern nation state." He points out that ideological contentions take place in Pakistan on many fronts. First, despite the imbalance in power, two competing ideologies are identifiable in Pakistan, namely the theocratic and liberal-democratic. Theocratic ideology defines good citizenship in religious terms and seeks to strengthen the Muslim *ummah* or Muslim community, and, as mentioned, is also a means of exporting Islam as a political ideology to other nations. In contrast, liberal-democratic ideology defines good citizenship in pluralist terms, emphasising citizenship as a secular concept, and the acquisition of religious knowledge is neither necessary nor sufficient for good citizenship.

Second, the two competing ideologies can be viewed in terms of Islamic nationalism and Pakistani nationalism. The former holds a dualist and bifurcated worldview, dividing the world into *Dar-al-Islam* (the land of peace) and *Dar-al-harb* (the land of war), whereby waging war against the non-Muslim nations is one of its central tenets. The latter views "Pakistan as a multi-faith, multi-cultural and multi-ethnic state, with equal rights for every citizen regardless of one's communal affiliation, faith or gender."

Third, ideological tension in the citizenship curriculum is expressed in terms of differential rights and responsibilities prescribed for the Muslim and non-Muslim citizens. For example, the list of duties for the non-Muslim citizens is only half of those for the Muslim citizens. This can be viewed as exclusion, but can also be a kind of compromise in not requiring the non-Muslim citizens to do what is expected of a Muslim. In the main, the contentions in citizenship ideology rest upon the issue of state and religion, and it is the contentions between those who argue that state and religion are two-in-one and those who argue that state and religion should be separated. Obviously, the former view is held by the politically dominant group in the society, and the latter view by their critics. These critics argue that when combining state with religion, the citizenship curriculum has twisted historical facts about the nation's cultural and political heritage, and discriminated against women and non-Muslim citizens.

While the ideological contentions are quite explicit in Pakistan, a nearly opposite picture is depicted by Fearnley-Sander and Yulaelawati (Chapter 7) in their analysis of citizenship curriculum in Indonesia:

> A salient feature of the momentous changes to the curriculum for citizenship since 1999 is that there has been next to no contestation or discussion in the educational world or the wider public about their implications for the civic identity of Indonesia's future citizens.

What is the reason for this lack of contention?

Their explanation is that citizenship curriculum has gone through a historical process of ideological development, leading to a rather common aspiration for citizenship today: "*Pancasila* Man" (a concept attached to the state religion, Islam) as the ideal citizen in the 1968 curriculum; the "good citizen" (who should possess the relevant knowledge and skill to support the country's science and technology development) in the 1975 curriculum; the design of citizenship curriculum in the form of "citizenship education" (*Pendidikan Kewarganegaraan*) as a reframing of "*Pancasila* and Citizenship Education" (*Pendidikan Pancasila dan Kewarganegaraan*) in 1998; and the introduction of competency-based citizenship, supported by a liberal-democratic ideology and a decentralisation policy in providing regional autonomy in curriculum development.

However, Fearnley-Sander and Yulaelawati also note that each epoch of curriculum development towards the acknowledgement of diversities in the society and the liberalisation of the curriculum was accompanied by a reinstatement of the principle of *Pancasila* in one way or another. They remark that the new citizenship curriculum has to cope with three different kinds of political values: a commitment to *Pancasila* as a source of national identity, a commitment of civic competency, and a rights-oriented view of citizenship. Moreover, despite a note of the absence of ideological contestation on the new curriculum, they also caution that "in a way that shows the limitations of a simple dichotomy between the powerful state and the powerless citizenry." They further add that the implementation of decentralisation has also been assisted by the reassertion of the national government as the watchdog of democratisation vis-à-vis district power. In the conclusion of the chapter, the authors express further queries about the true-heartedness of the decentralisation: "When educational decentralisation is looked at closely there docs not seem to be much scope for local autonomy as initiative-taking. The idea of service has guided the national department in a quality assurance role in the context of decentralisation." In other words, this can be regarded as recentralisation or the assertion of control in a different way.

Curriculum Tensions in Pacific Rim Societies

The discussion above shows that the Asian society cases examined in this volume fit well into the curriculum discourse in the international literature. Or putting it another way, the international curriculum discourse is found applicable to the analysis of citizenship curriculum in Asian societies. The citizenship curriculum agenda, like any society's curriculum agenda, is used by the governments to support the existing polity by emphasising the significance of cultural traditions or state ideology. Curriculum as a means of political socialisation is best illustrated in the development of citizenship curriculum in the Asian societies examined in this volume. As ideologies are always contentious in any society, employing the school curriculum as a tool of ideological transmission is also contentious, and this also takes place vividly in the citizenship curriculum development processes mentioned above.

Neo-conservative Civics versus Civic Renaissance

It is therefore not a surprise to find that the Pacific Rim societies included in this volume (the United States, Australia and New Zealand) manifest almost the same tensions, contentions and conflicts in citizenship curriculum development processes. Tensions and contentions in curriculum ideology are very well expressed in the title Kennedy (Chapter 11) chooses for Australia: "More Civics, Less Democracy: Competing Discourses for Civics and Citizenship Education in Australia." He starts his chapter by saying: "Australian politics in the 1990s was subject to successive waves of disparate ideological influences and these influences fundamentally altered the contexts in which the revival of civics has taken place." Kennedy describes Australia's current emphasis in the citizenship curriculum, *Discovering Democracy*, as a refocus on the appreciation of the institutions of the past that have shaped present-day Australia. To Kennedy, this is a kind of conservatism, or neo-conservatism that is consistent with the former Prime Minister John Howard's personal and political view in stressing Australian national identity and heritage. The Howard government abruptly brought a halt to the "civics renaissance" initiated by the previous Keating government, which acknowledged the need for reconciliation with indigenous people, and in general sought engagement with Asia and a new role for Australia in the global community. He deplores that "[c]onservatism triumphed and the Keating vision vanished." "Neo-conservatism, or at least its Australian equivalent, has fundamentally changed the Australian political and social landscape."

Dichotomies in Citizenship Ideology

Likewise, Mutch (Chapter 12) spots tensions and contentions in the development of citizenship curriculum in New Zealand. "Tensions" is the catchword for her summary of the historical development of citizenship curriculum in the country. She says:

> Elsewhere the author (Mutch, 2000) has described New Zealand curriculum history as consisting of three eras, each characterized by tensions between key social and political forces of the time. The first era (pre-European contact to the early 1900s) is titled "indigenous versus colonial," the second era (1900-1970s) "traditional conservative versus liberal progressive" and the third era (1980s-the present) is "new right versus liberal left."

Mutch's observation of the citizenship curriculum in New Zealand is very much in tune with Kennedy's. She remarks that the use of the term citizenship, and its multiple connotations, is itself a matter of debate:

> In recent discussion documents relating to a review of the social studies curriculum concern was raised about citizenship education introducing a coercive and political tone. This was seen as being at odds with the spirit of critical inquiry that social studies seeks to promote.

Mutch concludes her chapter by saying that because of its ideological nature, in developing the citizenship curriculum it is important for us to ask such fundamental questions as to whether citizenship education should enhance or detract from the current situation, what lessons we have learned from the past, and what should be the best direction for the future.

Democracy at the Crossroads

The U.S. chapter depicts a strikingly similar picture of citizenship curriculum development. Scott and Cogan (Chapter 10) highlight curriculum tensions in the U.S. in their chapter title, "Democracy at a Crossroads: Political Tensions Concerning Educating for Citizenship in the United States." They remark that the last two decades have seen a "hardening of conflicting ideologies regarding the structure, aims and content of the citizenship curriculum." Like Kennedy in the case of Australia, Scott and Cogan observe that the U.S. citizenship curriculum has increasingly been dominated by a neo-conservative agenda. They remark that "the curricular framework has increasingly come under the control of 'back to basics' conservatives who equate curricular reform with rote memorisation of factual information aligned to a set of quantifiably measured standards." With the standards movement, the epistemological nature of citizenship education was reversed from a progressive emphasis to an economic emphasis. Since September 11, the Bush citizenship curriculum has emphasised American patriotism, respect for the flag, a Christian national identity and an "America First" view on globalisation. Moreover, controversial content and politically sensitive issues have been eliminated, and the significance of dissent as a historical contribution to America is ignored. As a result, many teachers are hesitant to discuss controversial citizenship issues, and those teachers who engage in such "'subversive' activities [of discussing controversial issues] do so at their own risk."

Conclusion

This volume demonstrates that citizenship ideology is always complex and never straightforward. As Bajunid (Chapter 8) rightly puts it, the study of citizenship education is both exciting and perplexing:

> It is exciting because of the possibilities of fostering social and civic responsibilities. It is perplexing because of the complexity inherent in the relationship between the individual and the community at local, regional, national and international levels, as well as at the levels of civilization and the human species. … The search … for an understanding of citizenship education in Malaysia is a search across five decades of the development of an education system. … It is also a search for an understanding of the debates and agendas of politicians, intellectuals, and the definers of nationhood and citizenship.

Still, within the complexity, the diversity, and the debates, we can find some common themes. In our previous volume, Kennedy and Fairbrother (2004, p.293) identified the following emerging themes in citizenship education in Asian societies, namely:

1. Asian countries are characterised by multiple modernities that provide rich and complex contexts for the development of citizenship education.
2. Asian citizenship education is characterised more by conceptions of moral virtues and personal values than by civic and public values.
3. Civil society is constructed differently in the West and in Asian countries but it nevertheless can play an important role.
4. The nation-state plays the same role in Asian and Western countries in relation to citizenship education.
5. There is a tension between citizenship education, school subjects and the academic curriculum.
6. Teachers are key players when it comes to the implementation of citizenship education in school.
7. Student agency in responding to citizenship education needs to be taken into consideration.

Many of their observations have been reaffirmed in this volume, especially in relation to the emphasis on moral virtues and personal values, the same role played by the nation state in shaping the citizenship curriculum, and the tension between citizenship education, school subjects and the academic curriculum. Referring to the role of the state in shaping or manoeuvring the citizenship curriculum, our analysis of the society cases in this volume finds that they are aligned with the Western literature on curriculum, especially in relation to culture, state politics and political ideologies.

In sum, what we have found in this volume is another set of complicated pictures in relation to citizenship education. When we analyse the development of citizenship curriculum in the Asian cases, the general picture we can draw is a common emphasis on culture; a common understanding that civics and moral education are a twin relationship; a common expectation of the development of social responsibility to be supported by healthy and positive personal values; and a common concern about linking the cultural context to the modern challenges that these societies are facing. But what makes this volume exceptionally interesting are the complications underlying these commonalities. Underneath an emphasis on culture are tensions and contentions about what kind of culture should be upheld, and whether the younger generation should be socialised into the traditional culture or develop competency in critical cultural acculturation. More complicated still, the various chapters in this volume invariably reveal tensions and contentions in ideological discourse in relation to what kind of citizenship curriculum should be adopted for the younger generation relevant to the increasingly globalised environment of today. All the chapters touch upon the changing social and political circumstances of their societies, and the reaction to becoming a part of the globalised community. There are ongoing tensions between whether the traditional expectations towards good citizenship should be upheld or whether they need to be adapted to the globalised circumstances. There are ideological tensions between the state and the public, and between various social groups in the public. There are ideological contentions on many issues, such as the relationship between state and religion, localisation and globalisation, the historical past and the present society, and what is the priority of citizenship education: state-oriented, society-oriented, or individual-oriented?

These curriculum tensions and contentions are not unique to the Asian cases. The Pacific Rim cases are strikingly similar to the Asian cases, although the political backgrounds are different. This leads us to another major finding in the process of analysing the society cases in this volume. While I have argued that there can be fundamental differences in citizenship concepts between Asian and Western societies, when we come to the organisation of citizenship curriculum as a means of political socialisation, or transmission of political ideologies, the Asian and the Western societies tend to have more commonalities than differences. Thus, while citizenship concepts can be quite different between Asia and the West, we find that the citizenship curriculum agenda, or more correctly the political socialisation agenda, are pretty much the same across cultures. This analysis shows that the international curriculum discourse can be applicable to analysing the citizenship curriculum in Asian societies. Thus, when asked to write about the development of citizenship curriculum in their own societies, all chapter authors invariably identify tensions, contentions and conflicts related to citizenship ideologies in resolving curriculum issues.

Contributors

Iftikhar AHMAD is an Associate Professor and chair of the Department of Curriculum and Instruction, School of Education, Long Island University, New York. Dr Ahmad's research focuses on comparative citizenship, peace education, and the history of American social studies. He has contributed to journals such as *Teachers College Record, Social Education, The Social Studies,* and *Educational Studies.* His book, *Citizenship Education: Political Scientists' Struggle for the Social Studies Curriculum* was published in 2003 by University Colleges Press.

Ibrahim Ahmad BAJUNID is a Professor of Management, Leadership and Policy Studies at University Tun Abdul Razak (UNITAR). He is a former Director and Fellow Emeritus of The National Institute of Educational Management and Leadership. He is a Fellow of the Council of Education Management in Commonwealth Countries, Distinguished Fellow, Institute of Strategic and International Studies (ISIS) Malaysia, a Fellow of the National Research Institute on Youth and Senior Fellow of the Malaysian Social Institute. He has written over four hundred articles and academic papers and is currently engaged in several research projects.

Lee Chin CHEW graduated from the National University of Singapore (NUS) where she also received an MEd in educational counselling. She is currently an Assistant Professor in the Psychological Studies Academic Group of the National Institute of Education, Nanyang Technological University, Singapore, where she obtained her PhD in educational testing. Her interest continues to be in educational and psychological testing and measurement, as well as values education. She participated in a HKIEd-based study on citizenship education in Asia (2002-2004), and was Vice-President of the Educational Research Association of Singapore. She is a joint author of a curriculum review paper in the December 2004 issue of the *Journal of Moral Education.* She has in recent years been consultant to several Singapore secondary schools on "action research" by teachers, and has edited a volume of such research papers entitled *Action Research Across the Curriculum* (2006).

John J. COGAN is Professor Emeritus of International and Social Studies Education in the Department of Education Policy and Administration, University of Minnesota. He received his Ph.D. from The Ohio State University. His research specialisations are educating for citizenship, and educational reform in the Asia-Pacific Region. He is an internationally recognised authority on educating for citizenship and has directed two major international studies in this area in the last decade; both have been published as books and have influenced policy and curricula in the region. He recently directed a study on the Future of Schooling in six Asia-Pacific nations that was published in a Special Issue of the *International Journal of Educational Research* (Spring, 2006). He is the co-author of four books, 17 book chapters, and more than 100 published juried journal articles. He recently was awarded an Honorary Doctorate of

Education degree by Sukhothai Thammathirat Open University (Thailand) for his contributions to the improvement of education throughout the Kingdom.

Shiowlan DOONG received her PhD from the Department of Curriculum and Instruction at University of Minnesota. She specialises in citizenship/social studies education, and research on political education in particular. Dr. Doong has been a faculty member in the Department of Civic Education and Leadership at National Taiwan Normal University (NTNU) since 1989. Before that, she taught secondary school civics-related subjects in Taiwan for five years. Dr. Doong works closely with preservice and inservice teachers of civic education in Taiwan via teacher education courses at NTNU and locally sponsored in-service teacher workshops. She has also served as executive editor of *Bulletin of Civic Education*, consultant to the Taiwan's joint entrance examinations for senior high schools and vocational high schools, and external examiner for the Civic Education subject in the Postgraduate Diploma in Education Programme, the Hong Kong Institute of Education.

Mary FEARNLEY-SANDER was Chief Technical Advisor of the CLCC Program at the UNESCO Jakarta Office, Indonesia. She was formerly a Senior Lecturer in the Faculty of Education at the University of New England Australia and had taken up the work in Flores, Eastern Indonesia in a long-term AusAID project in primary education. She co-authored a chapter in the first book in this series, "Muslim Views of Citizenship in Indonesia during Democratisation."

David L. GROSSMAN is currently an Adjunct Senior Fellow of the Education Program of the East-West Center in Honolulu, Hawaii. Formerly Dr Grossman was Professor and Dean of the Faculty of Languages, Arts and Sciences at the Hong Kong Institute of Education (HKIEd). Prior to coming to HKIEd, Dr Grossman was Director of the Stanford University Program on International and Cross-Cultural Education (SPICE). He holds masters degrees in Chinese Studies and Social Sciences Education from Harvard University, and a PhD in International Development Education from Stanford University. In 1995 he joined HKIEd and later became Head of the Department of Social Sciences and Dean of the School of Foundations in Education. In 1999 he co-founded (with Lee Wing On) the Centre for Citizenship Education (CCE) at HKIEd, and served as Centre co-Head until 2007. With Wing On Lee, Kerry Kennedy, and Greg Fairbrother, he co-edited the first volume in this series, *Citizenship Education in Asia and the Pacific: Concepts and Issues*. He is also the co-Editor (with Joe Lo) of *Social Education in Asia*.

Kerry J. KENNEDY is currently the Acting Vice-President (Academic) at the Hong Kong Institute of Education where he is also the Dean of the Faculty of Professional and Early Childhood Education. Before coming to Hong Kong he was Pro Vice-Chancellor (Academic) at the University of Canberra in Australia. He is the author of *Changing Schools for Changing Times—New Directions for the School Curriculum in Hong Kong,* co-author (with Laurie Brady) of *Curriculum Construction* (3rd Ed) and *Celebrating Student Achievement—Assessment and Reporting* (2nd Ed). He edited

Citizenship Education and the Modern State and co-edited (with Wing On Lee, David Grossman and Greg Fairbrother) *Citizenship Education in Asia and the Pacific: Concepts and Issues.* He is a Fellow of the Australian College of Education and a Life Member of the Australian Curriculum Studies Association. His research interests are in citizenship education and curriculum policy and theory. His most recent work has focused on student conceptions of citizenship with a special focus on cross cultural contexts and the way these shape those conceptions.

Wing On LEE is currently Acting President and Vice-President (Academic) of the Hong Kong Institute of Education (HKIEd). Formerly Prof Lee was Professor of Education and Director (International) for Humanities and Social Sciences at the University of Sydney, where he continues to be an Honorary Professor. Prior to his Sydney appointment, Lee served at HKIEd as the founding Dean of the School of Foundations in Education, Head of two Departments, and co-Head of the Centre for Citizenship Education. He also served as Associate Dean of Education and Director of the Comparative Education Research Centre at the University of Hong Kong. He has published extensively in the areas of comparative and international education, civics and citizenship education, and values and moral education. Lee served as the Hong Kong representative and a member of the International Steering Committee of the IEA Civic Education Study. He co-founded the Centre for Citizenship Education at HKIEd, and was the lead editor (along with David Grossman, Kerry Kennedy and Gregory Fairbrother) of the first volume in this series, *Citizenship Education in Asia and the Pacific: Concepts and Issues.*

Carol MUTCH is Senior Advisor to the Chief Review Officer in the Educational Review Office, New Zealand Ministry of Education. She was formerly Director of Academic Developments and Research at the Christchurch College of Education, New Zealand. Her teaching and research interests are around curriculum theory, education policy and social education. Dr. Mutch is the author of *Doing Educational Research: A practitioner's guide to getting started* (2005) and publishes regularly in academic journals and edited books on citizenship education, social studies, curriculum, educational history and qualitative research methods. In 2003, Dr. Mutch received recognition from her institute for 'sustained excellence in tertiary teaching'; in 2004, a citation from Griffith University, Australia, for 'academic excellence' and; in 2005, an early career award from the American Educational Research Association for her contribution to 'critical issues in curriculum'. Through her work in the Pacific Circle Consortium, her time as a Visiting Professor at Nagoya University, and her work in Samoa, Dr. Mutch has fostered a strong interest in education in the Asia Pacific region.

Kazuko OTSU is a Professor of Global Education, Hokkaido University of Education, Sapporo, Japan. She is an acknowledged authority on civic and social studies education in Japan and an experienced researcher in the field of education. One of her publications *Through a banana—A lesson for global citizenship* (1987) has been a best-seller for years. She has developed a curriculum framework for international education, which is authorised by the Japan Association for International Education. Since 1995 she has conducted research on education in Sub-Saharan countries including Zambia, Tanzania, Uganda and South Africa.

Thomas SCOTT received his PhD from the University of Minnesota. He currently teaches social studies at Rosemount High School in Rosemount Minnesota. He is also Adjunct Associate Professor of Education at Saint Mary's University in Minneapolis and Adjunct Professor of Social Science at Metropolitan State University in St. Paul, Minnesota. His research interests include the study of globalization and its integration into the social studies curriculum, citizenship education, and the influence of the Internet on learning. Dr. Scott has conducted educational research in The People's Republic of China, India, Japan, and Thailand.

Tai Wei TAN has been in teacher education since 1974, specialising in teaching philosophy of education and moral education. He is currently an Associate Professor in the National Institute of Education, Nanyang Technological University, Singapore. He previously taught English literature and language in schools, having graduated from the then University of Singapore with BA (Hons) in English and Philosophy, and subsequently an MA in Philosophy. While teaching preservice teachers in the then Institute of Education, he obtained his PhD in philosophy from the National University of Singapore in 1981. His research interest is in philosophy of mind, religion and morals, both in themselves and in their relation to educational aims and practice. He has published several books and a number of papers in the U.S., U.K., Australia and Singapore on those subjects.

Ella YULAELAWATI completed her PhD in the Graduate School of Education, University of Queensland, Australia in 1998. From 1983 up to early 2004 she worked at the Curriculum Center, Office of Research and Development in Education and Culture, Ministry of National Education, Indonesia. Since February 2004 she has been the Deputy Director for Equivalency Program in Directorate of Community Education, Directorate General Out of School Education and Youth, Ministry of National Education, Indonesia. Since 2002 she has taught at Jakarta State University (Universitas Negeri Jakarta). Her recent publications include "Living Together for Indonesian Heterocultural Society: Contexts, Content, and Teaching Strategies," and "Curriculum and Instruction: Philosophy, Theory, and Application."

Minghua ZHONG is Dean and PhD Supervisor of the School of Education at Sun Yat-sen University in Guangdong, China. He is also Vice-chairman of the Ethics Association of Guangdong Province. His main fields of study are ethics and education. His major publications include: "Toward the Opening of Morality" (1994); "The Socialization of Culture and Youth Morality" (2003); and "The Historical Changes of School Moral and Citizenship Education" in *Educational Research* (October, 2004). He is also a co-author of "Deyu as Moral Education in Modern China, Ideological Functions and Transformations" in *Journal of Moral Education* (December, 2004).

References

Abdul Aziz, B. (2002). *Cabinet principles in Malaysia: The law and practice.* Kuala Lumpur: The Other Press.

Abdullah, A.B. (2004, April 19). *The challenges of multi-religious, multiethnic and multicultural societies.* Keynote Speech addressed at the Asia Media Summit, Kuala Lumpur.

Ahmad Sarji, A.H. (1994). *Perkhidmatan Awam Malaysia: Satu peralihan paradigma [The Malaysian public service: A paradigmatic change].* Kuala Lumpur: Percetakan Nasional Malaysia.

Ahmad, F., Javed, A., & Saeed (n.d.). *Pakistan studies: For 10th grade.* Peshawar: Pak Printing and Packages Corporation.

Ahmed, H. (2003). Teaching of social studies: Class 6 to 10. In A.H. Nayyar & A. Salim (eds.), *The subtle subversion: The state of curricula and textbooks in Pakistan* (pp.127-130). Islamabad: Sustainable Development Policy Institute.

Ahmed, I. (1987). *The concept of an Islamic state: An analysis of the ideological controversy in Pakistan.* New York: St. Martin's Press.

Al-Afendi, M.H., & Baloch, N.A. (1980). *Curriculum and teacher education.* London: Hodder and Stoughton & King Abdulaziz University Jeddah.

Al-Attas, M.N. (1979). *Aims and objectives of Islamic education.* London: Hodder and Stoughton & King Abdulaziz University Jeddah.

Alavi, H. (2002). *The rise of religious fundamentalism in Pakistan.* Retrieved March 17, 2007 from http://www.europe-solidaire.org/spip.php?article3054.

Alavi, H. (n.d.). *The rise of religious fundamentalism in Pakistan.* Retrieved August 7, 2004, from http://ourworld.compuserve.com/homepages/sangat/fundamen.htm.

Albert Shanker Institute. (2003). *Education for democracy.* Washington DC: Albert Shanker Institute.

Alcorn, N. (1999). *To the fullest extent of his powers: C. E. Beeby's life in education.* Wellington, New Zealand: Victoria University Press.

Altbach, P.G. (1991). The unchanging variable: Textbooks in comparative perspective. In P.G.. Altbach, G.P. Kelly, H.G. Petrie & L.W. Weis (eds.), *Textbooks in American society: Politics, policy and pedagogy* (pp.237-254). Albany, NY: State University of New York Press.

Althusser, L. (1971). Ideology and the Ideological State Apparatuses. In L, Althusser (ed.), *Lenin and philosophy, and other essays,* trans. Ben Brewster. New York: Monthly Review Press.

Ambigapathy, P. (1997). *Reading in Malaysia.* Bangi: Penerbit Universiti Kebangsaan Malaysia.

Ambigapathy, P., & Chakravarthy, G. (eds.). (2003). *New literacies, new practices and new times.* Serdang: Universiti Putra Malaysia Press.

Amer Hamzah, J., Hassan, S., Bajunid, I.A., Ibrahim, I., Shaharil, T., & Shansulbahriah, K.A. (eds.). (2002). *Integrated approaches to lifelong learning.* Kuala Lumpur: Asia-Europe Institute, Universiti Malaya.

America 2000 Excellence in Education Act, S.1141, 102nd Congress. (1991).

Anuar, A. (2004). The making of a good citizen in Malaysia. In W.O. Lee, D.J. Grossman, K.J. Kennedy, & G.P. Fairbrother (eds.), *Citizenship Education in Asia and the Pacific.* Hong Kong: Comparative Education Research Centre, The University of Hong Kong and Dordrecht: Kluwer Academic Publishers.

APEC Education Network. (2000, April 7). *Joint statement from the 2nd AEMM, education for learning societies in the 21st century, Singapore.* Retrieved May 9, 2004, from http://www.apecsec.org.sg/content/apec/.

Apple, M. (1979). *Ideology and curriculum.* London: Routledge and Kegan Paul.

Apple, M. (1990). The text and cultural politics. *The Journal of Educational Thought,* 24(3A), pp.17-33.

Apple, M. (1993). *Official knowledge: Democratic education in a conservative age.* New York: Routledge.

Apple, M. (1995). *Education and Power* (2nd ed.). New York: Routledge.

Apple, M. (1996). *Cultural Politics and Education.* Buckingham: Open University Press; New York: Teachers College, Columbia University.

Aquilina, J. (1997). Education Reform Further Amendment Bill, 1997. *Second Reading Speech in the NSW Legislative Assembly.* Retrieved June 15, 1997, from http://www.boardofstudies. nsw.edu.au/docs_stfreview/aquilina1.html.

Archer, E., & Openshaw, R. (1992). Citizenship as 'official' goals in social studies in New Zealand. In R. Openshaw (ed.), *New Zealand social studies: Past, present and future* (pp.19-33). Palmerston North, New Zealand: Dunmore Press.

Aronowitz, S., & Giroux, H. (1985). *Education under siege: The conservative, liberal and radical debate over schooling.* Mass a Chusetta: Bergin and Garvey Publishers Inc.

Association for Developing Japanese Education and Culture toward the World. (2003). *Statement against the amendment of Fundamental Law of Education.* Retrieved June 15, 2004, from http://www1.odn.ne.jp/kyoiku-bunka/.

Attorney General's Department. (2004). *National security Australia.* Retrieved October 24, 2004, from www.nationalsecurity.gov.au/agd/www/nationalsecurityHome.nsf/headingpagesdisplay/ 9F291545F46DC7B9CA256E43000565D4?OpenDocument.

Aung San Suu Kyi. (1999, May 27). *Address on the occasion of the 9th anniversary of the general election.* Address by Aung San Suu Kyi, General Secretary of the National League for Democracy, Rangoon. Retrieved March 29, 2004, from http://www.geocities.com/absdf_au/ assk/asskmsg15.html.

Australian Curriculum Studies Association. (2004). *2004 National discovering democracy forum report.* Retrieved November 30, 2004, form http://www.curriculum.edu.au/democracy/ prof_dev/forumreport2004.pdf.

Avery, P. (2002). Political tolerance, democracy, and adolescents. In W. Parker (ed.), *Education for democracy: Contexts, curricula, assessments* (pp.113-130). Greenwich, CT: Information Age Publishing.

Awang Had, S. (2002). Lifelong learning in the era of globalization. In J. Amer Hamzah, S. Hassan, I.A. Bajunid, I. Ibrahim, T. Shaharil & K.A. Shansulbahriah (eds.), *Integrated approaches to lifelong learning* (pp.xiii-xx). Kuala Lumpur: Asia-Europe Institute, Universiti Malaya.

Aziz, K.K. (1993). *Murder of history in Pakistan: A critique of history textbooks used in Pakistan.* Lahore: Vanguard Books.

Badr, A. (1993). *Etiquettes of Islamic life.* Karachi: Low Price Publications.

Bagnall, R. (2000). Lifelong learning and the limits of economic determinism. *International Journal of Lifelong Education,* 19(1), pp.20-35.

Bailey, C. (1977). A short summary of national education in New Zealand. *Education,* 9, pp.2-11.

Bajunid, I.A. (1980). Perubahan dan perkembangan kurikulum ke arah pembinaan negara. [Curriculum change and development towards nation-building]. In S. Awang Had (ed.), *Pendidikan ke arah perpaduan [Education for National Unity]* (pp.145-200). Kuala Lumpur: Penerbit Fajar Bakti.

Bajunid, I.A. (1995). Assessment of accountability systems in Malaysian education. *International Journal of Educational Research,* 23(6), pp.531-544.

Bajunid, I.A. (2001). The transformation of Malaysian society through technological advantage: ICT and education in Malaysia. *Journal of Southeast Asian Education.* 2(1), pp.104-146.

Bajunid, I.A. (2002a). *The global lifelong learning agenda: Reawakening the passion for knowledge in the Islamic world.* In Proceeding of the seminar on Islam, Globalisation and the Knowledge Economy: Issues and Challenges (pp.91-107). Shah Alam: International Institute of Public Policy and Management (INPUMA) and the Prime Minister's Department Malaysia.

Bajunid, I.A. (2002b, January 20). Pillars of a knowledge society – As I wonder. *New Sunday Times*, Higher education section, p.14.

Bajunid, I.A. (2002c, September 1). True meaning of independence – As I wonder. *New Sunday Times*, Higher education section, p.8.

Bajunid, I.A. (2003a, January). *The challenges of developing and implementing Peace Education Programmes in formal and non formal education and learning contexts in Malaysia.* Paper presented at the 2nd Southeast Asian Conflict Studies Network (SEACSN) Malaysian National Workshop, Penang.

Bajunid, I.A. (2003b, January 26). Gaining strength via multicultural literacy – As I wonder. *New Sunday Times*, Learning curve section, p.10.

Bajunid, I.A. (2003c, June 1). Whatever happened to civic consciousness – As I wonder. *New Sunday Times*, Learning curve section, p.10.

Bajunid, I.A. (2003d, November 2). The great Malaysian narrative – As I wonder. *New Sunday Times*, Learning curve section, p.8.

Bajunid, I.A. (2003e, December 21). The making of an enlightened citizenry – As I wonder. *New Sunday Times*, Learning curve section, p.12.

Bajunid, I.A. (2004a, March 14). The meaning of active citizenship – As I wonder. *New Sunday Times*, Learning curve section, p.12.

Bajunid, I.A. (2004b, March 28). The promise of an enlightened nationhood – As I wonder. *New Sunday Times*, Learning curve section, p.14.

Bajunid, I.A. (2004c, August 29). Know the true meaning of independence – As I wonder. *New Sunday Times*, Learning curve section, p.12.

Bakri, M.M. (2003). *An education system worthy of Malaysia.* Petaling Jaya: Strategic Information Research Development (SIRD).

Bakri, M.M. (2004). *Seeing Malaysia my way.* Petaling Jaya: Strategic Information Research Development (SIRD).

Banks, J.A. (2002). Teaching for diversity and unity in a democratic multicultural society. In W. Parker (ed.), *Education for democracy: Contexts, curricula, assessments* (pp.131-150). Greenwich, CT: Information Age Publishing.

Banks, J.A. (ed.). (2004). *Diversity and citizenship education: Global perspectives.* San Francisco: Jossey-Bass.

Barber, B. (2003). *Fear's empire: War, terrorism, and democracy.* New York: W.W. Norton & Company.

Barnard, T.P. (ed.) (2004). *Contesting Malayness.* Singapore: Singapore University Press.

Barone, T., & Bajunid, I.A. (2001). Malaysia: Strengthening religious and moral values. In W.K. Cummings, M.T. Tatto & J. Hawkins (eds.), *Values education for dynamic societies: Individualism or collectivism* (pp.229-242). Hong Kong: Comparative Education Research Centre, The University of Hong Kong.

Barr, H. (1997). From the Editor. *The New Zealand Journal of Social Studies*, 6(2), p.6.

Barr, H. (1998). Citizenship education without a textbook. *Children's Social and Economics Education*, 4(1), pp.28-35.

Barr, H., Hunter, P., & Keown, P. (1999, November). *The common good in the New Zealand social studies curriculum*. Paper presented to the Annual Conference of the National Council for the Social Studies, Orlando, Florida, U.S.A.

Bartlett, R., & von Zastrow, C. (2004, April 7). Academic atrophy. *Education Week*, 23(30), pp.58-59.

Battistoni, R. (1997). Service learning and democratic citizenship. *Theory into Practice*, 36(3), pp.150-156.

BBC. (2003). The future of the People's Republic of China - A perspective. Edited guide entry. Retrieved August 25, 2003, from www.bbc.co.uk/dna/h2g2/A1006480.

Benavot, A., & Braslavsky, C. (eds.). (2006). *School knowledge in comparative and historical perspective*. Hong Kong: Comparative Education Research Centre, The University of Hong Kong.

Bennell, P. (1998). Rates of return to education in Asia: A review of the evidence. *Education Economics*, 6(2), pp.107-120.

Bernama (2006, April 14). No 'Little Napoleon' in civil service please, says Abdullah. Pertubuhan Berita Nasional Malaysia (Malaysian National News Agency). Kuala Lumpur. Retrieved August 15, 2006, from www.pmo.gov.my/webdb.nsf/.

Blecher, R. (2003). *Intellectuals, democracy and empire – "Free people will set the course of history."* Retrieved September 3, 2004, from http://evatt.labor.net.au/publications/papers/ 87.html.

Bloom, B. (1956). *Taxonomy of educational objectives: The classification of educational goals*. By a committee of college and university examiners. New York: Longmans.

Board of Studies. (2001). *2001 Trial school certificate Australian history, geography, civics and citizenship official notice 29/01*. Retrieved September 3, 2004, from www.boardofstudies. nsw.edu.au/bulletins/on_2001.html.

Bottcher, W.A. (1980). Political and education. *Education*: Vol. 22, (pp.7-19). Germany: Institutes of Scientific Cooperation.

Brady, L., & Kennedy, K. (2003). *Curriculum construction* (2nd ed.). Sydney: Pearson Education.

Branson, M. (2003, January 31). *The importance of promoting civic education*. An Address to the 2nd Annual Scholars Conference, Pasadena, CA: Center for Civic Education. Retrieved March 30, 2004, from www.civiced.org/mb_scholarsconf_2003.pdf.

Brown, L.C. (2000). *Religion and state: The Muslim approach to politics*. New York: Columbia University Press.

Burchill, S. (2003, June 30). The perils of our US alliance. *Sydney Morning Herald*. Retrieved September 3, 2004, from www.smh.com.au/articles/2003/2006/2030/1056825317955. html?oneclick=true.

Bush, G.W. (2004). The essential work of democracy. *Phi Delta Kappan*, 86(2), pp.114-121.

Butts, R.F. (1977). Historical perspective on citizenship education in the United States. In National Task Force on Citizenship Education. (ed.). *Education for responsible citizenship: The report of the National Task Force on Citizenship Education* (pp.46-78). New York: McGraw-Hill.

Byron, I. (1999). *An overview of country reports on curriculum development in South and South-East Asia*. Retrieved August 18, 2005, from http://www.ibe.unesco.org/curriculum/ Asia%20Networkpdf/ndrep4.pdf.

Carson, C. (ed.). (1998). *The autobiography of Martin Luther King Jr.* (pp.187-204). New York: Warner Books, Inc.

Case, R., & Clark, P. (eds.) (1997). *Canadian anthology of social studies*. Vancouver: Pacific Education Press.

Center for Civic Education. (1991). *CIVITAS: A framework for civic education*. Calabasas, CA: Center for Civic Education.

Center for Civic Education. (1994). *National standards for civics and government*, Calabasas, CA: Center for Civic Education.

Center for Information and Research on Civic Learning and Engagement. (2003). *The civic mission of schools*. Carnegie Corporation of New York and Circle.

Center for Information and Research on Civic Learning and Engagement. (2004, November 8). *Youth Voting in the 2004 Election*. Retrieved November 18, 2004, from www.civicyouth.org/PopUps/FactSheets/FS-PresElection04.pdf.

Chang, C. (1999, April 12). Scholars and university professors questioned the Nine-Year Integrated Curriculum. *The China Times*, p.5.

Chen, H., & Chung, J. (2002). A study of the problems and coping strategies for school-based curriculum development. *Journal of Taiwan Normal University*, 47(1), pp.1-16.

Chen, I. (1968). *Japanese colonialism in Korea and Formosa: A comparison of its effects upon the development of nationalism*. Unpublished doctoral dissertation, University of Pennsylvania, Philadelphia.

Chen, W. (1997). National identity and democratic consolidation in Taiwan: A study of the problem of democratization in a divided country. *Issues and Studies*, 33(4), pp.1-44.

Chew, T.Y. (1980). *Propositions for a strategy for curriculum renewal – A study of Malaysian curriculum change process*. Unpublished Ph.D. dissertation. University of Malaya.

China Education Yearbook Editorial Board. (ed.). (Various Years). *Zhongguo jiaoyu nianbao [China education yearbook]*. Beijing: People's Education Press.

Chinese Communist Party Central Committee (1949a). Zhongguo renmin zhengzhi xieshang huiyi gongtong gangling [Common framework for Chinese people political negotiations]. In China Education Yearbook Editorial Board (ed.). *Zhongguo jiaoyu nianbao 1949-1981 [China education yearbook 1949-1981]*. Beijing: People's Education Press.

Chinese Communist Party Central Committee (1949b). 1949 nian diyici jiaoyugongzuo huiyi de jingshen [The spirit of the first education work conference in 1949]. In China Education Yearbook Editorial Board (ed.). *Zhongguo jiaoyu nianbao 1949-1981 [China education yearbook 1949-1981]*. Beijing: People's Education Press.

Cogan, J.J., & Derricott, R. (1998). *Citizenship for the 21st century – An international perspective on education*. London: Kogan Page.

Cogan, J.J., & Derricott, R. (2000). *Citizenship for the 21st Century: An international perspective on education* (paperback). London: Kogan Page; Sterling, Va.: Stylus Publishing.

Cole, P. (2003). *National discovering democracy forum – 2003 Final report*. Retrieved December 6, 2004, from http://www.curriculum.edu.au/ democracy/prof_dev/2003ddfinalreport.pdf.

Commission on Educational Reform (1996). *The general consultation report on educational reform*. Taipei, Taiwan: Commission on Educational Reform.

Conference of Asia Pacific Curriculum Policy Makers. (2002). *School based curriculum renewal for the knowledge society: developing capacity for new times : conference proceedings: program and papers*. Hong Kong: Dept. of Curriculum and Instruction, Hong Kong Institute of Education.

Constitution of the People's Republic of China. (1982). Adopted on December 4, 1982, *People's Daily Online*. Retrieved January, 10 2006, from http://english.people.com.cn/constitution/constitution.html.

Council of Indigenous Peoples (2004). *The tribes in Taiwan*. Retrieved May 23, 2004, from http://www.apc.gov.tw/en/tribes/indi/tribes.aspx.

Cummings, W.K., Tatto, M.T., & Hawkins, J. (eds.) (2001). *Values education for dynamic societies: Individualism or collectivism.* Hong Kong: Comparative Education Research Centre, The University of Hong Kong.

Curriculum Corporation. (1999). *Australian readers discovering democracy middle primary teacher guide.* Melbourne: Curriculum Corp.

Curriculum Corporation (2000). Studies of society and environment. Melbourne, Australia.

Curriculum Corporation. (2004a). *School show case 2003.* Retrieved September 3 2004, from http://www.curriculum.edu.au/democracy/showcase/showcase.htm.

Curriculum Corporation. (2004b). *National assessment - Professional development.* Retrieved September 3, 2004, from http://www.curriculum.edu.au/democracy/prof_dev/nat_assess/nat_assess.htm.

Curriculum Development Council. (1996). *Guidelines on civic education in schools.* Hong Kong: Education Department.

Curriculum Development Council. (1997). *General studies for primary schools curriculum guide (Primary 1 – Primary 6).* Hong Kong: Education Department.

Curriculum Development Council. (1998a). *Civic education – Secondary syllabus (F.1-3).* Hong Kong: Education Department.

Curriculum Development Council. (1998b). *Kecheng jianshi baogao: Xuexiao kechengnei de zhongguo yuansu [China elements in the school curriculum: Curriculum examination report].* Hong Kong: Education Department.

Curriculum Development Council. (2001). *Learning to learn: Lifelong learning and whole-person development.* Hong Kong: Curriculum Development Council.

Curriculum Development Council. (2002a). *General studies for primary schools curriculum guide.* Hong Kong: Curriculum Development Council.

Curriculum Development Council. (2002b). *Personal, social and humanities education KLA curriculum guide.* Hong Kong: Curriculum Development Council.

Curriculum Development Council. (2002c). *Four key tasks – Achieving learning to learn: 3A. Moral and civic education.* Hong Kong: Curriculum Development Council.

Curriculum Development Council. (2003). *Integrated humanities curriculum and assessment guide (Secondary 4 & 5).* Hong Kong: Curriculum Development Council.

Dale, R., & Robertson, S. (2004). Interview with Boaventura de Sousa Santos. *Globalisation, Societies and Education,* 2(2), pp.147-160.

Dahrendorf, Sir R. (1990, August 1). Decade of the citizen. *The Guardian.*

Delors, J. (1996). *Learning: The treasure within. Report to UNESCO of the International Commission on Education for the Twenty-First Century.* Paris: UNESCO.

Departemen Pendidikan Nasional. (2001a). Kurikulum Berbasis Kompetensi: Mata Pelajaran Kewarganegaraan Untuk Kelas I-VI, Buram 6, halaman.ii. [National Department of Education, Indonesia. The Competency-Based Curriculum: Citizenship Education for Class I-VI, Draft 6, p.ii].

Departemen Pendidikan Nasional. (2001b.) Kewarganegaraan SMP [Citizenship, Junior High School].

Departemen Pendidikan Nasional. (2001c) Pedoman Khusus Mata Pelajaran Kewarganegaraan SMA [Special Guidelines for the Study of Citizenship for Senior Secondary]. Jakarta.

Departemen Pendidikan Nasional. (2003). Kurikulum 2004 Standar Kompetensi Mata Pelajaran Pengetahuan Sosial, Sekolah Dasar dan Madrasah Ibtidaiyah, p.2. [Curriculum 2004: Competency Standards for Social Science in primary schools and madrasah].

Department of Education. (1954). *Social studies in history and geography.* Wellington, New Zealand: Department of Education.

Department of Education. (1961). *Social studies in the primary school.* Wellington, New Zealand: Department of Education.

Department of Islamic Development, Malaysia (2004). *The concept of Islam Hadhari.* Kuala Lumpur: Jabatan kemajuan Islam Malaysia (JAKIM).

Dirlik, A. (ed.). (1998). *What is a rim? Critical perspectives on the Pacific region idea* (2nd ed.). Lanham, Md: Rowman & Littlefield.

Dong, X.H. (1999). Zhuquan huiquixia de xianggang xuexiao gongmin jiaoyu [Civic education in Hong Kong after the return of sovereignty]. *Fujian Police Higher Education Journal – Social and Public Security Studies,* 13(5), pp.89-92.

Doong, S. (2002). *Reconstructing political education in Taiwan: A study on perspectives of teacher educators and senior high school teachers of civic education.* Unpublished doctoral dissertation, University of Minnesota.

Doong, S. (2003). School-based curriculum in the field of social studies: Retrospect and prospect. In S.J. Gau (ed.). *Kecheng gangyao shishi jiantao yu zhanwang lunwenji [The implementation of the curriculum guidelines: Retrospect and prospect]* (pp.607-624). Taipei, Taiwan: National Taiwan Normal University.

Douglass, F. (1967). *Narrative of the life of Frederick Douglass.* Cambridge, MA: Harvard University Press.

Drury, S. (2003). *Leo Strauss and the neoconservatives.* Retrieved September 3, 2004, from http://evatt.labor.net.au/publications/papers/112.html.

Dunstall, G. (1981). The social pattern. In W. Oliver (ed.), *The Oxford history of New Zealand* (pp. 396-429). Wellington, New Zealand: Oxford University Press.

Durkheim, E. (1956). *Education and sociology* (S.D. Fox, Trans.). Glencoe, Ill.: The Free Press.

Easton, P. & Klees, S. (1992). Conceptualizing the role of education in the economy. In R. Arnove, P. Altbach & G. Kelly (eds.), *Emergent issues in education* (pp.123-142). New York: State University of New York Press.

Education and Manpower Bureau. (1998). *Display of national flag and regional flag. EMB circular No. 2/1998, 27 May 1998.* Hong Kong: Education and Manpower Bureau.

Education and Manpower Bureau. (2004a). *National identity education.* Hong Kong: Education and Manpower Bureau circular.

Education and Manpower Bureau. (2004b). *Xianggang lingxiusheng jiangli jihua: Guoqing jiaoyu kecheng [Hong Kong student leaders award scheme: National Education Programme].* Retrieved January 8, 2006, from http://cd.emb.gov.hk/mce/ni_course/intro.htm.

Education and Manpower Bureau. (2004c). *Medium of instruction.* Hong Kong: Education and Manpower Bureau.

Education and Manpower Bureau. (2004d). *Display of national flag and regional flag. Education and Manpower Bureau circular memorandum No. 144/2004, 21 June 2004.* Hong Kong: Education and Manpower Bureau.

Education Commission. (2000). *Learning for life, learning through life: Reform proposals for the education system in Hong Kong: Education blueprint for the 21st century.* Hong Kong: Education Commission.

Education Department. (1997). *Medium of instruction: Guidance of secondary schools.* Hong Kong: Education Department.

Education Reforms displease parents. (2003, January 28). *Taipei Times.* Retrieved June 16, 2004, from http://www.taipeitimes.com.

Educational Reform Task Force Committee (1998). *Twelve education reform mandates.* Taipei, Taiwan: Executive Yuan.

Ehrlich, T. (1999). Civic education: Lessons learned. *PS: Political Science & Politics*, 32(2), pp.245-250.

Eisner, E.W. (1994). *The educational imagination* (3rd ed.). New York: Macmillan.

Eisner, E. & Vallance, C. (eds.). (1974). *Conflicting conceptions of curriculum*. Berkeley, CA: McCutchan.

Evans, R. (2004). *The social studies wars*. New York: Teachers College Press.

Faure, E. (1972). *Learning to be*. Paris: UNESCO.

Fearnley-Sander, M. (2000). Preparation for ethical community: Learning from education for Sittlichkeit in New Order Indonesia. *Citizenship Studies,* 4(3), pp.339-355.

Feizkhah, E. (2004, May 12). Laws and borders. New Zealand worries that its amiable image is attracting entirely the wrong kind of people. *Time*, 19, pp.38-39.

Fiala, F. (2006). Educational ideology and the school curriculum. In Benavot, A. & Braslavsky, C. (eds.), *School knowledge in comparative and historical perspective* (pp.15-34). Hong Kong: Comparative Education Research Centre, The University of Hong Kong.

Field, J. (2001). Lifelong education. *International Journal of Lifelong Education*. 20(1/2), pp.3-15.

Finn, C. (2004, Spring). Faulty engineering. *Education Next*, 4(2), pp.16-21.

Four More Years of Resistance. (2004-05). *Rethinking schools*, 19(2), p.4.

Franzosa, S.D. (1996). Civic education. In J.J. Chambliss (ed.), *Philosophy of education: An encyclopedia* (pp.79-82). New York: Garland Publishing.

Freire, P. (1970). *Pedagogy of the oppressed*. Harmondsworth: Penguin Books.

Freire, P. (1974). Education: Domestication or liberation? In I. Lister (ed.), *Deschooling* (pp.18-21). Cambridge: Cambridge University Press.

Gagnon, P. (2003). *Educating democracy: State standards to ensure a civic core*. Albert Shanker Institute. Retrieved March 15, 2004, from www.shankerinstitute.org/Downloads/gagnon/contents.html.

Galston, W. (2003). Civic education and political participation. *Phi Delta Kappan*, 85(1), pp.29-33.

Galston, W. (2004). Civic education and political participation. *PS: Political Science & Politics, 37*(2). Retrieved September 29, 2004, from http://www.apsanet.org.

Gandhi, M. (1958). *All men are brothers: Life and thoughts of Mahatma Gandhi*. K. Kripalani, (ed.), UNESCO.

Ghafoor, A., & Farooq, R.A. (1994). Pakistan: System of education. In *The international encyclopedia of education* (2nd ed., vol. 7, pp.4270-4263). New York: Elsevier Science Ltd.

Ghosh, B.N. (1998). *Malaysia: The transformation within*. Petaling Jaya: Addison Wesley Longman Malaysia.

Gibson, J.A. (1971). Teaching of citizenship. In *Encyclopedia of educational research* (6th ed.) (pp.135-138). New York: Macmillan Publishing Company.

Gilbert, R. (1996). *Studying society and environment: A handbook for teachers*. Melbourne, Australia: Macmillan Education.

Gillani, W. (2004, June 16). Curriculum controversy: Education ministry and textbook board blame each other. Retrieved August 24, 2004, from http//www.Dailytimes.com.pk/ default.asp?page=story_12-4-2004_2004_pg7_16.

Giroux, H. (1981). *Ideology, culture, and the process of schooling*. London: The Falmer Press.

Giroux, H. (1983). Theories of reproduction and resistance in the new sociology of education: A critical analysis. *Harvard Educational Review*, 53(3), pp.257-293.

Giroux, H. (2004). *Proto-fascism in America: Neoliberalism and the demise of democracy*. Bloomington, Indiana: Phi Delta Kappa Educational Foundation.

Glatthorn, A. (1999). Curriculum alignment revisited. *Journal of Curriculum and Supervision*, 15(1), pp.26-34.

Gleason, A. (2003). *The hard road to fascism - A turning point for the US?* Retrieved September 3, 2004, from http://evatt.labor.net.au/publications/papers/111.html.

Goals 2000 Educate America Act, 20 U.S.C., S5801. (1994).

Goh, C.T. (1997, June 2). *Shaping our future: Thinking schools, learning nation.* Speech delivered at the 7th International Conference on Thinking, Suntec City Convention Centre, Singapore. Retrieved October 28, 2005, from http://www.moe.gov.sg/speeches/1997/020697.htm.

Goodman, P. (1973). *Compulsory miseducation.* Harmondsworth: Penguin Books.

Goon, F.C., Naidu, R.D., & Lee A.B. (1977). *Sivik menengah baru: Buku 4-Malaysia Sebagai Sebuah Masyarakat [Civics for the new secondary curriculum: Book 4 – Malaysia as a society].* Petaling Jaya: Penerbit Fajar Bakti.

Gov't Plans to rewrite history texts, dropping China focus. (2004, November 11). *The China Post.* Retrieved December 1, 2004, from http://www.chinapost.com.tw.

Government of Indonesia. (1998). Broad guidelines of State Policy (GBHN).

Government of Pakistan. (2002a). *National curriculum: Civic for classes IX-X.* Islamabad, Pakistan: Curriculum Wing, Ministry of Education.

Government of Pakistan. (2002b). *National curriculum: Civic for classes XI-XII.* Islamabad, Pakistan: Curriculum Wing, Ministry of Education.

Gutmann, A. (2004). Unity and diversity in democratic multicultural education: Creative and destructive tensions. In J.A. Banks (ed.), *Diversity and citizenship education: Global perspectives* (pp.71-98). San Francisco: Jossey-Bass.

Hadiz, V.R. (2003, May). Decentralisation and democracy in Indonesia: A critique of neo-institutionalist perspectives (Working Papers Series No.47). The Southeast Asia Research Centre (SEARC), the City University of Hong Kong.

Hahn, C.L. (1999). Citizenship education: An empirical study of policy, practices and outcomes. *Oxford Review of Education*, 25(1-2), pp.231-250.

Hahn, C.L. (2003). Becoming political in different countries. In C. Roland-Levy, & A. Ross (eds.), *Political learning and citizenship in Europe* (pp.78-93). Stoke on Trent: Trentham Books.

Haj, S. (2002). Reordering Islamic orthodoxy: Muhammad ibn 'Abdul Wahab. *The Muslim world*, 92(3 & 4), pp.333-369.

Hanushek, E., & Luque, J. (2002). *Efficiency and equity in schools around the world. National Bureau of Economic research working papers (No. 8949).* Cambridge, MA: National Bureau of Economic Research. MA: National Bureau of Economic Research. Retrieved May 9, 2004, from http://www.nber.org/papers/w8949.

Haque, Z. (1987). Islamisation of society in Pakistan. In M.A. Khan (ed.), *Islam, politics and the state: The Pakistan experience* (pp.114-123). London: Zed Books Ltd.

Harper, T.N. (2001). *The end of empire and the making of Malaya.* Cambridge: Cambridge University Press.

Harrison, M., & Gilbert, S. (eds.). (1994). *Landmark decisions of the United States Supreme Court IV* (pp.90-104). La Jolla, CA: Excellent Books.

Hayama, K. (2003). Public spirit and nationalism in educational reform. *News of Osaka Society for Educational Law*, 29, pp.8-15.

Henderson, J., & Bellamy, P. (2002). *Democracy in New Zealand.* Christchurch, New Zealand: Macmillan Brown Centre for Pacific Studies.

Hikam, M.A.S. (1999). Politik Kewarganegaraan: Landasan Redemokratisasi di Indonesia [Citizenship politics: The basis for the redemocraticisation of Indonesia]. Jakarta: Penerbit Erlangga.

Hishammuddin, H.O. (2005, May 3). *Menjana Kecemerlangan Pendidikan Melalui Pentaksiran. [Generating educational excellence through assessment]*. Keynote Speech addressed at the Launch of the Golden Jubilee Celebrations of the Examinations Syndicate, Kuala Lumpur.

Hocking, J. (2003). Counter-terrorism and the criminalisation of politics: Australia's new security powers of detention, proscription and control. *Australian Journal of Politics and History*, 49(3), pp.355-371.

Hocking, J. (2004). National security and democratic rights: Australian terror laws. *The Sydney Papers*, 16(1), pp.89-95.

Hoodbhoy, P.A., & Nayyar, A.H. (1985). Rewriting the history of Pakistan. In M.A. Khan (ed.), *Islam, politics, and the state*: *The Pakistan experience* (pp.164-177). London: Zed Books.

Hsu, C. (2001, December 17). Reformists know nothing about students' pain and pressure. *United Daily News*, p.6.

Hu, S. (ed.). (1951). *Shehuikexue jibenzhishi [Basic knowledge of social sciences]* Changsha: Hunan Jiaoshi Bianjibu.

Huang, J. (2004, July 13). A natural approach to learning. *Taipei Times*, p.2.

Huang, P., & Chiu, L. (1991). Moral and civic education. In D.C. Smith (ed.), *The Confucian continuum: Educational modernization in Taiwan* (pp.367-420). New York: Praeger Publishers.

Hughes, R.K. (1993). *Disciplines of grace*. Wheaton, IL: Crossway Books.

Hunter, S.T. (ed.). (1988). *The politics of Islamic revivalism*. Bloomington: Indiana University Press.

Huntington, S.P. (1996). *The clash of civilizations and the remaking of world order*. New York: Simon and Schuster.

Hussein Hj. Ahmad. (1993). *Pendidikan dan Masyarakat [Education and society]*. Kuala Lumpur: Dewan Bahasa dan Pustaka.

Hywood, G. (2003, August 14). How Howard differs from Bush. *The Age*. Retrieved November 30, 2004, from www.theage.com.au/articles/2003/08/13/1060588456740.html.

Ikeda, D., & Tehranian, M. (2003). *Global civilization*. London: British Academic Press.

Illich, I.D. (1970). *Deschooling society*. Harmondsworth: Penguin Books.

Institut Kajian Sejarah dan Patriotisme Malaysia [Malaysian Institute of Historical and Patriotism Studies] (2004). Melaka: IKSEP. Retrieved February 8, 2006, from www.iksep.com.my/v2/page.asp>pageID+642.

Ip, P. (1996). Confucian familial collectivism and the underdevelopment of the civic person. In L.N.K. Lo & S.W. Man (eds.), *Research and endeavours in moral & civic education* (pp.39-58). Hong Kong: The Chinese University Press.

Irwin, K. (1994). Maori education, policy and teaching: Thinking globally, acting locally. In E. Hatton (ed.), *Understanding teaching: Curriculum and the social context of teaching* (pp.333-344). Sydney, Australia: Harcourt Brace.

Jalal, A. (1994). *The sole spokesman: Jinnah, the Muslim league and the demand for Pakistan*. New York: Cambridge University Press.

Jalal, A. (1995). Conjuring Pakistan: History as official imagination. *International Journal of Middle East Studies*, 27, pp.73-89.

Japan Federation of Bar Associations. (2002). *Statement against the amendment of Fundamental Law of Education*. Retrieved February 27, 2000, from www.nichibenren.or.jp/jp/katsudo/sytyou/iken/02/2002_24.html.

Jay, A. (2004, March 21). *Australia 2004. Continuing the drift to the far right*. Retrieved October 24, 2004, from www.zmag.org/content/ showarticle.cfm?SectionID=44&ItemID=5183.

Jenkins McElroy, L. (ed.). (1997). *Women's voices: A documentary history of women in America* Vol.2 (pp.238-247). Detroit: UXL.

Jiang Z.M. (2002). *Jiang Zemin's report at the 16th party congress*. Retrieved January 10, 2006, from http://www.china.org.cn/english/features/49007.htm#3.

Jiang, Z.M. (2000). *Jiang Zemin zai zhongyang sixiang zhengzhi gongzuo huiyishang fabiao zhongyao jianghua, 2000-6-28 [An important speech by Jiang Zemin delivered at the Central Committee Ideological and Political Work Conference, 28 June 2000]*. Retrieved August 25, 2006, fromwww.qlshx.sdnu.edu.cn/qlshx/news/news_view.asp?newsid=946.

Jinnah, M.A. (2000). *Jinnah: Speeches and Statements 1947-1948*. New York: Oxford University Press.

Johnson, R. (1979). Three problematics: Elements of a theory of working class culture. In J. Clarke et al. (eds.), *Working class culture: Studies in history and theory* (pp.201-237). London: Hutchinson.

Jones, E.B., & Jones, N. (eds.). (1992). *Education for citizenship: Ideas and perspectives for cross-curricular study*. London: Kogan Page.

Jones, O.B. (2002). *Pakistan: Eye of the storm*. New Haven: Yale University Press.

Kahn, J. (2006, August 31) A less ideological Chinese text puts Mao in his place. *The New York Times*. Retrieved September 5, 2006, from www.iht.com/articles/2006/08/31/news/china.php.

Kahne, J., Rodriquez, M., Smith, B., & Thiede, K. (2000). Developing citizens for democracy? Assessing opportunities to learn in Chicago's social studies classrooms. *Theory and Research in Social Education*, 28(3), pp.311-338.

Kahne, J., & Westheimer, J. (2003). Teaching democracy: What schools need to do. *Phi Delta Kappan*, 85(1), pp.34-40.

Kakakhel, M.N., Ahmad, F., Khan, N.M., & Abbas, S.Q. (n.d.). *Pakistan studies: Grade 10th*. Peshawar: Zeb Publishers.

Kellner, D. (1998), Globalization and the postmodern turn. In R. Axtmann (ed.), *Globalization and Europe* (pp.23-42). London: Cassell.

Kementerian Pelajaran Malaysia [Ministry of Education Malaysia] (1981). *Panduan am disiplin sekolah-sekolah [General guide for discipline in schools]*. Kuala Lumpur: Kementerian Pelajaran Malaysia.

Kementerian Pelajaran Malaysia [Ministry of Education Malaysia]. (1985). *Buku panduan pengurusan gerakerja ko-kurikulum sekolah menengah [Guidebook for the management of co-curricular activities in secondary schools]*. Kuala Lumpur: Kementerian Pelajaran Malaysia.

Kementerian Pendidikan Malaysia [Ministry of Education Malaysia]. (1994). *Surat Pekeliling Ikhtisas Bil.6/1994, 12 September, 1994: Usaha menanam semangat patriotisme di kalangan pelajar dan senaman ringkas dalam bilik darjah. [Professional circulars number 6/1994 12 September, 1994: Efforts to foster patriotism among students and physical exercise in classrooms]*.

Kementerian Pendidikan Malaysia [Ministry of Education Malaysia]. (2000). *Sukatan pelajaran Kurikulum Bersepadu Sekolah Rendah: Pendidikan Moral [Syllabus for the integrated curriculum for primary school: Moral education]*. Kuala Lumpur: Pusat Perkembangan Kurikulum.

Kementerian Pendidikan Malaysia [Ministry of Education Malaysia]. (2002a). *Huraian sukatan pelajaran Kurikulum Bersepadu Sekolah Menengah: Pendidikan Moral. [Analysis of the syllabus for the integrated curriculum for secondary school: Moral education]*. Kuala Lumpur: Pusat Perkembangan Kurikulum.

Kementerian Pendidikan Malaysia [Ministry of Education Malaysia]. (2002b). *Huraian sukatan pelajaran Kurikulum Bersepadu Sekolah Menengah: Sejarah Tingkatan 5. [Analysis of the syllabus for the integrated curriculum for secondary school: History Form 5]*. Kuala Lumpur: Pusat Perkembangan Kurikulum.

Kementerian Pendidikan Malaysia [Ministry of Education Malaysia]. (2002c). *Sukatan pelajaran Kurikulum Bersepadu Sekolah Menengah: Pendidikan Islam. [Syllabus for the integrated curriculum for secondary school: Islamic education]*. Kuala Lumpur: Bahagian Kurikulum Pendidikan Islam dan Moral.

Kementerian Pendidikan Malaysia [Ministry of Education Malaysia]. (2002d). *Sukatan pelajaran Kurikulum Bersepadu Sekolah Menengah: Pendidikan Islam [Syllabus for the integrated curriculum for secondary school: Islamic education]*. Kuala Lumpur: Bahagian Kurikulum Pendidikan Islam dan Moral.

Kementerian Pendidikan Malaysia [Ministry of Education Malaysia]. (2003a). *Huraian sukatan pelajaran Kurikulum Bersepadu Sekolah Rendah: Pendidikan Moral Tahun 1-6 [Analysis of the syllabus for the integrated curriculum for primary school: Moral education Year 1-6]*. Kuala Lumpur: Pusat Perkembangan Kurikulum.

Kementerian Pendidikan Malaysia [Ministry of Education Malaysia]. (2003b). *Huraian sukatan pelajaran Kurikulum Bersepadu Sekolah Menengah: Pendidikan Moral Tingkatan 1-5 [Analysis of the syllabus for the integrated curriculum for secondary school: Moral education Form 1-5]*. Kuala Lumpur: Pusat Perkembangan Kurikulum.

Kementerian Pendidikan Malaysia [Ministry of Education Malaysia]. (2003c). *Sukatan pelajaran Kurikulum Bersepadu Sekolah Menengah: Pendidikan Moral (Semakan) [Syllabus for the integrated curriculum for secondary school: Moral education (review)]*. Kuala Lumpur: Pusat Perkembangan Kurikulum.

Kementerian Pendidikan Malaysia [Ministry of Education Malaysia]. (2005a). *Sukatan pelajaran Kurikulum Bersepadu Sekolah Rendah: Pendidikan Siviks dan Kewarganegaraan). [Syllabus for the integrated curriculum for primary school: Civics education and citizenship]*. Kuala Lumpur: Pusat Perkembangan Kurikulum.

Kementerian Pendidikan Malaysia [Ministry of Education Malaysia]. (2005b). Sukatan pelajaran Kurikulum Bersepadu Sekolah Menengah: Pendidikan Siviks dan Kewarganegaraan). [Syllabus for the integrated curriculum for secondary school: Civics education and citizenship]. Kuala Lumpur: Pusat Perkembangan Kurikulum.

Kemp, D. (1994). A liberal vision for the next century. In B. Costar (ed.), *For better or for worse: The federal coalition* (pp.47-62). Carlton, Vic.: Melbourne University Press.

Kemp, D. (1997). *Discovering democracy: Civics and citizenship education, ministerial statement*. Canberra: Minister for Schools, Vocational Education and Training.

Kennedy, K. (2005a). *Changing schools for changing times – New directions for the school curriculum in Hong Kong*. Hong Kong: Chinese University Press.

Kennedy, K. (2005b). Civics and citizenship. In C. Marsh (ed.), *Teaching studies of society and environment* (4th ed.) (pp.299-315). Sydney: Pearson Education.

Kennedy, K. (2005c). Designing the school curriculum for tomorrow. In K. Kennedy. *Changing schools for changing times: New directions for the school curriculum in Hong Kong* (pp. 83-97). Hong Kong: Chinese University Press.

Kennedy, K.J., & Fairbrother, G.P. (2004). Asian perspectives on citizenship education in review: Postcolonial constructions or precolonial values? In W.O. Lee, D.L. Grossman, K.J. Kennedy, & G.P. Fairbrother (eds.), *Citizenship education in Asia and the Pacific: Concepts and issues* (pp.289-301). Hong Kong: Comparative Education Research Centre, The University of Hong Kong and Dordrecht: Kluwer Academic Publishers.

Kennedy, K., & Howard, C. (2004). Elite constructions of civic education in Australia. In J. Demaine (ed.), *Citizenship and political education today* (pp.90-106). Basingstoke: Palgrave Press.

Kennedy, K., Jimenez, S., Mayer, D., Mellor, S., & Smith, J. (2003). *Teachers talking civics – Current constructions of civics and citizenship education in Australian schools.* Canberra: Australian curriculum Studies Association.

Kennedy, P. (2004). The politics of 'lifelong learning' in post-1997 Hong Kong. *International Journal of Lifelong Education, 23*(6), pp.589-624.

Kennedy, P., & Sweeting, A. (2003). The education commission and continuing education in Hong Kong: Policy rhetoric and the prospects for reform. *Studies in Continuing Education, 25*(2), pp.185-209.

Kepel, G. (2002). *Jihad: The trail of political Islam.* Cambridge, MA: Harvard University Press.

Kerr, D. (2000, April). *Citizenship education: An international comparison across 16 countries.* Paper presented at the American Educational Research Association Conference, New Orleans.

Khairul Azmi M., & Faizal, F. (eds.). (2001). *Konsep pembangunan ummah dalam Islam: Perspektif Malaysia [Concept of the development of the Umma: Malaysian perspectives].* Johor Bahru: Ketua Penerangan Penyelidikan Kerajaan Negeri Johor.

Khoo K.K. (2001). *Malay society: Transformation and democratisation.* Kelana Jaya: Pelanduk Publications.

Kiang, C. (1992). *The Hakka odyssey and their Taiwan homeland.* Elgin, PA: Allegheny Press.

Kingston, M. (2002, April 26). Coming soon: Too many terrorists. *Sydney Morning Herald.* Retrieved November 30, 2004, from www.smh.com.au/articles/2002/04/26/ 1019441303758.html.

Kliebard, H.M. (1986). *The struggle for the American curriculum, 1893-1958.* Boston: Routledge and Kegan Paul.

Kliebard, H.M. (1992). Constructing a history of the American curriculum. In P.W. Jackson (ed.). *Handbook of research on curriculum* (pp.157-184). New York, NY: Simon & Schuster Macmillan.

Kohn, A. (2004). Test today, privatize tomorrow: Using accountability to "reform" public schools to death. *Phi Delta Kappan, 85*(8), pp.568-577.

Kua, K.S. (2002). *Malaysian critical issues.* Petaling Jaya: Strategic Information Research Development (SIRD).

Lapham, L. (2004). *Gag rule: On the suppression of dissent and the stifling of democracy.* New York: Penguin Press.

Law, F. (2002). *Speech by the Secretary for Education and Manpower, Mrs Fanny Law, at the 4th Kellogg – HKUST EMBA graduation ceremony, 14 April.* Retrieved October 28 2005, from www.info.gov.hk/gia/general/200204/14/0412243.htm.

Law, W.W. (2004). Globalisation and citizenship education in Hong Kong. *Comparative Education Review, 48*(3), pp.253-273.

Lee, H.P. (1995). *Constitutional conflicts in contemporary Malaysia.* Kuala Lumpur: Oxford University Press.

Lee, J. (2001). School reform initiatives as balancing acts: Policy variation and educational convergence among Japan, Korea, England and the United States. *Education Policy Analysis Archives, 9*(13). Retrieved February 27, 2004, from http://epaa.asu.edu/epaa/v9n13.html.

Lee, K.Y. (1965a). *The battle for a Malaysian Malaysia 1.* Singapore: Ministry of Culture.

Lee, K.Y. (1965b). *The battle for a Malaysian Malaysia 2.* Singapore: Ministry of Culture.

Lee, K.Y. (1965c). *Towards a Malaysian Malaysia.* Singapore: Ministry of Culture.

Lee, K.Y. (1966). *New bearings in our education system:* Singapore: Ministry of Culture.

Lee, K.Y. (1998). *The Singapore story: Memoirs of Lee Kuan Yew*. Singapore: Singapore Press Holdings.

Lee, W.O. (2002a). Moral education policy in China: The struggle between liberal and traditional approaches. *Perspectives in Education*, 18(1), pp.5-22.

Lee, W.O. (2002b). Moral perspectives on values, culture and education. In J. Carins, D. Lawton, & R. Gardner (eds.), *Values, culture and education. World Yearbook of Education 2001* (pp.207-266). London: Kogan Page.

Lee, W.O. (2002c). The emergence of new citizenship: Looking into the self and beyond the nation. In G. Steiner-Khamsi, J. Torney-Purta, & J. Schwille (eds.), *New paradigms and recurring paradoxes in education for citizenship: An international perspective*, 5 (pp.37-60). Oxford: Elsevier Science.

Lee, W.O. (2003). Xianggang huigui qianhou de gongmin jiaoyu: Shehui ziben de fansi [Civic education before and after 1997: Some reflections from social capital perspectives]. *Journal of Youth Studies*, 6(1), pp.112-125.

Lee, W.O. (2004). Concepts and issues of Asian citizenship: Spirituality, harmony and individuality. In W.O. Lee, D.L. Grossman, K.J. Kennedy, & G.P. Fairbrother (eds.), *Citizenship education in Asia and the Pacific: Concepts and issues* (pp.277-288). Hong Kong: Comparative Education Research Centre, The University of Hong Kong and Dordrecht: Kluwer Academic Publishers.

Lee, W.O., & Bray, M. (1995). Education: Evolving patterns and challenges. In J.Y.C. Cheng & S. Lo (eds.), *From colony to SAR: Hong Kong's challenge ahead* (pp.357-378). Hong Kong: Chinese University Press.

Lee, W.O., & Ho, C.H. (2005). Ideopolitical shifts and changes in moral education policy in China. *Journal of Moral Education*, 34(4), pp.417-435.

Lee, W.O., & Postiglione, G.A. (1994). The 'window effects' on education and development in South China. *Education Journal*, 21(2)/22(1), pp.111-122.

Lee, W.O., Grossman, D.L., Kennedy, K.J., & Fairbrother, G.P. (eds.). (2004). *Citizenship education in Asia and the Pacific: Concepts and issues*. Hong Kong: Comparative Education Research Centre, University of Hong Kong and Dordrecht: Kluwer Academic Publishers.

Leming, J. (2003). Ignorant activists: Social change, "higher order thinking," and the failure of social studies. In J. Leming, L. Ellington, & K. Porter-Magee, *Where did social studies go wrong?* (pp.124-142). Thomas Fordham Foundation.

Li, H.S., Chen, Y. & Chen, L. (2003). *"Daode yu shehui" xuesheng ketang qingyi jingyan yanjiu dagang [Research plan for "morality and society" lesson on student affective experience in class]*. Retrieved January 10, 2006, from www.cqslxx.com/jiaoshizhuye/lihais/ketifangan.htm.

Liu, J. (2005, December 12). Education key to 'transition crisis': Academic calls for teaching to smooth way for social change. *South China Morning Post*, p.A6.

Liu, J.S. (1998). *Zhongxue Deyu Cidian [Dictionary of moral education for secondary school]*. Beijing: Chinese People Public Security University Press.

Liu, M. (2004). A Society in transition: The paradigm shift of civic education in Taiwan. In W.O. Lee, D.L. Grossman, K.J. Kennedy, & G.P. Fairbrother (eds.), *Citizenship education in Asia and the Pacific: Concepts and issues* (pp.97-117). Hong Kong: Comparative Education Research Centre, The University of Hong Kong and Dordrecht: Kluwer Academic Publishers.

Liu, M., & Doong, S. (2002). Civic education reform in Taiwan: Directions, controversies, and challenges. *Pacific-Asia Education Journal*, 14 (1), pp.26-37.

Livingston, J.C. (1989). *Anatomy of the sacred*. New York: Macmillan Publishing.

Longstreet, W.S., & Shane, H.G. (1993). *Curriculum for a new millennium.* Boston: Allyn and Bacon.

Longworth, N., & Davies, W.K. (1996). *Lifelong learning.* London: Kogan Page.

Loque, C.M. (ed.). (1997). *Representative American speeches 1937-1997.* New York: H.W. Wilson Company.

MacDonald, M. (1977). *The curriculum and cultural reproduction.* London: The Open University Press.

Mahathir, M. (1970). *The Malay dilemma.* Singapore: Oxford University Press/The University of Singapore Press.

Mahayudin, H.Y. (2001). *Islam di alam Melayu [Islam in the Malay world].* Kuala Lumpur: Dewan Bahasa dan Pustaka.

Malaysia. (1988). *Dasar-Dasar utama kerajaan Malaysia. [Major policies of the Malaysian government].* Kuala Lumpur: National Institute for Public Administration (INTAN).

Malaysia. (1993). *Upholding the integrity of the Malaysian civil service.* Petaling Jaya: Pelanduk Publications.

Malaysia. (1997). *Etika Kerja Kementerian Pendidikan Malaysia. [Work ethics in the Ministry of Education Malaysia].* Kuala Lumpur: Kementerian Pendidikan Malaysia.

Malaysia. (1998). *Perkhidmatan awam Malaysia. [The Malaysian public service].* Kuala Lumpur: Malaysian Administrative Modernization and Management Planning Unit (MAMPU).

Malaysia. (2001). *Pembangunan pendidikan 2001-2010. [Education development 2001-2010].* Kuala Lumpur: Kementerian Pendidikan Malaysia.

Malaysia. (2003a). *Education development plan 2001-2010.* Kuala Lumpur: Ministry of Education.

Malaysia. (2003b). *Dasar Sosial Negara. [National social policy].* Kuala Lumpur: Kementerian Perpaduan Negara & Pembangunan Masyarakat.

Malaysia. (2006). The 9th Malaysia plan 2006 – 2010. Putrajaya: Government of Malaysia.

Malaysian Association for Education. (1968). *National seminar on civics education.* Kuala Lumpur: Persatuan Pendidikan Malaysia (PERPEMA).

Marciano, J. (2001). Civic illiteracy and education: The battle for the hearts and minds of American youth. *Theory & Research in Social Education,* 29(3), pp.532-540.

Mardiana, N., & Hasnah, H. (2004). *Pengajian Malaysia [Malaysian studies]* (2nd ed.). Shah Alam: Penerbit Fajar Bakti.

Marsh, C.J. (1997). *Key concepts for understanding curriculum: Vol. 1.* London: The Falmer Press.

Maududi, A.A. (1979). *Islamic Rayasat.* Lahore: Islamic Publications Ltd.

McGee, J. (1998). Curriculum in conflict: Historical development of citizenship in social studies. In P. Benson and R. Openshaw (eds.), *New horizons for New Zealand social studies* (pp.43-52). Palmerston North, New Zealand ERDC Press.

McMahon, W. (1998). Education and growth in Asia. *Economics of Education Review,* 17(2), pp.159-172.

Means, G. (1991). *Malaysian politics: The second generation.* Singapore: Oxford University Press.

Meier, D. (2002). *In schools we trust.* Boston: Beacon Press.

Mellor, S. (2004). *Solving some civics and citizenship education conundrums.* Retrieved November 30, 2004, from www.curriculum.edu.au/democracy/prof_dev/mellor.htm.

Mellor, S., Kennedy, K., & Greenwood, L. (2002). *Citizenship and democracy: Students' knowledge and beliefs, Australian fourteen year olds and the IEA Civic Education study.* ACER: Melbourne.

Michaelsen, C. (2003). International human rights on trial: The United Kingdom's and Australia's legal response to 9/11. *Sydney Law Review,* 25(3), pp.275-303.

Ministerial Council on Education, Employment, Training and Youth Affairs. (1999). *The Adelaide declaration on national goals for schooling in the twenty first century.* Retrieved November 30, 2004, from http://www.mceetya.edu.au/nationalgoals/natgoals.htm#nat.

Ministerial Council on Education, Employment, Training and Youth Affairs. (2003). *2002 National report on schooling - (Chapters being published progressively).* Retrieved November 30, 2004, from http://cms.curriculum.edu.au/anr2002/ch11_majordev.htm.

Ministry of Education, Culture, Sports, Science, and Technology. (1970). *The guidelines of the Courses of Study for junior high school social studies.* Tokyo: Ministry of Education.

Ministry of Education, Culture, Sports, Science, and Technology. (1998). *The Courses of Study for junior high school.* Tokyo: Ministry of Education.

Ministry of Education, Culture, Sports, Science, and Technology. (1999a). *The Guidelines of the Courses of Study.* Tokyo: Ministry of Education.

Ministry of Education, Culture, Sports, Science, and Technology. (1999b). *The Guidelines of the Courses of Study for junior high school moral education.* Tokyo: Ministry of Education.

Ministry of Education, Culture, Sports, Science, and Technology. (2001a). *The education reform plan for the 21st century---the Rainbow Plan 21.* Retrieved August 20, 2004, from www.mext.go.jp/a_menu/shougai/21plan/main_b2.htm.

Ministry of Education, Culture, Sports, Science, and Technology. (2001b). *Kokki oyobi kokka ni kansuru kankeishiryo [References to the national flag and anthem].* Retrieved March 3, 2001, from www.mext.go.jp/b_menu/houdou/11/09/990906b.htm.

Ministry of Education, Culture, Sports, Science, and Technology. (2003). *Report of Central Council for Education.* Tokyo: Ministry of Education, Culture, Sports, Science, and Technology.

Ministry of Education, Culture, Sports, Science, and Technology. (2005a). *The Fundamental Law of Education,* Retrieved March 1, 2005, from www.mext.go.jp/b_menu/kihon/about/index.htm.

Ministry of Education, Culture, Sports, Science, and Technology. (2005b). *Survey on moral education,* Retrieved March 1, 2005, from www.mext.go.jp/b_menu/houdou/16/11/04110503.htm.

Ministry of Education. (1972). *Education in the Republic of China.* Taipei, Taiwan: Ministry of Education.

Ministry of Education. (1975). *Guomin xiaoxue kechen biaozhun [Curriculum Standards for Elementary Schools].* Taipei, Taiwan: Ministry of Education.

Ministry of Education. (1979). Zhongxiao xuesheng shoze [Behavioural code for primary and secondary students]. In China Education Yearbook Editorial Board (ed.), (Various Years) *Zhongguo jiaoyu nianbao 1949-1981 [China education yearbook 1949-1981].* Beijing: People's Education Press.

Ministry of Education. (1983). *Guomin zhongxue kechen biaozhun [Curriculum Standards for junior high Schools].* Taipei, Taiwan: Ministry of Education.

Ministry of Education. (1993a). *Guomin xiaoxue kechen biaozhun [Curriculum Standards for Elementary Schools].* Taipei, Taiwan: Ministry of Education.

Ministry of Education. (1993b). *The New Zealand curriculum framework.* Wellington, New Zealand: Ministry of Education.

Ministry of Education. (1994a). *Guomin zhongxue kechen biaozhun [Curriculum Standards for junior high Schools].* Taipei, Taiwan: Ministry of Education.

Ministry of Education. (1994b). Zhonggong zhongyang guanyu jinyibu jiaqiang he gaijin xuexiao deyu de ruogan yijian [Opinions on further strengthening and improving moral education work in school]. Retrieved August 25, 2006, from www2.adca.edu.cn/sysd/zdhd/zhdb1.htm.

Ministry of Education. (1995). Zhongxue deyu dagang [Outline of moral education for secondary school] (Rev. ed.). In China Education Yearbook Editorial Board (ed.). (Various Years). *Zhongguo jiaoyu nianbao 1996 [China education yearbook 1996]*. Beijing: People's Education Press.

Ministry of Education. (1996). Quanrizhi putong gaozhong sixiang zhengzhi jiaoyu kecheng biaozhun [Curriculum standards for whole-day general senior secondary school ideopolitical education]. In China Education Yearbook Editorial Board (ed.). (Various Years). *Zhongguo jiaoyu nianbao 1997 [China education yearbook 1997]*. Beijing: People's Education Press.

Ministry of Education. (1997). *Social Studies in the New Zealand Curriculum.* Wellington, New Zealand: Learning Media.

Ministry of Education. (1999a). "Jiaoyubu guanyu jiaqiang zhongxiaoxue xinli jiankang jiaoyu de ruogan yijian [Several suggestions on reinforcing psychological health education in primary and secondary education]. Beijing: Ministry of Education. Retrieved August 25, 2006, from http://www.moe.edu.cn/edoas/website18/info1214.htm.

Ministry of Education. (1999b). *Health and Physical Education in the New Zealand Curriculum.* Wellington, New Zealand: Learning Media.

Ministry of Education. (2001a). Jiunian yiwujiaoyu xiaoxue sipinke ji chuzhong sixiangzhengzhikekecheng biaozhun [Curriculum standards for nine-year compulsory ideomoral education in primary school and ideopolitical education in junior secondary school]. In China Education Yearbook Editorial Board (ed.). (Various Years). *Zhongguo jiaoyu nianbao 2002 [China education yearbook 2002]*. Beijing: People's Education Press.

Ministry of Education. (2001b). *Jiunian yiwujiaoyu xiaoxue sipinke ji chuzhong sixiangzhengzhikekecheng biaozhun (xiugai gao) [Revised Curriculum standards for nine-year compulsory ideomoral education in primary school and ideopolitical education in junior secondary school]* Beijing: Ministry of Education.

Ministry of Education. (2001c). Jiunian yiwujiaoyu xiaoxue sipinke ji chuzhong sixiangzhengzhikekecheng biaozhun de tongzhi [Circular on curriculum standards for nine-year compulsory ideomoral education in primary school and ideopolitical education in junior secondary school]. In China Education Yearbook Editorial Board (ed.). (Various Years). *Zhongguo jiaoyu nianbao 2002 [China education yearbook 2002]*. Beijing: People's Education Press.

Ministry of Education. (2001d). *Education statistics of the Republic of China 2001.* Taipei, Taiwan: Ministry of Education.

Ministry of Education. (2002a). Zhongxiaoxue xinlijiankang jiaoyu zhidao gangyao [Outline of psychological health education for primary and secondary schools] Retrieved January 7, 2006, from http://www.moe.edu.cn/edoas/website18/info4604.htm.

Ministry of Education. (2002b). *Pinde yu shenghuoi kecheng biaozhun, chuxiao (Shixingban) [Morality and living curriculum standards (experimental version)]*. Beijing: Beijing Normal University Press.

Ministry of Education. (2002c). *Pinde yu sheshui kecheng biaozhun, gaoxiao [Morality and society curriculum standards (experimental version)]*. Beijing: Beijing Normal University Press.

Ministry of Education. (2002d). *Zhongxiaoxue xinli jiankang jiaoyu zhidao gangyao [Outline of psychological health education in primary and secondary school]*. Beijing: Ministry of Education.

Ministry of Education. (2002e). *Jiaokeshu kaifang shendingben yansheng wenti zhi jiantao yu gaijin zhuanan baogao [The Ministry of Education 2002 special report on the policy of textbook deregulation]*. Taipei, Taiwan: Ministry of Education.

Ministry of Education. (2002f, September). *Curriculum Stocktake Report to the Minister of Education*. Retrieved September 8, 2004, from www.minedu.govt.nz/index/recommendations.

Ministry of Education. (2003a). *Jiunian yiguan shehuike kecheng gangyao [The grade 1-9 curriculum guidelines for social studies]*. Taipei, Taiwan: Ministry of Education.

Ministry of Education. (2003b). *Guoxiaozu xuexiao jingying yanfa fudao shouce [School management and improvement manual for elementary schools]*. Taipei, Taiwan: Ministry of Education.

Ministry of Interior. (2004). *The 2003 census of the Republic of China*. Taipei, Taiwan: Ministry of Education.

Miralao, V.A., & Gregorio, L.C. (2000). Synthesis of country reports and general trends and needs. In *Final report of the training seminar on capacity-building for curriculum specialists in East and South-East Asia*. Bangkok: UNESCO. Retrieved January 9, 2006, from www.ibe.unesco.org/publications/regworkshops/thailand.htm.

Mohamed Suffian, T., Lee, H.P., & Trindade, F.A. (eds.). (1978). *The Constitution of Malaysia: Its development 1957-1977*. Kuala Lumpur: Oxford University Press.

Mottahedeh, R. (1985). *The mantle of the prophet*. New York: Pantheon Books.

Mouritsen, P. (2001, August). The liberty of the people: Three models of republican citizenship. Paper presented at the conference of Political Economy of Democracy Citizenship in an age of Globalisation, Copenhagen.

Munck, G., & Snyder, R. (2004). Mapping political regimes: How the concepts we use and the way we measure them shape the world we see. *Paper presented at Annual Meeting of the American Political Science Association*. Chicago, Il. Retrieved December 13, 2005, from www.asu.edu/clas/polisci/cqrm/APSA2004/MunckSnyder.pdf.

Munir, M. (1979). *From Jinnah to Zia*. Lahore, Pakistan: Vanguard Books Ltd.

Musharraf, P. (2004, June 1). A plea for enlightened moderation: Muslims must raise themselves up through individual achievement and socioeconomic emancipation. *Washington Post*, A23.

Musharraf, P. (2006). *In the Line of Fire: A Memoir*. New York: Free Press.

Mustafa, Z. (2004, April 4). A curriculum of hatred. *Pakistan Link*. Retrieved June 16, 2004, from www.Pakistanlink.com/letters/2004/april04/09/02.html.

Mutch, C. (2000). Old ideas in new garb: Values education in New Zealand. *Children's Social and Economics Education*, 4(1), pp.1-10.

Mutch, C. (2002). The contestable nature of citizenship in the New Zealand curriculum. *The International Journal of Social Education*, 17(1), pp.54-66.

Mutch, C. (2003). Citizenship education in New Zealand: Inside or outside the curriculum? *Citizenship, Social and Economics Education*, 5(3), pp.164-179.

Mutch, C. (2004, April). *Schooling for the future Phase 2 research: The New Zealand responses*. Panel presentation at the Pacific Circle Consortium Conference, Hong Kong.

Mutch, C. (2005). Developing global citizens: The rhetoric and the reality in New Zealand. In C. White & R. Openshaw (eds.), *Democracy at the crossroads: International perspectives on global citizenship education* (pp.187-210). Lanham, US: Lexington Books.

Nagendralingan, R., Rajendra, N., Sophia, M.Y., Lim, C.H., Norshah, S., & Idris, M.R. (2005). Pedagogical decision making as a basis for transforming teaching and learning: Practice and challenges of History teaching. Paper presented at Hong Kong.

National Commission on Excellence in Education. (1983). *A nation at risk*. Washington, DC: U.S. Department of Education.

National Commission on NAEP 12th Grade Assessment and Reporting. (2004, March 5). *12th Grade student achievement in America: A new vision for NAEP*. The National Assessment Governing Board.

National Council for the Social Studies. (1994). *Expectations of excellence*. Washington, DC: National Council for the Social Studies.

National Education Association. (1916). *The reorganization of the secondary school curriculum*. Washington, DC: Commission on the Reorganization of Secondary Education.

Nayyar, A.H. (2003). Insensitivity to the religious diversity of the nation. In A.H. Nayyar, & A. Salim (eds.), *The subtle subversion: The state of curricula and textbooks in Pakistan* (pp.9-63). Islamabad: Sustainable Development Policy Institute.

Nayyar, A.H. & Salim, A. (eds.). (2003). *The subtle subversion: The state of curricula and textbooks in Pakistan*. Islamabad: Sustainable Development Policy Institute. Nayyar, A.H. (2004, March 16). Debating education reform-1. *The News International*. Retrieved March 29, 2004, from http://www.jang.com.pk/ thenews/mar2004-daily/16-03-2004/oped/05.htm

Nazir, M., Khan, M.N., & Khan, F.A. (n.d.). *Social studies: Grade 7*. Peshawar: Rehmat Printers Publishers.

Niemi, R., & Smith, J. (2001). Enrollments in high school government classes: Are we short-changing both citizenship and political science training? *PS: Political Science & Politics*, 34(2), pp.281-288.

No Child Left Behind Act of 2001, 20U.S.C., S6301. (2002).

Noda, M. (2004). *Kokoro no kyouiku, Kokoro no Note*. Retrieved November 7, 2004, from www.ne.jp/asahi/manazasi/ichi/kyouiku/noda0210.htm.

Norton, A. (2003, August 19). Nothing neo about most conservatives. *The Australian*. Retrieved November 30, 2004, from http://www.cis.org.au/exechigh/Eh2003/EH15103.htm.

NSW Department of Education and Training. (2000). Discovering democracy – School projects – primary schools. Retrieved December 6, 2004, from www.abc.net.au/civics/democracy/ schools/SubjectIdx_Primary.htm.

Ohmae, K. (1996). *The end of the nation state: The rise of regional economies*. New York: Free Press.

Oliva, P.F. (1992). *Developing the curriculum* (3rd ed.). New York: Harper Collins Publishers Inc.

Omar, M.H. (2003). *Nilai-nilai Melayu dalam pendidikan [Malay values in education]*. In *Malaysia dari segi sejarah [Malaysia in history]*. Kuala Lumpur: Dewan Bahasa dan Pustaka.

Otsu, K. (1992). *International education – Curriculum and lessons for global citizenship*. Tokyo: Kokudosya.

Otsu, K. (1994). Four areas of global education in social studies. *Journal of Educational Studies*, 6(3), pp.75-82.

Pakistan Press International. (2004, April 23). Curriculum changes termed attack on Pakistan ideology. *Dawn*. Retrieved June 16, 2004, from www.dawn.com/2004/04/23/nat10.htm.

Pancasila (1945). http://indonesia.ahrchk.net/news/mainfile.php/Constitution/34?alt=english.

Parker, W. (1996). "Advanced" ideas about democracy: Toward a pluralist conception of citizen education. *Teachers College Record*, 98(1), Fall, pp.104-125.

Parker, W., Ninomiya, A., & Cogan, J. (1999). Educating world citizens: Toward multinational curriculum development. *American Educational Research Journal*, 36(2), Summer, pp.117-145.

Paterson, F. (2000). Building a conservative base-teaching history and civics in voucher supported schools. *Phi Delta Kappan*, 82(2), pp.150-155.

Patrick, J. (1997). *Global trends in civic education for democracy*. ERIC Clearinghouse for Social Studies/Social Science Education, ED410176.

Patrick, J. (2003). *Essential elements of education for democracy: What are they and why should they be at the core of the curriculum in schools?* Speech delivered on October 16, in Sarajevo, Bosnia and Herzegovina. Retrieved March 30, 2004, from www.civiced.org/pdfs/ EEOE-forDemocracy.pdf.

Patrinos, H. (1994). *Notes on education and economic growth: Theory and evidence. Human Resources Development and Operations Policy Working Papers No. 39*. Washington, DC: The World Bank.

Pederson, P., & Cogan, J.J. (2000). Developing democratic values: The case of the U.S.A. *Asia Pacific Journal of Education*, 20(1), pp.93-105.

Penerbit Universiti Malaya [University of Malaya] (2001). *Tamadun Islam dan Tamadun Asia [Islamic civilization and Asian civilization]*. Kuala Lumpur: Penerbit Universiti Malaya.

Pennington, M. (1999). Asia takes a crash course in educational reform. *The UNESCO Courier*, 52(7/8), pp.17-20. Retrieved May 9, 2004, from www.unesco.org/courier/1999_08/uk/somm/intro.htm.

Peters, M. (2001). National education policy constructions of the "knowledge economy": Towards a critique. *Journal of Educational Enquiry*, 2(1), pp.1-22. Retrieved May 9, 2004, from www.literacy.unisa.edu.au/jee/Papers/JEEVol2No1/paper1.pdf.

Pitchon, P. (1997). *Globalization versus localization*. Share International. Retrieved August 23, 2006, from http://www.share-international.org/archives/economics/ec_ppglobal.htm.

Popov, L.K. (1997). *The family virtues guide*. New York: Penguin Group.

Posner, G.J. (1998). Models of curriculum planning. In L.E. Beyer & M.W. Apple (eds.), *The curriculum: Problems, politics and possibilities* (2nd ed.) (pp.79-100). Albany: State University of New York Press.

Postman, N. (1995). *The end of education*. New York: Vintage Books.

Print, M. (1997). Renaissance in citizenship education. *International Journal of Social Education*, 11(2), pp.37-52.

Priyono A.E., Prasetyo, S.A., & Tornquist, O. (2003). Gerakan Demokrasi di Indonesia Pasca-Soeharto [The Democratic Movement in Post-Soeharto Indonesia]. Jakarta: DEMOS.

Psacharopoulos, G. (1993). *Returns to investment in education: A global update. World Bank Policy Research Working Paper No. 1067*. Washington, DC: The World Bank.

Purcell, V. (1967). *The Chinese in Malaya*. Kuala Lumpur. Oxford University Press.

Putnam, R. (2001). Community-based social capital and educational performance. In D. Ravitch & J. Viteritti (eds.), *Making good citizens: Education and civil society* (pp.58-95). New Haven: Yale University Press.

Putnam, R. (2002, February 11). Bowling together. *The American Prospect*, 13(3), pp.20-22.

Quaid-e-Azam Mohammad Ali Jinnah, (n.d.). *Speeches as governor general of Pakistan 1947-1948*. Karachi.

Queensland School Curriculum Council. (2000). *Studies of society and environment. Years 1 to 10 syllabus: with years 9 and 10 optional subject syllabuses*. Brisbane: Queensland School Curriculum Council.

Quigley, C. (2000, March 29). *Global trends in civic education*. A speech given at the Seminar for the Needs for New Indonesian Civic Education, Center for Indonesian Civic Education, Bandung. Retrieved March 21, 2004, from http://www.civiced.org/articles_indonesia.html.

Quigley, C. (2003, September 21). *What needs to be done to ensure a proper civic education?* A Presentation at The First Annual Congressional Conference On Civic Education, United States Senate, Washington, DC. Retrieved March 30, 2004, from www.civiced.org/pdfs/CongressConferenceSpeech.pdf.

Rajendran, N. (2001). The teaching of high order thinking skills in Malaysia. *Journal of Southeast Asian Education*, 2(1), July, pp.42-65.

Ramage, D. (1995). Politics in Indonesia: Democracy, Islam and the ideology of tolerance. London: Routledge.

Rashid, A. (1987). Pakistan: The ideological dimension. In M.A. Khan (ed.), *Islam, politics, and the state: The Pakistan experience* (pp.69-94). London: Zed Books.

Ratnam, K.J. (1965) *Communalism and the political process in Malaya.* Kuala Lumpur: University of Malaya Press.

Ravitch, D. (1990). *The American reader.* New York: Harper Collins.

Re-Generation. (2003, October). Special report: America's youth as a political force. *The American Prospect, 14*(9), A1-A23.

Reimer, E. (1974). School is dead. Harmondsworth: Penguin Books.

Report of the Malay Education Congress. (2001). Kuala Lumpur: Jawatankuasa Kongres Pendidikan Melayu.

Richter, F.J., & Mar, P.C.M. (2002). *Recreating Asia.* Singapore: John Wiley & Sons (Asia).

Ritchie, B.K. (2003). *Progress through setback? The Asian financial crisis and economic reform in Malaysia, Singapore, and Thailand.* Retrieved October 24, 2005, from www.msu.edu/~ritchieb/research/Progress_through_setback.pdf Subsequently published as: Progress through setback or mired in mediocrity? Crisis and institutional change in Southeast Asia. *Journal of East Asian Studies, 5*(2) (June), pp.273-314.

Roff, M.C. (1974). *The politics of belonging: Political change in Sabah and Sarawak.* Kuala Lumpur: Oxford University Press.

Roff, W.R. (1967). *The origins of Malay nationalism.* Yale: Yale University Press.

Romer, P. (1994). The origins of endogenous growth. *The Journal of Economic Perspectives, 8*(1), pp.3-22.

Ross, A. (2002). Citizenship education and curriculum theory. In D. Scott & H. Lawson. *Citizenship education and the curriculum* (pp.45-62). Westport, CO: Ablex Publishing.

Ross, E.W. (2004). Negotiating the politics of citizenship education. *PS: Political Science & Politics, 37*(2). Retrieved September 29, 2004, from http://www.apsanet.org.

Rosser, Y.C. (2004). Contesting historiographies in South Asia: The Islamization of Pakistani social studies textbooks. In S.C. Saha, (ed.), *Religious fundamentalism in the contemporary world* (pp.265-307). Oxford: Lexington Books.

Roszak, T. (1994). *The cult of information.* Berkeley: University of California Press.

Ruslan, A. (1975a). *Sivik Menengah Baru: Buku 1. [The new secondary school civics: Book 1].* Petaling Jaya: Penerbit Fajar Bakti.

Ruslan, A. (1975b). *Sivik Menengah Baru: Buku 2. [The new secondary school civics: Book 2].* Petaling Jaya: Penerbit Fajar Bakti.

Safire, W. (1992). *Lend me your ears: Great speeches in history.* New York: W.W. Norton & Company.

Saigol, R. (1995). *Knowledge and identity: Articulation of gender in educational discourse in Pakistan.* Lahore: ASR Publications.

Sakamoto, H. (1999). Discussion on Hinomaru and Kimigayo from a perspective of East Asian People. In H. Ishida (ed.), *Beyond Hinomaru and Kimigayo* (pp.29-33). Tokyo: Iwanami Shoten.

Saleem, F. (2003, December 27). Children of 'Jihad'. *Pakistan Facts.* Retrieved June 16, 2003 from www.pakistan-facts.com/article.php/2003122723374124.

Samsudin, O., Zulkurnain, A., & Sarojini, N. (eds.). (2000). *Good governance: Issues and challenges.* Kuala Lumpur: National Institute for Public Administration (INTAN).

Sarwar, B. (2004, June 16). Jehad and the curriculum. *Chowk.* Retrieved June 16, 2004, from www.Chowk.com/show_article.cgi?aid=00003311&channel=university%20ave&ord.

Satha-Anand, C. (2005). *The life of this world.* London: Marshall Cavendish.

Sato, T. (2000). *Japan unequal society.* Tokyo: Chuo Koronsya.

School term starts under "*Kimigayo*" cloud. (2004, April 7). *The Japan Times*, p.5.

Schubert, W.H. (1997). *Curriculum: Perspective, paradigm, and possibility*. Upper Saddle River: Prentice-Hall.

Scott, T. (2004). Pedagogy for global citizenship: Resisting standardization and high stakes testing in an age of globalization. *Pacific-Asian Education*, 16(1), pp.17-29.

Senu, A.R. (1971). *Mental revolution*. Subang Jaya: Pelanduk Publications.

Shahril @ Charil M., & Habib, M.S. (1999). *Isu pendidikan di Malaysia [Educational issues in Malaysia]*. Kuala Lumpur: Utusan Publications.

Shan, W. (2000). Causes and countermeasures for the resisting forces of educational reforms: The example of the nine-year integrated curriculum. *National Taiwan Normal University Educational Research Bulletin*, 45, pp.15-34.

Sheikh, M.H. (1995). *Civics: Grade 9th and 10th*. Peshawar: Shafiq Printers/Publishers.

Sheridan, G. (1999). *Asian values western dreams*. St. Leonards, NSW: Allen & Unwin.

Shorish, M.M. (1988). The Islamic revolution and education in Iran. *Comparative Education Review*. Retrieved April 29, 2004 from www.ed.uiuc.edu/EPS/people/Shorish_Islamic_Ed.html.

Shuker, R. (1992). Social studies as curriculum history. In R. Openshaw (ed.), *New Zealand social studies: Past, present and future* (pp.34-48). Palmerston North: Dunmore Press.

Simon, J. (1994). Historical perspectives on education in New Zealand. In E. Coxon, K. Jenkins, J. Marshall & L. Massey (eds.), *The politics of teaching and learning in Aotearoa-New Zealand*. Palmerston North, New Zealand: Dunmore Press.

Singapore Ministry of Education. (2000a). *Civics and moral education syllabus: Secondary*. Singapore: Ministry of Education Curriculum Planning and Development Division.

Singapore Ministry of Education. (2000b). *Civics syllabus for junior colleges and centralised institutes*. Retrieved March 15, 2004, from www1.moe.edu.sg/syllabuses/doc/Civics_PreU_1.pdf.

Singapore Ministry of Education. (2000c). *Civics and moral education syllabus: primary school*. Retrieved March 15, 2004, from www1.moe.edu.sg/syllabuses/doc/Civi_Pri.pdf.

Singapore Ministry of Education. (2000d). *Civics and moral education syllabus: secondary*. Retrieved March 15, 2004, from www1.moe.edu.sg/syllabuses/doc/CivicMoral_Lower%20&%20Upper%20Sec_1.pdf.

Singapore Ministry of Education, Curriculum Planning & Development Division. (2000-2002). *Civics and moral education series for secondary schools*. Singapore: Singapore National Printers.

Sinnema, C. (2004). *Social sciences, social studies or a new term?: The dilemma of naming a learning area*. An unpublished paper prepared for the Ministry of Education, New Zealand.

Smith, D.C. (1991). Foundation of modern Chinese education and the Taiwan experience. In D.C. Smith (ed.), *The Confucian continuum: Educational modernization in Taiwan* (pp.1-63). New York: Praeger Publishers.

Southern Taiwan Society, Eastern Taiwan Society, & PEN Taiwan (2003, September 12). Focus the education on Taiwan. *Taipei Times*. Retrieved June 16, 2004, from www.taipeitimes.com.

Spies, P. (2004). Action education: On the front line in Minnesota's Social Studies war. *Rethinking Schools*, 19(1), pp.21-24.

State Council Information Office. (2000). *China's population and development in the 21st century*. Retrieved January 7, 2006, from www.bjreview.com.cn/2001/Document/Files200052-China.htm.

State Council Information Office. (2005, October 19). *White paper on political democracy: Building of political democracy in China*. Retrieved August 8, 2006 from www.chinadaily.com.cn/english/doc/2005-10/19/content_486206.htm.

State Education Commission. (1988). *Zhongxue deyu dagang [Outline of Moral Education in Secondary School]*. Retrieved August 25, 2006, from http:222.16.142.1/gov/law/1/rules025.htm.

State Education Commission. (1990). *Guojiajiaowei guanyu jinyibu jiaqiang zhongxiaoxue deyugongzuo di jidian yijian [Opinions on further strengthening moral education work in primary and secondary schools], April 13.* In Q.J. Zhuo (ed.) (1992) *Zhongguo gaige quanshu: Jiaoyu gaige juan [Complete works on reform in China: Volume on education]* (pp.386-390). Dalian: Dalian Press.

State Education Commission. (1995). Zhongxue deyu dagang [Outline of moral education in secondary school] (Rev. ed.). In China Education Yearbook Editorial Board (eds.), *Zhongguo jiaoyu nianjian 1996 [China education yearbook 1996]*. Beijing, People's Education Press.

Stiglitz, J. (2002). Globalization and its discontents. London: Penguin Books.

SUHAKAM (2004). Akta Suruhanjaya Hak Asasi Manusia Malaysia, 1999, AkTA 597. [Human Rights Commission of Malaysia ACT, 1999, ACT 597]. Retrieved February 8, 2006, from www.suhakam.org.my/.

Syed Arabi A.I. (2005). *Study of youth not involved in associations*. Putrajaya: Youth Development Research Institute, Ministry of Youth and Sports.

Tanaka, Y. (1999). *Spell of hinomaru and kimigay: Beyond hinomaru and kimigayo* (pp.33-37). Tokyo: Iwanami Shoten.

Teacher Education Division. (1982). *The philosophy of teacher education in Malaysia.* Kuala Lumpur: Ministry of Education.

Teoh, H.J. (2005). *Mental health among youth in Malaysia.* Putrajaya: Youth Development Research Institute, Ministry of Youth and Sports.

Thanwi, M.A.A. (1992). *Adab-adab kehidupan bermasyarakat [Etiquette in social relations].* Kuala Lumpur: Darul Nu'man.

Toh, M.H., & Wong, C.S. (1999). Rates of return to education in Singapore. *Education Economics,* 7(3), pp.235-252.

Tokutake, T. (1999). *Ienaga saiban undo syoushi [A history of the Ienaga trial].* Tokyo: Shinni-hon-syuppansya.

Tolo, K. (1999). *The civic education of American youth: From state policies to school district practices.* A report by the Policy Research Project on Civic Education Policies and Practices, Lyndon B. Johnson School of Public Affairs, The University of Texas, Policy Research Project Report Number 133. Retrieved March 27, 2004, from www.civiced.org/ceay_ civiced-polict.pdf.

Torney-Purta, J. (2002). The school's role in developing civic engagement: A study of adolescents in twenty-eight countries. *Applied Developmental Science,* 6(4), 203-212.

Torney-Purta, J., Lehmann, R., Oswald, H., & Schulz, H. (2001). *Citizenship and education in twenty-eight countries: Civic knowledge and engagement at age fourteen.* Amsterdam: The International Association for the Evaluation of Educational Achievement.

Trowler, P. (1998). *Education policy: A policy sociology approach.* Eastbourne, UK: Gildredge Press.

Tsai, C. (2002). Chinese-ization and the nationalistic curriculum reform in Taiwan. *Journal of Educational Policy,* 17(2), pp.229-243.

Tsurumi, E.P. (1977). *Japanese colonial education in Taiwan, 1895-1945.* Cambridge, MA: Harvard University Press.

Tunku A.R. (1969). *May 13 – Before and after.* Kuala Lumpur: Utusan Melayu Press Limited.

Tyack, D. (2003). *Seeking common ground: Public schools in a diverse society.* Cambridge, MA: Harvard University Press.

Ubaidillah, A. (2004, March 29). Pendidikan Kewarganegaraan yang Membebaskan [Emancipatory Citizenship Education]. Kompas. Retrieved March 29, 2004, from www.kompas. com/kompas-cetak/0403/29/didaktika/906302.htm.

Ueno, C. (2004, April 30). The militants freed the hostages because they distinguished citizens from the government. Tokyo: *The Asahi Shimbun*, p.10.

Undang-Undang Republik Indonesia Nomor No. 22 Tahun 1999 Tentang Pemerintahan Daerah [Law No 22, 1999 of the Republic of Indonesia Concerning District Government].

Undang-Undang Republik Indonesia Nomor No. 25 Tahun 1999 Tentang Perimbangan Keuangan Antara Pemerintah Pusat dan Daerah. [Law of the Republic of Indonesia concerning Financial Balance between the Centre and the Districts].

Undang-Undang Republik Indonesia Nomor 20 Tahun 2003 Tentang Sistem Pendidikan Nasional [Law of the Republic of Indonesia No 20, 2003, on the National System of Education].

Unit Fasilitasi Desentralisasi Pendidikan (UFDP), Departemen Pendidikan Nasional. (2003). Konsep dan Strategi Menuju Desentralisasi dan Otonomi di Bidang Pendidikan [Concept and Strategy for attaining decentralisation and autonomy in the field of education]. Jakarta.

United Nations Common Country Assessment (2004). www.un.or.id/upload/CCA_30nov2004pdf. United Nations Development Programme. (2005). *Human Development Report 2005*. Retrieved October 24, 2005, from http://hdr.undp.org/reports/global/2005/pdf/HDR05_ complete.pdf.

United Nations Educational, Scientific and Cultural Organization. (1996). *Learning: The treasure within*. Paris: UNESCO.

United States Census Bureau. (2001). *Statistical abstract of the US: 2002* (122nd ed.). Washington, DC: United States Census Bureau.

Victorian Curriculum and Assessment Authority. (2002). *Curriculum priorities and the stages of schooling – Civics and citizenship education*. Retrieved November 30, 2004, from www.vcaa. vic.edu.au/csfcd/ov/ov-q.htm.

Vital Speeches of the Day, 60(16). (1994, June 1). Glory and hope: Let there be work, bread, water, and salt for all. Transcript of Nelson Mandela's speech to the People of South Africa, Pretoria South Africa, May 10, 1994, p.486.

Vital Speeches of the Day, 60(20). (1994, August 1). Post-modernism: The search for universal laws. Transcript of Vaclav Havel's speech delivered on the Occasion of the Liberty Medal Ceremony, Philadelphia, Pennsylvania, July 4, 1994, pp.613-615.

Walker, F. (2004, October 24). Tougher anti-terrorism laws on fast track. *Sydney Morning Herald*. Retrieved November 30, 2004, from http://www.smh.com.au/news/Anti-Terror-Watch/ Tougher-antiterrorism-laws-on-fast-track/2004/2010/ 2023/1098474928471.html.

Wan Arfah H., & Ramy, B. (2003). *An introduction to the Malaysian legal system*. Shah Alam: Penerbit Fajar Bakti.

Wei, L. (ed.). (1951). *Zhongguo geming chuxue duben [Beginners' readings on Chinese revolution]*. Shenyang: Northeast People's Press.

Weingartner, C., & Postman, N. (1969). *Teaching as a subversive activity*. Harmondsworth: Penguin Books.

Wellstone, P. (2001). *The conscience of a liberal*. Minneapolis: University of Minnesota Press.

Westbury, I. (1985). Textbooks: An overview. In J. Husen & T.N. Postlethwatte (eds.), *The international encyclopedia of education* (pp.5233-5234). New York: Pergamon Press.

Westheimer, J. (2004). Introduction – The politics of civic education. *PS: Political Science & Politics*, 37(2). Retrieved September 29, 2004, from http://www.apsanet.org.

Westheimer, J. (2006). Politics and patriotism in education. *Phi Delta Kappan*, 87(8), pp.608-620.

Westheimer, J., & Kahne, J. (2004). What kind of citizen? The politics of educating for democracy. *American Educational Research Journal*, 41(2), pp.237-269.

Williams, G. (2003). Australian values and the war against terrorism. *UNSW Law Review*, 26(1), pp.191-194.

Williams, G. (2004). Responding to terrorism without a Bill of Rights: The Australian experience. *AsiaRights 2*. Retrieved November 30, 2004, from http://rspas.anu.edu.au/asiarightsjournal/Williams.html.

Williams, R. (1976). Base and superstructure in Marxist cultural theory. In R. Dale, M. Esland & M. MacDonald (eds.), *Schooling and capitalism: A sociological reader*. London: Routledge & Kegan Paul.

Wilson, R.W. (1970). *Learning to be Chinese: The political socialization of children in Taiwan*. Cambridge, Mass: the M.I.T. Press.

Winaputra, U.S. (2000). *A needs-assessment for new Indonesian Civic Education: A National Survey 1999-2000*. Paper presented at the National Seminar on Citizenship Education, Bandung.

Wolpert, S. (1984). *Jinnah of Pakistan*. New York: Oxford University Press.

Wong, J.Y.Y. (1997). Rhetoric and educational policies on the use of History for Citizenship Education in England from 1880-1990. *Education Policy Analysis Archives*, 5(14). Retrieved February 2, 2006, from http://epaa.asu.edu/epaa/v5n14.html.

Wood, G. (1998). Democracy and the curriculum. In L. Beyer & M. Apple (eds.), *The curriculum: Problems, politics, and possibilities* (2nd ed.) (pp.177-198). Albany, NY: State University of New York Press.

Woodhall, M. (1987). Economics of education: A review. In G. Psacharopoulos (ed.), *Economics of education: Research and studies* (pp.1-10). Oxford: Pergamon Press.

World Bank. (2004). Indonesia education sector review: Education in Indonesia: Managing the transition to decentralisation, Vol.2.

Wu, J. (2002). Guozhong shehuilingyu jiaokeshu fazhan zhi linian kunjing yu yinying tujing [The development of the social studies textbooks at the junior high school level: Ideas, dilemmas, and alternatives. *Kecheng Yu Jiaoxue Jikan [Curriculum & Instruction Quarterly]*, 6(1), pp.73-94.

Wu, Q. (1998). Jeiyan yihou jiaoyu gaige yundong zhi tanjiu [An inquiry of the educational reform movement after the lifting of martial law]. *Jiaoyu Ziliao Jikan [Bulletins of Educational Information]*, 23, pp.261-275.

Xinhua News Agency. (2001a, October 24). Implementation outline on ethic building. *People's Daily*. Retrieved January 7, 2006, from www.people.com.cn/GB/shizheng/16/20011024/589496.html.

Xinhua News Agency. (2001b, October 24). Implementation outline on ethic building issued. *People's Daily (English version)*. Retrieved January 7, 2006, from http://english.people.com.cn/english/200110/24/eng20011024_83066.html.

Xu, N. (1993). *Taiwan jiaoyu shi [The history of Taiwan education]*. Taipei, Taiwan: Shi Da Press.

Yang, S., Wu, M., & Shan, W. (2001). *The historical development and current issues of teacher education in Taiwan*. Paper presented at the 46th International Council of Education for Teachers. Santiago, Chile.

Your own responsibility (2004, April 17). *The Hokkaido Shimbun*, p.39.

Yulaelawati, E. (2002). Education Reform in Indonesia: Contexts and challenges in New Times. In UNESCO IBE, Geneva, UNESCO, Asia and Pacific Regional Bureau for Education, Bangkok, Situational Analyses of the National Curricula for Basic Education in Easttaputra, U.S. (2000, March). A needs-assessment for new Indonesian Civic Education: A national survey 1999-2000. Paper presented at the National Seminar on Citizenship Education, Bandung.

Zaman, Y. (2003). The fight against terrorism: one step forward, two steps back. *Victorian Bar News*, 126, pp.38-41.

Zbar, V. (2004). *National discovering democracy forum – 2004 Final report.* Retrieved December 6, 2004, from http://www.curriculum.edu.au/democracy/ prof_dev/forumreport2004.pdf.

Zhang, A.L. (1995). Gaodeng yuanxiao de sixiangzheng jiaoyu [Ideopolitical education in higher institutes] In China Education Yearbook Editorial Board (ed.), (Various Years). *Zhongguo jiaoyu nianbao 2004 [China education yearbook 2004].* Beijing: People's Education Press.

Zhang, M.X. (2004). *Pinde yu shehui jiaoxue cankao ziliao [Morality and society: Teachers' reference materials].* Shanghai: Shanghai Education Press.

Zhu, R.J. (2001). *Report on the outline of the tenth five-year plan for national economic and social development (2001-2005).* Delivered at the fourth session of the ninth National People's Congress on 5 March 2001, Retrieved January 7, 2006, from www.chinatranslate.net/en1/ era/era04.htm.

Zinn, H. (1990). Declarations of independence: Cross-examining American ideology. New York: Harper Perennial.

Index